英汉互译原理

周方珠
卢志宏 编著

图书在版编目（CIP）数据

英汉互译原理／周方珠，卢志宏编著. —3 版. 合肥：安徽大学出版社，2008.8（2023.2 重印）
安徽省高等学校"十一五"省级规划教材
ISBN　978-7-81052-509-1

Ⅰ. 英…　Ⅱ：①周…　②卢…　Ⅲ. 英语—翻译　Ⅳ. H315.9

中国版本图书馆 CIP 数据核字（2008）第 116382 号

英汉互译原理

周方珠　卢志宏　编著

出版发行：	北京师范大学出版集团
	安 徽 大 学 出 版 社
	（安徽省合肥市肥西路 3 号 邮编 230039）
	www.bnupg.com
	www.ahupress.com.cn
印　　刷：	安徽昶颉包装印务有限责任公司
经　　销：	全国新华书店
开　　本：	787 mm×1092 mm　1/16
印　　张：	20.25
字　　数：	470 千字
版　　次：	2008 年 8 月第 3 版
印　　次：	2023 年 2 月第 4 次印刷
定　　价：	39.00 元

ISBN 978-7-81052-509-1

责任编辑：李　梅　钱来娥　　装帧设计：孟献辉　　责任印制：赵明炎

版权所有　侵权必究

反盗版、侵权举报电话：0551-5106311
外埠邮购电话：0551-5107716
本书如有印装质量问题，请与印制管理部联系调换。
印制管理部电话：0551-5106311

Preface

The 20th century witnessed an extraordinary boom in translation studies, which is marked by its interface with linguistics(including semantics, context, syntax, grammar, pragmatics, etc.), stylistics, culture, philosophy (including reading phenomenon, reception theory and hermeneutics), literature and communication theory. Before the 1970s, translation research was to a great extent treated as a branch of applied linguistics, and indeed linguistics in general was seen as the main discipline which is capable of informing the study of translation (the monograph entitled "A linguistic Theory of Translation" by Catford, J. C. published in 1965 is the typical example). Since the 1970s, translation scholars at home and abroad, especially those in the west, have begun to draw on the theoretical frameworks and methodologies borrowed from other disciplines mentioned above. In 1980s, scholars began to approach them from the perspective of culture, which marks the cultural turn in translation studies, and since then the interdisciplinary approaches to translation studies have gained sound ground. Up to the present, the growth of translation studies as a separate discipline becomes a success story.

In fact, translation has never been an activity that can be done in a vacuum. There is always a context in which translation takes place. Context varies with time and place, which determines the purpose of translation and shapes its form. In other words, translation as a means of cultural enrichment, the choice of works to be translated, the selection of strategies and methodologies, and the goals of translation activity are set by certain forces, power, or reason. There are many examples for illustration, such as translations done by Yan Fu, Lin Shu and other scholars in the late Qing Dynasty, the literary translation after the birth of the People's Republic of China, the translation of linguistic works and other works of social sciences at the turn of the century, to name but a few. Translation is therefore not the reproduction of the SL text in the target language, but rather a complex process of rewriting the original, which is influenced, or rather determined by the balance of power that exists between the SL culture and the TL culture.

In the 21st century, globalization has become one of the dominant "buzz words" in our life, especially in the areas of economy and marketing which influence all spheres of life. Economic globalization has become a trend as a result of the economic, scientific and technological development in the present-day world, which will certainly result in the cultural globalization. Needless to say, it is impossible for language to be free from the influence of the overwhelming trend of globalization. In fact, European English is emerging to fulfill the communicative needs of the EU member states. Snell-Hornby views the effect of the recent developments on the world language English from three different perspectives. Firstly, there is the free-floating lingua franca that has largely lost track of its original cultural identity, its idioms, its hidden connotations and its grammatical subtleties, and has become a reduced standardized form of language for supra-cultural communication. Secondly, there are many individual varieties, by and large mutually intelligible, but yet each an expression of a specific cultural identity (Indian English, British English, etc.). Finally, there are the literary hybrid forms as demonstrated in postcolonial literature, forging a new language "in between", adapted to its new surroundings. (Snell-Hornby, M. Translation Studies)

The new surroundings to which translation and translation studies must be adapted in the 21st century are cultural globalization. In the context of cultural globalization, translation proper that takes place between the source language and the target language is seen as the relationship between equal cultures. The increasing use of English as "lingua franca" in the global village decreases the authority of the native speaker, and the belief that English is a privileged language has been shaken as more and more people are rediscovering their cultural heritage and encouraged to present their cultural identity in translation. Against this background, the contents of this book are laid out to be adaptable to the new trend of cultural globalization, especially in Chapter Five and Chapter Six, where various strategies and methodologies are introduced to translation of different types of writings, and relative theories and principles are discussed for the feasibility of bridging the gap between Chinese and English cultures in translation of various types of literary works.

In order to demonstrate the possibility and feasibility of strategies and methods adopted in translation between Chinese and English, a large number of quotations are cited from various works. The authors of this book are grateful to all those copyright holders from whose works the quotations are cited. To those copyright holders whom the authors fail to contact with for various reasons they make sincere apology.

Zhou Fangzhu
Lu Zhihong
February 2008

内容提要

　　本书综合语言学、文体学、文化学和文学等相关学科的基础理论,从不同角度论证了英汉互译的基本原理及方法与策略。全书分为六章:第一章概述翻译的定义、功能、译者的必备条件及翻译标准。第二章介绍翻译策略、方法与技巧。第三章论述词语的翻译,内容包括:英汉词语的异同,语境与选词的关系,同义词的语义重叠及词汇的语体等级,成语、典故、谚语及文化负载词的翻译。第四章论述句子的翻译,内容包括:英汉句法结构的异同,形式对应的可行性,各种从句的翻译及特殊句型的转换机制。第五章从文体学的角度探讨不同文体作品的翻译,内容包括:广告翻译、新闻翻译、旅游文本翻译和科技及外交文献的翻译。第六章着力论述各类文学作品的翻译原理,作者以阐释学、接受美学及阅读理论为理据,探讨了小说、散文、诗歌、戏剧等文学作品翻译的可行性。本书融入了作者在翻译理论方面的部分研究成果。

List of abbreviations used in this book

ADJ =	adjectives
ADV =	adverbs
PREP =	prepositions
etc =	et cetera
sb =	somebody
SL =	the source language
SLT =	The source language text
sth =	something
TL =	the target language
TLT =	the target language text

Contents

Chapter One　Introduction ··· 1

  1.1　Definition ·· 1

  1.2　Qualification ·· 3

  1.3　Criteria of Translation ·· 6

Chapter Two　Strategies and Methods ································ 13

  2.1　Strategies ·· 13

    2.1.1　Domestication ·· 13

    2.1.2　Foreignization ·· 15

  2.2　Methods and Techniques ··· 19

    2.2.1　Literal Translation vs Free Translation ························ 19

    2.2.2　Extension ·· 25

    2.2.3　Conversion ··· 30

    2.2.4　Amplification ··· 36

    2.2.5　Simplification ·· 43

    2.2.6　Negation and Affirmation in Translation ······················ 48

    2.2.7　Shift Between the Concrete and the Abstract ············· 56

  2.3　Dictionary and Translation ··· 59

Chapter Three　Translation of Words ································· 65

  3.1　Semantic Change ··· 65

    3.1.1　Broadening ··· 65

    3.1.2　Narrowing ··· 65

    3.1.3　Melioration ··· 66

    3.1.4　Deterioration ·· 66

3.1.5　Antonomasia ·· 67
3.2　Gaps in Translation ·· 68
　3.2.1　Lexical Gap ·· 69
　3.2.2　Semantic Gap ·· 71
3.3　Context of Situation and Word Selection ································ 75
　3.3.1　Semantic Radiation ·· 75
　3.3.2　Direct Context and Word Selection ································ 76
　3.3.3　Indirect Context and Word Selection ································ 78
3.4　Synonyms and Choice of Words ································ 82
　3.4.1　Synonyms ·· 82
　3.4.2　Choice of Words ·· 85
3.5　Levels of Formality of Words and Diction ································ 89
　3.5.1　Semantic Overlap and Classification of Levels of Formality of Words ······ 90
　3.5.2　Levels of Formality and Diction ································ 92
3.6　Proper Use of Idioms in Translation ································ 96
　3.6.1　Similarities and Diversities between Chinese and English Idioms ······ 97
　3.6.2　Corresponding Idioms ································ 98
　3.6.3　Partly Corresponding Idioms ································ 100
　3.6.4　Modifiers Are Rendered into Idioms ································ 101
3.7　Translation of Proverbs and Two-part Allegorical Sayings ······ 106
　3.7.1　Proverbs ·· 106
　3.7.2　Two-part Allegorical Sayings ································ 110
3.8　Translation of Allusions ································ 113
　3.8.1　Traditional Allusions ································ 113
　3.8.2　New Allusions ································ 118
3.9　Translation of Culture-loaded Words ································ 121
　3.9.1　Similarity and Difference of Cultural Connotations between English and Chinese Culture-loaded words ································ 122
　3.9.2　Cognitive Schema Theory Applied to Translation of Culture-loaded Words ································ 125

Chapter Four　Translation of Sentences ································ 130

4.1　Differences and Similarities between English and Chinese in Syntax ··· 130

4.1.1　Difference and Similarity in Sentence Order ……………… 130
4.1.2　Difference and Similarity in Syntax ……………………… 135
4.2　Translation of Attributive Clauses ………………………………… 141
4.3　Comparison and Contrast …………………………………………… 150
4.4　Translation of Long Sentences ……………………………………… 156
4.5　Conversion between the Passive Voice and the Active Voice …… 163
4.5.1　Introduction ………………………………………………… 163
4.5.2　Conversion between the Passive Voice and the Active Voice …… 165

Chapter Five　Translation of Various Types of Writings ……………… 172

5.1　Translation of Advertisements ……………………………………… 172
5.1.1　Lexical Level ……………………………………………… 172
5.1.2　Syntactic Level …………………………………………… 176
5.1.3　Rhetorical Devices ………………………………………… 178
5.2　Translation of Journalistic Texts …………………………………… 188
5.2.1　Definition …………………………………………………… 188
5.2.2　Classification ……………………………………………… 188
5.2.3　Stylistic Features ………………………………………… 189
5.2.4　Major Components ………………………………………… 192
5.2.5　Translation Strategies …………………………………… 196
5.3　Translation of English for Tourism ………………………………… 198
5.3.1　Definition …………………………………………………… 198
5.3.2　Stylistic Features ………………………………………… 198
5.3.3　Translation Strategies …………………………………… 200
5.4　Translation of Scientific and Technical Writings ………………… 202
5.4.1　Linguistic Features of Scientific and Technical Writings …… 203
5.4.2　Increase or Decrease in Quantity ………………………… 210
5.5　Translation of Diplomatic Literature ……………………………… 214
5.5.1　Features of Diplomatic Language ………………………… 215
5.5.2　Translation of Diplomatic Literature …………………… 218

Chapter six　Translation of Literary Works ……………………………… 224

6.1　Introduction …………………………………………………………… 224

6.2　Fidelity to SLT Literary Messages ……………………………… 230
　　6.2.1　Fidelity to Semantic Information ……………………… 230
　　6.2.2　Fidelity to Grammatical Information …………………… 231
　　6.2.3　Fidelity to Rhetorical Information ……………………… 232
　　6.2.4　Fidelity to Pragmatic Information ……………………… 232
　　6.2.5　Fidelity to Cultural Information ………………………… 233
　　6.2.6　Fidelity to Syntactic Information ……………………… 234
　　6.2.7　Fidelity to Aesthetic Information ……………………… 235
6.3　Translation of Fiction ……………………………………………… 239
　　6.3.1　Introduction ……………………………………………… 239
　　6.3.2　Translation of Titles …………………………………… 240
　　6.3.3　The Stylistic Features Reproduced in Translation …… 241
6.4　Translation of Prose ……………………………………………… 245
6.5　Translation of Poetry ……………………………………………… 253
　　6.5.1　Opposite Opinions on Translation of Poetry …………… 253
　　6.5.2　Different Opinions on Subjectivity ……………………… 259
　　6.5.3　Translation of Poetry between English and Chinese … 260
6.6　Translation of Dramatic Texts …………………………………… 284
　　6.6.1　A Performance-oriented Translation vs. A Reader-oriented
　　　　　 Translation ……………………………………………… 284
　　6.6.2　Text vs. Subtext ………………………………………… 289

Appendix

翻译练习参考答案 ……………………………………………………… 293

Bibliography ……………………………………………………… 310

Chapter One

Introduction

1.1 Definition

This book is designed to give a sharp focus on translation between English and Chinese. But what is translation?

Translation is an incredibly broad notion which can be understood in many different ways. For example, in the broad sense, "translation" refers to the process and result of transferring a text from the source language into the target language.

In the narrow sense, it refers to rendering a written text into another language as opposed to simultaneously interpreting spoken language.

In foreign-language instruction, translation is considered, by some, "to be a fifth skill" (next to the traditional "four skills" of speaking, listening, reading and writing). Translation is a method used to practice and test competence and performance in a second language.

Different scholars, from different perspectives, define translation differently. Catford, for example, defines translation as "the replacement of textual material in one language (SL) by equivalent textual material in another language (TL)" (1965:20) as he tends to centre around the importance of maintaining some kind of equivalence between SLT and TLT. Peter Newmark, however, from the perspective of methods, classifies translation as follows:

Word-for-word translation

This is often demonstrated as interlinear translation, with the TL immediately below the SL words. The SL word-order is preserved and the words translated singly by their most common meanings, out of context. Cultural words are translated literally. The main use of word-for-word translation is either to understand the mechanics of the source language or to construe a difficult text as a pre-translation process.

Literal translation

The SL grammatical constructions are converted to their nearest TL equivalents but the lexical words are again translated singly, out of context. As a pre-translation process, this indicates the problems to be solved.

Faithful translation

A faithful translation attempts to reproduce the precise contextual meaning of the original within the constraints of the TL grammatical structures. It "transfers" cultural words and preserves the degree of grammatical and lexical abnormality" (deviation from SL norms) in the translation. It attempts to be completely faithful to the intentions and the text-realisation of the SL writer.

Semantic translation

Semantic translation differs from "faithful translation" only in as far as it must take more account of the aesthetic value (that is, the beautiful and natural sound) of the SL text, compromising on meaning where appropriate so that no assonance, word-play or repetition jars in the finished version. Further, it may translate, less important cultural words by culturally neutral third or functional terms but not by cultural equivalents—"une nonne repassant un corporal" may become "a nun ironing a corporal cloth"—and it may make other small concessions to the readership. The distinction between faithful and semantic translation is that the first is uncompromising and dogmatic, while the second is more flexible, admits the creative exception to 100% fidelity and allows for the translator's intuitive empathy with the original.

Adaptation

This is the freest form of translation. It is used mainly for plays (comedies) and poetry; the themes, characters, plots are usually preserved, the SL culture converted to the TL culture and the text rewritten. The deplorable practice of having a play or poem literally translated and then rewitten by an established dramatist or poet has produced many poor adaptations, but other adaptations have "rescued" period play.

Free translation

Free translation reproduces the matter without the manner, or the content without the form of the original. Usually it is a paraphrase much longer than the original, a so-called "intralingual translation", often prolix and pretentious, and not translation at all.

Idiomatic translation

Idiomatic translation reproduces the "message" of the original but tends to distort nuances of meaning by preferring colloquialisms and idioms where these do not exist in the original.

Communicative translation

Communicative translation attempts to render the exact contextual meaning of the original in such a way that both content and language are readily acceptable and comprehensible to the readership (1988:45-47).

Nida and Taber define translation as "translating consists in producing in the receptor language the closest natural equivalent of the source-language message, firstly in terms of meaning and secondly in terms of style" (1969/1982: 12). Functionists define translation as that "translation is the production of a functional target text maintaining a relationship with a given source text that is specified according to the demanded function to the target text (translation skopos)" (Nord 1991 a:28). *Dictionary of Translation Studies* provides readers with 82 definitions to translation. But the author believes that the translation process should be understood as a substitution of message in one language not for separate code units but for entire messages in some other language, so translation proper can be defined as the replacement of the information of the source language by its counterpart of the target language.

1.2 Qualification

Translation, no matter what sort of translation it may be, surely serves as an intermedium between two different languages, between the peoples of two countries, just like English-Chinese translation as a medium between English and Chinese. Translation works are somewhat like a matchmaker between a boy and a girl. To be a successful matchmaker one must be very familiar with both the boy and the girl. And in addition, one must learn some good methods and work flexibly. To do an adequate translation is very much like acting as a successful matchmaker. The translator must be well acquainted with both languages—the source language and the target language. Besides, one must learn the methods used in translating and the theory guiding translation. The modern theory is closely related to practical linguistics, stylistics, comparative linguistics (including bilingualism), sociolinguistics, semantics, psychology, semiotics, comparative literature and logic. Therefore, a qualified translator must be also good at linguistics, stylistics and semantics, and be a versatile scholar. Some people originally thought translation was a very easy job which could be done well as long as they learnt a foreign language. People with such point of view know not the implication of translation at all. Eugene A. Nida puts forth the following necessary qualifications which translators must have if they are to produce satisfactory translations:

1. A translator must be well acquainted with the source language.

Zhu Guangqian pointed out: We are inclined to feel too confident of our comprehension when we are reading foreign literary works. We think we know it from A to Z, yet when we start translating it we find it difficult and there are many points misunderstood by us. We are playing the fool with ourselves because of careless reading. Therefore translation serves as the best possible approach to the study of foreign languages.

2. A Translator must be well acquainted with the target language.

Let's take Yan Fu(严复) for instance:

When Yan Fu, a famous translator in the Qing Dynasty, was translating "Evolution and Ethics and Other Essays", the title turned out to be the crux that caused him to cudgel his brains day and night. His wife worried very much about it and said to him: "There is no need to sacrifice your health for a word." But Yan Fu said in reply: "Compared with the short life of a human being, a well-weighed word may enjoy eternal glory." He, then, went on to ponder over the proper representation of the title for quite some time and eventually had it translated into《天演论》which has since deserved high praise up till now. However the toiling he suffered was tasted by nobody but himself. No wonder he heaved a deep sigh when he completed his translation: "A new term established, ten days or a month spent"(一名之立,旬月踟蹰).

Only by acquainting oneself with both the source language and the target language, can one produce a satisfactory translation. An awkward translation is caused either by the poor source language or by the poor target language. But in addition, there are still some other causes. The main cause of them is the diversities between the two languages. So far as English-Chinese translation is concerned, there are great diversities between English and Chinese which are classified into two different families—the former, Indo-European Family; the latter, Sino-Tibetan Family. Great diversities lie in history, geography, politics, economy, culture, customs and so on: these diversities cause great difficulties in translation, and sometimes it is impossible to translate.

3. A translator must be armed with professional knowledge needed.

Besides the source and target languages, one must familiarize himself with the relevant disciplines such as mathematics, physics, chemistry, history, geography and so on. Otherwise one would often find himself at his wit's end in translation and the translation would be an awkward one. Dr Wang Zuoliang said, "Translation is actually a miscellaneous art." Such being the case, a translator should be a versatile scholar.

4. A translator must be armed with the ability to feel empathy for the SL writer and the characters portrayed.

As an actor, one must be wise enough to be aware of the role he (or she) is going to play, and capable enough to turn the available lines into action, gesture, sound and emotion. Just like an actor, a translator must be also capable of perceiving the true intention of the original author and change his works into the target language according to the author's intention.

The famous playwright Mary Ann Evans pointed out: "A translator must enter into the spirit of his character (identify himself with the role in a play)". That is to say, he seems to be

(1) present at the very spot. (身临其境)

(2) involved in the very occurrence. (亲历其事)

(3) witnessing the very parties concerned. (亲睹其人)

(4) iterating the very utterances. (亲道其法)

(5) experiencing the very joy. (亲尝其甘)

(6) and sorrow. (亲领其苦)

(7) sharing the very weal. (亲享其福)

(8) and woe. (亲受其祸)

(9) partaking of the glee. (亲得其乐)

(10) and grief. (亲感其悲)

5. A translator must be armed with the excellent ability of expressiveness and imagination. But how? Read and try to recite selections of ancient Chinese and English classics, and the poetry by the famous poets. "Toil yourself and endure hardship for obtaining a well-chosen word" and just as the famous poet Du Fu did, "never give up until an amazing poetic masterpiece is gained".

Apart from the above-mentioned qualifications, experience plays an important part in a good translation. Let's now analyse the following original and its translation.

When the literary gentleman, whose flat old Ma Parker cleaned every Tuesday, opened the door to her that morning, he asked after her grandson. Ma Parker stood on the doormat inside the dark little hall, and she stretched out her hand to help her gentleman shut the door before she replied, "We buried'im yesterday, sir," she said quietly.

巴克妈妈是替一个独身文学家收拾屋子的。一天早上那文学家替她开门的时候，他问起巴克妈妈的小外孙，巴克妈妈站在那间暗暗的小外房的门席子上，伸出手去帮着他关门再答话，"我们昨天把他埋了，先生"，她静静地说。

"Oh, dear me! I'm sorry to hear that," said the literary gentleman in a shocked tone. He was in the middle of his breakfast. He wore a very shabby dressing-gown and carried a crumpled newspaper in one hand. But he felt awkward. He could hardly go back to the warm sitting-room without saying something more. Then because these people set such store by funerals he said kindly, " I hope the funeral went off all right. "

"Beg pardon, sir?" said old Ma Parker huskily. Poor old bird! She did look dashed.

"啊，啊！我听着难过。"那文学家惊讶地说。他正在吃他的早饭。他穿着一件破烂的便袍，一张破烂的报纸，拿在一只手里。但是他觉得不好意思。要不再说一两句话，他不好意思走回他的暖和的"起坐间"去——总得再有一两句话。他想起了他们一班人下葬是看得很重的。他就和善地说，"我料想下葬办得好好儿的。"

"怎么说呢，先生？"老巴克妈妈嘎着嗓子说。

可怜的婆子！她看得怪寒伧的。

The original clearly tells us that "Old Ma Parker cleaned every Tuesday" for the literary gentleman. But the translator failed to put it into Chinese, and what is more, "我听着难过", "婆子", "怪寒伧的" are far from being proper; "他正在吃他的早饭", "一张破烂的报纸, 拿在一只手里", are far from being standard Chinese.

These are obvious mistakes, as for the syntax, choice of words and even the comprehension of the original, there is much to be desired. Nobody could believe that it was translated by Xu Zhimo, a famous poet and prose writer, who had once studied English in Columbia University in U. S. and Cambridge University in Britain. As Xu was good at both Chinese and English, the only explanation of his failure to translate the foregoing passage into good Chinese is his lack of "experience" which plays a considerably important part in translation. One might be armed with a good command of a foreign language and very capable of expressing himself in his mother tongue as well, but not necessarily a qualified translator. That's why we focus our effort on practice of translation.

In addition to all these qualifications mentioned above, we have to bear in mind one more point—"keep objectivity of the orginal and shun subjectivity"（保持原文的客观性而避免主观性）. This is a very important point to us. Because translators sometimes, out of the causes of politics, social system or religious belief, make some changes of the original text purposely or accidentally. But as a truly qualified translator, one should in no circumstances modify, let alone change, the will and attitude of the author of the original text.

1.3 Criteria of Translation

The subject of criteria of translation belongs to the practical theory of translation which is aimed to answer three fundamental questions:

(1) What is the nature of translation as linking together content and form? (This question has been discussed already.)

(2) What are the criteria for adequate and acceptable translations? (This is the very question we are going to take up in this chapter.)

(3) What are the problems which a translator ought to be able to recognize and resolve in order to produce a satisfactory translation? (This question will be dealt with in the following chapters.)

Early in the Tang Dynasty in our country, the learned monk Xuan Zang(玄奘)designed the criteria of translation with emphasis placed on accuracy and general knowledge. In the Qing Dynasty, Yan Fu established a three-character standard for translation:

"信"(faithfulness)

"达"(expressiveness)

"雅"(elegance)

which are similar to "tri-ness" by Herbert Rotheinstein(赫伯特·罗森斯坦): faithfulness, expressiveness and gracefulness which were considered the golden rule in the field of translation.

After the May 4th Movement, Lu Xun(鲁迅)proposed:

"信"(faithfulness) and "顺"(smoothness) as the criteria of translation.

After the birth of new China, quite a lot of translators put forward various criteria: such as "忠实","通顺","准确","流畅",重"神韵",而不是"形貌"(沈雁冰),"神似"与"形似"(许渊冲),"入化"(钱钟书) and so on. Among these criteria, however, Yan Fu's standard "faithfulness, expressiveness and elegance" is a highly influential theory which has given rise to a heated discussion. Quite some translators prefer Yan Fu's theory to others. Some disagree with it. Still some people make diverse interpretations of Yan Fu's three-character criterion of translation as:

"信"——Being faithful to the original(忠实于原文)

"达"——Being explicit and smooth(明白晓畅)

"雅"——Being elegant in words(词语的优雅)

which is different from Yan's own definition:

"信"——达旨(将原文说明)

"达"——前后引衬,以显其意

"雅"——尔雅(用汉以前字法,句法)

Translations done by Yan Fu and Lin Shu were based on this three-character criterion. Here is an example taken from his translation《天演论》"Evolution and Ethics and Other Essays"(by Henry Huxley).

It may be safely assumed that, two thousand years ago, before Caesar set foot in Southern

Britain the whole countryside visible from the windows of room, in which I write, was in what is called "the state of nature."

赫胥黎独处一室之中，在英伦之南，背山而面野，槛外诸境，历历如在几下。乃悬想两千年前，当罗马大将恺撒来到时，此时有何景物。计惟有天造草昧，人工未施。

Evolution and Ethics and Other Essays is a scientific work, and the translation by Yan Fu is full of smack of the Tongcheng School. That's why Wu Rulun(吴汝纶), the representative of the Tongcheng School, was willing to preface his translation and praised it to the skies. The three-character criterion put "Faithfullness" in the first place and "Elegance" in the last, but Yan Fu himself sometimes inverted the order and put "Elegance" in the first and "Faithfulness" in the last. From this example we can see it. So far as the explanation of Yan Fu's three-character criterion of translation is concerned, the author thinks only the first character "信" (faithful to the original) can be accepted; as for the second "达" and the third "雅", that all depends on the style of the original and the time when the original was published and translated.

Except for beautifully-written lyric prose or poetry, you can hardly find a novel or a film written only in elegant words. Local dialect, informal and colloquial English even awkward and vulgar words occasionally appear in masterpieces by great writers who succeeded in giving vivid pictures of his characters, such as Shakespeare, Dickens, Mark Twain, Thackeray, Isaac Bashevis Singer, 曹雪芹, 罗贯中, 施耐庵, 吴承恩 and so on. Now let's take "Gimpel the Fool" for instance.

Gimpel the Fool

I am Gimpel the fool. I don't think myself a fool. On the contrary. But that's what folks call me. They gave me the name while I was still in school. I had seven names in all: imbecile, donkey, flax-head, dope, gump, ninny, and fool. The last name stuck. What did my foolishness consist of? I was easy to take in. They said, "Gimpel, you know the rabbi's wife has been brought to childbed?" So I skipped school. Well, it turned out to be a lie. How was I supposed to know? She hadn't had a big belly. But I never looked at her belly. Was that really so foolish? The gang laughed and heehawed, stomped and danced and changed a goodnight prayer. And instead of the raisins they give when a woman's lying in, they stuffed my hand full of goat turds. I was no weakling. If I slapped someone he'd see all the way to Cracow. But I'm really not a slugger by nature. I think to myself. Let it pass. So they take advantage of me.

I was coming home from school and heard a dog barking. I'm not afraid of dogs, but of course I never want to start up with them. One of them may be mad, and if he bites there's not a Tartar in the world who can help you. So I made tracks. Then I looked around and saw the whole market-place wild with laughter. It was no dog at all but Wolf-Leib the Thief. How was I supposed to know it was he? It sounded like a howling bitch.

When the pranksters and leg-pullers found that I was easy to fool, every one of them tried his luck with me, "Gimpel, the rabbi gave birth to a calf in the seventh month; Gimpel, the Czar is coming to Frampol; Gimpel, the moon fell down in Turbeen; Gimpel, little Hodel Furpiece found a treasure behind the bathhouse." And I like a golem believed everyone. In the first place, everything is possible, as it is written in the Wisdom of the Fathers. I've forgotten just how. Second, I had to believe when the whole town came down on me. If I ever dared to say, "Ah, you're kidding!" there was trouble. People got angry. "What do you mean! You want to call everyone a liar?" What I to do? I believed them, and I hope at least that did them some good.

I was an orphan. My grandfather who brought me up was already bent toward the grave. So they turned me over to a baker, and what a time they gave me there! Every woman or girl who came to bake a batch of noodles had to fool me at least once. "Gimpel, there's a fair in heaven: Gimpel, a cow flew over the roof and laid brass eggs." A student from the yeshiva came once to buy a roll, and he said, "You, Gimpel, while you stand here scraping with your bakers shovel the Messiah has come. The dead have arisen." "What do you mean?" I said. "I heard no one blowing the ram's horn!" He said, "Are you deaf?" And all began to cry. "We heard it, we heard!" Then in came Rietze the Candledipper and called out in her hoarse voice. "Gimpel, your father and mother have stood up from the grave. They're looking for you."

To tell the truth, I knew very well that nothing of the sort had happened, but all the same, as folks were talking, I threw on my wool vest and went out. Maybe something had happened. What did I stand to lose by looking? Well, what a cat music went up! And then I took a vow to believe nothing more. But that was no go either. They confused me so that I didn't know the big end from the small.

I went to the rabbi to get some advice. He said, "It is written, better to be a fool all your days than for one hour to be evil. You are not a fool. They are the fools. For he who causes his neighbor to feel shame loses Paradise himself." Nevertheless the rabbi's daughter took me in. As I left the rabbinical court she said, "Have you kissed the wall yet?" I said, "No; what for?" she answered, "It's the law; you've got to do it after every visit." Well, there didn't seem to be any harm in it. And she burst out laughing. It was a fine trick. She put one over on me all right.

I wanted to go off to another town, but then everyone got busy matchmaking, and they were after me so they nearly tore my coat tails off. They talked at me and talked until I got water on the ear. She was no chaste maiden, but they told me she was a virgin pure. She had a bastard, and they told me the child was her little brother. I cried, "You're wasting your time. I'll never marry that whore." But they said indignantly, "What a way to talk! Aren't you ashamed of yourself? We can take you to the rabbi and have you fined for giving her a bad name." I saw then that I wouldn't escape them so easily and I thought: they're set on making me their butt. But when you're married the husband's the master, and if that's all right with her it's agreeable to me too. Besides, you can't pass through life unscathed, nor expect to.

I went to her clay house, which was built on the sand, and the whole gang, hollering and chorusing, came after me. They acted like bear-baiters. When we came to the well they stopped all the same. They were afraid to start anything with Elka. Her mouth would open as if it were on a hinge, and she had a fierce tongue. I entered the house. Lines were strung from wall to wall and clothes were drying. Barefoot she stood by the tub, doing the wash. She was dressed in a worn hand-me-down gown of blush. She had her hair up in braids and pinned across her head. It took my breath away, almost, the reek of it all.

Evidently she knew who I was. She took a look at me and said, "Look who's here! He's come, the drip, Grab a seat." I told her all: I denied nothing. "Tell me the truth," I said, "are you really a virgin, and is that mischievous Yechiel actually your little brother? Don't be deceitful with me, for I'm an orphan."

"I'm an orphan myself," she answered, "and whoever tries to twist you up, may the end of his nose take a twist. But don't let them think they can take advantage of me. I want a dowry of fifty guilders, and let them take up a collection besides. Otherwise they can kiss my you-know-what." She was very plainspoken, I said, "Don't bargain with me. Either a flat "yes" or a flat "no"—Go back where you came from."

I thought: No bread will ever be baked from this dough. But ours is not a poor town. They consented to everything and proceeded with the wedding. It so happened that there was a dysentery epidemic at the time. The ceremony was held at the cemetery gates, near the little corpse-washing hut. The fellows got drunk. While the marriage contract was being drawn up I heard the most pious high rabbi ask, "Is the bride a widow or a divorced woman?" And the sexton's wife answered for her, "Both a widow and divorced." It was a black moment for me. But what was I to do, run away from under the marriage canopy?

There was singing and dancing. An old granny danced opposite me, hugging a braided white chalah. The master of revels made a "God a mercy" in memory of the bride's parents. The schoolboys threw burrs, as on Tishe b'Av fast day. There were a lot of gifts after the sermon: a noodle board, a kneading trough, a bucket, brooms, ladles, household articles galore. Then I took a look and saw two strapping young men carrying a crib "What do we need this for?" I asked. So they said, "Don't rack your brains about it. It's all right, it'll come in handy." I realized I was going to be rooked. Take it another way though, what did I stand to lose? I reflected:

I'll see what comes of it. A whole town can't go altogether crazy.

This story starts with a very terse and colloquial prologue with few modifiers and Gimpel makes a self-introduction at the very beginning.

(1) "I am Gimpel the fool."

But how to put it into proper Chinese? Let's pick out another sentence in the prologue.

(2) If I slapped someone he'd see all the way to Gracow.

If we are to translate it into proper Chinese, we must take into consideration the style of the original, especially the levels of formality of words used in the story.

Elka is another character in the story, who is a fierce lustful vixen (shrew). Her first appearance in the story makes a striking impression on readers. The following is the conversation between Gimpel and Elka during their first arranged meeting.

I told her all; I denied nothing. "Tell me the truth," I said, "are you really a virgin, and is that mischievous Yechiel actually your little brother? Don't be deceitful with me, for I'm an orphan."

我可是什么话都给她说了,(什么)一点儿也没隐瞒。"喂,说真的,你真的是处女吗!(姑娘吗,黄花闺女吗?)那个捣蛋的叶切尔底是不是你弟弟?别骗俺(别哄我,)埃尔卡,俺可是个孤儿。"

"I'm an orphan myself," she answered, "and whoever tries to twist you up, may the end of his nose take a twist. But don't let them think they can take advantage of me. I want a dowry of fifty guilders, and let them take up a collection besides. Otherwise they can kiss my you-know-what."

(1) 我自己不也是孤儿,她答道。谁要是捉弄你,谁的鼻子尖就会弄歪。不过,别让他们以为他们可占我的便宜,我要价值50盾的嫁妆,还要他们拿一份彩礼。否则,让他们来吻我的那个玩意儿。

(2) 我不也是孤儿,她答道。谁要是捉弄你,就要谁的鼻子尖歪了。不过,别让他们以为他们可占我的便宜,我要价值50盾的嫁妆,还要他们凑一份彩礼。不然的话,就让他们来吻我的那个吧。

(3) 人家不也是孤儿,她答道。谁骗你啊,谁就不得好死。不过,他们要是认为能占我的便宜(他们要是想占我的便宜)没门。我要的是50盾的嫁妆,外加一份彩礼,要是没有这笔钱,就让他们来舔本姑娘的屁股。(姑奶奶的屁股)

Compare the different versions, you will find that (3) is much more faithful to the original with regard to the style of the story and the language used in it. By comparing "舔" in (3) with "吻" in other versions, we can see "舔" used here not only rude, rough but vulgar, used together with "屁股" even more vulgarer and rougher. By using "舔" here, the translation vividly and thoroughly expresses the way the shrew speaks. If "kiss" is put into "吻", it seems a little bit more elegant, but not in harmony with the way Elka speaks. "You-know-what", of course, can be put into "那个" or "那个玩意儿". But here it is extended into "屁股" out of the mouth of a vixen, it seems more faithful to the original so far as the deep structure of the original is concerned.

Having sworn and cursed, Elka showed Gimpel the door. "Either a flat 'yes' or a flat 'no' —Go back where you came from."

(1) 要么干脆说"行",要么干脆说"不行";要不然你从什么地方来,还回到什么地方去吧。

(2) 干脆说"行"或者"不行"——否则,你从哪里来就回哪里去。

(3) 要就要,不要就拉倒——你请便吧。

(4) 行就行,不行就拉倒,你好滚了。

Gimpel and Elka got married at last. But the little apprentice flirted with his wife and made love together. Gimpel said he had heard gossip about his wife. But the little apprentice said to him.

"Ignore it as you ignore the cold of last winter."

(1) 你别去理他,就像别理上一个冬天有多冷一样。

(2) 别去理睬它,就像你不理睬去年冬天的寒冷那样。

(3) 管他们干什么?他们的话当作耳边风好了。(管他们说什么,当耳边风好了。)

Four months after their marriage, Elka gave birth to a baby, then, Gimpel said to his wife "A fine thing you have done to me"!

"If my mother had known of it she'd have died a second time."

(1) 如果我的母亲知道这件事,她会再死一次。

(2) 我母亲要是有知,她会再一次死去。

(3) 要是俺娘知道,她一定会气得从棺材里跳出来。

Comparing the original with the various versions, we can see easily which is more faithful to the original in words, form, style, and deep structure, and in a word, in essence. The so-called three-character criterion is actually one key character which contains"达","雅"in fact. "达", "雅"must be based on the changing context. In the above-mentioned story there are quite a few rude, rough even vulgar words, which can't be translated into elegant, beautiful Chinese words, considering the original style, it will otherwise spoil the aesthetic effect of the original, which is opposite to the author's real intention and far from being faithful to the original in deep structure and essence. Disregard of faithfulness and too much care of elegance and smoothness are no more than penny-wise and pound-foolish for a translator.

The criteria of translation must be definite and practicable, otherwise they could badly be fulfilled. For instance, Yan Fu's "Elegance" is by no means definite. Elegance varies with place and time. It varies with the individual, too. As for the criteria put forward by foreigners, two of them should be mentioned: one is proposed by Alexander Fraser Tytler, professor of history at Edinburgh University. He laid down three fundamentals by which a translation should be made or judged in the last decade of the 18th century. They are:

(1) A translation should give a complete transcript of the ideas of the original work.

(2) The style and manner of writing should be of the same character as that of the original.

(3) A translation should have all the ease of original composition.

The other famous translator who establishes influential criteria of translation is Eugene A. Nida(尤金·奈达) who took part in translating the "Bible" and devoted himself to studies of linguistics, semantics, anthropology, etc. He accomplished many important works, such as "Componential Analysis of Meaning", "The Theory and Practice of Translation" (co-authored with Charles R. Taber), "Towards a Science of Translating" of which the last one is regarded one of his representative works. In this book, Nida lays down the following fundamentals:

(1) True to the original 忠实原文

(2) Vivid 传神

(3) Smooth and natural 语言顺畅自然

(4) Equivalence of response 同等效应

Of these fundamentals, the last one is the key point. I think the so-called equivalence of response means that a good translation can call forth the response of his readers equivalent to that of the readers of the original work. The response of a good translation and that of the orginal should be equivalent to each other. Of course, to fulfill these criteria is no easy task. It deserves a painstaking effort, but it is by no means impossible. It can be regarded as a pearl at the crown of the science of translation, but it's different from the pearl of mathematics crown which nobody, up to now, has laid his hands on it. It has been touched by quite a few well-known translators: such as 朱生豪,郭沫若,卞之琳,傅雷,王佐良,杨必 and others.

Now some examples for us to appreciate.

Studies serve for delight, for ornament, and for ability. Their chief use for delight is in privateness and retiring; for ornament, is in discourse; and for ability, is in the judgment and disposition of business.

(Francis Bacon:Of Studies)

读书足以怡情,足以傅采,足以长才。其怡情也,最见于独处幽居之时,其傅采也,最见于高谈阔论之中,其长才也,最见于处世判事之际。

Histories make men wise; poets witty; the mathematics subtle; natural philosophy deep; moral grave; logic and rhetoric able to contend. Abeunt Studia in mores.

(Francis Bacon:Of Studies)

读史使人明智,读诗使人灵秀,数学使人周密,科学使人深刻,伦理学使人庄重,逻辑修辞学使人善辩,凡是所学皆成性格。

The original here is taken from an excellent piece of prose by Bacon, a well-known British philosopher. The style of writing is characterized by explicitness, conciseness, terseness and philosophy. With well-whetted Chinese words, sentences and structure, which are in harmony with those of the original version, Wang Zuoliang's translation is faithful to the original not only in form, in style, but in essence. We can surely say that Wang's version can call forth the same response among his readers equivalent to that of the original.

Now one more example taken from Shakespeare's work A Midsummer Night's Dream(《仲夏夜之梦》) translated by Dr. Zhu Shenghao(朱生豪).

Quince: Yea, and the best person, too and he is a very paramour for a sweet voice.

Flute: You must say "paragon". A paramour is a thing of naught.

昆斯:对,而且也是顶好的人,有一副好喉咙,吊起膀子来真是顶呱呱的。

鲁特:你说错了,你应该说"吊嗓子",吊膀子,老天爷! 那是一种难为情的事。

In the original the author uses alliteration to gain the peculiar effect, Flute puts Quince right when he mispronounces "paragon" as "paramour". Without expression of alliteration in the translation, the dialogue would not make any sense, and the translation can not call forth the equivalent response. The translator, however, by using the well-chosen words "吊膀子", "吊嗓子" which are homphonic words(谐音字), keeps his version very faithful to the original, not only in form, but in style, structure, and what's more, in rhythm and phonology. It's really an all-time wonderful touch, unmatched subtlety, ever read in translated works.

Chapter Two

Strategies and Methods

2.1 Strategies

Unlike methods of translation, strategies of translation involve the basic tasks of choosing the text to be translated and developing a method to translate it. Both of these tasks are determined by various factors: cultural, economic, political, but the translator's attitude towards the source language text, its writer in particular turns out to be the leading factor. The strategies that have emerged since antiquity can perhaps be divided into two large categories: domesticating strategies and foreignizing strategies. Domesticating strategies may conform to values currently dominating the target-language culture, taking a conservative and openly assimilationist approach to the foreign text, appropriating it to support domestic canons, publishing trends, political alignments. Alternatively, foreignizing strategies may resist and aim to revise the dominant by drawing on the marginal, restoring foreign texts excluded by domestic canons, recovering residual values such as archaic texts and translation methods, and cultivating emergent ones (for example, new cultural forms). Strategies in producing translations inevitably emerge in response to domestic cultural situations. But some are deliberately domesticating in their handling of the foreign text, while others can be described as foreignizing, motivated by an impulse to preserve linguistic and cultural differences by deviating from prevailing domestic values.

2.1.1 Domestication

Domestication is a term used to describe the translation strategy in which a transparent, fluent style is adopted in order to minimize the strangeness of the foreign text for target language readers. It has been implemented at least since ancient Rome, when, as Nietzsche remarked, translation was a form of conquest and Latin poets like Horace and Propertius translated Greek texts into the Roman present: "they had no time for all those very personal things and names and whatever might be considered the costume and mask of a city, a coast, or a century" (Nietzsche 1974: 137). As a result, Latin translators not only deleted culturally specific markers but also added allusions to Roman culture and replaced the name of the Greek poet with their own, passing the translation off as a text originally written in Latin.

It is evident that domestication is culture-oriented, to be exact, it is target language culture-oriented. The translator leaves the reader in peace, as much as possible, and moves the author towards him. However, for some scholars such as Venuti, the term domestication has negative connotations as it is identified with a policy common in dominant cultures which are "aggressively monolingual, unreceptive to the foreign", and which he describes as being "accustomed to fluent translations that invisibly inscribe foreign texts with English-language values and provide readers with the narcissistic experience of recognizing their own culture in a cultural other" (1995:15).

Domestication finds its strongest and most influential advocates in the French and English translation traditions, particularly in Anglo-American culture, sometimes for cultural consideration, sometimes for economic consideration or sometimes for religion. The multi-volume English version of Cao Xueqin's novel《红楼梦》(The Story of the Stone) by David Hawkes is the typical example translated by means of domestication. Some examples:

1. 上下人等,打扮得花团锦簇。

(1) As for the inhabitants of the mansion, all of them, both masters and servants, seemed, in their dazzling holiday array, like walking flower-gardens of brilliant embroidery and brocade.

(2) High and low alike were splendidly dressed.

2. "巧媳妇做不出没米的饭来",叫我怎么样呢?

(1) I don't see what I am supposed to do without any capital. Even the cleverest housewife can't make bread without flour!

(2) Even the cleverest housewife can't cook a meal without rice. What do you expect me to do?

In translating Example 1, Hawkes takes readers into consideration. He leaves readers in peace as much as possible, and moves the author towards readers. In translating Example 2, Hawkes' version conforms to the way of living of the target text readers by choosing "bread" and "flour" instead of "meal" and "rice".

Another typical example of domesticating translation is Yan Fu's translation of *Evolution and Ethics and Other Essays*《天演论》

The source language text:

That which endures is not one or another association of living forms, but the process of which the cosmos is the product, and of which these are among the transitory expressions. And in the living world, one of the most characteristic features of this cosmic process is the struggle for existence, the competition of each with all, the result of which is the selection, that is to say, the survival of those forms which, on the whole, are best adapted to the conditions which at any period obtain, and which are, therefore, in that respect, and only in that respect, the fittest.

Yan Fu's Version

虽然天运变矣,而有不变者行乎其中。不变惟何,是名天演。以天演为体,而其用有二:曰物竞,曰天择。此万物莫不然,而于有生之类为尤著。物竞者,物争直存也;以一物以与万物争,或存或亡,而其效则归于天择。天择者,物争焉而独存;则其存也,必有其所以存。必其所得于天之分,自致一己之能;与其所遭值之时与地,及凡周身以外之物力,有其相谋相剂者焉。夫而后独免于亡,而足以自立也。而自其效而观之,若是物特为天之所厚而择焉以存也者,夫是之谓天择。

The version from *A History of Translation in China* (Volume I) by Ma Zuyi:

能够持续下来的并不是各种生命形式的这种或那种结合,而是产生宇宙本身的过程。而各种生命形式的不同结合,不过是这个过程的一些暂时表现而已。在生物界,这种宇宙过程的最大特点之一就是生存斗争及物种间的相互竞争,其结果就是选择。这就是说,那生存下来的生命形式,总的说来,都是最适应于在任何一时期的环境条件的。因此,在这方面,也仅仅在这方面,它们是最适者。

The comparison between the two versions helps us to learn that Yan Fu's version is characterized by the conscious adoption of a fluent, natural-sounding TL style, the adaptation of TT to conform to target discourse types, the interpolation of explanatory material, the removal of SL realia and the general harmonization of TT preconceptions and preferences, which speak volume for Wu Rulun's prefacing his translation《天演论》。

Economic and religious considerations sometimes underlie a domesticating strategy in translation, but they are always qualified by current cultural and political developments. Translation of the Bible turns out to be the typical example. For Eugene Nida, domestication assists the Christian missionary: as translation consultant to organizations dedicated to the dissemination of the Bible, he has supervised numerous translations that relate the receptor to modes of behavior relevant within the context of his own culture. (1964:159;see also BIBLE TRANSLATION)

Therefore we can say for sure that domestication is a TL culture-oriented strategy in translation.

2.1.2 Foreignization

As a strategy in translation, foreignization was first formulated in German culture during the classical and Romantic periods, perhaps most decisively by the philosopher and theologian Friedrich Schleiermacher(F. 施莱尔玛赫)(Berman 1992). In an 1813 lecture "On the Different Methods of Translating", Schleiermacher argued that "there are only two. Either the translator leaves the author in peace, as much as possible, and moves the reader toward him. Or he leaves the reader in peace, as much as possible, and moves the author toward him" (quoted in Lefevere1992b:149). Schleiermacher acknowledged that most translation was domesticating, an ethnocentric reduction of the foreign text to target-language cultural values, bringing the author back home. But he very much preferred a foreignizing strategy, an ethnodeviant pressure on those values to register the linguistic and cultural difference of the foreign text, sending the reader abroad. From its origins in the German tradition, foreignizing translation has meant a close adherence to the foreign text, a literalism that resulted in the importation of foreign cultural forms and the development of heterogeneous dialects and discourse. However, different scholars have different opinions on foreignization. Those who propose that the strategy should be adopted believe that foreignization would entail not only a freedom from absolute obedience to target linguistic and textual constraints, but also where appropriate the selection of a non-fluent, opaque style and the deliberate inclusion of ST realia or TL archaisms; the cumulative effect of such features would be to provide TL readers with an alien reading experience, which would thus enrich TL and promote the intercultural communication. Some people think otherwise. They exemplify the risk of incomprehension that is involved in challenging literary canons, professional standards, cultural connotations and ethical norms in the target language. It is generally admitted that domestication and foreignization, each has its advantages and disadvantages, which speaks volumes for the fact that the same TL text has different versions based on different translation strategies. The translations of 《红楼梦》is the typical example. The title has been respectively translated into *The Story of the Stone* by David Hawkes and *A Dream of Red Mansions* by Yang Xianyi out of various considerations; Yang adopts foreignization as he aims to preserve the cultural connotation of the original title which will lead readers to vivid associations; David Hawkes adopts domestication to free his readers from misunderstanding of the title, the culture-specific term "red mansions" (红楼) in particular. He believes that the term will surely lead the English-speaking readers to quite different associations. Therefore, whenever he comes across the term "红楼梦", he adopts domestication and has it translated into *The Dream of Golden Days*, and "怡红院" translated into "The House of Green Delight". Some more examples:

第四十一回　贾宝玉品茶栊翠庵
　　　　　　刘姥姥醉卧怡红院

(1) Baoyu Sips tea in Green Lattice Nunnery

　　Granny Liu Succumbs to Wine in Happy Red Court

(2) Jia Baoyu tastes some superior tea at Green Bower Hermitage

　　And Grannie Liu Samples the sleeping accommodation at Green Delights

第一百二十回　甄士隐详说太虚情
　　　　　　　贾雨村归结红楼梦

(1) Chen Shihyin Expounds the Illusory Realm

　　Chia Yutsun Concludes the Dream of Red Mansions

(2) Zhen Shiyin expounds the nature of Passion and Illusion

　　And Jia Yucun concludes the Dream of Golden Days

Determining whether a translation project is domesticating or foreignizing clearly depends on a detailed reconstruction of the cultural formation in which the translation is produced and consumed; what is domestic or foreign can be defined only with reference to the changing hierarchy of values in the target language culture. For example, a domesticating translation may constitute a historical interpretation of the foreign text that conforms to prevailing critical opinion. Yan Fu's lexicon and syntax, while intelligible to the contemporary readers of the Tongcheng School, make use of archaisms favoured by the élite then. The distinction between the strategies adopted by Yang Xianyi and David Hawkes are evident, but both of them adopt domestication and foreignization interchangeably as neither one can accomplish the translation of a novel with one and only strategy.

Translation Exercises

Ⅰ. *Compare the following English with its Chinese version, then give your opinion on the strategy adopted by the translator.*

When standing by a lake-side in the moonlight, you see stretching over the rippled surface towards the moon, a bar of light which, as shown by its nearer part, consists of flashes from the sides of separate wavelets. You walk, and the bar of light seems to go with you. There are, even among the educated classes, many who suppose that this bar of light has an objective existence, and who believe that it really moves as the observer moves—occasionally, indeed, as I can testify, expressing surprise at the fact. But, apart from the observer there exists no such bar of light; nor when the observer moves is there any movement of this line of glittering wavelets. All over the dark part of the surface the undulations are just as bright with moonlight as those he sees, but the light reflected from them does not reach his eyes. Thus, though there seems to be a lighting of some wavelets and not of the rest, and though, as the observer moves, other wavelets seem to become lighted that were not lighted before, yet both these are utterly false seemings. The simple fact is that his position in relation to certain wavelets brings into view their reflections of the moon's light, while it keeps out of view the like reflections from all other wavelets. （Herbert Spencer：Study of Sociology）

（望舒东睇,一碧无烟,独）立湖塘,（延赏）水月,见自彼月之下,至于目前,一道光芒,溰漾闪烁,（谛而察之）,皆细浪沦漪,（受月光映发而为此也）。（徘徊数武）,是光（景）者乃若随人。颇有明理士夫,谓是光（景）为实有物,故能相随,且亦有时以此（自）讶。（不悟是光景者）,从人而有,使无见者,则亦无光,更无光（景）,与人相逐。盖全湖水面,受月映发,一切平等,（特人目与水对待不同,明暗遂别。不得以所未见,即指为无）。是故虽所见者为一道光芒,他所不尔。又人目易位,前之暗者,乃今更明。然此种种,无非（妄见）。以言其实,则由人目与月作二线入水,（成等角者,皆当见光。其不等者）,则全成暗。（惟人之察群事也亦然,往往以见所及者为有,以所不及者为无。执见否以定有无,则其思之所不赅者众矣）。

II. *Make a comparative study of the following English versions to the same Chinese text, then analyse the translation strategies adopted by translators.*

1. 可知我"井底之蛙",成日家只说现在的这几个人是有一无二的;谁知不必远寻,就是本地风光,一个赛似一个。

（1）I've been like the frog living at the bottom of the well who thought the world was a little round pool of water. Up to now I've always believed that the girls in this household were without equals anywhere; but now, even without my needing to go outside, here they come, each one more beautiful than the last!

（2）Why, I've been like the frog at the bottom of a well, imagining that our girls here were unmatched; but now, without searching far afield, here on this very spot I see others who surpass them.

2. 等我性子上来,把这"醋罐子"打个稀烂,他才认的我呢!

（1）One of these days when I really lose my temper, I'm going to give that vinegary bitch a good beating to show her who's master here.

（2）One of these days when I get my temper up I'm going to lay into that jealous bitch and break every bone in her body. Then perhaps she'll know who's master round here.

（3）好了歌

世人都晓神仙好，	世人都晓神仙好，
惟有功名忘不了！	只有娇妻忘不了！
古今将相在何方？	君生日日说恩情，
荒冢一堆草没了。	君死又随人去了。
世人都晓神仙好，	世人都说神仙好，
只有金银忘不了！	只有儿孙忘不了！
终朝只恨聚无多，	痴心父母古来多，
及到多时眼闭了。	孝顺子孙谁见了？

ALL GOOD THINGS MUST END

All men long to be immortals

Yet to riches and rank each aspires;

The great ones of old, where are they now?

Their graves are a mass of briars.

All men long to be immortals,

Yet silver and gold they prize

And grub for money all their lives

Till death seals up their eyes.

All men long to be immortals

Yet dote on the wives they've wed,

Who swear to love their husband evermore

But remarry as soon as he's dead.

All men long to be immortals

Yet with getting sons won't have done.

Although fond parents are legion,

Who ever saw a really filial son?

WON-DONE SONG

Men all know that salvation should be won,

But with ambition won't have done, have done.

Where are the famous ones of days gone by?

In grassy graves they lie now, every one.

Men all know that salvation should be won,

But with their riches won't have done, have done.

Each day they grumble they've not made enough.
When they've enough, it's goodnight everyone!

Men all know that salvation should be won,
But with their loving wives they won't have done.
The darlings every day protest their love,
But once you're dead, they're off with another one.

Men all know that salvation should be won,
But with their children won't have done, have done.
Yet though of parents fond there is no lack,
Of grateful children saw I ne'er a one.

2.2 Methods and Techniques

2.2.1 Literal Translation vs Free Translation

Literal translation and free translation are of frequent occurrence in translation and also methods frequently adopted in translation proper. Literal translation is a type of translation in which great attention is paid to producing the form of the SLT while being faithful to the exact contextual meaning and pragmatic effect of the original, whereas free translation is a type of translation in which more attention is paid to producing a naturally reading TLT than to preserving the SLT wording and syntax intact. Different scholars from different perspectives define the two differently: Catford argues that literal translation takes word-for-word translation as its starting point, although because of the necessity of conforming to TL grammar, the final TT may also display group-group or clause-clause equivalence(1965:25). Nabokov, however, describes it as "rendering, as closely as the associative and syntactical capacities of another language allow, the exact contextual meaning of the original", and claims that only this strategy can be considered true translation(Nabokov 1964/1975:viii). Some people have suggested alternative contrasts based on related though different notions: e. g. House's (1977) Covert Translation vs Overt Translation, Gutt's (1991) Direct Translation vs Indirect Translation, Nida's (1964) Dynamic and Formal Equivalence. It is evident that different scholars have different opinions on the adoption of literal translation or free translation. Peter Newmark once pointed out that "I believe literal translation to be the basic translation procedure, both in communicative and semantic translation, in that translation starts from there. However, above the word level, literal translation becomes increasingly difficult. Literal translation above the word level is the only correct procedure if the SL and TL meaning correspond, or correspond more closely than any alternative; that means that the referent and the pragmatic effect are equivalent, i. e. that the words not only refer to the same "thing" but have similar associations (Mama, "mum"; le prof, "the prof") and appear to be equally frequent in this type of text (1988:70). Chukovsky believes that adoption of literal translation leads to a "complete distortion of the meaning of the original" (Chukovsky 1966:

242).

However, it is generally agreed nowadays that literal translation and free translation do not form a binary contrast, and that the most appropriate translation method will vary according to the text-type being translated and the purpose of translation. The author of the book believes that literal translation and free translation should be adopted in co-operation with each other, sometimes they can be adopted interchangeably. Sometimes we may come across some expressions or sentences which are identical, both in the meanings given to corresponding symbols and in the ways in which such symbols are arranged in phrases and sentences. Such being the case, literal translation can be adopted. Some examples:

Phrases

1. Noah's ark   诺亚方舟
2. Judas' kiss   犹大之吻
3. crocodile tears   鳄鱼的眼泪
4. Trojan horse   特洛伊木马
5. armed to the teeth   武装到牙齿
6. to kill two birds with one stone   一石二鸟
7. to flog a dead horse   鞭打死马
8. to teach a fish how to swim   教鱼游泳
9. 竭泽而渔   to drain a pond to catch all the fish
10. 望梅止渴   to gaze at plums to quench one's thirst
11. 危如累卵   as dangerous as a pile of eggs
12. 悲喜交集   with joy and sorrow mingled
13. 过河拆桥   Burn the bridge when one is safely over the river.
14. 否极泰来   The extreme of adversity is the beginning of prosperity.
15. 一国两制   one country, two systems

Sentences

1. Smashing a mirror is no way to make an ugly person beautiful, nor is it a way to make social problems evaporate.

砸镜子不能使丑八怪变漂亮,也不能使社会问题烟消云散。

2. A: Still waiting here? Seems you have waited a long time.

   B: Have to wait, C told me he would come and I have something to tell him. It won't wait.

   A: 还等在这儿? 好像你已等了很久了。

   B: 得等着,C 告诉我他会来的;而我还有事要告诉他,那可不能等。

3. Partly as a result of the recently increasing demand, wholesale tea prices have almost doubled.

部分由于最近日益增长的需求,批发茶价几乎翻了一番。

4. "巧媳妇做不出没米的饭来",叫我怎么样呢?

Even the cleverest housewife can't cook a meal without rice, what do you expect me to do?

5. 卧榻之侧岂容他人酣睡。
How can I let another sleep alongside my bed?
6. 月满则亏,水满则溢。
The moon waxes only to wane, water brims only to overflow.

Poems

A RED, RED ROSE
Robert Burns

O my luve is like a red, red rose,
That's newly sprung in June;
O my luve is like the melodie
That's sweetly played in tune.

As fair thou art, my bonie lass,
So deep in luve am I;
And I will luve thee still, my dear,
Till a'the seas gang dry.

Till a'the seas gang dry, my dear,
And the rocks melt wi'the sun;
And I will luve thee still, my dear,
While the sands o'life shall run.

And fare thee weel, my only luve,
And fare thee weel a while;
And I will come again, my luve,
Tho'were ten thousand mile!

一朵红红的玫瑰
罗伯特·彭斯

啊,我爱人像红红的玫瑰,
在六月里苞放;
啊,我爱人像一支乐曲,
乐声美妙、悠扬。

你那么美,漂亮的姑娘,
我爱你那么深切;
我会永远爱你,亲爱的,
一直到四海涸竭。

直到四海涸竭,亲爱的,
直到太阳把岩石消熔!
我会永远爱你,亲爱的,
只要生命无穷。

再见吧,我唯一的爱人,
再见吧,小别片刻!
我会回来的,我的爱人,
即使万里相隔!

天净沙

春

白朴

青山暮日和风,
阑干楼阁帘栊,
杨柳秋千院中。
啼莺舞燕,
小桥流水飞红。

Spring

To the Tune of Sky-clear Sand

Green hills, setting sun and breeze blows,
Pavilions, banisters and curtained windows,
Swings in the courtyard and weeping willows.
Orioles are singing, dancing swallows,
Tiny bridge, petals flying and stream flows.

Sometimes the use of literal translation seems acceptable, but translation in this way actually fails to convey the essence of the SLT to readers.

Some examples:

1. He bent solely upon profit.
   (A) Surface:他只屈身于利润之前。
   (B) Shallow:只有利润才使他低头。
   (C) Deep:他惟利是图。

2. We are here today and gone tomorrow.
   (A) Surface:我们今天在这里,明天就到别处去了。
   (B) Shallow:今日在世,明日辞世。
   (C) Deep:人生朝露。

3. John is tall like I am the Queen of Sheba.

（A）Surface：约翰高得像我是西巴皇后。

（B）Shallow：约翰高的话,我就是西巴皇后。

（C）Deep：要说约翰个头高,没那回事。

In the above-mentioned examples, translation (A) is only a surface translation, and (B) is merely a shallow translation. Neither succeeds in seeing through the surface structure of the original grammatical structure, not to speak of penetrating into the deep structure of the original. Translation (C), however, not only breaks the crust of the original, but gains an insight into the deep structure through the surface structure. Only by doing so, can a translation be really faithful to the original in equivalence of implication. Such method used in the above-mentioned examples is called free translation or liberal translation.

On condition that the source language is in harmony with the target language neither in form nor in content, translating in the original form will fail to preserve the integrity of the source text, and what is more, when there is something implicated behind, between, beyond the lines we have to be free from the yoke of the form of the source text and translate it in the form of the target language for the sake of taking the advantages of the receptor language. That's to say, when essence is in contradiction with form in translation and the two can't be harmonized, essence should be stressed, and free translation can be adopted. Some examples：

4. Cast pearls before swine.

对牛弹琴。

5. Barbara was born with a silver spoon in her mouth.

巴巴拉出生在富贵人家。

6. But no one forces you to go to sea. It gets in your blood.

可是没人强迫你出海,是你心甘情愿嘛。

7. I gave my youth to the sea and I came home and gave her (my wife) my old age.

我把青春献给了海洋,等我回来见到妻子时,已是两鬓如霜了。

8.   Finis

  Walter Savage Landor

  I strove with none, for none was worth my strife.

  Nature I loved and next to Nature, Art：

  I warm'd both hands before the fire of life；

  It sinks, and I am ready to depart.

终曲

沃尔特·萨凡基·兰多

与世无争兮性狷介。
钟情自然兮游心艺苑；
生命之火兮暖我心田,
爝火熄兮羽化而归天。

Literal translation and free translation can be generally adopted as they are mentioned above but the fact of matter is that neither literal translation nor free translation is adopted absolutely in translation practice. Instead of being mutually exclusive, literal translation and free translation are mutually complementary in translation practice. Example 6 and Example 7 are typical examples, the first part of Example 6 is translated literally, but the second part liberally complementary. The same is true of the translation of Example 7. Hence we can come to the conclusion that literal translation and free translation are mutually complementary, they can be adopted interchangeably in translation practice, neither can be adopted absolutely.

Translation Exercises

I. *Translate the following sentences into Chinese literally or liberally, or with the proper methods interchangeably used.*

1. My uncle remembered me on my birthday.
2. Would there be any possibility of having breakfast on the train before we are decanted at Munich?
3. Their accent couldn't fool a native speaker.
4. This season saw an ominous dawning of the tenth of November.
5. There is no love lost between them.
6. We must claim extraordinary insight for Hegel.
7. Truth lies at the bottom of the decanter.
8. Darkness released him from his last restraints.
9. He was seized with the despairing sense of his helplessness.
10. Most of us, however, take life for granted. We know that one day we must die, but usually we picture that day as far in the future. When we are in buoyant health, death is all but unimaginable. We seldom think of it. the days stretch out in an endless vista. So we go about petty tasks, hardly aware of our listless attitude toward life.

II. *Translate the following poems literally, if possible, or liberally, if not, or with both literal translation and free translation properly adopted.*

1. Pippa's Song
   Robert Browning

The year's at the spring,
And day's at the morn;
Morning's at seven;
The hillside's dew-pearled;
The lark's on the wing;
The snail's on the thorn:
God's in His heaven—
All's right with the world!

2. 天净沙

秋

白　朴

孤村落日残霞，

轻烟老树寒鸦，

一点飞鸿影下。

青山绿水，

白草红叶黄花。

2.2.2　Extension

In the translation between English and Chinese, we sometimes come across some words that are easy to understand but difficult to express the exact meanings in accurate Chinese. Now some examples:

1. Mr. Li will be a valuable acquisition to the teaching staff of our school.
2. Now you can meet good Samaritans here, there and everywhere.

"Acquisition" in Example 1 and "Samaritans" in Example 2 are the key words in translation, we can easily find the Chinese interpretations or the interpretations in English provided by dictionaries. But only relying on interpretations provided by dictionaries, translation of these sentences would be dull, obscure, and occasionally misunderstood. Such being the case, we have to extend the meanings of the key words in order to have the original naturally and smoothly expressed in the target language. Extension of the meaning of a word must be in harmony with the original in essence. It can not go beyond the semantic range of the original, otherwise it will misrepresent the original meaning.

Let's try to extend "acquisition" and "Samaritan" and put these sentences into Chinese.

"Acquisition" is interpreted as 1) acquiring, 2) sth. or sb. acquired or added. The subject of the sentence is a person. Thus we can extend the word into "不可多得的新成员"(or 新的骨干) as it is modified by "valuable". The sentence can thus be translated as follows:

李先生是我校教师队伍中不可多得的新成员。

(or 李先生是我校一位新的骨干教师。)

"Samaritan," taken from the Bible, was later quoted as an allusion which means a person who pities and gives practical help to persons in trouble. According to the meaning, we can extend the word into "助人为乐者"，"乐于助人的人". The second sentence can be expressed in Chinese as:

现在助人为乐者比比皆是，处处可见。

(or 眼下，走到哪里都能遇到热心人。)

Some of the words extended are rather abstract, some are concrete. Abstract words are usually extended into concrete words and vice versa.

- **From the concrete and specific into the abstract and general**

3. Every life has its <u>roses</u> and <u>thorns</u>.

4. The emergence of the peoples of the third world and their struggle for identity will lead to the flowering of diverse concepts of life in the future.

第三世界人民的兴起,及其为争取合法地位而进行的斗争将丰富未来生活的各种观念。

5. Since then, our relations based on the anti-imperialist struggle have blossomed and have been diversified and considerably reinforced.

从那时起,我们之间建立在反帝斗争基础上的关系便有了发展,而且是多方面的发展,同时也得到了极大的加强。

"Flowering" and "blossom" are concrete words that give specific form and shape, but share a general and abstract concept when extended into "丰富" and "发展" respectively.

6. Arabs rub shoulders with Jews, and have been doing so from the earliest settlement of the territories.

阿拉伯人与犹太人生活一起,自从这块土地有人居住以来一直就是这样。

7. Their life style could seem Spartan to a city family with their assets.

他们的生活方式对城市里的殷实人家来说似乎过于简朴了。

The Spartan people are well-known for caring little for the ordinary comforts of life, fearing neither pain nor hardship, living a very simple life. So we extend its meaning into "简朴" in Chinese.

Now try to translate the following three sentences into Chinese and have the meanings of the underlined words extended.

8. There were times when emigration bottleneck was extremely rigid and nobody was allowed to leave the country out of his personal preference.

9. You will never work it out by that method; you are off the track altogether.

10. When the new president tried to become dictator, the generals soon clipped his wings.

• **From the abstract and general into the concrete and specific**

11. As the Politburo gave the go-ahead to Brezhnev, Nixon and Kissinger were meeting in President's Kremlin apartment, prepared to accept a setback on SALT.

政治局向勃列日涅夫开放绿灯时,尼克松和基辛格正在克里姆林宫的总统下榻处开会,准备承受限制战略武器会谈失败的挫折。

12. Vietnam was his entree to the new Administration, his third incarnation as a foreign policy consultant.

越南战争成了他进入新政府的敲门砖。他担任政府的对外政策顾问已是第三次了。

13. I say this because of the bleak consensus, albeit (although) only among some in the West, about the future.

我之所以这样说,是因为即便是在一些西方人士中间也普遍存在着一种对人类前途的悲观的看法。

14. Alas, an examination of the international situation does not warrant optimism.

可惜的是,国际局势看来并不使人乐观。

"Alas", an interjection used very flexibly to express regret, sorrow, fear, sadness… shares a strong hue of mood. The exact implication of the word in given contexts can be perceived only by chewing the cud of the original and whetting it carefully. Here "alas", extended into "可惜的是", is much more obvious in meaning.

15. Saudi Arabia has had problems with Iraq and South Yemen but he tried hard to remain in touch with leaders of both states.

沙特阿拉伯与伊拉克南也门之间早有纠葛,但它仍竭尽全力与两国领导人保持接触。

"Problem" is very general and flexible in meaning, when extended into "纠葛" in Chinese, its meaning is fixed.

16. Death ends all things and so is the comprehensive conclusion of a story, but marriage finishes it very properly too and the sophisticated are ill-advised to sneer at what is by convention termed a happy ending. It is a sound instinct of the common people which persuades them that with this all that needs to be said is said. When male and female, after whatever vicissitudes you like, are at least brought together, they have fulfilled their biological function and interest passes to the generation that is to come.

死是一切的了结,所以是一个故事的总收场。但用结婚来结束也很合适,那些世俗的所谓大团圆,自命风雅的人大可不必嗤之以鼻。普通人有一种健全的本能,总相信这么一来,一切该交代的都交代了,男的女的,不论经历怎样的悲欢离合,终于被撮合在一起,两性的生物功能已经完成,兴趣也就转到下一代。

In this long sentence, "sophisticated" and "vicissitudes" are two key words worth much of our thought. The first one is generally paraphrased as "worldly wise", "老于世故的", "洞悉世情的"; "矫揉造作的" in Chinese. Here it's extended into "自命风雅的人" on the basis of reading between the lines of the context and the artistic problem involved. Generally speaking, most people like a happy ending, but those who think themselves towering above the rest consider happy endings too vulgar, unbearably vulgar. This is, of course, a subjective point of view. The happy ending may not necessarily turn out to be vulgar and those who have objection to the happy ending may not necessarily tower above the rest. Therefore it is extended into "自命风雅的人", which is regarded as an extension in deep structure that calls for a thorough digestion of the original.

"Vicissitude" means change, esp in sb's fortunes; such as changes from wealth to poverty, from success to failure (荣辱兴衰 in Chinese). But it is here used to indicate the joys and sorrows of love, thus "悲欢离合" in Chinese is a very appropriate extension.

Idioms and idiomatic phrases can also be extended and sometimes it's necessary to have their meanings extended. For example:

17. Their stock had gone down, but Nasser, who had bought off the arms deal with the Soviet block, was riding high.

The idiomatic phrase "ride high" means to enjoy a feeling of success and well-being. e.g. Our team are really riding high after all their victories. 在取得一连串胜利之后,全队上下,喜气洋洋,兴高采烈。Here Example 17 is used to describe the mood after his success in buying off the arms deals with the Soviet block.

英国人的本钱所剩不多了。但是纳塞尔在同苏联集团达成军火交易之后,洋洋得意。

18. Sadat whisked all of his—and Heikal's—enemies off to jail on charges of trying to

overthrow the government, and Heikal was left riding higher than ever.

萨达特不费吹灰之力将他的——也是海卡尔的那些敌人,以图谋颠覆政府的罪名全部送进监狱,而海卡尔则是平步青云,飞黄腾达。

Extension of meaning of allusions.

Allusions(典故) are words or phrases abstracted from historical facts, popular legends, anecdotes or famous classics. Allusions are the cream of language refined in diction, but profound in meaning, and hence frequently quoted by various writers. The implied meaning of a specific allusion is usually difficult for a reader to understand, even more difficult for a TLT reader, or over his head. Such being the case, it is necessary for the translator to have the meanings of the allusions extended according to the context. Some examples:

1. In times of peace, a large part of the dictator role would be as a sort of national Aunt Sally, a symbol on which its citizens could vent their frustration.

和平年代,独裁者的作用充其量不过是众矢之的,只能是国民们受挫时发泄怨恨的出气筒。

2. It was another one of those catch-22 situations, you're damned if you do and you're damned if you don't.

这真是又一个左右为难的尴尬局面,做也倒霉,不做也倒霉!

3. He's a real Jekyll and Hyde: at home he's kind and loving, but in business he's completely without principles.

他真是个具有双重人格的人,在家里他和蔼可亲,可在做生意时他却完全不讲道义。

4. The scientist was widely respected for many years, and not until after his death was it realized that most of his discoveries were mare's nests.

这位科学家多年来一直为人们所尊崇,可直到他死后人们才意识到他的发现原来大多是子虚乌有的骗人把戏。

5. He poked his head forward like a born Paul Pry, put out his hand and said "Good afternoon, won't you sit down?"

他向前探出头来,生就一副爱管闲事的样子,伸出手说道:"下午好,您请坐。"

6. The rich man met with Saint Nicholas' clerks on his way home and got robbed.

那位腰缠万贯的富人在回家的路上遇上了拦路的强盗,钱财被抢劫一空。

7. He was picked up by the police as a peeping Tom.

他因为窥视(女人)被警察抓住。

8. 先生大名,如雷贯耳。小弟献丑,真是班门弄斧了。

Your great fame long since reached my ears like thunder. I am ashamed to display my incompetence before a connoisseur like yourself.

9. 怪不得老爷说我是"管窥蠡测"!昨夜说:你们的眼泪单葬我,这就错了。看来我竟不能全得。

I'm not surprised that Father tells me I have a "small capacity but a great self-conceit". I mean, that staff about all of you making a river of tears for me when I die: I realize now that it's not possible.

In a word, allusions can't be translated too literally, nor mechanically, their implied meanings are supposed to be extended properly in translation for the sake of a better understanding of TLT readers.

Translation Exercises

I. *Translate the following sentences into Chinese, extending the meanings of the underlined words by reading between the lines.*

1. The invention of machinery had brought into the world a new era—the Industrial Age. Money had become <u>king</u>.

2. They met again in April at Bandung. It was a considerable occasion for Nehru. He was <u>riding high</u>.

3. China is today <u>the tabernacle of</u> justice and the hope of oppressed people.

4. There are more <u>smiles</u> in the world than there are <u>tears</u>.

5. The mountain plateau <u>laughs with verdure</u>.

6. <u>Brain drain</u> has been Egypt's Number One <u>concern</u>—as a matter of fact it has become an <u>epidemic</u> in that area of the world.

7. With scores of journals and magazines published on nationwide scale and more coming off the press at a later date, an <u>Augustan Age</u> for China's literature and art can well be expected.

8. What will it be when the increase of yearly production is brought to a complete stop? Here is the vulnerable place, <u>the heel of Achilles</u>, for capitalistic production.

9. Many took to gambling and got in over their heads, borrowing from <u>Shylocks</u> to pay their debts.

10. His meeting with this film director was the <u>open sesame</u> to a successful life as an actor.

II. *Translate the following passage into Chinese with enough attention to the choice of words and extension of the underlined words.*

How to Grow Old

Some old people are oppressed by <u>the fear</u> of death. In the young there is a <u>justification</u> for this feeling. Young men who have reasons to fear that they will be killed in battle may <u>justifiably</u> feel bitter in the thought that they have been cheated of the best things that life has to offer. But in an old man who has known human <u>joys</u> and <u>sorrows</u>, and has achieved whatever work it was in him to do, the fear of death is somewhat abject and ignoble. The best way to overcome it—so at least it seems to me is to make your interests gradually wider and more impersonal, until bit by bit the walls of <u>the ego recede</u>, and your life becomes increasingly merged in the universal life. An individual human existence should be like a river—small at first, narrowly contained within its banks, and rushing passionately past boulders and over waterfalls. Gradually the river grows wider, the banks recede, the waters flow more quietly, and in the end, without any visible break, they become merged in the sea; and painlessly lose their individual being. The man who, in old age, can see his life in this way, will not suffer from the fear of death, since the things he cares for will continue. And if, with the decay of vitality, weariness increases, <u>the thought of rest</u> will be not unwelcome. I should wish to die while still at work, knowing that others will carry on what I can no longer do, and content in the thought that what was possible has been done.

2.2.3　Conversion

In the translation from English into Chinese, some sentences can be translated without converting the parts of speech of the original words. Some examples:

1. Mr. Ford called on Americans to bite the bullet and make personal sacrifices. This, he said, would help to halt inflation.

福特先生号召美国人咬紧牙关,做出个人牺牲,他说,这将有助于制止通货膨胀。

2. The manager was a nervous anxious little man, always ready to cry wolf if the shop takings went down a pound or two.

经理是个身材矮小、神经过敏、焦急不安的人,只要商店营业收入下降一两镑,他就要大喊大叫。

3. Fred said he could beat the new man in boxing, but he lost and had to eat crow.

费雷德说他能在拳击中击败那个新对手,但他却被击败了,只好承认自己吹牛。

4. One after another, speakers called for the down-fall of imperialism, abolition of exploitation of man by man, liberation of the oppressed of the world.

发言人一个接一个表示要打倒帝国主义,要消灭人剥削人的制度,要解放世界上被压迫的人民。

5. For two years I have only had insults and outrage from her. I have been treated worse than any servants in the kitchen. I have never had a friend or a kind word, except from you. I have been made to tend the little girls in the lower schoolroom, and to talk French to the Misses, until I grew sick of my mother-tongue.

两年来她羞辱我虐待我,厨房里的佣人过的日子比我还强些呢。除了你,没有一个人把我当朋友,也没有人对我说过一句好话,我得伺候低班的小姑娘,又得跟小姐们说法文,说得我一想起自己的语言就头痛。

"Downfall", "abolition", "exploitation", "liberation" in Example 4 and "insults" and "outrage" in Example 5 are all nouns, but they are turned into verbs in the Chinese version. All these words in the original are nouns, yet they share the function of verbs, which are called "verbal nouns"(动作名词). Verbal nouns are usually changed into verbs when translated into Chinese.

For examples:

6. Franklin had a deep conviction that we must learn to understand and to get on with our neighbours in this hemisphere.

富兰克林深信,我们必须学会了解本半球的邻居并学会同他们友好相处。

7. Ordinarily a territorial claim requires physical possession of the territory by one or more explorers.

在一般情况下,提出任何一种领土要求都要由一个或更多先驱者实地占有这块土地。

8. Nuclear warfare would leave no time for the old-style mobilization of the armed forces.

核战争将不让你有时间照老样子按部就班地动员武装部队。

9. He was a voracious reader, spending much of his days and evenings devouring books.

他读起书来,不分昼夜,废寝忘食。

10. I will say the very thought of you makes me sick, and that you treated me with miserable cruelty.

我会说,我一想起你就恶心,你对我残酷到了可耻的地步。

"Conviction", "possession", "reader" and "thought" in sentences from 6 to 10 are all nouns whose parts of speech are changed. In addition to this (n-v), we can also convert parts of speech as follows:

- **Turn nouns into adjectives**

11. We are deeply convinced of the correctness of this policy and firmly determined to pursue it.

我们深信这一政策是正确的,并决定继续奉行这一政策。

12. Belannde's admission brought to light the entire hypocrisy of the statement made by the representatives of the Anglo-American bloc about the defence of rights of individual freedom.

贝朗迪所承认的事实证明,英美集团代表的所谓保护人自由权的说法完全是假的。

13. Japanese guests are immensely impressed by the splendor and warmth of our reception at the airport, along the boulevard and in the Great Hall of the People.

日本客人对于我们在机场、街道以及人民大会堂所给予的盛大热情的接待(款待)非常感激(深表感激)。(日本客人在机场、街道和人民大会堂都受到我们盛大的热情的接待,对此他们深表感激)

14. There is increased demoralization.

士气比以前更消沉。

- **Turn verbs into nouns, adverbs, adjectives**

15. They argue that regimes come and go, that political issues are always transient, that the Olympic spirit is transcendent.

他们说,政府无非是走马灯,政治问题总是朝生夕逝的,只有奥林匹克精神才是永世长存的。(v-n)

16. Quick decision characterized him.

当机立断是他的特点。

17. He was always smartly dressed.

他穿着一直很考究。(v-n)

18. A well-dressed man, who looked and talked like an American, got into the car.

一个穿着讲究的人上了车,他外表和谈吐都像个美国人。(v-n)

19. He was motivated by a desire to reach a compromise.

他的动机是希望达成某种妥协。(v-n)

20. They thought differently.

他们的想法不同。(v-n)

21. In his six consecutive speeches, Nasser indulged in violent attacks on the Baghdad government.

在六次一连串的演说中,纳塞尔一味对巴格达政府进行猛烈的攻击。(v-adv)

22. He said, if this was the case, he would be tempted to try.

他说：如果情况是这样，他颇有跃跃欲试之意。(v-adv)

23. Let me see if it works.

让我瞧瞧它是不是坏了。(v-adj)

- Turn adjectives into verbs, nouns, adverbs

24. It is a two-way street in politics. When you ignore people, they are going to ignore you.

这是政治上的一种有来必往的现象，如果你不理睬人们（家），人们（家）也就不会理睬你。(a-v)

25. The State Department's top-ranking Asian specialist said Monday that China's opening to the West is a helpful policy that should be encouraged by close ties with United States.

国务院最高级的亚洲问题专家星期一说，中国向西方开放的政策是一项好政策，应该通过加强中国同美国的关系来加以鼓励。(a-v)

26. The noon sun clarified the air, I became aware of two surfers well out from the shore, patiently paddling their boards while they waited for a perfect wave.

正午时天气晴朗，我瞥见两个冲浪者离岸很远，耐心地踏着滑板，等候一个最理想的浪头。(a-v)

27. Shortly after Jimmy Carter's election as President, his advisers were reported as recommending lower taxes and higher government spending.

在吉米·卡特当选总统后不久，据说他的顾问们就建议应当降低税收，扩大政府开支。(a-v)

- Adjectives can sometimes be converted into nouns

28. Most of us think him very hypocritical.

我们大家都认为他是一个十足的伪君子。(a-n)

29. The new treaty would be good for ten years.

新条约的有限期为 10 年. (a-n)

30. Official Cairo is taking pains to create impression as if its relations with the East have remained untouched.

开罗官方千方百计想制造一种印象，好像他同东方国家的关系仍然没有受到影响。(adj-n)

- Adjectives are occasionally changed into adverbs

31. There is a big increase in demand for all kinds of consumer goods in every part of our country.

目前，我国各地对各种消费品的需要量已大大增加。(a-adv)

32. I've often wondered in the years since whether I made the right choice.

究竟这步棋我是走对了，还是走错了？几年来我经常纳闷。(a-adv)

33. We must make full use of the natural resources available.

我们应当充分利用现有的自然资源。(a-adv)

- Turn adverbs into verbs, adjectives and nouns

34. There are more people in India sleeping in the streets than any place else in the world.

A dominant power is dominant inherently.

在印度,要饭的人比任何国家都多,那里的统治阶层是靠血统一代一代传下去的。(adv-v)

35. The performance is on.

演出已经开始了。(adv-v)

36. In those years the Republicans were in.

那些年是共和党执政。(adv-v)

37. Why should we let in foreign goods when Americans walk the streets because they can't sell their own goods?

在美国人由于推销不出自己的产品而失业之际,为什么我们还要让外国货进口呢?(adv-v)

38. Traditionally, there had always been good relations between them.

他们之间一直有着传统的友好关系。(adv-a)

39. The electronic computer is chiefly characterized by accuracy and quick computation.

电子计算机的主要特点是运算正确、迅速。(adv-a)

40. It was officially announced that they agreed on a reply to the Soviet Union.

官方宣布,他们就给苏联的复信取得了一致意见。(adv-n)

41. The paper said editorially that Mcmillan has stolen the Western leadership during Dulles' absence.

这家报纸的社论说,麦克米伦在杜勒斯卧病期间窃走了西方领导权。(adv-n)

• **Conversion of prepositions**

Prepositions are usually converted into verbs when translated into Chinese. Some examples:

42. Out of all the glorious tales written about the revolution for independence from Britain, the fact is hardly know that a black man is the first to die for American independence.

读遍关于(有关)美国为摆脱英国统治争取独立而进行革命的堂皇纪事,也很难了解到第一个为美国独立而牺牲的(捐躯者)原来是黑人。

43. Some longtime associates and friends wanted to protect him from the White House; some, to protect him from the public; and others, to protect him from himself.

有些老同事和老朋友想保护他,使他免受白宫的连累,有的想保护他,使他不受到公众的攻击,还有一些人则想保护他,使他本人不要说错话或做错事。

44. Now, ten years later, she has gained her master's degree from Harvard's School of Education and is finally off welfare.

现在经过十年寒窗之苦以后,她已获得了哈佛大学教育学院的硕士学位,并终于摆脱了救济。

45. The most Panamanians are after at this time is a change to get more income from the Canal.

这一次巴拿马人所追求的最大目标是希望有机会从运河那里得到更多的收入。

46. Downstairs, then, they went, Joseph very red and blushing, Rebecca very modest, and holding her green eyes downwards. She was dressed in white with bare shoulder as white as snow—the picture of youth, unprotected innocence, and humble virgin simplicity.

他们一路下楼,乔瑟夫涨红脸,利蓓加举止端正,一双绿眼望着地下,她穿了一件白衣服,露出雪白的肩膀,年纪轻轻,越发显得天真烂漫,活是一个娴静又纯洁的小姑娘。

Conversion of part of speech is frequently and flexibly used in the translation from English into Chinese. Whether or not it is to be used seems not determined by the original, instead, it is determined by the target language. Some examples for illustration as follows:

(verb-to-noun conversion)

1. 语言这个东西不是随便可以学好的,非下苦功不可。

The mastery of language is not easy and requires painstaking effort.

2. 林则徐认为,要成功地禁止鸦片买卖,就得首先把鸦片焚毁。

Lin Zexu believed that a successful ban of the trade in opium must be preceded by the destruction of the drug itself.

3. 革命是解放生产力,改革也是解放生产力。

Revolution means the emancipation of the productive forces, and so does reform.

4. 他酷爱古典音乐。

He is an ardent lover of classical music.

5. 谁负责翻译第一章?

Who is responsible for the translation of Chapter One?

(verb-to-adj, prep or adv conversion)

6. 他们充分意识到这一法案的重要性。

They are fully aware of the importance of the bill.

7. 全世界爱和平的人民都反对战争。

Peace-loving people all over the world are against war.

8. 他们的试验已经结束。

Their experiment is over.

(n-to-v conversion)

9. 橄榄枝是和平的象征。

Olive branch symbolizes peace.

10. 改革的目的在于提高生产力。

Reform aims at improving productivity.

11. 这位总统的特点是当机立断。

A prompt decision characterizes the president.

(conversion between adjective and adverb)

12. 他的首次演讲给学生留下了深刻的印象。

The students were deeply impressed by his first speech.

13. 小说中的人物惟妙惟肖,栩栩如生。

The characters in this novel are vividly depicted.

14. 我们必须充分利用现在的自然资源。

We must make full use of the natural resources available.

15. 她慢条斯理地点了一下头,表示同意。

She agreed with a slow nod.

(some other conversions)

16. 学生应德、智、体全面地发展。

All the students should be well developed morally, intellectually and physically.

17. 老人家好心好意地给我们指路。

The old man had the kindness to show us the way.

18. 快收拾一下吧！厨房太脏了！

Get cleaned up, the kitchen's a mess!

19. 我们决不屈服。

Under no circumstances shall we give in.

Translation Exercise

I. *Translate the following passage into Chinese.*

The First Snow

The first snow came. How beautiful it was, falling so silently all day long, all night long, on the mountains, on the meadows, on the roofs of the living, on the graves of the dead! All white save the river, that marked its course by a winding black line across the landscape; and the leafless trees, that against the leaden sky now revealed more fully the wonderful beauty and intricacies of their branches. What silence, too, came with the snow, and what seclusion! Every sound was muffled, every noise changed to something soft and musical. No more tramping hoofs, no more rattling wheels! Only the chiming of sleigh-bells, beating as swift and merrily as the hearts of children.

II. *Translate the following sentences into Chinese, converting the parts of speech of the underlined words.*

1. The very earth trembled as with <u>the tramps of horses</u> and <u>murmur of angry men</u>.

2. You don't turn sick <u>at the sight of blood</u>?

3. I shuddered <u>at the thought of</u> Grace Poole bursting out upon me.

4. She promptly shepherded them out of the crowded living room and into the <u>privacy of the library</u>.

5. <u>The pallor of her face</u> indicated clearly how she was feeling at the moment.

6. Bingley was endeared to Darcy by <u>the easiness, openness</u> and <u>ductility of his temper</u>.

7. I recognized the <u>absurdity of dealing with them through intermediaries</u>.

8. It is a truth <u>universally acknowledged</u>, that a single man in possession of a good fortune must be in want of a wife.

9. The President had <u>prepared meticulously</u> for his journey.

10. Boys <u>think differently</u> from girls.

III. *Translate the following sentences into English, converting the parts of speech of the underlined words and phases.*

1. 希望你们<u>考虑</u>一下我们的意见。

2. 他犹豫了一会,终于决定还是自己送我去。
3. 我意识到这项投资要冒风险。
4. 我们一致赞成他的建议。
5. 他在剧中的精彩表演给我们留下深刻的印象。
6. 这种行为举止是罪犯的心理特征。
7. 年轻人迟早要取代老年人。
8. 他的新书十分成功。
9. 他们热烈欢迎这位著名的作家。
10. 她急切地希望见到他。

2.2.4　Amplification

A good translation, generally speaking, is a bit longer than the original (We don't mean that a good translation must be longer than the original) primarily because a translator must faithfully turn the obvious form of the original language into the target language, and at the same time, he must convey what is implied in the original context, especially the message that is closely connected with the background of the original culture and history in the target language.

The difficulties to readers of translation lie in what's implied in the original, and the translator should make some adaptations in the light of specific conditions to enable readers to understand more easily, which is similar to a boa that twines itself around an animal and squeezes it hard to make it longer and thinner before it can swallow the animal more easily. Nothing is lost in the animal itself but the shape of the animal is changed by being squeezed and pressed. A translator must, sometimes, add something (that is implied but not obviously expressed in words) to the original in his translation to give explanations, translation is thus lengthened, form changed, but the meaning of the original remains unchanged, which is only adapted to capability of readers. The method adopted this way is called amplification.

The words added in translation must be indispensable (absolutely necessary) either syntactically or semantically. Thus, amplification can be classified as:

(1) Words supplied for syntactic construction(结构性增补)

(2) Words supplied for semantic completion(语义性增补)

The former is to meet the needs of syntax of the target language and the latter for the clearness and completion of the original meaning expressed in the target language, but both are used for good readability.

Some examples:

1. 人民犯了法,也要受处罚,也要坐班房,也有死刑。

When anyone among the people breaks the law, he too should be punished, imprisoned or even sentenced to death.

Instead of turning "人民" into "the people", a collective noun in English, we put it into "anyone among the people" by adding "anyone among" and "when" which are actually involved in the original. Suppose we put "人民" into "the people" (without adding "when" and "anyone among") the meaning of the original will be misrepresented.

2. 其实地上本来没有路,走的人多了,也便成了路。

For actually the earth had no roads to begin with, but when many men pass one way, a road is made.

Without "to begin with", the parts of translation would fail to be logically connected with each other, without adding "but when", the translation would not be in agreement with the syntax of the English language. Therefore, the phrases "to begin with" in Example 2 and the words "anyone among" in Example I are the words supplied for semantic completion, and the words "when", "he" in Example 1 and "but when" in Example 2 are for syntactic construction.

3. You got a prejudice all right-against a race that's black. That's why I called you white racist that night. But when you deal with a black person, I don't feel any bad vices.

你这个人确有偏见。你(结构性增补)对整个(语义性增补)黑人种族抱有偏见(结构性增补)。那天晚上,我说你是个白人种族主义者,道理就在这里。但是当你跟一个具体的(语义性增补)黑人打交道时,我倒不(修辞性增补:语气补足词)觉得你有什么恶意。

4. The V sign itself is a challenge, for the famous Churchillian invention that used to mean Allied Victory is no longer valid. Instead of having to do with war, V today is made to mean peace.

V形手势(语义性增补)本身就是一种挑战。因为丘吉尔的这个著名的发明当年(语义性增补)曾作为盟国胜利的标志。如今这层(省略"与战争有关的")意思已不复存在。今天(修辞性重复)V形手势语是被用来表示和平。

5. My audiences vary from tens to thousands. I expected opposition but got hardly any.

我的听众从几十人到几千人不等(修辞性补足),我希望持有异议的人起来跟我辩论(语义性增补),但几乎没有遇到(结构性增补)。

6. But, if this world is not merely a bad joke, life a vulgar flare amid the cool radiance of the stars, and existence an empty laugh braying across the mysteries; if these intimations of something behind and beyond are not evil humour born of indigestion, or whimsies sent by the devil to mock and madden us; if, in a word, beauty means something, yet we must not seek to interpret the meaning.

但是,即使现实世界不仅仅是一个拙劣的玩笑,生命不仅仅是(结构性重复)天体间交织的寒光中的一点平庸的火花,人生也不仅仅是(结构性重复)喧噪于神秘之乡的空虚的一笑,即使这一切高深莫测的启示不是由于内在的失调而迸发的邪界之念,也不是(结构性重复)魔鬼用来嘲弄和激怒我们的奇思怪想,一句话,即使美确实(修辞性增补:语气补足词)具有某种意义,我们还是不要试图去解释它的意义为好(修辞性增补:语气补足词,落在句尾,使句子意思更完整)。

7. What is feared as failure in American society, is, above all, aloneness. And aloneness is terrifying because it means that there is no one, no group, no approved cause to submit to.

在美国社会中作为失败而为人们所(语义及结构上的增补。汉语通常要求"为……所有"结构中置入施事者)恐惧的莫过于孤独了。而孤独之所以可怕,就因为那意味着没有一个可服从的人,没有一个可服从的公认的大义("可服从的"重复两次,皆因结构上的需要,原文中 to submit to 修饰三者。因此重复是必要的)。

8. Long, anxious days passed, during which I hoped that Dave would see that white was not

always white nor black always totally black. Time was running out; his decision could not be indefinitely postponed.

我过着漫长的、焦虑的日子,一直(语义增补词)希望戴夫能明白,世事(语义结构上的需要)并非处处皂白分明。时光流逝,他不能这样(修辞性补足词)无限期地延宕下去,而不作(结构性增补)决定。

9. I remember the first time we talked as woman to woman.

我还记得我们之间那第一次女人之间的知心会意(结构性增补)的谈话。

10. "And before you go to beg their pardon, change those trousers for a dress. You know how your mother-in-law feels about pants on a woman. She always says, 'What was hatched a hen must not try to be a rooster!'"

"在你去向他们赔礼之前,先用女服('女'是结构性增补)换掉男裤('男'亦是语义性增补,类似涉及不同文化差异的语义问题,要特别注意增补,以利中国读者理解)。你知道你婆婆对女人穿长裤是怎么看的,她总是说:'孵出来是母鸡就别想当公鸡!'"

From all these examples we can see that amplification in translation is the further explanation of the unspoken words involved in the original to the understanding of the original, the words supplied are in harmony with the original in essence and in agreement with the target language in syntax. This is closely correlated with the translator's sense of his mother tongue, but free from the personal will of the translator.

Amplification can be done by supplying the words that are omitted in the original, such as relative pronouns, adverbs, possessive pronouns and some other connecting words, by supplying category words and by supplying overlap words.

- **Supply what's omitted in the original in translation**

Omission is frequently used in English out of rhetorical device or to meet the needs of the English syntax. But, in nine cases out of ten, what's omitted must be supplied in translation, which will otherwise disagree with the syntax of the receptor language or misrepresent the original meaning. Some examples:

11. Histories make man wise; poets witty; the mathematics subtle; natural philosophy deep; moral grave; logic and rhetoric able to contend. Abeunt studia in mores.

读史使人明智,读诗使人灵秀,数学使人周密,科学使人深刻,伦理学使人庄重,逻辑修辞学使人善辩:凡有所学,皆成性格。

12. We recognize—and share—China's resolve to resist the attempts of any nation which seeks to establish global or regional hegemony.

我们认识到中国有决心反对任何国家谋求建立全球霸权或地区霸权的企图,我们也有这样的决心。

13. We, in Britain, have every reason to wish for better relations with the states of Eastern Europe. And we do sincerely want them.

我们英国人有充分理由同东欧国家改善关系,我们衷心希望改善同他们的关系。

14. These problems had to be weighed up under varying, sometimes uncertain, factors.

这些问题必须根据变化着的因素,有时是捉摸不定的因素来进行衡量。

15. Mr. Sedley was neutral. Let Jos marry whom he likes, he said; it's no affair of mine, this girl has no fortune; no more had Mrs Sedley. She seems good-humoured and clever, and will keep him in order perhaps. Better she, my dear, than a black Mrs Sedley, and a dozen of mahogany grandchildren.

赛特立先生是无可无不可的,他说乔斯爱娶谁就娶谁,反正不是我的事,那女孩子没有钱,可当年赛特立太太也一样穷;她看上去性情温顺,也很聪明,也许会把乔斯管得好好的。亲爱的,还是她吧,总比娶个黑不溜秋的媳妇养出十来个黄黑脸皮的孙子孙女们好些。

16. He may go back and tell Miss Pinkerton that I hate her with all my soul and I wish he would, and I wish I had a means of proving it, too.

他不妨回去告诉平克顿小姐,说我恨她恨得入骨。我巴不得她回去搬嘴,巴不得叫老太太知道我的厉害。

17. And the fear of death, of God, of the universe, comes over him—the hope of the Resurrection and the life, the yearning for immortality, the vain striving of the imprisoned essence—it is then, if ever, man walks alone with God.

于是,对死神的恐惧,对上帝的敬畏,对宇宙的惶惑纷纷萦绕心头(一齐袭来),对复活的希冀,对生活的向往,对永生的渴望,这一切犹如多囚徒的徒劳奋争,若临此境,人也只好听天由命了。

18. 三个臭皮匠,顶个诸葛亮。

Three cobblers with their wits combined equal Zhuge Liang the master mind.

19. 知不知,上,不知知,病。夫惟病病,是以不病。圣人不病,以其病病,是以不病。

老子《道德经》

To know when one does not know is best.

To think one knows when one does not know is a dire disease.

Only he who recognizes this disease as disease

Can cure himself of the disease.

The Sage's way of curing disease

Also consists in making people recognize their

Diseases as diseases and thus ceasing to be diseased.

20. 宝玉盘着腿,合着手,闭着眼,撅着嘴,道:"讲来。"黛玉道:"宝姐姐和你好,你怎么样?宝姐姐不和你好,你怎么样?宝姐姐前儿和你好,如今不和你好,你怎么样?今儿和你好,后来不和你好,你怎么样?你和他好,他偏不和你好,你怎么样?你不和他好,他偏要和你好,你怎么样?"

Baoyu sat with his legs crossed his hand folded, his eyes closed and his mouth pouting, saying, "say as you please." Daiyu said, "How do you behave, if endeared to elder sister Bao or not? How if once endeared to her, but not now? How if endeared to her now, but not in the future? How if she's endeared to you but gives you a rebuff? How if she's not endeared to you, but strives to win your endearment?"

- **Supply category words**

Most of the category words are conceptional nouns with rather abstract meanings. The translators must be famililar with the category of the words they are going to deal with. Such as "tension", is generally put into Chinese "紧张" and if need be, we can add "局势" to "紧张"; "jealousy" is generally put into Chinese "嫉妒" and we can add "心理" to it if necessary according to the context.

Now the following words are put into Chinese by supplying category words:

fatuity	顽愚状态
allergy	过敏反应
necessity	必要性
readability	可读性
assimilation	同化作用
alienation	异化现象
relativity	相对论
transformation	转化过程
indifference	冷漠态度
lightheartedness	轻松愉快的心境(情)
gayety	欢乐气氛
arrogance	傲慢态度
hostility	敌对情绪(行为)
antagonism	对抗性,对抗作用
irregularities	越轨行为
corrosive	腐蚀剂
dripping	滴注,滴注法
dejection	沮丧情绪
complexity	复杂性,复杂局面

Now translate the following sentences into Chinese, adding some category words.

1. The gathering glow of a November evening heightened the sadness of this desolation.

2. Gayety prevailed among the fugitives.

3. He was apprehensive, moreover, of irritating the jealousy of military sway prevalent throughout the country.

4. He looked at me in an amazement.

5. They are sanguine about building up a near peace.

6. The doctor's face expressed a kind of doubting admiration.

7. "I'll beat you to a pulp, you dogs," said Quilp, vainly endeavouring to get near either of them for a parting blow.

- **Supply reduplicated words or numerals to express the plural form of nouns**

Unlike the English language that has the inflectional forms such as the plural form of nouns as well as that of verb tenses, the Chinese language has no change of the plural form of nouns which is usually expressed by supplying reduplicated words or numerals, such as "朵朵鲜花", "百花齐放", "阵阵寒风", "徐徐凉风", "微风习习" etc. Sometimes Chinese words "们", "诸

位","大家","大伙",are used in translation to express the plural form of English nouns. Even uncountable nouns can also be expressed in Chinese reduplicated words or numerals as the Chinese language owes a lot of idioms and proverbs partly composed of numerals, such as "一鳞半爪","一叶知秋","两袖清风","两小无猜","两全其美","三心二意","三顾茅庐","三思而行","三教九流","四面楚歌","四分五裂","五体投地","五光十色","五马分尸","五脏六腑","六神无主","六亲不认","七窍生烟","七零八落","七嘴八舌","八拜之交","八面玲珑","八仙过海,各显神通","九牛一毛","九九归一","九霄云外","十年寒窗","十恶不赦","十室九空","百步穿杨","百废俱兴","百孔千疮","千夫所指","千呼万唤","万水千山","万代千秋","万劫不复","万籁俱寂","万象更新"。

Now turn the following words, phrases or sentences into Chinese by supplying reduplicated words or numerals.

Songs

flowers

ripples

cheers

a chilly wind

a cold wind

a murmuring stream(brook)

deadly still

galloping horses

a golden opportunity

throughout ages

Even Homer sometimes nods.

Flowers of all sorts are blooming in a riot of colour.

The audience left one after another.

In Spring, a gentle wind rippled the tranquil lake.

Translation Exercises

Ⅰ. *Translate the following sentences into Chinese, supplying some words in your versions if need be.*

1. Forms leaned together in the taxis as they waited, and voices sang, and there was laughter from unheard jokes, and lighted cigarettes outlined unintelligible gestures inside.

2. The seasons came and went and they revolved around Joshua. He was the center of Jennifer's world. She watched him grow and develop day by day and it was a never-ending wonder as he began to walk and talk and reason. His moods changed constantly and he was in turn, wild and aggressive and shy and loving.

3. ... in a word, the whole baronetage, peerage, commonage of England, did not contain a more cunning, mean, selfish, foolish, disreputable old man. That bloody-red hand of Sir Pitt

Crawley's would be in anybody's pocket except his own.

4. A still wintry night: Upon this wintry night it is so still, that listening to the intense silence is like looking at intense darkness. If any distant sound be audible in this case, it departs through the gloom like a feeble light in that, and all is heavier than before.

5. Ingrid Bergman(英格丽·褒曼) became a myth, but not in the same way as Greta Garbo (葛利泰·嘉宝) whose entire life is surrounded by secrets, Ingrid became a myth exactly because she dared to live. Openly.

II. *Translate the following sentences into English, supplying some connectives if necessary.*

1. 没有调查就没有发言权。
2. 虚心使人进步,骄傲使人落后。
3. 跑了和尚跑不了庙。
4. 送君千里,终有一别。
5. 知己知彼,百战不殆;不知彼而知己,一胜一负;不知彼不知己,每战必殆。

III. *Translate the following passage into Chinese, supplying reduplicated words if necessary.*

The Night Storm
Charles Dickens

On wintry evening a keen north wind arose as it grew dark, and night came on with black and dismal looks. A bitter storm of sleet, dense and ice-cold, swept the wet streets, and rattled on the trembling windows. Sign-boards, shaken past endurance in their creaking frames, fell crashing on the pavement; old tottering chimneys reeled and staggered in the blast; and many a steeple rocked again that night, as though the earth were troubled.

It was not a time for those, who could by any means get light and warmth, to brave the fury of the weather. In coffee-houses of the better sort, guests crowded round the fire forgot to be political, and told each other with a secret gladness that the blast grew fiercer every minute. Each humble tavern by the waterside had its group of uncouth figures round the hearth, who talked of vessels foundering at sea, and all the hands lost; related many a dismal tale of shipwreck and drowned men, and hoped that some they knew were safe, and shook their heads in doubt. In private dwellings, children clusterd near the blaze; listening with timid pleasure to tales of ghosts and goblins, and tall figures clad in white standing by bedsides, and people who had gone to sleep in old churches and being overlooked and found themselves alone there at dead hour of the night, until they shuddered at the thought of the dark rooms upstairs, yet loved to hear the wind moan too, and hoped it would continue bravely. From time to time these happy in-door people stopped to listen, or one held up his finger and cried. "Hark!" And then above the rumbling in the chimney, and the fast pattering on the glass, was heard a wailing rushing sound, which shook the walls as though a giant's hand were on them; then a hoarse roar as if the sea had risen; then such a whirl and tumult that the air seemed mad and then, with a lengthened howl, the waves of wind swept on, and left a moment's interval of rest.

Cheerily, though there were none abroad to see it, shone the May-pole Tavern light that evening. Blessings on the deep-red, ruby-glowing red, old curtains of the window, blending into one rich stream of brightness, fire a candle, meat, drink, and company, and gleaming like a jovial eye upon the bleak waste out of doors! Within, what carpet like its crunching sand, what music merry as its crackling logs, what perfume like its kitchen's dainty breath, what weather genial as its hearty warmth! Blessings on the old house, how sturdily it stood! How did the vexed wind chafe and roar about its stalwart roof; how did it pant and strive with its wide chimneys, which still poured forth from their hospitable throats great clouds of smoke, and puffed defiance in its face; how, above all, did it drive and rattle at the casement, emulous to extinguish that cheerful glow, which would not be put down and seemed the brighter for the conflict.

Notes:

(1) May-pole:五月柱,又称五朔节花柱,用花装饰的柱子,少年男女在五朔节绕此柱舞蹈游戏,庆祝春天,此处用作旅馆的名字。

(2) Blessing on...:一般用来表示其人或物因某中缘故而应得到祝福(有福气)

2.2.5 Simplification

Simplification, just like amplification, is one of the useful techniques used in the translation from English into Chinese and vice versa. By simplification, we don't mean "Cutting the feet to fit the shoes", instead, we try to make our translation more expressive and explicit. Liu Xie(刘勰), a famous ancient Chinese literary critic pointed out "善删者字去而留意,善敷者辞殊而义显". That is to say simplification is supposed to be made just to the point, to convey the essence of the original more effectively. Otherwise, it would spoil the meaning of the original. For example: "Judges are supposed to treat every person equally before the law." Suppose we put the sentence into "法律面前人人平等", "judges" and "to be supposed to" are omitted in the translation, and then the original meaning is thus misrepresented. It may well be that simplification out of rhetoric alone will not be the main emphasis in the translation either from English into Chinese or vice versa.

As English is greatly different from Chinese in syntax, what is regarded as a natural or indispensable form of repetition in Chinese may be regarded as superfluous or even a stumbling block in English.

Consider the following examples:

1. 要维护世界和平,就要反对侵略者的绥靖政策,不管是军事的、政治的绥靖,还是经济的绥靖,都要反对。

To safeguard world peace, it is essential to oppose the policy of appeasement towards the aggressors, militarily, politically and economically.

"绥靖""反对"are mentioned twice respectively, which sounds very natural in Chinese. However, the English equivalents "appeasement" and "oppose" are mentioned only once, which is in agreement with the target language.

2. 我们党结束了那个社会动荡和纷扰不安的局面。

Our Party has put an end to the social unrest and upheaval of that time.

It's necessary to supply "局面" after the Chinese phrase "动荡和纷扰不安", but it's unnecessary to find an English equivalent for "局面" in the translation as "the social unrest and upheaval" share the meaning of "局面" per se. On the contrary, if we put the above-mentioned versions back into Chinese, repetition and amplification would be preferably used.

3. For the bound man's fame rested on the fact that he was always bound, that whenever he washed himself he had to wash his clothes too and vice versa, and that his only way of doing so was to jump in the river just as he was every morning when the sun came out, and that he had to be careful not to go too far for fear of being carried away by the stream.

被捆缚的人的名声就在于(the fact that 是英语结构关联词,故省略)他总是被捆着,他每次要洗澡,总得连衣服一起洗,每次洗衣服,也得连带洗个澡(语义及结构性增补)。(and that his only way of doing so 的意思已经被融入上下文,故省略)每天清晨,太阳刚露面,他就跳进河里去洗澡但他总是非常小心,不敢离岸太远,以免被激流冲走。

4. We think we have freed our slaves, but we have not. We just call them by a different name. Every time people reach a certain status in life they seem to take pride in the fact that they now have a secretary.

我们自以为奴隶(省略 our)已经解放了,实际上并没有(省略了 we)。我们只不过用一种不同的名字来称呼他们罢了(修饰性增补:语气补足词)。每当人们上升到一定的地位(省略了"in life",词义已被融入),他们似乎就以有了一名秘书而感到自豪(省略了结构关联词"in the fact that")。

Some more examples:

5. He put his hands into his pockets and then shrugged his shoulders.

他把双手放进口袋,然后耸了耸肩膀。

Even the subject can be sometimes omitted.

6. I have never begun a novel with more misgiving. If I call it a novel, it is only because I don't know what else to call it. I have little story to tell and I end neither with a death nor a marriage.

我以前动手写小说从未像现在感到惶惑过。我叫它做小说,只是因为除了小说之外,想不出能称它做什么。故事几乎没有可述的,结局既不是死,也不是结婚。

Two subjects of the first person in the original are omitted because "I", as the subject, has been repeated for three times. If the syntax of the original is changed to "There is little story to tell and the end is neither a death nor a marriage", it is much more harmonious with the Chinese usage.

7. Anyone who does not recognize this fact is not a materialist.

不承认这个事实,就不是唯物主义者。

To avoid unnecessary repetition simplification is needed.

8. And what is the first attempt of the infamous man who had got at the government by a surprise of the people and who continue to hold it by conspiracy with the foreign invader, what is the first attempt?

这批趁人惊慌失措时攫取政权、勾结外国侵略者而继续控制政权的无耻之徒,他们的首要企图是什么呢?

9. But certain circumstances and inflexibility in the attitudes and behaviour of some nations in the past have tried to delay the effective performance of this role in the past.

但是,过去某些情况和某些国家的僵硬态度和行为,曾试图推迟这种作用的实现。

10. If omens are of significance, surely this presents <u>a bright future</u> with promise for the friendship of the Canadian and Chinese people.

如果征兆有意义,那么今天这个吉兆肯定预示加中人民的友谊有光明的未来。

Simplification used in the above-mentioned examples is easy to master. But when used out of rhetorical conciseness and briefness, simplification is far from being easy to learn. Yet it is true simplification to some extent.

11. In the course of the same year, war broke out in that area.

同年,该地区爆发了战争。

cf.(在同一年的过程中)

12. Before the night was far advanced, they began to move against the enemy.

入夜不久,(cf. 在天色已晚,但是夜还不深的时候)他们开始进攻敌人。

13. At the earliest opportunity he ordered the cavalry to ride out and clear the level ground in the occupation of the enemy.

机会一到,他便下令骑兵出击平原上的敌人阵地。

(cf. 在最早的机会出现时)

14. Their respective destinies are becoming increasingly interdependent.

他们的命运日益休戚相关。

(cf. 他们各自的命运……)

15. China is also a country of people with a passionate love of flowers and trees and intense dedication to the welfare of children and to the work ethic.

中国人还热爱鲜花和树木,专心致志献身于造福于儿童的事业,并恪守工作道德。

(cf. 中国也是这样的国家,它的人民……)

16. These developing countries cover vast territories, encompass a large population and abound in natural resources.

这些发展中国家,土地辽阔,人口众多,资源丰富。

Simplification is more often used in translating literary works, but interchangeably used with repetition and amplification.

17. If Miss Rebecca Sharp had determined in her heart upon making the conquest of this big beau, I don't think, ladies, we have any right to blame her; for though the task of husband-hunting is generally, and with becoming modesty, entrusted by young persons to their mammas, recollect that Miss Sharp had no kind parent to arrange these delicate matters for her, and that if she did not get a husband for herself, there was no one else in the wide world who would take the trouble off her hands.

利蓓加打定主意要收服这个肥大的花花公子,请各位太太小姐别怪他。一般说来,娴静知礼的小姐少不得把物色丈夫这件工作交给妈妈去做,可是夏泼小姐没有慈爱的母亲替她处理这么细致烦难的事,她自己不动手,谁来代替呢?

The original ends affirmatively, but the translator transforms the original syntax and ends his version with a rhetorical question by means of omission, as a result of this, the meaning of the phrase "recollect that" is involved.

18. Do you think I have no heart? Have you all loved me, and been so kind to the poor orphan-deserted-girl, and am I to feel nothing? O my benefactors! May not my love, my duty, try to repay the confidence you have shown me? Do you grudge me even gratitude, Miss Crawley? It is too much—my heart is full; and she sank down in a chair so pathetically, that most of the audience present were perfectly melted with her sadness.

"难道你以为我没有心肝吗？我是一个没爹没娘没人理的女孩子，(增译)你们大家待我这么好，难道我连个好歹都不知道吗？唉，我的好朋友！我的恩人！你们对我这么推心置腹，我这一辈子服侍你们，爱你们，把命拼了也要补报的。克劳莱小姐，别以为我连良心都没有，我心里太激动了，我难受！"她怪可怜地倒在椅子上，在场的人倒有大半看着不忍。

19. In Miss Jemima's eyes an autographic letter of her sister, Miss Pinkerton, was an object of as deep veneration as would have been a letter from a sovereign. Only when her pupil quitted the establishment, or when they were about to be married, and once, when poor Miss Birch died of the scarlet fever, was Miss Pinkerton known to write personally to the parents of her pupils; and it was Jemima's opinion that if anything could console Mrs Birch for her daughter's loss, it would be that pious and eloquent composition in which Miss Pinkerton announced the event.

在吉米玛小姐看来，她姐姐亲笔签字的信和皇帝的上谕一样神圣，平克顿小姐难得写信给家长，只限于学生离校，或是结婚，或是像有一回那可怜的白却小姐害猩红热死掉的时候，她才亲自动手。吉米玛小姐觉得她姐姐那一回通信里的句子又虔诚又动听，世界上如果还有能够使白却太太略述悲怀的东西，那就是这封信了。

From the perspective of functionalism simplification is frequently applied to translation of tourist text. In order to give prominence to the focus of information, unimportant and insubstantial message is often omitted.

Some examples:

20. 水映山容,使山容益添秀媚,山清水秀,使水能更显柔情,有诗云:岸上湖光各自奇,山舫水酌两相宜。只言游舫浑如画,身在画中原不知。

English Version: The hills overshadow the lake and the lake reflects the hills. They are in perfect harmony, and more beautiful than a picture.

21. 崂山,林木苍翠,繁花似锦,到处生机盎然,春天绿芽红花,夏天浓荫蔽日,秋天遍谷金黄,严冬则玉树琼花。其中,更不乏古树名木。景区内,古树名木有近300株,50%以上为国家一类保护植物,著名的有银杏,桧柏等。

English Version: Laoshang Scenic Area is thickly covered with trees of many species, which add credit for its scenery. Among them over 300 are considered rare and precious, half of which are plants under State-top-level Protection. The most famous species include gingko and cypress.

22. 团结湖北京烤鸭店为全聚德挂炉烤鸭。为保证宾客品尝精美风味,全部现吃现烤。精选纯北京白鸭,以果木挂炉烤制,只40分钟就能品尝到为你特别烤制的色泽枣红,香酥脆嫩,浓香四溢的正宗烤鸭。

English Version: Tuanjiehu Beijing Roast Duck Restaurant uses only the finest Beijing Ducks which are only roasted after you place your order. Preparation takes 40 minutes after which we will serve you with a delicious, golden red Beijing Duck with crunchy skin.

Translation Exercises

I. *Analyse and appreciate the following passage.*

Beauty

Not less excellent, except for our less susceptibility in the afternoon, was the charm, last evening, of a January sunset. The western clouds divided and subdivided themselves into pink flakes modulated with tints of unspeakable softness, and the air had so much life and sweetness that it was a pain to come within doors. What was it that nature would say? Was there no meaning in the live repose of the valley behind the mill, and which Homer or Shakespeare could not reform for me in words? The leafless trees become spires of flame in the sunset, with the blue cast for their background, and the stars of the dead calices of flowers, and every withered stem and stubble rimed with frost, contribute something to the mute music.

The inhabitants of cities suppose that the country landscape is pleasant only half the year. I please myself with the graces of the winter scenery, and believe that we are as much touched by it as by the genial influences of summer. To the attentive eye, each moment of the year has its own beauty, and in the same field, it beholds every hour, a picture which was never seen before, and which shall never be seen again. The heavens change every moment, and reflect their glory or gloom on the plains beneath. The state of the crop in the surrounding farms alters the expression of the earth from week to week. The succession of native plants in the pastures and roadsides, which makes the silent clock by which time tells the summer hours, will make even the divisions of the day sensible to a keen observer. The tribes of birds and insects, like the plants punctual to their time, follow each other, and the year has room for all. By watercresses, the variety is greater. In July, the blue pontederia or pickerel-weed blooms in large beds in the shallow parts of our pleasant river, and swarms with yellow butterflies in continual motion. Art cannot rival this pomp of purple and gold. Indeed the river is a perpetual gala, and boasts each month a new ornament.

But this beauty of Nature which is seen and felt as beauty, is the least part. The shows of day, the dewy morning, the rainbow, mountains, orchards in blossom, stars, moonlight, shadows in still water, and the like, if too eagerly hunted, become shows merely, and mock us with their unreality. Go out of the house to see the moon, and "it's mere tinsel; it will not please as when its light shines upon your necessary journey. The beauty that shimmers in the yellow afternoons of October, who ever could clutch it? Go forth to find it, and it is gone ;" its only a mirage as you look from the windows of diligence.

昨天黄昏,我又观赏一次日落美景,时虽冬令正月,但景物不减春秋,只是下午人的灵智不顶清明罢了。西方云散,纷纷化为绛色碎片,其色调之柔和,非言辞所能表达,空气清新,充满了活力。回到屋子里来,真成了受罪。大自然有什么话要对我说呢? 磨坊后面山谷安闲中有无限生机,虽荷马或莎士比亚重生,也不能将它化为文字——这里面难道没有意吗？霞光照处，秃树皆熠熠如尖塔着火，东方一片蔚蓝，成为极妙的背景，花朵谢落，然点点犹如繁星，败枝残干，风霜之踪斑斑——这一切都构成了我面前无声的音乐。

久居都市的人，总以为乡间景色，只有半年可观。我独对于冬日风光，亦有癖好，夏日气候温和，风光固然明媚，然而冬天肃杀之气未尝没有动人之处。对于有心人来说，一年四季无时无刻没有它的美处，乡间一角，景色时时变换，这一个钟头所看见的，以前从未见。以后再也不会见到了。天色刻刻变换，其光暗明晦，就反映在下界大地上。四周田亩中的五谷，自萌芽及于成熟，每星期景况不同，大地也因此每星期换一番面目。牧场上，官道旁，野草杂树，四季代谢，宛然替大自然摆下一架无言的大钟，假如观察的人目光锐利，非但可以看见四时更替，而且还可以看出一天的朝夕变化，十二时辰的运行呢。植物兴衰，固然系于时令，鸟群虫群的出没，又何独不然？可是一年四季里头，总有地位给它们安插罢了，水涯河上，变化之迹更为显著：以七月为例，河中水浅之处，丛生的梭子鱼草兰花盛开，黄色蛱蝶蹁跹不断，飞翔其间，与水光相掩映。满眼金紫之色，其富丽堂皇，决非画师所能描绘。清溪一曲，其风光旖旎，四时不辍，每天好像都是令节佳日，每月都有新的点缀。

可是凡是耳目所能辨认出来的美，只是自然之美的最低部分。一天的阴晴变化，多露的早晨，虹彩与星星，青山一抹，桃李满园，碧潭疏影等美景，假如求之过切，反而只成了一皮相之美，美景犹如幻境看者未免扫兴。步出斗室以望月，月亮就像一面铜盘，你不会感觉到征程旅人偶然发现月色照人的那一种快乐。十月下午那金光闪闪的美，谁能把握得住呢？你若出去找寻它。它就会化为乌有了，你从公共马车窗外望出去，秋日的美景就只成了过眼云烟。

II. *Translate the following passage into Chinese by means of amplification and simplification where necessary.*

April advanced to May, a bright, serene May it was, days of blue sky, placid sunshine, and soft western or southern gales filled up its duration. And now vegetation matured with vigour: Lowood shook loose its tresses; it became all green, all flowery. Its great elm, ash, and oak skeletons were restored to majestic life. Wood land plants sprang up profusely in its recesses; unnumbered varieties of moss filled its hollows, and it made a strange ground sun shine out of the wealth of its wild primrose plants; I have seen their pale gold gleam in evershadowed spots like scatterings of the sweetest lustre. All this I enjoyed often and fully, free, unwatched and almost alone: for this unwonted liberty and pleasure, there was a cause, to which it now becomes my task to advert.

2.2.6 Negation and Affirmation in Translation

Please answer the following question first and then translate them into Chinese.

You don't know it, do you?

(1) No, I don't.

(2) Yes, I know a bit.

It seems easy to answer it, but how to translate it into Chinese, then?

Here "no" is put into Chinese "是的"（对）whereas "yes" is put into "不". The translation and the original seem contradictory to each other, but they are actually in harmony with their own respective syntax and the translation is faithful. From this example we can see that "negation" in the original is not always expressed in a negative way, and "affirmation" always in an affirmative way either. Sometimes negation can be expressed in an opposite way in the receptor language and vice versa. Suppose you see a board on which "Wet Paint" are written. How, then, to put the words into Chinese to your companion who knows nothing of English.

(1)"湿的漆"
(2)"油漆是湿的"
(3)"油漆未干"

Versions (1) and (2) are, of course, awkward Chinese and Version (3) is pleasant to ear and acceptable to most Chinese readers. By comparison we can find Version (3) is opposite to the original in the way of expression, which is necessary. Quite some words, phrases even sentences can be expressed in this way.

1. | Original | Affirmation | Negation |
| --- | --- | --- |
| loathe | 讨厌 | 不乐意 |
| fail | 失败 | 没成功,没做成…… |
| deny | 拒绝 | 不相信,不接受 |
| complain | 发牢骚 | 不满意 |
| munificence | 慷慨,大度 | 毫不吝惜 |
| low-spirited | 情绪低落 | 无精打采的 |
| look blue | 愁眉紧锁,面带愁容 | 愁眉不展 |
| break one's promise | 食言 | 不履行诺言 |
| A danger lurks. | 潜伏着危险。 | 隐患未除。 |
| It's all Greek to me. | 这简直是天书。 | 这玩意儿我压根儿不懂。 |

2. | Original | Negation | Affirmation |
| --- | --- | --- |
| carelessness | 不注意,不细心 | 粗心大意,疏忽 |
| illiterate | 不识字的人 | 文盲 |
| incomplete | 不完全的 | 残缺的 |
| infrequently | 不经常的 | 偶尔有之的 |
| disagree | 不同意,不符合 | 争执,有害 |
| Never is a long word. | 不要说 不干了。 | 坚持到底。 |
| Let's not phrase in the absolute. | 咱们别把话说死了。 | 咱们说话留点余地。 |
| He does not find himself. | 他很不得志。 | 他甚感茫然。 |
| He is no idiot. | 他又不是白痴。 | 他很明白。 |
| The station is no distance at all. | 车站没多远。 | 车站很近。 |

Some more examples:

3. He was indeed a good riddance. 他还是不在的好。
4. That thermometer must be lying. 这个温度计一定不准。
5. The explanation is pretty thin. 这种解释站不住脚。

Some of the above-mentioned phrases and sentences express the negative meaning with the help of prefixes and some share the negative meaning themselves, negation is involved in these phrases and sentences instead of being expressed by the negation words. They are affirmative in form but negative in essence, which is worth our special care in translation. The following sentences can be translated into Chinese from affirmative into negative.

1. February 17,1915 was just another day at the Western Savings Bank in Chicago. That is, until 2:30 PM.

1915年2月17日,芝加哥的西方储蓄银行里一切如常,但到下午两点半钟情况就不同了。

2. Other (committees) such as the Committees on Small Business of the House of Representatives and the Senate, are committees dealing with problem areas in national life rather than with the work of particular departments of the federal government.

其他委员会,例如众议院和参议院的"小企业委员会",处理的是国民生活中的困难问题,而不是联邦政府某一特定部门的工作。

In English, "rather than", "but", "far from", "free from", "beyond" are often translated in a negative form.

3. As he lay awake, he realized that he was in trouble; other men in his predicament, he knew, had panicked, exhausted themselves and not survived.

他醒过来了。躺在地上,明白自己处境不妙,他知道,有人因为迷路,张皇失措,弄得精疲力竭而丧生。

4. Just then there came a vague vibration in the earth and air, quickly changing into a violent pulsation, and an oncoming rush that caused me to start back, as though it had force to draw me down.

接着一列火车风驰电掣般向我冲来,我禁不住惊吓得往后退缩,好像这股巨大力量要席卷我而去。

"Caused me to start back" is expressed in the negative in Chinese.

5. But Edwards can be partially excused for doing violence to human feelings. It is better to confess that he was an imitator and a generous borrower than to allow him the credit of originality at the expense of his better human attributes.

爱德华兹如此刺激我们的感觉,也有可原谅之处。我们不得不承认:爱德华兹并没有独创一家之言来吓唬我们,他只是摭拾他人之言而已。

6. It's a sick joke if the West thinks he's a liberal—he is anything but liberal; he's very big on making people perform, at every level.

如果西方把他看作一个自由派人士,那无异于开令人厌恶的玩笑,他根本不是什么自由主义者。在驱使底下各级的人按他的指令办事方面,他是一把好手。

7. She has an incisive manner of speaking, happily free from urs and ers, and perhaps, a tribute to the elocution lessons she took while still a young girl.

她说话嘴尖舌利,完全没有哼哼哈哈的拖腔,或许应归于她少女时代所受的演讲术的训练。

8. Were the RAF, Goering once proclaimed in prouder days, ever to get past the Luftwaffe and bomb a German city "my name is Meyer".

戈林在神气活现的日子里曾经说过,(……在他得势时,曾经神气活现地说过)如果英国皇家空军有一天能突破德国空军防线并在德国城市上空投下炸弹,我就不姓戈林。

9. ... in a word, the whole baronetage, peerage, commonage of England, did not contain a more cunning mean, selfish, foolish, disreputable old man. That blood-red hand of Sir Pitt Crawley's would be in anybody's pocket except his own.

总而言之,英国所有的从男爵里面,所有的贵族和平民里面,再也找不出比他更狡猾、卑鄙、自私、糊涂、下流的老头儿了。毕脱·克劳莱爵士血红的手在任何人的口袋里都想捞一把,只有他自己的口袋是不能碰的。

10. He hurried upstairs to Amelia in the highest spirits. What was it that made him more attentive to her on that night than he had been for a long time—more eager to amuse her, more tender, more brilliant in talk? Was it that his generous heart warmed to her at the prospect of misfortune; or that the idea of losing the dear little prize made him value it more?

他兴冲冲地上楼来找爱米丽亚,那夜对她分外殷勤,又温存,又肯凑趣,谈锋又健。他已经有好多时候没有对她这么好,为什么忽然改变了态度呢?莫非是他心肠软,想着她将来的命苦而怜惜她吗?还是因为这宝贝不久就会失去而格外看重它呢?

Quite some English verbs can be expressed in Chinese in an opposite way to the original, e. g. fail, refuse, keep off, reject, deny, prevent from, refrain from, give up, withhold, avoid, stop, turn down, fall short of, lose sight of, wash one's hands of, shut one's eyes to, turn a deaf ear to and so on.

Now try to turn the following sentences into Chinese by means of negation.

1. You are telling me!
2. Catch me ever telling him anything again.
3. It takes two to make a quarrel.
4. She modelled between roles.
5. Before I take the city into financial deficit position, the elephant will roost in the trees.
6. He seemed to be at a loss for the precise word to complete his thought.
7. Shortness of time has required the omission of some states.
8. He dived into the water fully clothed and rescued Mr. and Mrs. Smith.
9. Foreign Minister Ismail Fahmy accused the Israelis of bad faith.
10. Their action amounted to treason.

• **The following sentences can be translated from negative into affirmative**

Negation in English can be, sometimes, expressed in Chinese in the affirmative. Some examples:

1. You can't be too careful.

你要特别小心。

cf. (你不管多么小心都不算过分。)

2. He never spared himself and so he made me work hard.

他一向都是拼命干的,所以我也只能拼命地干。

3. Mexico City is an earthquake zone and earth tremors are not unusual.

墨西哥城处于地震带，在那里地震是家常便饭。

4. Evidently he had the first quality of an angler, which is not to measure the pleasure by the catch.

他显然已具备了钓鱼者最重要的品质，那就是以钓为乐，钓多钓少一个样。

5. The process is too risky not to be checked in time.

这一过程危险性太大，应及时加以制止。

6. Knowledge about the most powerful problem-solving tool man has ever developed is too valuable not to share.

人类业已开发出功率极大的解决问题的电脑，这方面的知识极其可贵，应为人类所共享。

We are familiar with the structure "too...to", but here in Sentences 5 and 6, "not" is placed before infinitive "to" respectively, so it shares the meaning of affirmative.

- **Translation of special negation and negation of negation**

Special negation and negation of negation sometimes amount to a trap into which Chinese readers would easily fall if they fail to be aware of what is negated. Sentences such as "All is not tight", "Everybody cannot do it" and "I don't know both" are often misunderstood or misrepresented. To have a correct understanding and expression in Chinese, one must be aware of what is negated, partly negated, or totally negated.

Now translate the following sentences into Chinese, with enough attention to special negation.

1. All that glitters is not gold.

2. Romulo said that all American proposals would not be acceptable.

3. And yet, all was not lost. In London, Churchill told the House of Commons that De Caulle's conduct and bearing had made his confidence in the general greater than ever.

4. Everything is not a joke.

5. The whole city was not occupied.

6. No, everything is not straightened out.

7. But you see, we both cannot go.

8. Both read the same Bible, and pray to the same God; and each invokes his aid against the other. The prayers of both could not be answered.

9. He explained his silence by his absence at the battle front.

10. The long absence in New England, he explained, "put my business so much behindhand, that I have been in a continual hurry ever since my return."

- **Negation of negation**

A proverb goes: "Two noes make a yes" (否定之否定为肯定). Negation of negation, however, is sometimes not equal to an affirmation.

Analyse the following examples:

1. Once Mrs. Graig asked him something about Stalin, and his reply was, "May, I don't write no social column".

有一次格兰夫人要他谈谈斯大林,他回答说:"梅,我可不是社会新闻版的撰稿人。"

2. "I don't know nothing about what's waiting for me", said Thrash.

施腊希说:"我不知道我未来的命运如何。"

In the above-mentioned examples, double-negation is used in each one, and they are still turned into "negation" instead of affirmation, because the true meaning of negation is involved in them. Some English grammarians take this kind of negation for a vulgar speech. Even some contemporary grammarians regard it as substandard English. At any rate, it is the speech of the native speakers of English, particularly that of the working people in England and the United States. And it even presents itself in English literary works such as Mark Twain's *The Adventures of Tom Sawyer*, and *The Adventures of Huckleberry Finn*, and even in *W. M.* Thackeray's works. For example: "We never thought of nothing wrong", which is thus translated into "我们从来没想到什么错误" instead of "我们从来没有想到没有什么错误". Otto Jespersen holds that in repeating these negations, the speakers are only taking pains to make his negative meaning clear and unmistakable for fear that one negation alone might not be heard.

We should, however, recognize that double negation generally shows an affirmation which sometimes denotes "Euphemism" and sometimes "Emphasis".

For Euphemism

The British people are said to express often in reserved forms their ideas which other people express in rather strong forms, for example: "Not half bad."(很不错。)

Her singing isn't half bad. 她唱得很不坏(错)。

By doing so their ideas are expressed in a mild, moderate, humorous and euphemistic way instead of calling a spade a spade. Some more examples:

3. Not unexpectedly, the accounts of the two leading personages——Mr. Smith and Mr. Simon are strikingly at variance.

两个主要角色——史密斯先生和西蒙先生的叙述大相径庭,这并不出人意料。

4. The fact, however, remains that, though seemingly a big military power, she (U.S.A) is far from invulnerable in her air defence.

然而,现实情况仍旧是,虽然她(美国)貌似一个军事强国,她的防空却远远不是无懈可击的。

(此句中 far from 与 invulnerable 构成委婉而又含蓄的双重否定,若译为"她的防空却总是无懈可击的"则与原意和事实都有较大出入。例18 中的双重否定若译成肯定,"这完全在意料之中",语气未免太强,与原意不符。)

For Emphasis

In regard to double negation which denotes emphasis, no fundamental difference in the way of thinking exists between Chinese and English. No complication, therefore, would arise in translation. For examples:

5. There is no smoke without fire.

无风不起浪。

6. You can't make something out of nothing.

巧妇难为无米之炊。

7. Nothing venture, nothing have.

不入虎穴,焉得虎子。

8. No roses without thorns.

没有不带刺的玫瑰。

9. Daring burglaries by armed men, and highway robberies, took place in the capital itself every night; families were publicly cautioned not to go out of town without removing their furniture to upholsterer's warehouses for security...

大胆持械行动和拦路抢夺财物的事,每天晚上,就发生在英国的京城,政府告诫每户人家,除将家具运往货栈以策安全外,不得离城外出。

〔持械夜盗和拦路抢劫(的)妄为之举在英国京城每晚均有发生,政府告诫百姓……〕

But there are times when double negation is not in harmony with the way of thinking in Chinese, flexibility in this case is necessary for a translator.

Translation Exercises

Ⅰ. *Translate the following sentences into Chinese.*

1. There is no place like home.
2. He was nothing if not a hypocrite.
3. I never see her but I want to kiss her.
4. Nasser was astonished, this was the first time he had heard of any special fund.
5. I have read your articles. I expected to meet an older man.
6. They will be ice-skating in hell the day when I vote the aid for them.
7. You can never be too strong.
8. Appearances are deceptive.
9. All these nations are not neutral.
10. They were Chou's welcoming party, they had been in the capital for three days, but had remained in seclusion.
11. More than any other poet, Lord Byron has been identified with his own heroes—with Childe Harold, the romantic traveller; with Manfred, the outcast from society; with Don Juan, the cynical heartless lover.
12. Elliott was too clever not to see that many of the persons who accepted his invitations did so only to get a free meal and that of these some were stupid and some worthless.

Ⅱ. *Translate the following passage into Chinese, giving attention to the expression of the underlined parts.*

The Whisper Test

I grew up knowing I <u>was different</u>, and I hated it. I was born with a cleft palate, and when I started to go to school, my classmates—who were constantly teasing—made it clear to me how I must look to others: a little girl with a misshapen lip, crooked nose, lopsided teeth, and <u>somewhat garbled speech</u>.

When schoolmates asked, "What happened to your lip?" I'd tell them that I'd fallen as a baby and cut it on a piece of glass. Somehow it seemed more acceptable to have suffered an accident than to have been born different. By age seven I was convinced <u>no one outside my family could ever love me. Or even like me.</u>

And then I entered Grade 2, and Mrs. Leonard's class.

Mrs. Leonard was round and pretty and fragrant, with chubby arms and shining brown hair and warm, dark, smiling eyes. Everyone adored her. <u>But no one came to love her more than I did. And for a special reason.</u>

The time came for the annual "hearing tests" given at our school. <u>I was barely able to hear anything out of one ear, and was not about to reveal yet another problem that would single me out as different. And so I cheated.</u>

I had learned to watch the other children and raise my hand when they did during group testing. The "whisper test", however, required a different kind of deception: Each child would go to the door of the classroom, turn sideways, close one ear with a finger, and the teacher would whisper something from her desk, which the child would repeat. Then the same thing was done for the other ear. I had discovered in kindergarten that nobody checked to see, how tightly <u>the untested ear was being covered</u>, so <u>I merely pretended to block mine.</u>

As usual, I was last, but all through the testing I wondered what Mrs. Leonard might say to me. I knew from previous years that the teacher whispered thing like "The sky is blue" or "Do you have new shoes?"

My turn came. I turned my bad ear to her, plugging up the other solidly with my finger, then gently backed my finger out enough to be able to hear. I waited, and then came the words that God had surely put into her mouth, seven words that changed my life forever.

Mrs. Leonard, the pretty fragrant teacher I adored, said softy, "I wish you were my little girl."

III. *Translate the following passage into Chinese, then compare your own version with given Chinese.*

The Old Manse

Gentle and unobtrusive as the river is, yet the tranquil woods seem hardly satisfied to allow its passage. The trees are rooted on the very verge of the water, and dip their pendent branches into it. At one spot there is a lofty bank, on the slope of which grow some hemlocks declining across the stream and outstretched arms, as if resolute to take the plunge. In other places the banks are always on a level with the water; so that the quiet congregation of trees set their feet in the flood, and are fringed with foliage down to the surface. Cardinal flowers kindle their spiral flames and illuminate the dark nooks among the shrubbery. The pond-lily grows abundantly along the margin—that delicious flower, which, as Thoreau tells me, opens its virgin bosom to the first sunlight and perfects it s being through the magic of that genial kiss. He has behind beds of them unfolding in due succession as the sunrise stole gradually from flower to flower—a fight not to be hoped unless when a poet adjusts his inward eye to a proper focus with the outward organ.

Grapevines here and there twine themselves around shrub and tree and hang their clusters over the water within reach of the boatman's hand. Oftentimes they unite two trees of alien race in an inextricable twine marrying the hemlock and the maple against their will, and enriching them with a purple offspring of which neither is the parent. One of these ambitious parasites has climbed into the upper branches of a tall, white pine, and still ascending from bough to bough unsatisfied till it shall crown the tree's airy summit with a wreath of its broad foliage and a cluster of its grapes.

译文：溪流十分安静，与世无争，可是两岸同样安静的树林，却似乎不让它静静地流过，树根生在水边，下垂的树枝就浸入水里。有一处地方，崖岸很高，斜坡之上，长了几株铁杉，树枝外伸，斜依水面，似乎作姿欲跳，准备纵身入水。有些地方，河岸几乎和水面相齐，河岸的树密密地聚在一起，脚都伸到水里去了，树叶也都接触到水面。半边莲点燃起螺旋形的火焰，照亮了灌木丛中幽暗的角落。溪旁荷花盛开，据梭罗告诉我，荷花须经清晨的阳光照射后方始开放，阳光轻轻地吻着它，娇嫩的荷花也像少女似的成熟了。他曾经看见这样一个奇景：天色刚刚发亮，清晨太阳渐渐东升，阳光所及之处，荷花一朵朵地依次开放，好几处的荷花，无不皆然——可是假如不是诗人内心的法眼和身体的肉眼取得一致的焦点，这种奇景平常休想能看得到，荷花之外，岸上高矮树木之上，到处绕满了葡萄，葡萄累累下垂，就挂在水面之上，船上的人垂手可得，藤蔓纠缠，有时把两根不同种族的树缠在一起，难解难分，有一株铁杉和一株枫树就这样结合起来了，树上长满了葡萄藤，虽依人作嫁，倒真有凌云之志，它爬上一棵高高的白皮松，爬到了树顶梢还不算，还要一棵一棵树跨过去，以致松树凌虚缥缈的树顶，挂满了一串串葡萄，绕满了阔大的葡萄叶，好似戴了一顶皇冠。

2.2.7 Shift Between the Concrete and the Abstract

In the course of human history, the cognition of the objective world is subjected to the shift from objectivity to subjectivity, from perceptional knowledge to rational knowledge and the shift from the concrete to the abstract as well. Cognition of the material or physical forms comes earlier than that of the insubstantial ones, that is to say, the concrete objects are first cognized, and in the course of learning the nature of the concrete objects and indicating the quality or state of them, people came to learn the abstract attribute of the concrete things. Hence the words denoting the concrete objects are gradually invested with abstract senses and the words denoting the abstract senses are also gradually vested with the sense of concrete objects, which can be shown as follows:

From the concrete to the abstract

英语词语	具体语义	抽象语义
brain	脑	智力
chair	椅子	主持
coat	外套	掩饰
dove	鸽子	鸽派
flowering	开花	繁荣,丰富
hawk	鹰	鹰派
head	头	领导,带领
king	国王	主宰,统治
muscle	肌肉	体力,力气

rose	蔷薇,玫瑰	舒服,愉快
thorn	刺,荆棘	苦恼,挫折
tie	领带,结礼	联系,约束
yoke	轭	奴役,束缚

From the abstract to the concrete

英语词语	抽象语义	具体语义
acknowledgement	承认,感谢	收条
acquaintance	相识,心得	熟人
acquisition	获得,习得	获得物(人)
admission	允许进入,承认	入场(会)费
antiquity	古代,古旧	古物,古迹
beauty	美丽,美感	美人,珍品
comfortable	合适的,愉快的	鸭绒被,绒线围巾
entree	入场权,入场许可	正菜,开场舞
gay	欢快的,华美的	同性恋者
justice	正义,公平	法官,审判员
licence	许可,特许	许可证,执照
wanton	恶意的,放荡的	放荡的人

In translation practice, the shift between the concrete and the abstract should be carried out according to the context of situation. The translator is supposed to be well aware of the context in which the key word is placed. Some examples for illustration of shift from the concrete to the abstract.

1. I was practically <u>on my knees</u> but he still refused.

我几乎是苦苦哀求,但他依然不答应。

2. He is a <u>rolling stone</u>. I don't think he can go far.

他是个见异思迁的人,我想他不会有多大出息。

3. I'll <u>break my neck</u> to get this done by Friday, but I can't promise for sure.

我一定尽最大努力在星期五前完成此事,但我不能完全肯定。

4. I <u>have no head</u> for music.

我没有音乐天赋。

5. If you dare to <u>play the fox with me</u>, I'll shoot you at once.

你小子敢给我耍滑头,老娘我一枪崩了你。

6. 别人家里<u>鸡零狗碎</u>的事情你都知道得这么全,你真是个顺风耳啊!

You know all the bits and pieces of trifles of other families. You are really well informed.

7. 爷们儿怪罪下来,大不了我一个人拉着家小逃之夭夭,可天津卫还有我的老宅院,还有我的<u>姑姨叔舅</u>,让人家受我连累,我对不起人。

Should the locals take umbrage, I can just disappear together with my family. But I have an old house and some relatives in Tianjing. It would be unfair to implicate my relatives. I certainly don't want to get them into trouble.

8. 官场不好混。左右逢源，上下照应，按下葫芦起来瓢，没有金刚钻还真揽不了瓷器活儿。

Steering through official waters, placating right and left, attending to the high and the low. It's no joke, I'm telling you! Getting rid of one thorny problem and another crops up. It's not any diamond that can work on such delicate china.

9. 孩子是张大妈从一把屎一把尿侍弄出来的，像亲生儿子一样，孩子也把张大妈当亲妈，冷不丁把娘俩拆开，孩子能受得了吗？

She had nursed him ever since he was a small baby and loved him as her own; and the child, too, regarded her as as his own mother. What would happen to him if he was taken away from her?

10. 上海，这个灯红酒绿的花花世界，对于一个初上舞台的青年女演员，处处都是陷阱。

Shanghai was a dazzling world of myriad temptations, yet for a young and inexperienced actress like herself, it seemed a place more of pitfalls than of opportunities.

Some examples for illustration of shift from the abstract to the concrete.

11. All the wit and learning in this field are to be present at the symposium.

这一领域里的全部学者都将出席这次专题研讨会。

12. By experimentation and reasoning, mathematics is discovering new facts and ideas that science and engineering are using to change our civilization.

通过实验、想象和推理，数学家们在寻求新观念，从而使科学家和工程师们用之以促进人类文明的发展。

13. There had been too much violence in that region.

那个地区发生了许多暴力事件。

14. Vietnam was his entree to the new Administration, his third incarnation as a foreign policy consultant.

越南战争成了他进入新政府的敲门砖，他担任政府的对外政策顾问，那是第三次了。

15. 他每天都要处理许多棘手的问题。

He has many hot potatoes to handle every day.

16. 我知道你现在是进退两难。

I know you are holding a wolf by the ears.

17. 第五个人说："何必那么激动！你以为当官那么愉快？你以为当官的都活得挺舒坦？没有那事儿。"

The fifth expostulates: why get all worked up? An official's life is not a bed of roses!

18. 妈妈卖掉最后一件首饰，送她到上海去自谋生路。

The last piece of her mother's jewelry was sold to buy her train ticket for Shanghai, where Huang Zhongying would earn her own bread and butter.

19. 在城里，我不是什么大人物，可现在在乡下，我被认为是了不起的人物。

In the city I was nothing, but there in the countryside I was considered a big fish.

20. 我们决不能姑息养奸。

We should never warm snakes in our bosoms.

Translation Exercises

Ⅰ. *Translate the following sentences with enough attention to shift from concrete nouns to abstract ones.*

1. I need to pick your brains: what can you tell me about credit unions?
2. He held the Chair of Botany at Cambridge University for thirty years.
3. We wanted to buy a bigger house than this but we had to cut our coat according to our cloth.
4. He has a good head for figures.
5. In 1783, the American Colonies threw off the yoke of England.
6. 真正的好朋友应该雪中送炭。
7. 他们和群众血肉相连,休戚与共。
8. 处理这些复杂的问题,你应快刀斩乱麻。
9. 可见我糊涂了！正经说的都没说,且说些"陈谷子,烂芝麻"的。
10. 人家是醋罐子,他是醋缸,醋瓮!

Ⅱ. *Translate the following sentences with enough attention to shift from abstract nouns into concrete ones.*

1. I didn't receive an acknowledgement of my application.
2. The school has valuable new acquisition in Mr. Smith.
3. She was a famous beauty in her youth.
4. Her wealth and beauty gave her entree into upperclass circles.
5. 且莫惹是生非。
6. 人生有苦有甜。
7. 不要高兴得太早,棘手的问题还在后头呢。
8. 他这个人只管自己的事。
9. 等他自作自受,少不得要自己败露的。
10. 他说的事一点把握也没有。

2.3 Dictionary and Translation

It is important for a college student to have a good dictionary. It's more important for a teacher to be armed with some good dictionaries. It's even more important for a translator to have some good dictionaries available as no translator can do without. However, no dictionary is so good as to solve all the problems that a translator faces, even the best one is by no means a master key. Nobody can do without the help of a dictionary in his translation, but on the other hand, no translator can be a great success if he can't free himself from the yoke of dictionary explanation, which is the relation between translation and dictionary. But what is the good of a dictionary to a translator? How to make a proper use of a dictionary ? We are going to make a study of these problems as follows.

• **Language Meaning, Parole Meaning and Dictionary Explanation**

As we all know, translation is an information transmission from one language into another, which is far from being a simple interchange, but an interpretation of the original from various angles, especially the cultural angle. Therefore, translation involves almost all the factors between different cultures, especially various factors concerning langue and parole.

Modern linguistics holds that language is composed of langue and parole. The British linguists R. R. K. Harmann and F. C. Stork point out:"Langue is a system of language which is passed from one generation to another, including grammar, syntax and vocabulary; parole, however, refers to all parts of the content spoken and comprehended by the speaker. Langue means something established by popular usage, or something accepted through common practice of public, but parole means various expressions with individuals. In other words, langue is different from parole in that langue is code, but parole is message." Translation is an indirect information transmission to the greatest possible extent between different languages, which is attributed to the category of parole or that of langue; dictionary explanation, however, is attributed to the category of langue, no matter whether the explanation is given by a monolingual dictionary or a bilingual dictionary. Langue meaning is different from parole meaning in that the former is corresponding to concepts, which is established and accepted by the public, and appears in a dictionary as the fixed and accepted by the public, and appears in a dictionary as the fixed interpretation that can't be changed individually; whereas the latter is corresponding to concrete objects of the objective world, which shares individual flavour and greatly concerns the status, self-cultivation and experience of the speaker, to some extent, also special context of situation and background. Take the following as example:

甲:昨天进城逛商店去了。
乙:买啥了？
甲:一双男牛,一双女猪。
乙:老婆喜欢女牛。

In no dictionary can we find the words or phrases like"男牛"and"女猪"as they are not attributed to langue words, but to parole words. However, these words share specific meanings when used by a specific group of people in a specific situation. Of course, scholars and professors will never use this kind of words, but they are frequently used by part-time manual workers and hippies in town. Each individual speaker has his own small circle of vocabulary. The vocabulary circle of each language is one and only, but there are innumerable small circles of parole words in each language. The sum total of the innumerable small circles of parole words is certainly larger than the vocabulary circle of a language. A monumental dictionary can contain most or almost all words of a vocabulary circle of a language, but it can never contain all the parole words of innumerable small circles of a language. Therefore, we can come to a conclusion that langue vocabulary is not so large as parole vocabulary. As mentioned above, the meaning of a langue word is fixed and diachronic, and already accepted by the public, whereas the meaning of a parole word is changeable and synchronic, sometimes with a striking regional character, for example,"空嫂","人流","内矛","贼好","阿诈里","白相",etc. Samuel Johnson, the originator of modern dictionary compiling and the representative of the Prescriptive School, believed that a dictionary compiler was obliged to develop what is useful and correct, to discard what is useless and wrong so as to preserve the purity of a language; dictionary explanation should be up to the standard of tradition and history so as to preserve the relative stability of a language. In the light of the viewpoint of the Prescriptive School, it is impossible for the above mentioned Chinese phrases to be accepted by a Chinese dictionary. Quite a few scholars in our country prefer to banish this fashionable dregs of language for the sake of purity of our mother tongue. The above-mentioned words, however, are used from time to time on the occasion of social intercourse by a specific group of people, which turns out to be the specific difficulty in translation as it involves both langue words and parole words. Just imagine how one can suppose himself to find in the target language the corresponding words to these brand-new words which are not yet accepted as the established ones in the source language. A perfect dictionary may provide its readers with various explanations such as word meaning, grammatical meaning, pragmatic meaning and even stylistic meaning. These meanings, however, are only limited to explanations within the langue category, and explanations attributed to parole category are seldom made in any kind of dictionary. Thus it can be seen that the range of dictionary explanation is, generally speaking, smaller than the semantic range of parole words. And in addition, there are lexical gaps and semantic gaps caused by various factors of cultural diversities. So dictionary explanations are of limited help to translators, who are sometimes disappointed at his failure to find the corresponding words in a dictionary. Such being the case, translators can only seek the help from the thorough comprehension and the correct analysis of the context of the original (the direct context and the indirect context as well) before he makes sure of the accurate meanings of the words in question.

- **Context Meaning and Dictionary Explanation**

Polysemy characterizes almost all languages in the word. A single word is characterised by great vacillation so far as its semantic range is concerned; it is characterized by great flexibility, so far as its pragmatic value is concerned, and it is characterized by multiplicity so far as its senses of a dictionary entry are concerned. The meaning of a word, to a great extent, is conditioned by context. B. Malinowsky pointed out: "They regard context as the sole determiner of meaning without which meaning does not exist". J. R. Firth, a linguist of London School believed that : "Each word when used in a new context is a new word". Thus it can be seen that the meaning of a word is influenced and conditioned by context. The contextual meaning of a word is exact and fixed, and only the exact and fixed meaning of a word can prove its value of pragmatics. But, how many contexts a single word (with the exception of terminologies) can be placed, how many fixed meanings a single word can get from various contexts, remain unknown, as most words can radiate semantically into various fields around their centres of semantic cores, which forms semantic circles that cover all the meanings of words in question. Dictionary explanation, even if that of great dictionary can only provide readers with most of the meanings of a word at most. Therefore there are times when one makes a choice of words in translation for a given word in a certain context, he can hardly find its semantic equivalent and he can not find the proper corresponding word even if he has consulted almost all the big dictionaries. Take "philosophize" in the following sentence for instance:

Not that the parting speech caused Amelia to philosophize, or that it armed her in any way with a calmness, the result of argument; but it was intolerably dull, pompous, and tedious...

倒并不是平克顿小姐的临时赠言使她想得通丢得开,因此心平气和,镇静下来,却是因为她说的原是一派门面话,又长又闷,听的人难受。

The English-Chinese Dictionary(英汉大词典) with Lu Gusun as the editor-in-chief provides two senses of the word entry as follows:

1. 哲学家似的思考(或推理)性的思考(或推理);

2. 肤浅地谈论哲理,卖弄大道理。

Oxford English Dictionary, which is rated as the perfect dictionary of all, provides explanations as: "to play the philosopher; to think, reason or argue philosophically; to speculate, theorize, to moralize;" Horizon Ladder Dictionary explains "philosophize" as "to take a calm, quiet attitude towards life even in the face of unhappiness, danger, difficulty, etc.".

Yang Bi translated "philosophize" into "想得通丢得开", which seems not in harmony with the explanations made by the above-mentioned dictionaries on the surface. Making a comparison between the dictionary explanation and the word selection by Yang Bi, one can hardly come to the conclusion which is right. Generally speaking, monolingual dictionary explanation is descriptive, concrete and unchangeable, whereas billingual dictionary explanation is general, abstract and changeable. Accuracy of monolingual dictionary explanation mentioned above is beyond doubt as it can't be substituted. Compared with monolingual dictionary explanation, billingual dictionary explanation can be substituted to some extent as it is not so accurate as monolingual dictionary explanation. However, it is the changeability that sheds a new light on translators, which enables them to draw inferences about other cases from one instance and think of the proper corresponding equivalent in various contexts. A translator can't count on any bilingual dictionary to provide a ready-made explanation that is suitable and corresponding to the original word in all possible contexts. Yang Bi's version seems not in harmony with the bilingual dictionary explanation on the surface, but it is in conformity with the monolingual dictionary explanation semantically. Analyzed on the basis of the explanations of Horizon Ladder Dictionary and Oxford English Dictionary, the phrase "想得通丢得开" is just within the semantic range of "philosophize", the translator merely concretized the abstract meaning of the original on the basis of the context. Taking dictionary explanation as reference and based on the specific context, the process of semantic analysis and word selection is carried out from generality to specification, from abstract to concrete, which is the complete and only process of word selection in translation. Carrying out each step of the process well to the point is of great importance to accuracy of word selection in translation.

- **Reference, Discrimination and Word Selection**

To a translator, a dictionary is a teacher. But depending too much on it, one would be harmed. Samuel Johnson, the famous English lexicographer, believed that "Dictionaries are like watches, the worst is better than none and the best can not be expected to be quite true". What

Johnson said above not only summarized the function of dictionaries, but explained indirectly the dialectical relation between translation and dictionaries. Translators can't expect one hundred percent accuracy of dictionary explanation. In fact, errors and mistakes are common in dictionary explanation at present. Translators can't be too careful when they make use of dictionary explanation for word selection. They would be otherwise taken in.

With 520,000 word entries and 40 million words, "The English-Chinese Word-Ocean Dictionary" compiled by Wang Tong-yi remains the biggest bilingual dictionary up to now in China. However there are quite some mistakes in explanation and translation of the original explanation. Some mistakes picked out from it as follows:

1. hatchment:丧事标志,一块对角放着的正方形板或菱形板,上面放着死者的两个衣服袖子,通常暂时挂在死者住宅墙的外面。

2. Corps de ballet[F]:群舞演员,芭蕾舞剧团不同于独舞者和主角的集体舞者或群舞者。

3. by 8b:[现主苏格兰]和……相比:BESIDE.

(was but as a fly by an eagle-Shake 而是像一只鹰那样飞行)

11a[现主苏格兰]相反地:DESPITE(I could not deny him but was forced by myself to give Samual Pepys 我不能拒绝他,但是我得强迫自己让步)

Compared with the original explanation, the examples mentioned above are wrong or far from being accurate. Some are wrong in explanation, some are inaccurate, some translations are far from being faithful to the original explanation. In Example 1, the phrase "coat of arms"("纹章") is rendered into"死者的两个衣服袖子", which is a square tenon to a round mortise. In Example 2, the phrase "corps de ballet"(芭蕾舞团,芭蕾团中的伴舞队)is explained as"群舞演员", which is an inaccurate ambiguous conception, causing confusion among readers. In Example 3, explanation of 8b is correct, but the meaning of "by" in the example sentence totally disagrees with the word entry explanation, the original means "与苍鹰相比,他只不过是一只苍蝇". But it is translated into"而是像一只鹰那样飞行". It can thus be seen that the dictionary compiler not only fails to have a correct comprehension of the original meaning, but fails to have a clear framework of the original syntax. The correct translation of the "Word Entry 11 A" should be "我无法拒绝他,只能违心地作出让步" instead of "我不能拒绝他,但是我得强迫自己让步". Examples mentioned above are only part of mistakes discovered by the author, which can speak volumes for the author's view that a translator can't be too careful when he makes use of dictionary explanation for word selection in translation. Whether dictionary explanation is accurate or not is an important criterion of judging dictionary quality. Mistakes and errors in dictionary explanation will do a lot of harm to readers. Therefore readers are obliged to judge, to discriminate, to distinguish the good from the poor, the accurate from the inaccurate, the correct from the incorrect. Dictionary explanation, even correct and accurate explanation is not necessarily the ready-made equivalent corresponding to the original. Take the word "committed" for instance, which is explained in The English-Chinese Dictionary by Lu Gusun as:(1)受托付的,承担义务的。(2)忠于某一立场的,坚定的,忠诚的。(3)(政治上)有密切关系的,结盟的。(4)(作品,作家

等)根据一定(政治或宗教)观点写作的,介入的。These four senses of the the word entry show the denotation of "committed" and its connotation as well, which proves to be correct in explanation. But in actual translation, ready-made corresponding words can't be easily discovered in a dictionary:

1. He said, "I feel that my existence in the world is completely mine, more than when I was a committed Nazi."

2. If there are those who don't want to vote for me because I am a deeply committed Christian, I believe they should vote for someone else.

Analysing the word "committed" used in the above mentioned sentences, one can hardly select the ready-made corresponding words from the four explanations given. But basing himself on the second sense of the word entry, one can easily associate Nazi with"死心塌地",and think of"虔诚的基督徒"as the corresponding equivalent for"committed Christian" with the help of the frame of words and the contexts. These two sentences can thus be translated as follows:

1. 我感到今天的我完完全全属于我自己,与当年一个死心塌地的纳粹分子的我相比,简直判若两人。

2. 如果有人因为我是一名十分虔诚的基督徒而不投我的票,那我认为他们就该去投他人的票。

It thus can be seen that generality, abstraction and changeability of bilingual dictionary explanation are of great importance. Correctness and accuracy of dictionary explanation are shown from its generality, abstraction and changeability, as no dictionary can provide the complete meanings corresponding to all possible contexts. It is generality, abstraction and changeability of dictionary explanation that enlighten readers on diction and enable translators to select from general and abstract dictionary explanations proper words corresponding to the original words in specific contexts.

Mario Pei, an American linguist, points out,"Dictionaries are of limited help, because most words in one language have a dozen possible translations in another."Dictionary is a tool instead of an open sesame. One can make use of this tool to attain his object directly or indirectly, but he can't regard a dictionary as an Aladdin's cave, still less an Aladdin's lamp.

Chapter Three

Translation of Words

3.1 Semantic Change

Language is changing, it changes on the basis of semantic change which happens along with the advance of science and technology, and development of history. In the course of semantic change, meanings of some words are generalized, some of them are narrowed, some are changed from good sense to bad sense and vice versa, and still some radiate their meanings to the various branches of learning. Semantic change result in polysemy which leads to difficulty of translation.

3.1.1 Broadening

Broadening refers to the shift of meaning of a word from specific reference to general reference, so it is also called generalization. "Dog", for example, in Old English refers to "hound", but in Middle English, it refers to all sorts of dogs, it has up to now more than 20 meanings. "Butcher" in English originally refers to "killer of sheep" only, but now it can be used to indicate person whose job is killing animals for food or selling meat, besides it sometimes refers to "slaughter" or "slaughterer". The same is true of semantic change in Chinese. Take the following for example:

饭桌上一盘炒鸡毛菜,一盘番茄炒鸡蛋,一碗汤是极清爽的豆腐丝瓜汤。下课回家用餐的走读大学生紫云见了,却噘嘴:怎么又是"老三篇"呢?

"老三篇" refers to the three essays: "the Foolish Old Man Removed the Mountains", "Serve the People" and "In Memory of Dr. Bethune" (《愚公移山》,《为人民服务》,《纪念白求恩》) by Mao Zedong during the Cultural Revolution. The term, which was vulgarly misused by Lin Biao and the Gang of Four, is now invested with the meaning of stereotype which is fresh and new to readers today.

3.1.2 Narrowing

Just opposite to broadening, narrowing refers to the change of meaning from general reference to specific reference, hence it is also called specialization. "Girl", for example, in Old English means "child", which can be used to refer to both the female child and the male child without distinction of sex. But now it only refers to female child or young, usually unmarried woman. "Deer", in Old English used as a collective noun, refers to small creatures, but it only indicates stag or doe today.

Now consider the following example:

But mice and rats and such small deer,

Have been Tom's food for seven long years.

(W. Shakespeare: King Lear, Act Ⅲ)

长达7年之久,汤姆仅靠老鼠耗子之类的小动物为食。

Semantic change from general reference to specific reference is of common occurrence which should be taken into consideration from the perspective of diachrony and synchrony.

3.1.3 Melioration

Another term for amelioration, melioration means making something bad or unsatisfactory better, or the change of meaning from bad sense to good sense, such as the meaning of "knight" changes from "servant" to a man awarded a non-hereditary title by the sovereign in recognition of merit or service and entitled to use the honorific "Sir" in front of his name. "Queen" in Old or Middle English means "woman", but now it means "the female ruler of an independent state". The word "fond" originally refers to "foolish" and "insane", it indicates now "kind and loving". The most typical example of melioration is the semantic change of "nice" as follows:

Stupid→ignorant→lazy→foolish→wanton→coy→modest→fastidious→

refined→precise→subtle→slender→critical→attentive→minute→accurate→

dainty→appetizing→pleasant→agreeable.

Diachronic analysis of meanings of such words as "nice" must be made carefully, the choice of words would be otherwise improper even though the translator is a mastermind. Consider the following example:

These are complements, these are humours; these betray nice wenches,—that would be betrayed without these.

朱生豪译文:这是台型,这是功夫,可以诱动好姑娘们的心,虽然没有这些她们也会被人诱动。

梁实秋译文:这就是功夫,这就是派头,这就可以诱惑娇羞的少女,其实没有这一套她们也会被诱惑的。

Along the semantic chain of "nice" above-mentioned, readers can easily find the equivalent corresponding to "好" or "娇羞" (such as "dainty" and "pleasant"), yet we have to say that neither "好" nor "娇羞" is proper as this example is taken for illustration of "wanton", "loose-mannered" or "lascivious", one of the leading meanings of nice, especially in the time of Shakespeare by the compiler of Oxford English Dictionary. We can thus say for sure that "nice" in the above example means "wanton" or "loose-mannered" ("放荡的","行为不检点") and hence the choice of words for nice is improper as it does not match the contextual meaning of the word, nor the logical explanation.

3.1.4 Deterioration

Just opposite to melioration, deterioration refers to change of meaning from good sense to bad sense. For example, cunning originally means "person who is learned", but now it means "clever at deceiving people" or "skill in deceiving"; "gossip" originally means "godfather", "godmother", it refers to "casual talk about affairs of other people, typically including rumour and critical comments", or "person who is fond of doing so". The word villain originally refers to "tenant", and then its meaning changes to "slave", but now it indicates "person guilty or capable of great wickedness" or "criminal" in the great majority of cases. Both "churl" and "peasant" have the meaning of "person who does farm work" without bad sense originally, but now they share the meaning of "an impolite and mean-spirited person" in most cases. Hence the English native speakers choose "farmer" or "farm-worker" instead of "peasant" when they refer to "农民".

3.1.5 Antonomasia

Antonomasia refers to the use of a proper name instead of a common noun to express a general idea, which is a kind of rhetorical devices and a way of semantic change as well. In the course of history a lot of proper names have been invested with implicatures on the basis of their conceptual meanings, among which some are proper names of true historical figures, some are proper names selected from literary works, some are the names of historical spots, some are the names of places of literary writings, still some are the names of trade marks or book titles. Examples are listed as follows:

Proper Name	Implication
Don Juan	philanderer
Hamlet	the star role
Helen	the beautiful woman
Hitler	tyrant or fascist
Jekyll and Hyde	single person with good and bad personalities
Jordan	sound basketball player
Judas	traitor
Napoleon	ambitious tyrant
Shylock	cruel loan shark
Solomon	sage
Uncle Tom	flatterer
诸葛亮	sage
伯乐	good judge of talent
王祥	filial son
西施	beautiful woman
Babel	scene of noise and confusion
Dunkirk	notorious retreat
Eden	beautiful garden
Shangri-La	earthly paradise
Watergate	political scandal
Waterloo	decisive defeat or failure

Cadillac   product of name brand

Catch-22   a dilemma

In translation of these proper names enough attention must be paid to the relationship between their conceptual meanings and their implications as the implications are closely correlated with the conceptual meaning and at the same time different from each other to some extent. Some examples:

1. He is a fascist who out-Hitlers Hitler.

他是个比希特勒还残暴的法西斯分子。

2. In ambition, arrogance, astuteness and effectiveness, the new military dictator already out-Napoleons Napoleon.

这位新的军事独裁者野心勃勃,傲气十足,奸诈狡猾,专横跋扈,他已经比拿破仑还拿破仑了。

3. He did a Jordan!

他投篮如乔丹一样快捷准确。

4. He's a real Jekyll and Hyde: at home he's kind and loving, but in business he's completely without principles.

他是个具有双重人格的人,在家里他和蔼可亲,可做生意时他却完全不讲道义。

5. Many took to gambling and got in over their heads, borrowing from Shylocks to pay their debts.

许多人染上赌博的恶习,愈陷愈深,不能自拔,于是向高利贷者借钱还债。

6. Smith often Uncle Tommed his boss.

史密斯常对老板阿谀奉承。

7. Such a Babel! Everyone talking at once and nobody listening to anyone.

一片嘈杂!大家同时都在讲,谁也不听谁的。

8. It was another one of those catch-22 situations, you're damned if you do and you're damned if you don't.

这真是一个左右为难的尴尬局面,做也倒霉,不做也倒霉。

9. Jobson played the Judas and turned on his partner.

乔布森当了叛徒,与他的伙伴为敌。

10. The candidate met his Waterloo in the national elections.

那位候选人在全国大选中遭到惨败。

3.2 Gaps in Translation

Early in the 18th century, some scholars believed that precise interchange was absolutely possible between any two languages. They said they could find a corresponding equivalent of any term in another language. However, the American translator E. A. Nida disagrees with the above opinion, he points out: "Effective communication in one language is difficult enough... Absolute equivalence in translating is never possible (Nida. 1969)." Incompatibility actually exists between any two languages, it is more obviously shown in the translation from English into

Chinese and vice versa. Though English has a large vocabulary of over a million words, lexical gaps and semantic gaps are of frequent occurrence in communication between English and Chinese.

3.2.1 Lexical Gap

English possesses a much larger vocabulary than Chinese, but lexical gaps are of common occurrence in English-Chinese translation. There are too many examples to mention one by one. As we know, in English, the term "rose" refers to roses that bloom only once during a season and to those that bloom throughout a growing season as well. But in Chinese, an important distinction is made. Roses that bloom only once and normally are highly fragrant, they are called "玫瑰", but roses that bloom throughout the growing season and are not so fragrant are called "月季".

Some of the most complicated problems of segmentation reflect important distinctions in culture. This is particularly well illustrated by kinship terminologies. It is known to all that the feudal society lasted for several thousand years in China and a peculiar and close patriarchal clan system was formed. Distinction between sexes is clear enough, the order between the old and the young is precisely classified, and blood relationship is distinctively marked by kinship terminologies.

In English the term "brother" serves quite well as a designation for anyone of male sex who has the same father and mother as the so-called "reference person". Chinese, however, makes an additional distinction between terms for "elder brother" and "younger brother". The normal expression for an older brother is "哥哥", and for a younger one is "弟弟". It is also possible to use a monosyllabic "哥" or "弟" particularly in combination with an ordinal number, e. g. "二哥" and "三弟", which are literally "second older brother" and "third younger brother", but actually imply two systems incorporated in one term. "Second" or "third" refers to the second or third in age among the brothers, but "older" or "younger" refers to comparison with the person using the term, so that the same man will be "二哥", ("second older brother") to brother and sisters younger than him and "二弟" ("second younger brother") to those older.

In translating the English term brother into Chinese, one must attempt to determine from the context whether the person in question is older or younger, and then to decide on the Chinese term which would be most suitable for the relationship. There is simply no Chinese term which means "brother" and at the same time is completely vague with regard to relative age. In translating a novel, one may not be able to determine from the immediate context the relative age of the persons involved, in fact, one may have to read the whole book in order to make certain about some of these features of kinship. In some languages the evidence with regard to relative age may be given indirectly, as in the case of ancient Hebrew, in which the order of names of brothers follows the pattern of listing first the older brother and then a younger brother. In some texts, however, there may be no indication at all as to whether a brother is an older or a younger brother, and the translator simply has to guess.

Some translators might conclude that, in the case of kinship terms, it is much easier to translate from Chinese into English, for whether the man in question is older or younger, he is nevertheless a brother. From the standpoint of simple denotation, the English term brother is sufficient, but when one considers differences of emotive impact in the various Chinese expressions, then something significant is lost in using a generic term such as brother. Even if one translates the Chinese term"大哥" as "eldest brother," something is lost in the rendering, for the Chinese term has an associative meaning of respect and intimacy which is not found in the corresponding English expression. The English expression "big brother" does carry some of the connotations of "大哥", but it is ambiguous with regard to whether he is the first brother in the family. Similar distinctions exist in speaking of one's sisters, and even greater complexities are found in Chinese terms for uncles, aunts and cousins.

In Chinese, term"伯父","舅父","姑父","姨父","表叔"are remarkably different from each other not only in age, but in blood relationship. Thus they can be confused under no circumstances. But in English, the term "uncle" is always used as the corresponding word to all the Chinese terms mentioned above. We often feel at our wits' end when translating Chinese terms such as "嫂子","连襟","内弟","大伯子","小叔子","姐夫","妹婿","小姨子","小姑子","妯娌", etc., as no equivalent words in English precisely correspond to them. The so-called translation of them is no more than an explanation in another language. However, in Chinese, no words can be selected as equivalent words exactly corresponding to "uncle", "brother", "sister-in-law" and "cousin" either, because these English words are loaded with greater volume of information than Chinese terms "叔叔","弟弟","嫂子"and"堂弟". In view of this, we can say that lexical gaps exist both in translation from English into Chinese and vice versa.

In cross-culture communication, the diversity reflected in patriarchal clan system should be taken into careful consideration and cultural clashes caused by lexical gaps should be carefully fathomed before you can figure out a method to adapt the target language to the source language. Consider the following example as follows:

"况且这通身的气派竟不像老祖宗的外孙女儿,竟是嫡亲的孙女儿似的……"

As we know, Lin Daiyu is Jia Min's daughter, and Jia Min is the Old Ancestress' daughter. In feudal China, the married daughter was like water sprinkled. Only sons' children could be taken as family members of direct blood relations, daughters' children could be only regarded as relatives (of indirect blood relations). The patriarchal clan relationship in feudal China is thoroughly expressed in the above-mentioned words by Wang Xifeng, whose words subconsciously emphasize the core of the male blood relationship instead of the female. But both"外孙女"and "孙女"in English are expressed with "granddaughter". Thus it is by no means easy to have the difference between direct blood relationship(嫡亲) and indirect blood relationship(外姓亲戚) clearly expressed in translation. David Hawks translated it into English as follows:

"And everything about her so distingue! She doesn't take after your side of the family, Grannie, She is more like a Jia."

The English version "she doesn't take after your side of the family" aims at a clear expression of direct blood relationship, unfortunately it fails to, it even fails to mention the relation between

Lin Daiyu and the Old Ancestress; what is more, it misrepresents the meaning of the addresser: what Wang Xifeng said is to flatter the Old Ancestress. However, Hawkes' version, instead of flattering, is rather offensive to the Old Ancestress, which is just opposite to Wang Xifeng's characteristic of snobbery. This suggests that the translator is far from being acquainted with Chinese patriarchal clan system, is not familiar with the cultural difference reflected in this aspect. Comparatively speaking, the translation by Yang Xianyi is more accurate.

"Her whole air is so distinguished! She doesn't take after her father, son-in-law of our Old Ancestress, but looks more like a Chia".

This version shows less respect for the Lins, but it flatters the Jias. Amusing the Old Ancestress is the very intention of the addressor, also the key point of the original. Through the explanation of the relation between Daiyu's father and the Old Ancestress, the translator makes a clear account of the relation between Lin Daiyu and the Old Ancestress by means of changing the angle of expressing (viewing from different aspect), in the meanwhile, the addresser's intention and characteristic are precisely conveyed to readers. The author believes that this is the translator's success and it is an effective approach to overcoming the barrier of the cultural clash caused by the lexical gap.

With the development of society and advance of science, more and more new words come into being. Coinage of new words in one language often leads to a lexical gap in another language. Therefore introduction and loan of newly-coined words from other languages are the ways commonly used in translation. For example, "尼龙"(nylon), "激光"(laser), "青霉素"(penicillin), "电脑"(computer) and "特洛伊木马"(Trojan horse) in Chinese are loan words from English, whereas "tea", "kowtow", "Wushu", "Great Leap Forward" and "paper tiger" are loaned from Chinese. These words used in the target language, like newly-brewed wine, must be mellowed for some time before they can be easily accepted. The fact shows that introduction of newly-coined words from one language into another and loan of newly-coined words from other languages are effective approaches to making up lexical gaps in translation.

3.2.2 Semantic Gap

Herder pointed out: "A nation's language and culture were manifestations of its distinctive national spirit of mind." Mode of thinking and values of various nations are different from each other, as they are deeply rooted in the soil of national culture. The same thing to different peoples shares different implications. Take "green" for instance: when green means "a colour between blue and yellow", "young", "tender", "flourishing" and "full of vigour", it is in agreement with meanings of its Chinese equivalent "绿色"; but when it means "envious and jealous", it is not in harmony with the meaning of the Chinese word "绿色", which leads to a semantic gap in Chinese. Thus the English word "green-eyed" is rendered into "嫉妒", "眼红" instead of "绿眼的". In the Yuan and Ming Dynasties in China, a man whose wife made love with others had to wear a green scarf; a prostitute's husband had to do so similarly. Since then, those whose wives flirt or make love with others have been called "戴绿头巾" or "戴绿帽子". In Chinese, this implication is closely connected with "绿色"(green colour), but in English, "green cap" is totally different from the implication of the Chinese phrase "绿帽子", and its semantic equivalent corresponding to "绿帽子" is "cuckold" which, however, has nothing to do with "绿色" (green colour). In view of this, "green cap" can never be used as the corresponding equivalent of Chinese phrase "绿帽子" because of the semantic gap between the two. The effective approach to making up this kind of semantic gap is to select the semantic equivalent by penetrating into the deep structure of the original instead of word-for-word translation. Such being the case, "戴绿帽子" should be rendered into "cuckold" instead of "wear a green cap". Colours in one language can't be mechanically expressed with its corresponding ones in another language. Cultural factors must be carefully weighed. Otherwise the semantic gap can't be made up.

Semantic gap sometimes occurs in expression of moral concepts and ethnical disposition. In dealing with this kind of semantic gap, meaning comes first. If translation can be done faithfully both in meaning and in form, so much the better. But sometimes it's not necessary to make such an excessive demand on a perfect translation, sometimes it is impossible to select the absolute equivalent in translation. For example, there are a lot of phrases like "菲酌", "薄礼", "寒舍", "拙作", "敝人", "贱内", "小女", "犬子" in Chinese, which suggest the intrinsic disposition of the Chinese people who are honest, lenient and modest. However, the English-speaking people are quite different, they never depreciate themselves, instead, they appreciate individual importance and give enough attention to self-expression and even self-glorification. This kind of cultural clash caused by the intrinsic ethnical character often leads to a semantic gap. It's hard for a translator to find the semantic equivalents corresponding to "菲", "薄", "寒", "拙", "敝", "贱", "小", "犬" in the above examples. In author's opinion, it's not necessary to have these Chinese characters translated, what is needed is to have the key words (characters) clearly expressed. Judging from pragmatics, it's by no means necessary to make up the semantic gap caused by intrinsic ethnical character mentioned above; an excessive emphasis on accuracy of self-depreciatory expression will lead to the misunderstanding of readers.

Polysemy characterizes both English and Chinese words (with the exception of some specific terminologies). Each polysemous word can radiate its meaning to various branches of learning, which forms a semantic radiation range, therefore, polysemous words im one language usually overlap the meaning of their corresponding words in the target language to some extent, but not completely, because the semantic radiation range of a polysemous word in one language is different from the range of its corresponding word in another language. Take "flower" and its Chinese equivalent "花" for instance: flower and "花" are more or less the same in the basic meaning, as the English word "flower" means "that part of a plant that produces seeds" and "finest part", and in Chinese, "花" means "种子植物的有性繁殖器官" 和 "精华". But in practical social intercourse, "flower" is greatly different from "花": "flower" can be used as a verb that means "开花", "发育", "成熟", "繁荣", "丰富", etc.; whereas "花" can't be used this way in modern Chinese. When "花" is used as a verb it means "spend" (花钱、花费). Thus a semantic gap exists between "flower" and "花" when they are used as verbs. Besides, the semantic radiation range of "flower" is different from that of "花" to a great extent when they are placed in different contexts respectively. In Chinese "花" shares many meanings when collocated with various words, such as "花魁", "花仙", "寻花问柳", "花街柳巷", "拈花惹草", "花枝招展", "花天酒地", "花好月圆", "花柳病"; "黄花" shares the meaning of the yellow flower (黄颜色的花儿), it also implies a virgin or a boy who has not yet experienced sexual intercourse; "野花" may mean "wild flowers by the roadside", it also implies "concubine" in a given context. As for "挂花", "出花", "眼花", "花镜", their meanings are quite different from the essential meaning of "花", yet it is within the semantic radiation range of "花". By comparison, the great difference in semantic range can be clearly seen. The semantic gap between "flower" and "花" can be clearly shown as follows:

△ ABC stands for the semantic radiation range of "花".

△ DBE stands for the semantic radiation range of "flower".

The overlapped part stands for the semantic equivalent part corresponding to each other, the semantic gaps to each other are clearly shown as Quadrilateral AFEC and △DBF.

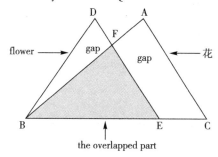

In translation, the key point to make up this kind of semantic gap is to make sure of the fixed meaning of a word when placed in certain context. The contextual meaning of a word may be similar to its essential meaning, it may be different to some extent; it may be the extended meaning based on the essential meaning, it may be totally different from its essential meaning. If the contextual meaning branches too far away from its essential meaning, word-for-word equivalence can hardly convey the original information to readers of the target language, not to speak of semantic equivalence.

Some examples:

1. 他父亲给他娶了个媳妇,今年才20岁,也有几分人才,又兼生性轻薄,最喜拈花惹草。

2. 那媳妇子故作浪语,在下说道:你们姐儿出花儿,供着娘娘,你也该忌两日,倒为我腌臜了身子,快离开我这里罢。

3. The emergence of the peoples of the Third World and their struggle for identity will lead to the flowering of diverse concepts of life in the future.

In the example sentences mentioned above, "花" in Example 1 and "flowering" in Example 3 share extended meanings, "花儿" in Example 2 has almost nothing to do with its conceptual meaning. Such being the case, contextual meaning is of great importance and word-for-word translation turns out to be meaningless. Therefore the above-mentioned examples are rendered into:

1. His parents had found him a wife who was now just about twenty and whose good looks were the admiration of all. But she was a flighty creature who loved nothing better than to have affairs.

2. To inflame him further, the woman under him teased, "your daughter has smallpox and they're sacrificing in your home to the goddess. You ought to lead a clean life for a couple of days, not dirty yourself for me. Hurry up and get out of here."

3. 第三世界人民的兴起,以及他们为争取合法地位而进行的斗争将丰富未来生活的各种观念。

Judging from what is mentioned above, it can be seen that in communication between languages, semantic gaps between corresponding words can only be made up by contextual meanings which are influenced by langue factors and conditioned by parole factors as well; they are corresponding to the concrete facts in the objective world and closely correlated with the identity, cultivation, qualification and experience of the addresser (speaker) in question. As a translator, one has to take all those factors into consideration before he bridges the lexical gap and semantic gap in cross-culture communication.

Translation Exercises

Ⅰ. *Translate the following passage into Chinese, paying enough attention to choice of words.*

Beautiful and plentiful August: There is no month in the whole year, in which nature wears a more beautiful appearance than in the month of August! Spring has many beauties, and May is a fresh and blooming month, but the charms of this time of year are enhanced by their contrast with the winter season. August has no such advantage. It comes when we remember nothing but clear skies, green fields and sweet-smelling flowers—when the recollection of snow, and ice, and bleak wind, had faded from our minds as completely as they have disappeared from the earth—and yet what a pleasant time it is! Orchards and corn-fields ring with the hum of labour; trees bend beneath the thick clusters of rich fruit which bow their branches to the ground; and the corn, piled in graceful sheaves, or waving in every light breath that sweeps above it, as if it wooed the sickle, tinges the landscape with a golden hue. A mellow softness appears to hang over the whole earth; the influence of the season seems to extend itself to the very waggon, whose slow motion across the well-reaped field, is perceptible only to the eye, but strikes with no harsh sound upon the ear.

Ⅱ. *Translate the following phrases into English.*

1. 西部大开发
2. 生态农业
3. 环保产业
4. 拳头产品
5. 三角债
6. 三个代表

7. 使中国经济与国际接轨
8. 实现小康目标
9. 豆腐渣工程
10. 大包干

3.3　Context of Situation and Word Selection

　　Translation is the end of learning a foreign language. Chinese students of English may believe that translation is easy so long as you know something about English, and foreign students of Chinese may believe that translation is not so difficult so long as you have a good grasp of Chinese. However, well-experienced translators are often baffled by meanings of words, especially the accuracy of word selection in translation as most of English words and some of Chinese characters are polysemous. Eric Partridge said："Words do not have meanings；people have meanings for words". An individual word when used in different context may share various meanings. Just take "chair" for instance, it may mean"椅子","轿子","电刑","马车","主席、议长"or"总统","教授"；and what is more, it can be used as a noun, and a verb as well, which depends on the concrete context, without which it enjoys great vacillation(游移性). The British linguist Firth points out "Each word when used in a new context is a new word", which means that meanings of words are conditioned and influenced to a great extent by the context. Without being placed in context, meanings of words enjoy great flexibility. But in a given context, they enjoy little independence.

3.3.1　Semantic Radiation

　　Polysemy characterizes flexibility of English words. With the development of science and technology, more and more English words become polysemous words with more and more meanings. The meaning of an ordinary word can range from daily life to physical culture, to chemical industry, to medical science and military science as well. Besides the meanings we are familiar with, it may have some specific meanings new to us. Take "carry" for instance, apart from its essential meanings in Chinese："运","带","传送",it means"结转","生息","赎卖" in economics；"进位" in mathematics；"负荷"in physics；"怀胎"in medical science；"控制球" in physical culture and "射程","攻克"in military science as well. If we take"运","带","送" as its semantic core(语义核), "carry" then forms its semantic radiation range(语义辐射),like a circle. The semantic radiation range may be large or small, large as a circle, or small as a point, that all depends. For example, "zori" means no more than "草履"；so its semantic radiation range is a point. However, "good", its semantic radiation range is a large circle as "good" means respectively qualified, exciting, capable, convincing, fresh, proper, devoted, handsome, fertile, wholesome, amusing and competent when used respectively as modifiers of teacher, news, wife, excuse, eggs, manners, Christian, looks, soil, exercise, joke and worker. But how to make an accurate choice of words in translation?

　　(1) Be familiar with the semantic range of the word you are to focus on.
　　(2) Make a careful analysis of the frame of words and its context.

3.3.2 Direct Context and Word Selection

Context is composed of many factors. It can be classified into context of culture and context of situation according to Malinowsky's viewpoint. But the British linguist M. A. K. Halliday has it classified into field(场景), tenor(交际者) and mode(方式), which are different in form, but similar in essence. The author believes that context, according to its influence on meanings of words and its limitation to them, can be classified into direct context and indirect context.

Direct context may be a few words juxtaposed with the key word you are to focus on, which are called juxtaposed words(左右相邻的词). Sometimes the juxtaposed words concern greatly the determination of the meaning of a word. Take the Chinese character"打"for example, we are not sure of the exact meaning of"打"here if it is placed in no context as it is a polysemous character. But when we have it used in the following phrases, its meanings are fixed:"打家具"(制作—make,manufacture),"打毛衣"(knit),"打酱油"(buy),"打游击"(be engaged in),"打鼓"(beat, strike),"打渔杀家"(catch). In these phrases,"家具","毛衣","酱油","游击","鼓"and"渔"are juxtaposed with"打", which concern a great deal in determining the meanings of"打". Without the juxtaposed words,"打"enjoys great vacillation in meaning.

Direct context may be a short sentence or a long sentence, or a paragraph in which the word is placed. However short the sentence is, it also concerns greatly in determination of the meanings of a word. Just take the English word "fox" for instance, without being used in the given context, nobody knows its meaning or its parts of speech as it is a polysemous word that can be used both as a noun and as a verb:

(1) It is a fox behind the tree.

(2) Don't trust that man, he is an old fox.

(3) She foxed him.

(4) He was completely foxed with the problem.

From these four sentences we can see that in what way and to what a great extent meanings of a word are conditioned and influenced by context. Malinowsky pointed out: "They regard context as the sole determiner of meaning without which meaning does not exist."(语境是决定语义的惟一因素,舍此别无意义可言。) The close relation between context and word selection in translation is clearly revealed here. Context not only exercises a great influence on determination of meanings of words, but sometimes changes the essential meanings of words, For example:"他一气之下,看破红尘,遁入深山,索性在一个小庙里削了发。不多久,有人说他和山麓的尼姑发生了友谊,沸沸扬扬,流言蜚语,愈传愈盛。"(徐铸成:《哈同外传》,1982. 2. 16《新民晚报》)."友谊"in Chinese usually means friendship between friends. In the feudal days, a man should not touch the hand of a woman in giving or accepting anything(男女授受不亲),let alone build up"友谊"between a monk and a nun. In this specific context, the meaning of"友谊"turns naturally into flirtation or flirtatious behavior (or flirting with each other) between the monk and the nun as it is conditioned by the direct context.

The close relation between context and determination is clearly revealed. But how to make an accurate choice of words in translation is the question we are going to discuss next. Some examples:

1. "How old was I when you first took me in a boat?" "Five and you nearly were killed when I brought the fish in too green and nearly tore the boat to pieces. Can you remember?"

"你头一次带我上船,那时我多大岁数?"

"五岁。当年我把一条活蹦乱跳的大鱼拖上船的时候,那家伙险些儿把那只船撞得粉碎,你也险些儿送了命。还记得吗?"

Here, let's focus on "green".

Consulting a dictionary we can learn that "green" can be used as an adjective, a noun, and a verb as well. It is not so difficult for us to determine its part of speech with the help of the frame of words and its juxtaposed word——"too". But it takes time to make an accurate choice of words even though we know it is used as an adjective as it is polysemous because of various collocations such as green plants, green duck (young), green hand (inexperienced, naive), green eye (jealous), green winter (mild, not very cold), green old age (flourishing, active), green bananas (unripe), green horse (youthful, vigorous, full of vigor). From its context "you nearly were killed... and nearly tore the boat to pieces" we can learn that the fish must be big enough, must be strong and active enough. If not, how could it nearly tear the boat to pieces? That is why we supply one more character "大" collocated with 鱼 and put "green" into "活蹦乱跳"。

Relying on context is of great importance in determination of meanings of words and diction. But only relying on the context in which the key word is placed is not enough. Sometimes we have to seek help from other sentences or even the neighbouring (or other) paragraphs.

2. So that when lieutenant Osborne, coming to Russel Square on the day of the Vaux hall party, said to the ladies, "Mrs. Sedley. Ma'am, I hope you have room; I've asked Dobbin of ours to come and dine here, and go with us to Vaux hall. He is almost as modest as Joe".

到游乐场去的那一天,奥斯本中尉到了勒塞尔广场就对太太小姐们说:"赛特笠太太,我希望您这儿有空位子。我请了我们的都宾来吃饭,然后一块儿上游乐场。他跟乔斯差不多一样怕羞。"

"Modest" in this sentence is the key word we are going to focus on. We usually take "谦虚"、"谨慎"as the equivalent translation corresponding to "modest". Consulting the dictionary we can find the possible choices of words such as "客气","羞怯","端庄","淑静","贞节" and so on besides "谦虚"、"谨慎". But why did the translator choose "羞怯"as the equivalent of "modest" here? Of course, he took context into consideration. However, "context" here is by no means the only sentence where "modest" is placed. In a broad sense, the context must be enlarged to the neighbouring sentences, paragraphs, even the chapters relevant to the key word "modest". The above-mentioned sentence is taken from Chapter 5 (*Vanity Fair*)and at the end of Chapter 3, there is a sentence that can serve as a clear explanation to Joe's(乔斯) disposition: "Poor Joe, why will he be so shy?"(可怜的乔斯,他干吗那样怕羞呢?) And at the end of Chapter 5 there is another sentence confirming that Dobbin is shy and timid: "he had arrived with a knock so, very timid and quite"(都宾他来的时候怯生生地敲,声音很轻). In view of the foregoing analysis, it can be seen that by translating "modest" into "怕羞" instead of "谦

虚"、"端庄"… the translator took into consideration all the possible factors relevant to the key word.

3.3.3 Indirect Context and Word Selection

Indirect context means additional linguistic factors relevant to the contents of a book (or an article) but not yet expressed in written form by the author. It consists of the author's point of view, his common sense, historical background, local conditions and customs relevant to the key words. The other factors including the self-cultivation and qualification of the characters of works, and even the mood, emotion, gesture, the manner of the speaker and the intonation of the addresser and addressee.

The author's point of view and experience usually exercise a great influence upon the style of his works. Whether or not the translator can exactly represent author's viewpoint and the style of the original in his translation, the key factor is that to what extent the translator is acquainted with the author and his works, e. g.

3. Rebecca thought in her heart, Ah, mon beau monsieur! I think I have your gauge—the little artful minx.

利蓓加暗暗想道:"哈,我的漂亮少爷,你是块什么材料可给我捉摸出来了。"这小姑娘是个诡计多端的狐媚子。

According to the dictionary explanation, "artful" shares the meanings of "skillful" and "clever" in good sense, and "deceitful", "cunning" in bad sense. Why did the translator put it into "诡计多端"? That all depends on the translator's leaning about the author and his work *Vanity Fair*. William Thackeray, the famous critical realist of the 19th century, flogged vanity of ugly features of the bourgeois aristocratic society in his representative work *Vanity Fair*, which gave a vivid picture of all kinds of snobs. Of them, Rebecca Sharp was the notorious example. She spared no efforts to flatter her master. In order to worm her way into the upper class, she flirted with her senior and junior masters and even offered her body to them. She was the typical representative of that time in England, whom the author loathed very much. The translator knew all this only too well. Thus Yang Bi put "artful" into "诡计多端". Perhaps out of the similar reason, he translated Example 4 as follows:

4. "You men perceive nothing, you silly, blind creature if anything happens to Lady Crawley, Miss Sharp will be your mother-in-law: and that's what will happen."

"你们这些男人什么都看不见。你这糊涂瞎眼的人哪,克劳莱夫人要有个三长两短,夏泼小姐就要做你的后娘了。你瞧着吧!"

In spite of his mother's serious disease which was beyond cure, Crawley went on flirting with Rebecca Sharp. But Crawley did not know that his father was also planning to marry Rebecca Sharp if Lady Crawley went west. The onlooker sees the most of the game. So Mrs Bute said to Crawley something mentioned above as a warning. "If anything happens to Lady Crawley" was put into "克劳莱夫人要有个三长两短" instead of "如果克莱太太发生了什么事情", it is really an excellent choice of words and proper weighing of diction, which suggests that the translator is aware of the word "death" as a taboo to foreigners just like"死"to Chinese patients. By making a proper choice of words he gave a vivid picture of the manner of speech, the expression and bearing of the addressor, which suggests that a thorough analysis of the linguistic factors, such as the social position, the background and the state of mind of the relevant characters of the work are of great importance to accuracy of word selection in translation. The additional linguistic factors such as expression, manner of speech, gestures, mood and intonation form an important part of indirect context of situation, which can be expressed and enhanced to the full by means of video and audio effects in TV programs and films, even implied meanings and meanings between the lines, behind the lines and beyond the lines can be vividly expressed. Without the help of video and audio effects, however, expression of additional linguistic factors would be more difficult in translation. e. g.

5. The Flower Girl: Will ye-oo py me f'them?

(Will you pay me for them?)

The Daughter: Do nothing of the sort, mother. The idea!

(George Bernard Shaw: Pygmalion)

These are lines taken from *Pygmalion*(《卖花女》). The word selection for "The idea!" is something knotty indeed! There are a lot of additional factors attached to it: The mother, daughter and the son were well dressed then, waiting for a cart (taxi cart) in a storm, and nearby was a flower girl: the mother sent the son to get the taxi cart; having left in a hurry, the son had the flower girl's flowers trodden into the mud; without paying her for the flowers, the son ran away. The flower girl cursed him angrily: "Fletty, are you blind?" The mother was puzzled, and asked: "How do you know Fletty, my son?" The flower girl learnt that the lady was the young man's mother, and then asked her to pay for the flowers which were trodden into the mud by her son. The daughter, instead of the mother, said the above-mentioned sentence which just shows the daughter's contempt for the flower girl, and the former's superiority over the latter.

The daughter's wrath, resentment, her spoiled manner and her arrogance are fully revealed in this simple sentence. How to express such plentiful implications between the lines in translation? Please appreciate the following version.

卖花女:你肯给钱吗?(你肯替他付钱吗?)

女儿:妈,一个子儿也别给。她想得倒美!

"她想得倒美"seems a very simple sentence. Ponder over it carefully, you will find that it conveys the complete information of the original to readers. The mood, feelings, emotion, manner of speech and even the expression of the speaker's eyes are vividly shown to readers as if one could hear her voice, see her in the pouts and squinting, and enjoy her vivid performance in a theatre. The translation produces such a good effect just because the translator took all the additional factors possible into consideration. If one fails to do so and only has "The idea!" put into Chinese by means of word-for-word translation, the Chinese version must be very dull or a misrepresentation of the original.

Additional linguistic factors work only when key words are well weighed and polished. By comparing "The idea!" with its corresponding Chinese, one will find "The idea!" is rich enough in information. It suggests the wide gap between the daughter and the flower girl in social position; it suggests the daughter's contempt for the flower girl and the former's arrogance and superiority. But in no dictionary can one discover the Chinese explanation "她想得倒美" corresponding to "idea". However, just these 5 Chinese characters have the original implication completely conveyed, and the style of the original thoroughly and vividly expressed in translation. It can thus be seen that relying only on the dictionary explanation, the original, if with plenty of implications and complicated additional factors, can't be well translated. Just as Lü Shuxiang pointed out: "In no language, the meaning of a sentence is equal to the sum total of each individual word, sometimes more than that. According to mathematics, 2 + 2 is 4, instead of 5. But it is something possible in linguistics." An individual word or sentence when used in a certain context its meaning is often different from its dictionary explanation. Its implication between the lines may be much more than the dictionary explanation. The same is true of Chinese. Now something quoted from *A Dream of Red Mansions*(《红楼梦》). When Baoyu was beaten black and blue by his father, Daiyu was late enough to go to see him. She had thousands of words to say to Baoyu but not one word could she utter. At long last she sobbed: "Never do such things again" ("你可都改了罢!"). The sentence is short enough, but it is meaningful and worth pondering as it reveals on the one hand deep sorrow and bitterness in Daiyu's bosom, and implied her grievance and retreat when she has no way out, and on the other hand, it expresses the heartfelt sympathy and great consolation from the bosom for Baoyu in the meanwhile it also shows the great suffering after the failure in revolt against feudalism, the deep hatred after the wreck of an ideal life, and to some extent, a slight reproach to her lover at the time of being panic-stricken. All this can only be sensed between the lines. Without the concrete situation in Jia's mansions as the background, without the contrast between the characteristics of Baoyu and Daiyu and the special relation between the two, all the above-mentioned factors can be hardly sensed.

Indirect context and direct context are closely connected with each other. Indirect context can't exist in isolation. No direct context, no indirect context, only by making a thorough analysis of the direct context in which the key words are placed, can one have an insight into the complicated indirect context of situation through the surface of language and then have a grasp of the accurate meanings implied in the relevant words, changes of mood and emotion, and vicissitudes of life, and then have all these important factors well expressed in the target language.

Translation Exercises

I. *Turn the following sentences into Chinese. Be sure to catch the fixed meanings of "wet" in various contexts.*

1. As the ship righted herself I got up, half strangled with the brine I had swallowed and wet to the skin.

2. To Big Tim that day Roosevelt looked like a cocky college kid, still wet behind the ears.

3. In private Thatcher scoffed at her continental allies as "bloody wets".

4. The weatherman throws a <u>wet blanket</u> on picnic plans when he forecasts rain.

5. Uncle Willie told John to wait outside for a minute while he went in to the cafe <u>to wet his whistle</u>.

6. You <u>are all wet</u> if you think the governor will approve this scheme.

7. She can be scornful of those who are not tough in either performance or philosophy, reserving for them her ultimate pejorative "wet", which in her lexicon is an accusation of gutlessness.

Ⅱ. *Translate the following passage into Chinese, giving enough attention to the meanings of underlined words.*

China's modern humiliations began with the early nineteenth century, with the Opium Wars. Thereafter the great <u>powers</u>, as occasion permitted, worked industriously to carve it up into spheres and areas for exploitation. China's central government was a <u>mockery</u>, capable only of feeble response. So out of tune with the world of nation-states was China that it did not even possess a ministry of foreign affairs until as 1858. It continued officially in the dream word of former times when a ministry of tribute and capitulations was all that was really needed for dealing with "barbarians". With a curious arrogance, made even stranger by its weakness, China at first continued to refuse to accept the West on equal terms and negotiate with them as such. When ultimately it began to negotiate, China's only real strength lay in playing the powers off against one another—a tactic only partially successful. Despite the spheres of influence and territorial concessions it was driven to concede, China remained a nominally independent state primarily because its very size made it difficult to <u>digest</u> and there were many who wished to attempt it.

America may have fondly imagined that its 1899 Open Door policy toward China, to which the other powers gave lip service, had stayed the process of division. But this was more or less self-delusion. In 1898, Britain, Germany, Russia, and France had forced concessions from China, which, combined together, destroyed China's future as an economic unit. These leases, which were to run for ninety-nine years (Russia's lease on the southern Liaotung Peninsula was for only twenty-five), provided for Chinese employment of a British inspector general of Chinese customs, exclusive rights (to Germany) to build railroads and open mines in Shantung, the giving over of control of Port Arthur (to Russia), Kwangchow (to France), and Kowloon and Weihaiwei (to Britain). Italy's demand for a port in 1899 the Chinese government felt strong enough to reject. The complete colonization of China was stayed only by its great mass and by the inability of the powers to agree readily on how to divide it up.

In October 1911 the long-delayed Chinese Revolution began, and in 1912 the six-year-old boy emperor abdicated. Sun Yat-sen, who had been elected president on December 30, 1911, resigned when Yuan Shih-kai was selected in mid-February as president by the national assembly. Yuan Shih-kai, a would-be Oriental Bonaparte, now attempted to consolidate his power. At the end of 1915 he announced his assumption of imperial powers, was forced to cancel this, and, in the middle of 1916, died. After this date the struggle for power became more and more confused. Not only were there governments at both Canton and Peking, but between 1920 and 1926 war lords fought one another in equal disregard of both.

(Frederick H. Hartmann: *The Relation of Nations*: *The Asian Powers*).

3.4 Synonyms and Choice of Words

3.4.1 Synonyms

Many English words possess synonyms which express more or less the same meaning. But there are no synonyms that are entirely the same, just as you can never find a leaf that is entirely the same with another. There is some difference between any pair of synonyms, however slight it may be. We have a lot of synonyms for "laugh" as follows:

Laugh		
	smile	微笑
	grin	嘴笑,露齿笑
	chuckle	暗笑,轻声笑
	giggle	痴笑,吃吃地笑
	chortle	哈哈大笑
	titter	傻笑,嗤嗤地笑
	snigger	嬉皮笑脸地笑
	guffaw	哄笑,放声大笑
	cackle	尖声笑,咯咯地笑
	roar	狂笑

All these words share the meaning of "laugh", but they are different from each other in manner, volume, degree, mood, connotation, passion and appeal（方式,音量,程度,心情,涵义,感情及感染力）. To have your translation faithful to the original in accuracy, you must be well acquainted with shades of difference of synonyms.

Now try to tell the shades of difference of the underlined words used in the following sentences and then turn them into Chinese.

1. Child <u>cried</u> himself to sleep.
2. She <u>sobbed</u> herself to sleep.
3. The girls <u>wept</u> with joy after their volleyball team won.
4. Her eyes are always <u>weeping</u> for the loss of her beauty.
5. She <u>wept</u> copiously over the loss of her lover.
6. A child your age shouldn't sit about <u>blubbering</u> over a lost toy.
7. There she collects the force of female lungs, sighs, <u>sobs</u> and passion.
8. The film ends with the heroine <u>sobbing</u> desperately as her lover walks away resolutely.
9. The headmaster said to her, "if you have something to say, have it out clearly. It's no use <u>weeping</u> and <u>wailing</u> endlessly."
10. The wind was <u>wailing</u> in the woods.

This cluster of words are synonyms for each other that share something in common—shedding of tears indicative of grief, pain or other strong emotions. All these words can be expressed in a Chinese character—哭 as there exists a semantic overlap（语义重叠）which enables some of them to be interchangeably used in some of the given contexts (Note: only some) without causing confusion and remarkable difference in meaning. For example, "tremble" and "shudder", their overlapping relationship between meanings can be illustrated as follows:

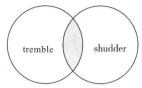

The overlapped parts of synonyms may be large or small, but they are similar to each other in meaning as long as the non-overlapped parts are not opposite to each other in meaning. "Cry", "sob", "weep", "blubber" and "wail" are overlapped in meaning to some extent, but there are, after all, the non-overlapped parts though they are not opposite to each other. Such being the case, synonyms must be carefully chosen when interchangeably used as the non-overlapped parts share the shades of difference in manner, degree, mood, connotation, passion, appeal, etc.

Now let's analyse the shades of difference of the above-mentioned synonyms.

"Cry" and "weep" are close synonyms which are often used interchangeably. "Weep", however, is more frequently used in writing than in speech, and gives greater emphasis to the shedding of tears than to the accompanying sounds. From the above-mentioned examples we can see that "weep" is usually used to express one's profound feelings, deep sorrow, grief-stricken feelings (mental grief). "Cry", on the other hand, usually gives primary emphasis to the sound (she cried loudly in despair). From this and above mentioned Example 1, we can see that "cry" does not always indicate depth of feeling. Babies often "cry" but never "weep".

"Sob" means to weep with audible convulsive catches of breath and the heaving of one's chest. Sobbing is usually accompanied by gasps (喘粗气), and akin to sighing (抽泣,泣不成声). "Sob", stronger than weep or cry in degree, implies pathetic circumstances (令人怜悯的,哀怜的), e.g. she sobbed out the story of her son's death in a traffic accident. (她泣不成声地哭诉着自己的儿子如何在一次车祸中丧生。)

"Blubber" and "wail" stress the sounds accompanying weeping. "Blubber" means to weep or sob noisily; the word reflects an attitude of ridicule of contempt on the part of the person using it, and is thus more abusive than descriptive, e.g. the above-mentioned Example 6.

"Wail" suggests a loud, unbroken, usually high-pitched cry. Wailing is traditionally associated with grief, sorrow, misfortune, and "wail" is a formal cry of mourning, e.g.

  to wail a person's death   痛悼,哀悼
  to wail over one's misfortune   为……不幸而恸哭

Many wailed at the funeral for Premier Chou En-lai. 在周总理的追悼会上许多人失声痛哭。

Through the above-mentioned analysis, you may have a clear idea of the overlapped parts and the non-overlapped parts of these synonyms, which will throw more light on the interchangeable use of synonyms. The overlapping relationship between them can be illustrated as the following Diagram:

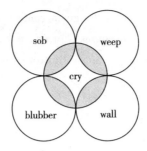

Distinguish the shades of meaning of the underlined words or phrases in the following sentences and translate them into proper Chinese.

1. Come to the theatre with me and <u>laugh off</u> your worries.
2. At this moment another <u>smile</u> of deep meaning passed between her and him.
3. Spring awakened all nature <u>smiled</u>.
4. The waters of a brook...
Limpid and <u>laughing</u> in the summer's sun.
5. He <u>chuckled</u> at himself for having worn his wife's shirt.
6. The girls couldn't stop <u>giggling</u> when the boy answered that Cao Cao was a sound tennis player.
7. Why do teenage girls <u>giggle</u> so much?
8. Father used to <u>chortle</u> over the funny papers every Sunday.
9. We whisper, and hint, and <u>chuckle</u>, and <u>grin</u> at a brother's shame.
10. Since the famous portrait, the Mona Lisa was painted, people have been fascinated by the mysterious <u>smile</u> on the face and by the strange background of fantastic rocks.

Translation Exercises

I. *Analyse and compare the meanings of the following words, distinguishing the shades of difference, and try to make sure of the speech levels of them.*

1. curious, nosy, inquisitive, prying
2. daring, bold, cocky, audacious, foolhardy
3. dog, canine, cur, mongrel, hound, hunter, pup, puppy, bowwow, bitch, shut
4. foe, enemy, opponent, rival, competitor
5. associate, colleague, companion, comrade, ally, accomplice, cooperator
6. teacher, pedagogue, schoolmaster, instructor, mentor, educator
7. girl, maid, maiden, lass, lassie, damsel, gal, damoiselle, miss, missy, doll, baby, cute, jill, flapper, puss, pussy, chicken, tomboy, bobbysoxer
8. woman, lady, female, dame, member of the fair, weaker sex, wench, hussy, broad, vampire, bitch
9. father, sire, pater, the old man, governor, papa, pa, dad, daddy, pop, patriarch, male parent
10. walk, stroll, march, saunter, crawl, amble, tramp, trudge, traipse, plod, promenade,

perambulate

II. *Translate the following into Chinese, focus your efforts on dealing with the underlined parts.*

1. You have both pleased and angered me.
2. The surly insolence of the waiters drove him into a rage, and he flung his serviette to the floor and stalked out of the restaurant.
3. Mad with fury, he pounded his fists on the wall and beat his breast.
4. Abolitionists viewed the institution of slavery with indignation.
5. He heard the weltering of the waves of wrath.
6. Mrs. Brown's daughter looked out... and there were wrath and vengeance in her face.
7. He strode out of the house.
8. Will you join us for a stroll in the park?
9. Whistling as he sauntered along the beach.
10. The blister on my heel made walking painful.
11. The drunken man tottered down the street.
12. We ambled across the meadow enjoying the fresh air.
13. The fat woman waddled down the street carrying a load of groceries.
14. We trudged a hundred yards or so through deep, untrodden snow.
15. Three or four elephants, loaded with hay, swaggered down the crowded street.
16. Pompous little dictator swells with pride and importance as he struts up and down his study.

3.4.2 Choice of Words

Polysemy is characteristic of English words and polysemous words often share more than one part of speech, which takes time to determine the fixed meaning and its given part of speech in a certain context, and even more time to make a final decision of the Chinese equivalent of the original word. After a thorough analysis of the original syntax and the general idea of the original text, choice of words becomes the determining factor in a good translation. To have a proper choice of a word is easier said than done. The choice of the equivalent to "and" seems easy enough, the actual practice, however, is very different from what one might imagine.

1. war and peace
2. eat and drink
3. to work arduously and skillfully
4. The girls came over talking and laughing.
5. She is the Party secretary and manager as well.
6. It was not easy to carry such a heavy load, and during the dog days.
7. The earth rotates and it revolves.
8. fine and thin
9. rare and hungry
10. The sun came out and the grass dried.

11. Reading the text many times and you will be able to recite it.

12. He came here by bike and I walked here.

13. He did it, and did it well.

14. They walked two and two.

15. many and many a time

16. They talked and talked until small hours.

17. There are men and men.

"And" in each of the above phrases and sentences is used as a conjunction, and the essential meaning is more or less the same, but the choice of the Chinese equivalent of each "and" is different from one another. Expression instead of comprehension, viewed from this angle, is the crux of translation, which is correlated closely with rhetoric as both translation and rhetoric are devoted to techniques of applying languages. To have every word well expressed in Chinese, one must acquaint himself with rhetoric, especially the active rhetoric whose essential task is to have words well chosen, which is just in agreement with the key link of expression in translation. Whether a word is well chosen affects greatly the accuracy of expression. Now let's have one more example:

good will	good sense
good wife	good year
good mother	good match
good gold	good player
	good deeds
good teacher	good points
good friend	good husband
good neighbor	good boy(child)
good heart	good looks

"Good" collocated respectively with the above words shares the same connotation—"having the right or desired quality, giving satisfaction" which appear in the same semantic range. However it can not be expressed in the same Chinese character "好", instead, it is respectively translated into "慈","贤","德","真","良","益","丰","高","优", and so on, by which the advantage of receptor language has been brought into full play and the unnecessary repetition avoided. This turns out to be the most effective way in translating a polysemous word, especially when used repeatedly in the same text. Now let's have a try by putting the following sentences into Chinese.

19. It was a good dinner.

20. He proved to be a very good listener.

21. The captain of the jet came back, saluted and in very good English, said to the President, "To Cairo, Sir?"

22. He (Dulles) was told, when complaining that he could not follow Nasser's moves, that Nasser was a good chess player.

23. Although schoolmistresses' letters are to be trusted no more nor less than churchyard epitaphs; yet, as it sometimes happens that a person departs this life, who is really deserving of all the praises the stone-cutter carves over his bones; who is a good Christian, a good parent, child, wife or husband; who actually does leave a disconsolate family to mourn his loss; so in academies of the male and female sex it occurs every now and then, that the pupil is fully worthy of the praises bestowed by the disinterested instructor.

一般地说来,校长的信和墓志铭一样靠不住。不过偶然也有几个死人当得起石匠们刻在他们朽骨上的好话,真的是虔诚的教徒,慈爱的母亲,孝顺的儿女,尽职的丈夫,贤良的妻子。他们家里的人也真的哀思绵绵地追悼他。同样的,不论在男学校女学校,偶然也会有一两个学生当得起老师毫无私心的称赞。

"Good" in this sentence is respectively translated into"虔诚的","慈爱的","尽职的","孝顺的"and"贤良的"by Yang Bi. What a good choice of words! It's so precise and accurate that you can make no nit-picking about the choice of words for "Good". It would be quite inferior if "good" be expressed in the same Chinese character"好". One more example:

24. One of our ancient prayers says:

"Common be your prayer;

Common be your purpose;

Common be your deliberation;

Common be your desires;

Unified be your hearts;

Unified be your intentions;

Perfect union among you."

This is an ancient prayer of India, with neat words and well-knit syntax. The word "common" is repeatedly used but with essentially the same meaning which can be expressed in Chinese as"共同的","一致的". The translator, however, shows ingenuity in expressing these "commons" in Chinese as follows:

我国古代的一篇祷文说道:

"愿同祈祷,

目标无二,

意志合一,

谋虑与共,

冀求相通,

一体同心,

众志成城,

固此联盟。"

By expressing "commons" in various Chinese synonyms the translation is not only faithful to the original in essence, in form and in syntax (the use of four-Chinese-character structure), but avoids monotony caused by unnecessary repetition. It is really an excellent model in translation. One more example:

25. As the manager of the performance sits before the curtain on the boards, and looks into the Fair, a feeling of profound melancholy comes over him in his survey of the bustling place. There is a great quantity of eating and drinking, making love and jilting, laughing and the contrary, smoking, cheating, fighting, dancing, and fiddling: there are bullies pushing about, bucks ogling the women, knaves picking pockets, policemen on the look-out, quacks (other quacks, plague take them!) bawling in front of their booths, and yokels looking up at the tinselled dancers and poor old rouged tumblers, while the light-fingered folk are operating upon the pockets behind. Yes, this is Vanity Fair...

领班的坐在戏台上幔子前面,对着底下闹哄哄的市场,瞧了半天心里不觉悲惨起来,市场上的人有的在吃喝,有的在调情,有的得到新宠就丢了旧爱;有在笑的,也有在哭的,还有抽烟的、打架的、跳舞的、拉提琴的、骗哄人的。有些是到处横行的强梁汉子;有些是和女人飞眼儿的花花公子,也有扒手和到处巡逻的警察,还有走江湖吃十方的,在自己摊子前扯起嗓子嚷嚷(这些人骗我同行,真该死!)。跳舞的穿着浑身漂亮的衣服,可怜的翻筋斗老头儿,涂着两腮帮子胭脂,引起那些乡下佬睁着眼瞧,不提防后面就有三只手的家伙在掏他们的口袋。是了,这就是我们的名利场。

The very beginning of the translation turns out to be attractive to readers by means of proper choice of words faithful to the original but not rigid, flexible but not excessive (忠实而不呆板,灵活而不过分). By contrast between the original and the translation, we will come to know what an excellent, vivid representation of the original the translation is.

Words and sentences can be handled this way, so can be phrases.

26. He woos both high and low, both rich and poor.

他追起女人来,不分贫贱富贵。

27. High and low, all made fun of him.

上上下下没有一个不捉弄他。

(上上下下没人不拿他开心。)

28. Here were high and low, slaves and masters.

这里高低贵贱的人都有,有奴仆,也有主人。

In a word, the key point of expression is choice of words. Proper choice of words on the basis of a thorough digestion of the original will surely lead to a successful translation.

Translation Exercises

I. *Translate the following passage into Chinese with painstaking effort on the choice of the underlined words.*

The afternoon wore on, and with the awe, born of <u>the white silence</u>, the voiceless travelers bent to their work. Nature has <u>many tricks</u> where-with she convinces man of his finity—the ceaseless flow of the tides, <u>the fury</u> of the storm, <u>the shock</u> of the earthquake, the long roll of heaven's artillery—but the most tremendous, the most stupefying of all, is <u>the passive phase</u> of the white silence. All movement ceases, the sky clears, the heavens are as brass: the slightest whisper seems sacrilege, and man becomes timid, affrighted at the sound of his own voice. Sole speck of life journeying across the ghostly wastes of a dead world, he trembles at his audacity, realizes that his is a maggot's life, nothing more. Strange thoughts arise unsummoned, and the mystery of all things strives for utterance. And the fear of death, of God, of the universe, comes over him—the hope of the Resurrection and the life, the yearning for immortality, the vain striving of the imprisoned essence—it is then, if ever, man walks alone with God.

Ⅱ. *Translate the following passage into English with enough attention to the choice of the underlined words.*

月光如流水一般,静静地泻在这一片叶子和花上。薄薄的青雾浮起在荷塘里。叶子和花仿佛在牛乳中洗过一样;又像笼着轻纱的梦。虽然是满月,天上却是一层淡淡的云,所以不能朗照;但我以为这恰是到了好处——酣眠固不可少,小睡也别有风味的。月光是隔了树照过来的,高处丛生的灌木,落下参差的斑驳的黑影,峭楞楞如鬼一般;弯弯的杨柳的稀疏的倩影,却又像是画在荷叶上。塘中的月色并不均匀;但光与影有着和谐的旋律,如梵婀铃上奏着的名曲。

荷塘的四面,远远近近,高高低低都是树,①而杨柳最多。这些树将一片荷塘重重围住;只在小路一旁,漏着几段空隙,像是特为月光留下的。树色一侧是阴阴的,乍看像一团烟雾;但杨柳的丰姿,便在烟雾里也辨得出。树梢上隐隐约约的是一带远山,只有些大意罢了。树缝里也漏着一两点路灯光,没精打采的,是渴睡人的眼。这时候最热闹的,要数树上的蝉声与水里的蛙声;但热闹是它们的,我什么也没有。

忽然想起采莲的事情来了。采莲是江南的旧俗。似乎很早就有,而六朝时为盛;从诗歌里可以约略知道。采莲的是少年的女子,她们是荡着小船,唱着艳歌去的。采莲人不用说很多,还有看采莲的人。那是一个热闹②的季节,也是一个风流的季节。梁元帝《采莲赋》里说得好:

于是妖童媛女,荡舟心许:鹢首徐回,兼传羽杯;棹将移而藻挂,船欲动而萍开。尔其纤腰束素,迁延顾步;夏始春余,叶嫩花初③,恐沾裳而浅笑,畏倾船而敛裾。

3.5 Levels of Formality of Words and Diction

Language in works and articles can be classified into the classical or the vernacular; the elegant or the popular. Their styles are different from each other with various writers, but the style of writing to a great extent is determined by diction, Liu Xie believed that "辞尚体要,弗惟好异,盖防文滥也", which means that diction is valued for expression of essential meaning instead of queer writing, and this is for avoiding superfluousness. Works full of flowery words are not necessarily fine pieces of writing, in most cases, a masterpiece handed down from ancient times is well polished in diction. Jonathan Swift, a famous English writer, pointed out "Proper words in proper places make the true definition of a style."

Applying a right word to a right context is too strict a demand on a student learning a foreign language. It is far from being easy even to a native speaker. It is said that the mayor of Chicago made an ebullient speech at the sending-off ceremony for a queen of a European country, at the end of which he said to the queen: "The next time you come, bring the kids along."

No sooner had the mayor finished his speech than the atmosphere of the ceremony utterly changed: some people were struck dumb with surprise, some were ashamed of the mayor's words, the queen and her entourage were filled with fury, looking at each other in blank dismay.

What made such a great change of the atmosphere? It was nothing but the word "kids" used in the mayor's speech. As a noun, "kid" means"孩子","小子","年轻人"in Chinese. It is classified into a colloquial word by many dictionaries such as the English-Chinese Dictionary by Lu Gusun, Webster's New World Dictionary and so on. It is classified into a slang by Oxford Advanced Learners' Dictionary of Current English. Considering the status of the mayor and the queen, and the situation then, the word "kids" is obviously incompatible with the atmosphere. It is evident that the mayor failed to use a proper word in the proper context of situation. If the mayor had replaced "kids" with "princes" or "princesses", the embarrassment could have been avoided.

"Kid" and "prince (or princess)" are similar to each other in meaning, but they are classified into different levels of formality. Because of this they should be applied to different contexts. Words used in different contexts will produce different pragmatic effects, which is worth enough attention in translation and composition, otherwise it will lead to pragmatic failure.

3.5.1 Semantic Overlap and Classification of Levels of Formality of Words

There are some semantic similarities between "kid" and "prince (or princess)" in expression of "子女", which is the so-called semantic overlap. Semantic overlap is the fundamental attribute of synonyms. In other words, words that belong to the same semantically synonymous field(语义同义场) are different from each other in the overlapped part, as some are large, some small. Take the following words for instance: anger, rage, indignation, fury, ire and wrath are in the same semantically synonymous field, but the overlapped parts between each pair are different; the overlapped part between "anger" and "fury" is obviously different from that between "rage" and "fury", as the former is small and the latter is comparatively large.

Generally speaking, the overlapped part changes with the degree of semantic similarity. The more similar in meaning they are, the larger the overlapped part will be, and as a result, synonyms enjoy greater possibility to be interchangeably used. However, there are no synonyms whose meanings cover one another completely. You can hardly find a pair of synonyms whose meanings are one and the same. In fact, apart from the overlapped part between synonyms, there is also the non-overlapped part between any pair of synonyms however similar they are in meaning. This is due to the different shades of meaning between synonyms. Interchangeable use between synonyms is conditioned by the coexistence between semantic overlap and different shades of meaning. It means that most words can only be replaced by their synonyms by adding some adverbs, adjectives or some other words to make up the semantic deficiency in degree or intensity, e.g., we can replace "rage" with the phrase "in a fit of anger"; replace "fury" with "a frenzied rage". Making up semantic deficiency is the basic condition of interchangeable use of synonyms. In addition to this, another important factor, that is levels of formality of words, must be taken into consideration, which is the key point that will be discussed further.

There are different views on classification of levels of formality of words. Some linguists prefer five categories (classification):①scientific and technical(科技语体);②literary(书面语体);③common(中性语体);④colloquial(口语体);⑤slang(俚语). Take "horse" and its synonyms for instance, they can be classified as follows:

同义词例	语体分类
charger	technical
courser, steed, palfrey	literary
horse	common
nag	colloquial
plug	slang

Martin Joos classifies levels of formality of words into five categories in his paper "Five Clocks" as follows:

(1) frozen(拘谨) (2) formal(正式) (3) consultative(商议) (4) casual(随意) (5) intimate(亲密)

For example:

Frozen: Visitors should make their way at once to the upper floor by way of the staircase.

Formal: Visitors should go up the stairs at once.

Consultative: Would you mind going upstairs right away, please.

Casual: Time you all went upstairs now.

Intimate: Up you go, chaps.

The differences between the above-mentioned levels of formality of words are mainly shown in syntax and diction. From the frozen to the intimate, the complex degree of syntax is getting progressively less. In the example for the frozen, "make their way to", "upper floor", "by way of" and "staircase" are chosen, which are more formal in degree of formality than "go up the stairs" in the next sentence, and much more formal than "going upstairs" and "up you go" in the other sentences. Degree of formality is also getting less and less successively.

In addition to the above-mentioned, there are some other kinds of classification of levels of formality of words. But in practice, words are actually classified into three categories as (1) colloquial(口俗语)(2)common(常用语)(3) formal(书面语). Take "wife" for instance:

Colloquial: woman, old woman, better half, gray mare, squaw, missus.

Common: wife.

Formal: consort, spouse, helpmate, helpmeet.

There are many Chinese expressions corresponding to "wife", which can be similarly classified as follows:

口俗语:老婆,媳妇,老伴,婆娘,婆姨,娘子。

常用语:爱人,妻子。

书面语:夫人,内人,内子,玉雪,敝房,荆房,荆布。

Words of different levels of formality are actually different in many points, discrimination of which is of great importance to accuracy of diction both in translation and composition.

3.5.2 Levels of Formality and Diction

Accurate discrimination of levels of formality of words is by no means easy to Chinese students, as most words they have learnt are the common core of English. They share the common characteristic of various levels of formality, but strictly speaking, are lacking in their own distinctive characteristic. These words can be applied almost in all contexts of situation, which attains the aim of communication although they are pedestrian. Most of these words are attributed to superordinate words(上义词) such as "horse", "anger" and "wife" mentioned above. Superordinate words are typical and general enough but not so specific and accurate. Just opposite to superordinate words are hyponyms(下义词)in the semantically synonymous field. The relation between superordinate words and hyponyms is a kind of semantic inclusion(语义内包关系) as follows:

(Ⅰ)

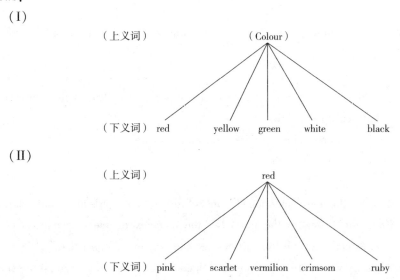

(Ⅱ)

Superordinate words and hyponyms are relative to each other. For example, "red" is a hyponym in diagram Ⅰ, but in diagram Ⅱ it is a superordinate word. Some superordinate words and their corresponding hyponyms are in the same semantic field (e.g. Diagram I), some in the same semantically synonymous field (e.g. Diagram II). The two are different from each other. The words of the former express a general conception(e.g. colour), but they are different from each other semantically, and they do not overlap each other in meaning; the words of the latter, however, while expressing a general conception (e.g. red), are similar to each other in meaning and overlap each other semantically. Comparatively speaking, choice of words of the latter is more difficult as synonyms are different from each other in many points (such as shades of meaning, degree of formality, levels of formality and so on) besides semantic similarity. Accurate choice of words is based on the following two points:

First, make sure of the correct levels of formality of words. Generally speaking, words with distinctive levels of formality are marked with ready-made classification of categories in dictionaries, especially in big dictionaries. For example, "steed", "courser" and "nag" are respectively marked with "liter", "poet"and "colloq" in Oxford Advanced Learners' Dictionary of Current English;《英华大词典》, a bilingual dictionary provides readers with clear marks of (诗)(俚)and so on, which make discrimination of levels of formality much easier for readers as they narrow the range of choice of words and make word selection more accurate. If putting the Chinese lines "乱花渐欲迷人眼,浅草才能没马蹄" into English, one will certainly select "steed" instead of "horse", "nag" or "plug" as the English equivalent corresponding to"马". Of course, word selection is by no means such an easy question. Some English words have a great many synonyms; a word may have a dozen, or even dozens of synonyms. It is possible sometimes that several synonyms are graded at the same level of formality. Take "absurd" for instance, it has a lot of synonyms such as "insupportable, preposterous, incredible, ludicrous, groundless, silly, false, crazy, loony, bull". If they are graded at three levels, "insupportable, preposterous and incredible" are attributed to formal words, "ludicrous, groundless, absurd, silly and false" are common words, the other words are colloquial words. As a result of this, there are at least three words at each level of formality. Such being the case, an accurate choice of words for the following paragraph is much more difficult.

"Fears based on ignorance can sometimes be conquered by scientific fact. In 1983, a radio program called War of the Worlds actually terrified large numbers of Americans by pretending to report that the earth was being invaded by men from Mars. But as we now know from unmanned exploration of Mars itself, the idea that Martians' could invade the earth is _____."

What is the correct selection for the last space? Some big words such as"conquer","invade" and"exploration" are used in this paragraph, which suggests that the level of formality of the paragraph is not a colloquial one. Analysing the original syntax, one can find that the original syntax is not very complex and the degree of formality of words is not very formal, which show us that the original is written in common standard English. Therefore the level of formality of the last word is neither colloquial nor formal and it should be common. Such being the case, we can rule out three formal words and three colloquial words, and just select one from five common words. To make an accurate selection from five synonyms at the same level of formality one must discriminate the different shades of meaning between any pair of them. It is as difficult as distinguishing one pea from another in a pot. A good dictionary may provide you with clear explanations as follows:

"Ludicrous" means "worthy of scornful laughter".

"Groundless" means "unsupported by evidence". A groundless belief is not necessarily silly, absurd, or ludicrous, or even false. It simply has no basis in what is known.

"Absurd" means "irrational" or "nonsensical" but not "frivolous", deadly serious people can sometimes have absurd ideas.

"Silly" means "frivolous", "foolish", or "thoughtless".

"False" means "not true". A statement may be false without being either silly, ludicrous, or absurd.

Based on the above-mentioned explanations and analysis of the context, it can be determined that the last space should be filled with "groundless".

Secondly, two factors concerning levels of formality must be taken into consideration: the direct context of situation and the indirect context of situation.

The direct context of situation may be a few words juxtaposed with the key word in question, or a few sentences, paragraphs, chapters, or even the relevant content concerning the key word in question. It involves the field of discourse(话语范围), subject(话题) and content(话语内容)。

The indirect context of situation means the additional linguistic factors relevant to the contents of a book(or an article) but not yet expressed in written form. The additional linguistic factors involve many factors: so far as social cultural situation is concerned, it includes traditional conditions, customs and some knowledge concerning history and geography; so far as situation of communication is concerned, it involves specific situation(交际场合), manner of discourse(话语方式), the social position, self-cultivation, mood, emotion and gestures of the addresser(说话人) and addressee(受话人)。

The direct context of situation and indirect context of situation share the function that not only conditions the meaning of a word, but limits the degree of formality of a word to a certain level. Neglecting this function will lead to incompatible word selection. Suppose a primary school teacher asks his pupil "贵庚了？令尊在何处高就？", the level of formality of his choice of words will be obviously incompatible with the specific situation of communication.

There is an English story about a discussion between a young woman and an old granny on sucking eggs. It goes as follows: The young woman said to the granny, "Take an egg, and make a perforation in the base and a corresponding one in the apex, then apply the lips to the aperture, and by forcibly inhaling the breath, the shell is entirely discharged of its contents." On hearing this, the old granny replied, "When I was a gal they made a hole in each end and sucked."

The old granny used some colloquial words and slang, whereas the young woman chose a lot of big words such as "perforation", "aperture", "corresponding", "apex", "inhale" and so on. Considering the context and the specific situation of communication, the young woman was obviously showing off by making a mountain out of a mole-hill. On the contrary, the old granny spoke to the point by means of colloquial words and a simple sentence. Sometimes similar mistakes can be discovered in translations and compositions by Chinese students as follows:

I wanted to go off to another town, but then everyone got busy matchmaking, and they were after me so they nearly tore my coat tails off. They talked at me and talked until I got water on the ear. She was no chaste maiden, but they told me she was a virgin pure.

鄙人意欲远走他乡，然而，此时人人皆忙于为在下做月下老儿。在下所到之处红娘紧随其后，形影不离，几乎将在下之燕尾扯下。他们滔滔不绝，口若悬河，致使在下双耳嗡鸣。此女既非大家闺秀，亦非小家碧玉，本无贞操可言。然而，他们却言称此女乃圣洁之贞女也。

The above-mentioned original is taken from a short story *Gimpel the Fool* by the American writer Isaac Bashevis Singer, a Nobel Laureate in literature. Gimpel, the hero of the story, is an orphan, a baker and almost illiterate, who is regarded as a fool, a butt of the public. The quotation cited above is taken from what Gimpel says. Analysing the original, one can find that it is flexible in syntax and full of simple short sentences and colloquial words. Compared with the original, the translation is incompatible with the original in meaning and in style as well as too many classical Chinese characters such as "之", "乎", "者", "也" are used in it. These classical Chinese characters are so formal that readers will surely believe that Gimpel is a learned man rather than an illiterate fool. In the translator's opinion the short story is a literary work that is formal in style, therefore it should be translated into a classical, elegant version. However the translator little realizes that literary works are different from one another with various writers, styles and even heroes of the works. As literary works, some short stories are written in classical and delicate words, some in popular and plain words, some in coarse and rough words. Xue Baochai, one of the main characters in *A Dream of Red Mansions* has always something of refined prosperity in her language, but her brother Xue Pan never opens his mouth without speaking vulgarly. Both Xue Baochai and Xue Pan have left a deep impression on readers, which suggests a great success of the author in diction. An author can beautify a maid of honour by making her up heavily; he can similarly grace a village girl by a spray of wild flowers. The same goal can be reached by different approaches to writing. The gifted girls pictured by Li Ruzhen with refined language and flowery words are as charming as fairies; but the country folk described by Zhao Shuli with plain language and colloquial words are similarly vivid and true to life. Just take a few sentences for example: "三仙姑却和大家不同,虽然已经四十五岁,却偏爱当个老来俏,小鞋上仍要绣花,裤腿上仍要镶边,顶门上的头发脱光了,用黑手盖起来,只可惜官粉涂不平脸上的皱纹,看起来好像驴粪蛋上下上了霜。"San Xiangu (the sorceress) described by Zhao Shuli is so distinct that readers can see her and talk to her in her face.

Summing up the above-mentioned, the author believes that a clear discrimination of attribution of formality levels is of great importance to accuracy of diction both in translation and composition. Diction is like carving and painting, a vivid touch comes from a sound awareness of formality levels of words and overall balance of different colours.

Translation Exercises

I. *Translate the following prose into Chinese with enough attention to the levels of formality of words.*

An October Sunrise

I was up the next morning before the October sunrise, and away through the wild and the woodland. The rising of the sun was noble in the cold and warmth of it ; peeping down the spread of light, he raised his shoulder heavily over the edge of gray mountain and wavering length of upland. Beneath his gaze the dew-fogs dipped and crept to the hollow places, then stole away in line and column, holding skirts and clinging subtly at the sheltering corners where rock hung over grassland, while the brave lines of the hills came forth, one beyond other gliding.

The woods arose in folds; like drapery of awakened mountains, stately with a depth of awe, and memory of the tempests. Autumn's mellow hand was upon them, as they owned already, touched with gold and red and olive, and their joy towards the sun was less to a bridegroom than a father.

Yet before the floating impress of the woods could clear itself, suddenly the gladsome light leaped over hill and valley, casting amber, blue, and purple, and a tint of rich red rose, according to the scene they lit on, and the curtain flung around; yet all alike dispelling fear and the cloven hoof of darkness, all on the wings of hope advancing, and proclaiming, "God is here!" Then life and joy sprang reassured from every crouching hollow; every flower and bud and bird had a fluttering sense of them, and all the flashing of God's gaze merged into soft beneficence.

So, perhaps, shall break upon us that eternal morning, when crag and chasm shall be no more, neither hill and valley, nor great unvintaged ocean; when glory shall not scare happiness, neither happiness envy glory; but all things shall arise, and shine in the light of the Father's countenance, because itself is risen.

Ⅱ. *Translate the following passage into English.*

老屋离我愈远了；故乡的山水也都渐渐远离了我，但我却并不感到怎样的留恋。我只觉得我四面有看不见的高墙，将我隔成孤身，使我非常气闷；那西瓜地上的银项圈的小英雄的影像，我本来十分清楚，现在却忽地模糊了，又使我非常的悲哀。

我躺着，听船底潺潺的水声，知道我在走我的路。我想：我竟与闰土隔绝到这地步了，但我们的后辈还是一气，宏儿不是正在想念水生么。我希望他们不再像我，又大家隔膜起来……然而我又不愿意他们因为要一气，都如我的辛苦展转而生活，也不愿意他们都如闰土的辛苦麻木而生活，也不愿意都如别人的辛苦恣睢而生活。他们应该有新的生活，为我们所未经生活过的。

3.6 Proper Use of Idioms in Translation

Both the English and the Chinese languages are abundant in idioms and idiomatic phrases. The proper use of them in the translation from English into Chinese can serve as the critical touch (like dotting an eyeball in painting a dragon) and your version will be well supplied with brevity. e. g.

1. Spare the rod and spoil the child.
2. The two teams went halves with each other in the game.
3. The other girls disliked her way of making eyes at their boy friends instead of finding one of her own.
4. Now, gentlemen, I an not a man who does things by halves. Being in for a penny, I am ready, as the saying is, for a pound.

As it happens there are ready-made Chinese idioms available that can be used in translating the above-mentioned sentences into Chinese. It is true that we have some ready-made Chinese idioms and phrases available that are nearly corresponding to English idioms. However, they amount to only a small number. Most of English idioms, however, are different from those of

Chinese. Now let's analyse the similarity and diversity between the two.

3.6.1 Similarities and Diversities between Chinese and English Idioms

One would naturally associate "idiom" with "成语" in Chinese, but the dictionary defines it as follows:

"Succession of words whose meaning is not obvious through knowledge of the individual meanings of the constituent words but must be learnt as a whole." e.g.

  give way 让步,屈服,失败,倒塌

  in order to 以便,为了,为……起见

  be hard put to it 左右为难,陷于窘境

Compare the English definition of "idiom" with the Chinese one of "成语":

"熟语的一种,习用的固定词组,在汉语中多数由四个字组成,组织多样,来源不一。有些可以从字面理解,如"万紫千红"、"乘风破浪";有些要知道来源才懂,如:"青出于蓝"出于《荀子·劝学》、"守株待兔"出于《韩非子·五蠹》。"

The above-mentioned definitions show the obvious diversity and similarity between the idioms of the two languages. Particularly in structure, Chinese idioms are greatly different from English idioms as most of the former are composed of four characters, whereas some of the latter are made of only two words, and some, of many words, even a complete sentence.

  give a dog a bad name and hang him 谗言可畏

  make a mountain out of a molehill 小题大做

  You lose on the swings what you make on the roundabouts. 失之东隅,收之桑榆

These idioms are quite long, but the following rather short.

  dog-tired 精疲力竭

  go to the dogs 完蛋,毁灭,破灭

  Love me, love my dog. 爱屋及乌

There are still some Chinese idioms that are not composed of four characters, but three, five, six or even more characters. e.g.

  马后炮 马前卒

  中山狼 老皇历

  执牛耳

  一退六二五 三下五除二

  小巫见大巫 久旱逢甘露

  坐山观虎斗 快刀斩乱麻

Some Chinese idioms are composed of six, seven or even more characters.

  风马牛不相及

  一蟹不如一蟹

  不登大雅之堂

  醉翁之意不在酒

  说曹操曹操就到

  此地无银三百两

庆父不死,鲁难未已

塞翁失马,安知非福

司马昭之心,路人皆知

以其人之道,还治其人之身

踏破铁鞋无觅处,得来全不费功夫。

Idioms of this kind, however, add up to only a small number. Most Chinese idioms are well-knit four-character idioms. On the other hand, Chinese idioms are obviously different from proverbs and common sayings whereas English idioms include proverbs, slangs and collocations. For examples:

"一丘之貉" is an idiom, but "天下乌鸦一般黑" which is similar in meaning to "一丘之貉" is a proverb, whereas "大河有水小河满,大河无水小河干"; "靠山吃山,靠水吃水"; "巧妇难为无米之炊"; "解铃还须系铃人"; "天上下雨地上流,小两口吵架不记仇" are common sayings.

Since English idioms include proverbs, slang and collocations, only some of them can be rendered into corresponding ready-made Chinese idioms which are different from proverbs and common sayings.

On the basis of a comparative study of Chinese idioms and English idioms, we can classify them into corresponding idioms, and partly corresponding idioms.

3.6.2 Corresponding Idioms

There are some English idioms corresponding to ready-made Chinese idioms both in meaning and in structure. Such idioms can be turned into corresponding Chinese ones and vice versa.

1. In ancient times if a man's eye was put out by his enemy, he might get revenge by putting his enemy's eye out. This was the rule of an eye for an eye and a tooth for a tooth.

古时候要是一个人的眼睛被敌人挖去了,对方可以把敌人的眼睛挖下来作为报复。这就是以眼还眼,以牙还牙的原则。

2. None of the children have any love for the old man. They would be pleased if he kicked the bucket tomorrow.

他的子女对老子全都毫无感情(无情无义)。他们巴不得他明天就翘辫子呢。

3. No more than three days after that dirty dog returned he turned up toes. (variation)

4. You pretended that you were helping them out of their difficulty, but actually you are pouring oil on the fire and making matters worse.

你自称帮助他们摆脱困境,实际上你是在火上浇油,把事情搞得更糟。

5. "Doesn't he know that his wife's being unfaithful to him, and doesn't she know he is being unfaithful to her? If they don't, everybody else does."

"The onlooker sees the most of the game."

"难道他不知道他老婆对他不忠,而她也不知道她丈夫对他不忠?如果他们不知道,别人可都知道!"

"当局者迷,旁观者清嘛!"

also: "他们夫妻互相不忠对此难道他们各自都蒙在鼓里?他们如果不知,别人可都清楚。"

"旁观者清,当事者迷嘛!"

6. If it is a wet summer the firm making mackintoshes will find good markets, if there is a heat wave there will be a special big demand for bathing suits, if we have shares in both we need not feel unduly anxious about the weather, for what we lose on the swing we shall gain on the roundabouts.

要是夏天雨水多,做雨衣的厂商就大有销路,要是热浪袭人,游泳衣便特别吃香。如果我们两头都有股份,那就用不着为天气担心。因为失之东隅可以收之桑榆。

English idioms used in (1) through (6) are directly translated into ready-made Chinese idioms as they are corresponding to each other. Some of Chinese idioms can be translated Similarly. Some examples:

过河拆桥	kick down the ladder
乳臭未干	be wet behind the ears
格格不入	be like square pegs in round holes
魂不附体	jump out of one's skin
小题大做	make a mountain out of a molehill
赴汤蹈火	go through fire and water
洗心革面	turn over a new leaf
七颠八倒	at sixes and sevens
横行霸道	throw one's weight about
大发雷霆	blow one's top
如履薄冰	be on the thin ice
一丘之貉	birds of a feather
胆小如鼠	as timid as a rabbit
趁热打铁	strike while the iron is hot

In English, some idioms are synonymous, and the same is true of some Chinses idioms. Such being the case, translation of them can be done very flexibly as follows:

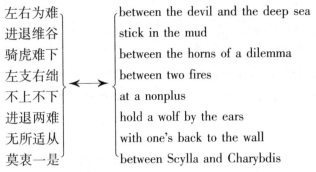

3.6.3 Partly Corresponding Idioms

Some of English idioms are only partly corresponding to those of Chinese in meaning, use and structure. Some of them can be still interchangeably translated, but some can not be directly put into ready-made Chinese idioms without making appropriate adaptations. Some examples:

1. The man is neither fish nor fowl; he votes Democrat or Republican according to which will do him the most good.

这个人什么也不是；他投民主党的票还是共和党的票完全根据谁对他最有利。

(这人什么党也不是,他投民主党的票还是共和党的票其根据就是谁对他最有利。)

(比较:非驴非马,不伦不类,四不像)

2. Willy: You are my foundation and my support, Linda.

Linda: Just try to relax, dear, You make mountains out of molehills.

维利:你是我的(靠山)基础,我的支柱,林达(心肝)。

林达:亲爱的,轻松一下吧,(别这么紧张)你夸大其词了。

(你讲得也太邪乎了。)

(比较:小题大做)

3. The news that the firm was closing down came as a bolt from the blue to the staff.

商行要倒闭的消息对该行职员来说犹如晴天霹雳。

4. News of their marriage was a bolt from the blue—we don't know they were engaged.

他们结婚的消息真是令人感到意外,我们压根儿就不知道他们订婚的事。

5. George was the apple of his father's eyes. He did not like Harry, his second son, so well.

乔治是他父亲的心肝宝贝(宠儿)。他父亲对老二哈里就不那么喜欢。

(比较:掌上明珠)

6. The two party system is the apple of the capitalists' eye, so far as maintaining their political control of the worker is concerned.

就资产阶级维护对工人的政治控制而言,两党制是资本家的法宝。

(比较:掌上明珠)

From the above-mentioned examples we can come to a conclusion that English idioms corresponding to those of Chinese add up only to a small number. Most of idioms of the two languages can not be rendered interchangeably. Some idioms in the SLT seem corresponding to those in the TLT on the surface, their contextual meanings are actually different from the meanings of those in the TLT. Such being the case, the contextual meaning must be taken into consideration.

However, in translation between English and Chinese, there is a common occurrence that the modifiers in the SLT are rendered into idioms in the TLT, that is to say, the idioms in the TLT have no corresponding ones in the SLT, yet the meanings of the original modifiers can be clearly expressed and the TLT can be well accepted.

3.6.4 Modifiers Are Rendered into Idioms

1. She has beauty still, and, if it is not in its heyday, it is not yet in its autumn.

她依然很美,如果不是芳华正茂,也还不到迟暮之年。(……纵然不是芳华正茂,也还未到花落叶黄。)

2. ... loss of virtue in a female is irretrievable, one false step involves her in endless ruin.

……失去贞操对于一个女性是万劫不复的,一失足成千古恨。

"Heyday", "autumn" in (1) and "irretrievable", "one false step involves her in endless ruin" in (2) are not at all idioms themselves, they are, however, expressed in Chinese idioms naturally and faithfully. Of course, properly using Chinese idioms this way requires sufficient capability of mastering both the Chinese and the English languages, especially, the former (to the students of English major). One would otherwise get into trouble through clever means if he has idioms overused or improperly.

Some more examples with idioms properly used:

3. Seeing that he evidently wished her at the end of the earth, Gemma hastened to state her business.

琼玛看到他那副明显的拒人千里之外的神色,就立即说明来意。

4. If France can have two or preferably three years time, she can reconstitute herself...

如果法国有两年,最好是三年时间,它就能重新组织自己。

(比较:重整旗鼓;东山再起)

5. Russian intervention will thus find justification.

俄国的干涉因此而找到正当理由。

(比较:……因此而名正言顺)

6. No greater misfortune can befall a country than to be governed by an old tyrant.

一个国家的最大不幸莫过于被一个暴君所统治。

(比较:国之横祸莫过于暴君当政。)

By comparison we can see the versions with idioms properly used are better than the versions without. By using idioms and four-character structure, our versions are smooth, concise and well-knit in syntax and diction.

Some more from literary works:

7. If she did, she need not coin her smiles so lavishly; flash her glances so unremittingly; manufacture airs so elaborate, graces so multitudinous.

如果是爱他的话,她根本用不着这样满脸堆笑,不停地滥送秋波;这样煞费苦心地故作姿态,摆出那么斯文的样子。

8. ... the sun was just entering the dappled east and his light illumined the wreathed and

dewily orchard trees shone down the quiet walks under them.

……太阳刚刚进入霞光灿烂的东方。阳光照耀着枝叶缠绕、露珠晶莹的果树。洒落在树下静悄悄的小径上。

also：太阳刚刚升起，东方霞光万道（灿烂）。阳光洒在枝叶缠绕、露珠晶莹的果树上，洒落在幽静的小径上。

9. While such honey-dew fell, such silence reigned, such gloaming gathered. I felt as if I could haunt such shade for ever, but in threading the flower and fruit-parterres at the upper part of the enclosure, enticed there by the light the new-rising moon casts on this more open quarter, my step is stayed—not by sound, not by sight, but once more by a warning fragrance.

译文（1）在这样蜜露降落，沉默统治，暮色渐深的时候，我觉得我仿佛可以永远在这荫处常留，但是被照在更开朗的地方初升的月光所吸引，我在这隐蔽地底上部踏着花果的平台时，我的脚步不是被声音，也不是因为看见什么，却又被一种警告的香味停住了。

译文（2）在这样蜜露降落，这样万籁俱寂，这样暮色渐浓的时候，我觉得我仿佛永远在这树荫下徘徊下去；但是初升的月亮把月光倾泻在比较开阔的地方，我受引诱，正穿过园里较高的花丛和果林的时候，我的脚步被阻止了——不是被声音，不是被景象，而是再一次被一阵警告性的香味阻止了。

亦可以改译为：甘露洒落，万籁俱寂，暮色渐浓，此时此刻，我仿佛觉得可以永远在这树荫下徘徊下去，然而初升的月儿，把（迷人）皎洁的月光洒在一片开阔的去处，令人神往。穿过园子里高处的花丛与果林，我却停住了脚步，不是因为听到了什么，也不是因为看见了什么，而是因为另一种香味的警告。

10. They began to talk; their conversation eased me completely; frivolous, mercenary, heartless, and senseless, it was rather calculated to weary than enrage a listener.

他们开始谈话；他们谈话使我完全安下心来，琐琐碎碎，利欲熏心，言不由衷，毫无意义，那只会叫听的人（听话者）感到厌倦，而不会感到愤怒。

11. I suppose he will be awfully proud, and that I shall be treated most contemptuously. Still I must bear my hard lot as well as I can...

我猜他是骄气凌人，不把我放在眼里，我有什么办法呢？只能逆来顺受了……

cf.（"忍受我不幸的命运"则大为逊色）

12. But my kind reader will please to remember that this history has "Vanity Fair" for a title, and that Vanity Fair is a very vain, wicked, foolish place, full of all sorts of humbugs and falseness and pretensions.

请忠实的读者务必记住，这本书的名字是《名利场》。"名利场"当然是穷凶极恶，崇尚浮华，而且非常无聊的地方，到处是虚伪欺诈还有各式各样的骗子。

In nine cases out of ten, Chinese is different from English in the way of expression, which requires the translator to have the original rearranged in syntax creatively on the basis of perfect digestion of the original. e. g.

13. Whilst our friend George and his young wife were enjoying the first blushing days of the honeymoon at Brighton...

乔治和他的年轻夫人新婚燕尔，在布拉依顿度蜜月的时候……

14. His blood boiled with honest British exultation, as he saw the name of Osborn ennobled in the person of his son, and thought that he might be the progenitor of a glorious line of baronets.

这老头是老实的英国人本色。一想到儿子光宗耀祖,成了贵人以后一脉相传,世代都是光荣的从男爵,自己便是老祖宗,不禁得意得浑身暖融融的了。

Whether or not an idiom is properly used can not be judged only by a word, a phrase or a single sentence. One must take many factors into consideration—style of writing and its background, the social position and characteristic of the hero you are going to describe and even his (or her) age or temperament.

e. g.

15. In fact, the lexicographer's name was always on the lips of this majestic woman, and a visit he had paid to her was the cause of her reputation and her fortune.

这位威风凛凛的女人嘴边老是挂着词汇学家的名字。原来他曾经拜访过他一次,从此使她名利双收。

16. He had time to note the light, fluffy something that hid her greeny head, the tasteful lines of her wrapped figure, the gracefulness of her carriage and of the hand caught up her skirts...

他来得及看清她雍容华贵的头上裹着一条薄薄的毛茸茸的头巾,身子裹在衣服里(那衣着,那身段),线条优美,仪态万方,一只手提着裙子边,姿态真美……

17. She gazed at him with new approval when she stopped, the lush, responsive tissues of her dark face turning darker still and blooming somnolently with a swelling and beautifying infusion of blood.

等止住笑后。她用新的赞许的神气凝视着他。那张本来黝黑的脸上富有肉感,富有弹性的肌肉显得更黑了。虽然她有点儿倦意,但由于高兴激动,却显得春风满面,分外骄艳(妖艳、妖冶)。

(此处骄艳宜改为妖艳为好)

Three female characters are respectively pictured in (15) (16) and (17). The first one was a schoolmistress, the second, a young American lady of the upper class in the early 20th century and the third, a prostitute who served in an American military base area in the 60s of the 20th century. Such being the case, different idioms should be used in describing them as the above-mentioned examples do.

Some more examples:

18. He was able to outsmart the political analysts by suddenly unveiling a major adviser who was not a Nixon regular, and, for the first time in his political career, he was able to attract a widely respected intellectual to his service.

他能出奇制胜,突然命令一个与尼克松素无瓜葛的人出任重要顾问,这一招是政治家们所意料不到的。他能把一个佼佼盛名的知识分子罗织到自己手下,这在他的政治生涯中还是头一遭。

19. I had brought the press to tears, having six appointments a day, every day, and never saying a word. They had to stand there in that heat watching me go in, come out, go in, come

out, and never saying anything.

我把记者们弄得哭笑不得,一天六次会晤,对他们却一(只)字不漏。他们站在外边头顶骄阳,眼巴巴看着我出出进进,就是守口如瓶。

20. Zeena herself, from an oppressive reality, had faded into an unsubstantial shade.

连细娜这人也由咄咄逼人的实体(有血有肉)褪成一个虚无缥缈的影子。

21. 士隐那禁得贫病交攻,竟渐渐地露出了那下世的光景来。

Aging and a prey to poverty and ill health, he began to look like a man with one foot in the grave.

22. 雨村闲居无聊,每当风日晴和,饭后便出来闲步。

Then Yucun, finding time hang heavy on his hands, used to take a walk after his meals when the weather was fine.

23. 谁知这拐子又走不脱,两家拿住,打了个半死。

Before he could get away with this, they nabbed him and beat him within an inch of his life.

24. 那衣裳虽是旧的,我也没大很穿,你要嫌弃,我就不敢说了。

The clothes may not be new, but they haven't been worn much. Still, if you turn up your nose at them, I shan't complain.

25. 那疯跛道人听了,拍掌大笑道:"解得切,解得切!"

The lame, eccentric Taoist clapped his hands. "You have hit the nail on the head," he cried.

26. 彼时贾政已看了妹丈之书,即忙请入相会。

Jia Zheng, who had received his brother-in-law's letter, lost no time in asking him in.

27. 不是那日我眼错不见,不知那个没调教的,只图讨你的喜欢,给了你一口酒喝,葬送的我挨了两天骂!

But I haven't forgotten the way they scolded me for two days on end just because some irresponsible fool who wanted to get on the right side of you gave you a sip of wine behind my back.

28. 黛玉接了,抱在怀中,笑道:"也亏了你倒听他的话!我平日和你说的,全当耳旁风;怎么他说了你倒依,比圣旨还快呢!"

Nursing the stove in her arms Daiyu retorted, "So you do whatever she asks, but let whatever I say go in one ear and out the other. You jump to obey her instructions faster than if they were an Imperial edict."

29. 林黛玉自在荣府,贾母万般怜爱,寝食起居,一如宝玉,把那迎春、探春、惜春倒且靠后了。

Since her coming to the Rong Mansion, the Lady Dowager had been lavishing on her, treating her in every respect just like Baoyu so that Yingchun, Tanchun and Xichun, the Jia girls, all had to take a back seat.

30. "这小厮那里害什么病!想是翟家这奴才走下乡狐假虎威,着实恐吓了他一场。"

"How can the fellow be ill? It's all the fault of this rascal Chai. He goes down to the villages like a donkey in a lion's hide, and he must have scared this painter fellow out of his wits."

In a word, a good translation with nothing to be further desired is easier said than done. By using idioms properly we can have our translation more naturally, flexibly and expressively done. But bear in mind: never have idioms overworked, never use an idiom unless you are sure of its meaning and implication, or you will be trapped by your own clever means.

Translation Exercises

Ⅰ. *Translate the following sentences into Chinese, using Chinese idioms if possible.*

1. Like a peacock among sparrows, the film flaunts its differences.

2. Tired of the pomps and vanities of this heartless world, he chose to live in obscure loneliness.

3. Almost all managers are in the position of having easy access to a special benefit.

4. The clouds over the land now rose like mountains and the coast was only a long green line with the gray-blue hills behind it.

5. You told me the other day that you weren't going to write anything about him yourself. It would be rather like a dog in a manger to keep to yourself a whole lot of material that you have no intention of using.

6. Despair seized him at the thought of her setting out alone to renew the weary quest for work.

7. Linton lavished on her the kindest caresses, and tried to cheer her by the fondest words; but vaguely regarding the flowers, she let the tears collect on her cheeks unheeding.

8. Her knowledge of love was purely theoretical, and she conceived of it as lambent flame, gentle as the fall of dew or the ripple of quiet water, and cool as the velvet-dark of summer nights. Her idea of love was more that of placid affection, serving the loved one softly in an atmosphere, flower-scented and dim-lighted, of ethereal calm.

Ⅱ. *Translate the following passage into Chinese, using Chinese idioms if possible.*

Jane Eyre, who had been an ardent, expectant woman—almost a bride—was a cold, solitary girl again: her life was pale; her prospects were desolate. A Christmas frost had come at midsummer: a white December storm had whirled over June; ice glazed the ripe apples, drifts crushed the blowing roses; on hayfield and corn-field lay a frozen shroud: lanes which last night blushed full of flowers, today were pathless with untrodden snow; and the woods, which twelve hours since waved leafy and fragrant as groves between the tropics, now spread, waste, wild, and white as pine-forests in wintry Norway. My hopes were all dead—struck with a subtle doom, such as, in one night, fell on all the first born in the land of Egypt, I looked on my cherished wishes, yesterday so blooming and glowing; they lay stark, chill, livid—corpses that could never revive. I looked at my love: that feeling which was my master's—which he had created; it shivered in my heart, like a suffering child in a cold cradle; sickness and anguish had seized it: it could not seek Mr. Rochester's arms—it could not derive warmth from his breast. Oh, never more could it turn to him; for faith was blighted—confidence destroyed! Mr. Rochester was not to me what he had been; for he was not what I had thought him. I would not ascribe vice to him; I would not say he had betrayed me, but the attribute of stainless truth was gone from his idea; and from his presence I must go: that I perceived well. When—how—whither, I could not yet discern, but he himself, I doubted not, would hurry me from Thornfield. Real affection, it seemed, he could not have for me; it had been only fitful passion: that was balked; he would want me no more. I should fear even to cross his path now. My view must be hateful to him. Oh, how blind had been my eyes! How weak my conduct!

Ⅲ. *Translate the following idioms into English idioms if possible, or translate them literally.*

1. 竭泽而渔
2. 打草惊蛇
3. 易如反掌
4. 玩火自焚
5. 挥金如土
6. 对牛弹琴
7. 守口如瓶
8. 雪中送炭
9. 画蛇添足
10. 井底之蛙
11. 甘拜下风
12. 半斤八两
13. 捕风捉影
14. 本性难改
15. 过河拆桥
16. 患难见真情
17. 既往不咎
18. 捷足先登
19. 事难两全
20. 水底捞月

3.7 Translation of Proverbs and Two-part Allegorical Sayings

3.7.1 Proverbs

A Dictionary of Contemporary Chinese defines proverb as: 在群众中流传的固定语句。用简单而通俗的话反映出深刻的道理。如:"三个臭皮匠,赛过诸葛亮";"三百六十行,行行出状元";"天下无难事,只怕有心人"。 The New Oxford Dictionary Of English defines proverb similarly: "A short pithy saying in general use, stating a general truth or piece of advice." In *A Dictionary of English Proverbs Annotated Bilingually* by Sheng Shaoqiu and Li Yongfang there are quite a few proverbs which can serve as interpretation to the attribute of proverb. Examples are listed as follows.

A proverb is a true word.
谚语乃真言。

A proverb is an ornament to language.
谚语为语言增色。

A proverb is much matter decocted into few words.
谚语言简意赅。

There is no proverb without a grain of truth.
条条谚语都含哲理。

Proverbs are the lamps to words.
谚语为语言增色。

A proverb is a short sentence based on long experience.
谚语是长期经验的结晶。

From the proverbs mentioned above it can thus be seen that ①all proverbs express truth, ②proverbs are short in form but rich in meaning, ③proverbs make language more beautiful, ④most proverbs are used as sentences, which is different from idioms of which most are used as words or phrases. The attribute of proverbs and their linguistic features can be preserved in translation by means of substitution, literal translation, liberal translation or literal translation plus liberal translation.

Substitution

1. A friend is known in necessity.

患难见知交。

2. A good example is the best sermon.

身教重于言教。

3. A near neighbour is better than a far-dwelling kinsman.

远亲不如近邻。

4. A single fact is worth a shipload of arguments.

事实胜于雄辩。(cf. Facts speak louder than words.)

5. A single spark can start a prairie fire.

星星之火,可以燎原。

6. Rivers run into the sea.

条条江河归大海。

7. All things whatever ye would that men should not do to you, do ye even not to them. (Do not do to others as you would not be done by.)

己所不欲,勿施于人。

8. Better die standing than live kneeling.

宁可站着死,决不跪着生。

9. Do unto him as he do unto others. (Do unto him as he does unto you.)

以其人之道还治其人之身。

10. Failure is the mother of success.

失败是成功之母。

11. 趁热打铁

Strike while the iron is hot.

12. 祸不单行

Misfortune never comes singly.

13. 水火无情

Fire and water have no mercy.

14. 憨人有憨福。

Fortune favours fools.

15. 得寸进尺

Give him an inch and he will take a yard.

16. 良药苦口

Good medicine always tastes bitter.

17. 入乡随俗

When in Rome, do as the Romans do.

18. 有其父必有其子

Like father, like son.

19. 学习如逆水行舟，不进则退。

Learning is like rowing upstream: not to advance is to dropback.

20. 不入虎穴,焉得虎子。

If you don't enter a tiger's den, you can't get his cubs.

Literal translation

21. A bird in the hand is worth two in the bush (or wood).

双鸟在林,不如一鸟在手。

22. A contented person is happy with his status quo.

满足现状,心情舒畅。

23. A soft answer turns away wrath.

婉言可息盛怒。

24. A stitch in time saves nine.

一针及时省九针。

25. All covet, all lose.

样样都想要,样样得不到。

26. All roads lead to Rome.

条条道路通罗马。

27. Among the blind the one-eyed man is king.

盲人国里,独眼称王。

28. As you brew, so shall you drink.

自己酿的酒自己喝。

29. Better poor with honour than rich with shame.

宁可清贫而有德,不可为富而不仁。

30. Better to reign in hell than serve in heaven.

宁在地狱为王,不在天堂为臣。

31. 猛药起沉疴。

Desperate diseases must have desperate cures (or remedies)

32. 自己最了解自己

Every man is best known to himself.

33. 一向不生病,生病就要命。

He who never was sick dies the first fit.

34. 骑虎难下。

He who rides a tiger is afraid to dismount.

35. 万事开头难。

It is the first step that costs.

36. 学而不思则罔,思而不学则殆。

Learning without thought is useless, thought without learning is dangerous.

37. 什么树结什么果。

Like tree, like fruit.

38. 旁观者清,当局者迷。

Lookers-on see more than players.

39. 光阴一去不复返。

Lost time is never found again.

40. 金钱乃万恶之源。

Money is the root of all evil.

Liberal translation

41. As well be hanged for a sheep as for a lamb.

一不做,二不休。

42. Beauty is in the beholder's eye.

情人眼里出西施。

43. Better be the head of an ass than the tail of a horse.

宁为鸡首,不为牛后。

44. Do as you would be done by.

己所不欲,勿施于人。

45. Good wine needs no bush.

酒好客自来。

46. He bit the hand that fed him.

恩将仇报。

47. Heaven's vengeance is slow, but sure.

天网恢恢,疏而不漏。

48. It is a wise man that never makes mistakes.

智者千虑,必有一失。

49. It is never too late to mend.

改过不嫌晚。

50. Let another's shipwreck be your sea mark.

沉舟侧畔千帆过。

51. 防患于未然。

Lock the stable before you lose the steed.

52. 谋事在人,成事在天。

Man proposes; God disposes.

53. 欲速则不达。

More haste, less speed.

54. 不劳则无获。

No pains, no gains (or profit).

55. 前人栽树,后人乘凉。

Plant pears for your heirs.

56. 醉翁之意不在酒。

Many kiss the baby for the nurse's sake.

57. 言为心声。

Speech is the picture of mind.

58. 班门弄斧。

Teach your grandmother to suck eggs.

59. 江山易改,本性难移。

The leopard cannot change its (or his) spots.

60. 酒后吐真言。

Truth is at the bottom of the decanter.

In order to have the linguistic features of a proverb well preserved, sometimes it's necessary to have both literal translation and liberal translation simultaneously applied to translation of one proverb as follows:

61. A horse may stumble on four feet.

人有失手,马有失蹄。

62. A little pot is soon hot.

壶小易热,量小易怒。

63. Words are but wind, but seeing is believing.

耳听是虚,眼见为实。

Translation of proverbs must be based on thorough understanding, never translate a proverb according to its superficial meaning. Such as the proverb "the child is father of the man" means "the experiences of childhood determine a person's character as an adult", which is similar to Chinese proverb "从小看大,七岁看老", so it can't be translated to "有其父必有其子". Another point that should be emphasized is the style and national tint of proverbs. If the SL proverb is tinged with strong national tint and shares high level of formality, the translator is supposed to have this style reproduced in his translation. Consider the following examples:

64. The Trojans became wise too late.

(1) 事后诸葛亮,为时已太晚。

(2) 待到醒悟时,为时已太迟。

65. 说曹操,曹操到。

(1) Talk of the devil and he is sure to appear.

(2) Talk of Caocao and he is sure to appear.

Considering the style and the national tint of the original, the second versions of both proverbs are better than the first versions.

3.7.2 Two-part Allegorical Sayings

A two-part allegorical saying, a vivid humorous rhetorical device peculiar to Chinese language, is composed of two parts, of which the first is a metaphor, and the second functions as an interpretation to the first. As a pause is used between the two parts, the device is thus called as its name implies "歇后语"。

Structurally the two-part allegorical sayings are classified to the simplified sayings and the complete sayings. A simplified two-part allegorical saying usually has the second part omitted as its meaning is simple and easy enough, and known to all, for example,"你水山不用对我这么客气,给我磕头,我也不会把侄女给你,想占我的房产……哼!黄鼠狼给鸡拜年"。

A complete two-part allegorical saying has the two parts, the metaphor and the interpretation well balanced, for example,"人嘛,药材店里的抹台布——甜酸苦辣样样都得沾点。"(张贤亮:《河的子孙》) So far as the way of expression is concerned, two-part allegorical sayings are classified to metaphorical sayings and homonymous sayings. A metaphorical saying is based on making use of the second part for illustration of the first part, such as "骑驴看唱本——走着瞧"。A homonymous saying usually serves as a pun based on homophony whose meaning is implied between the lines and sounds, such as "我看你是贾家的姑娘嫁贾家,贾(假)门(假)氏!明是熊蛋包,还要往自己脸上贴金"。(杨朔:《三千里江山》) As two-part allegorical sayings are peculiar to Chinese language, there is no equivalent corresponding to them in English. Hence translation of them must be done flexibly. Some of them can be translated literally, some liberally, and some should be translated by means of adaptation.

Some examples:

1. 那个宝玉是个"丈八的灯台——照见人家,照不见自己"的,只知嫌人家脏。这是他的房子,由着你们糟蹋。

As for Baoyu, he's like a ten-foot lampstand that sheds light on others but none on itself. He complains that other people are dirty, yet leaves you to turn his own rooms topsy-turvy.

2. 没良心的!"狗咬吕洞宾——不识好歹"。

You ungrateful thing! Like the dog that bit Lü Tung-pin—you bite the hand that feeds you.

3. 这件事,除了他三儿子和几个经手的人以外,谁也不知道。他也不对任何人提起。哑巴吃黄连,有苦说不出。

No one knew of these transactions apart from his youngest son and the few people who had handled them, nor was he going to mention the matter to anyone else. He was like the dumb man eating the bitter herb: he had to suffer the bitterness of it in silence.

4. 去设埋伏我们都没有信心,想他一定在昨天晚上就早溜了,今天去是瞎子点灯白费蜡。

We had no confidence in today's ambush because we were sure he had escaped last night. It seemed as useless as a blind man lighting a candle.

The above four examples are translated literally. But the translated versions are smooth and vivid. So they can be easily accepted by readers. Some more examples:

5. 怪不得人说你们"诗云子曰"的人难讲话!这样看来,你好像"老鼠尾巴害疖子,出脓也不多!"

No wonder they say you bookworms are hard to deal with: one might just as well try to squeeze water out of a stone.

6. 生活的海里起过小小的波浪,如今似乎又平静下去,一切跟平常一样,一切似乎都是外甥打灯笼,照舅(旧)。

The even tenor of their life had been disturbed, but things seemed to be setting done again. The villagers felt themselves back in the old rut.

7. 可是谭招弟心中却想:骑着毛驴看书——走着瞧吧,看究竟是什么原因。

But Tan Chao-ti was still thinking to herself: Let's wait and see what the reason for it turns out to be in the end.

The above three examples are translated liberally as great difference lies between the SLT and TLT in tenor and vehicle, literal translation would lead to misunderstanding of the implied meaning. Some two-part allegorical sayings are supposed to be translated by means of literal translation plus annotation or by adaptation as follows.

8. 耗子进书房,咬文嚼字。

A rat entering a library—gnawing characters. The phrase (咬文嚼字) "gnawing sentences and chewing characters" is applied to one who lays great stress on externals in study, a pedant. The mention of "a rat in a study", is intended to suggest this meaning.

9. 一根筷子吃藕,挑眼。

Eating lily root with only one chop-stick—picking it up by the holes. This root has many apertures, called "eyes". The expression tiao-yen(挑眼) means to "pick flaws", in which sense the proverb is employed.

10. "……回来你一个人怎么着?这白洋淀可容易失迷呢。"

"看你,隔着门缝儿瞧人,把人看扁啦。"

"... how would you find your way back alone? It's easy to get lost on Baiyang Lake!"

"Humph! If you peer at a person through a crack, he looks flat! Don't be so prejudiced."

From analysis of the above examples we can see that harmony between the first part and the second part of a two-part allegorical saying, especially that between the implied meaning and the interpretation, is the basis on which an allegorical saying is formed. Hence the translator is supposed to give top priority to the effective approaches that lead to harmony between the implied meaning of the first part and the interpretation to the second part of an allegorical saying.

Translation Exercises

I. *Translate the following proverbs literally or liberally.*

1. You cannot eat your cake and have it (too).
2. You cannot clap with one hand.
3. Yesterday will not be called again.
4. Wine and judgement mature with age.
5. Who keeps company with wolves, will learn to howl.
6. In wine there is truth.
7. Unpleasant advice is a good medicine.

8. True gold fears not the fire.

9. There is no rule without an exception.

10. The pen is mightier than the sword.

11. 无风不起浪。

12. 为人不做亏心事,夜半敲门人不惊。

13. 人要衣装,佛要金装。

14. 天无绝人之路。

15. 天下无不散之筵席。

16. 一个和尚挑水吃,两个和尚抬水吃,三个和尚没水吃。

17. 一次被蛇咬,三年怕草绳。

18. 少壮不努力,老大徒伤悲。

19. 饱汉不知饿汉饥。

20. 巧妇难为无米之炊。

Ⅱ. *Translate the following two-part allegorical sayings into English with enough attention to harmony between the two parts.*

1. 你可倒好!"肉包子打狗,一去不回头啊!"

2. 日本曹长心里像有十五个吊桶打水,七上八下地不安宁。

3. 他必审问我,我给他个"徐庶入曹营——一语不发"。

4. 穷棒子闹翻身,是"八仙过海,各显其能"。

5. 等他们赶来增援时,已是"正月十五贴门神——晚了半月啦"。

6. 他吗,"棺材里伸出手来——死要钱"。他哪会借钱给我?

7. 对新药业,老实讲,我是"擀面杖吹火——一窍不通"。

8. 我哪里管的上这些来!见识又浅,嘴又笨,心又直,"人家给个棒槌,我就拿着认针(真)了"。

9. 我是想:咱们是"孔夫子搬家,净是书(输)"。

10. 蒋介石本人是"泥菩萨过江——自身难保"。

3.8 Translation of Allusions

3.8.1 Traditional Allusions

Allusions are lustrous pearls in the palace of literature which shine brightly in the literary classics of writers and poets at home and abroad. In the works by Shakespeare there are about 1000 allusions; there are as many as 700 allusions from the Bible which are included as lexical entries of a dictionary; in the Complete Collection of the Tang Poetry there are around 20000 allusions cited by over 2200 poets. Allusions are used not only by men of letters, but also by writers of various types of writings. Some examples:

1. All roads to Venice.

The journalist made clever use of the allusion "All roads lead to Rome" in his comment on Venice Conference in 1980.

2. What would not a man give, O judges, to be able to examine the leader of the great

Trojan expedition; or Odysseus or Sisyphus, or numberless others, men and women too!

The philosopher cited the allusions to make his essay more logic and profound.

3. There are no dragon's teeth so prolific as mutual misunderstandings.

The elocutionist cited allusion to make his speech more philosophical and inviting. The above examples speak volume for the extensive use of allusions in various types of works.

Allusion, either an English one or a Chinese one, usually derives from the condensed story that is vivid and interesting. It may be a word, or a phrase, however simple or complex it may be, it must be deep in meaning and thought-provoking when used in literary works. Hence the proper use of an allusion is based on the correct understanding of the implied meaning which is usually read between the lines, beyond the lines and sometimes behind the lines. Translation of allusions is usually based on the awareness of the difference and similarity between English allusions amd Chinese allusions.

China boasts a long history and Chinese culture goes back to time immemorial, so most Chinese allusions are deeply rooted and can be traced back to the same origin—Chinese culture. English allusions, however, are different from Chinese allusions in the source, some of them are of the English origin, some derive form other cultures, such as Greek-Roman culture, French culture, and cultures of some other European Countries, and still some from the Bible, which result in the difference between the two in form and structure. English allusions are flexible and elastic in structure, some of them are long, some short, some of them are well-knit and compact, some loose. Some examples:

4.
- Hair by hair you will pull out the horse's tail.
  (矢志不移,定能成功)
- What one loses on the swings one gets back on the roundabouts.
  (失之东隅,收之桑榆)
- Ark （避难所）
- Eden （乐园）

Chinese allusions, however, are fixed in form, most of them are composed of two, three or four characters, there are few cases in which allusions are used as sentences, most of Chinese allusions function as words or phrases. Examples are as follows:

5.
- 貂不足,狗尾续。
- 韩信用兵,多多益善。
- 解铃还须系铃人。
- 南山可移,此案不动。
- 塞翁失马,焉知非福。
- 太公钓鱼,愿者上钩。
- 项庄舞剑,意在沛公。
- 一人得道,鸡犬飞升。
- 以子之矛,攻子之盾。

Comparatively speaking, there are more cases in which English allusions are used as sentences, especially the allusions derive from the Bible and the works by Shakespeare.

Metaphorically speaking, English allusions are quite similar to Chinese ones. The metaphors of some English allusions are based on historical events or historical figures, such as "Trojan horse", "meet one's Waterloo", "Helen of Troy". Some take the typical characters of famous literary works as metaphors, such as "Shylock", "Hamlet"; some metaphors are based on the tales or legends such as "kick the bucket", "skeleton in the cupboard". The same is true of Chinese allusions, some examples are as follows:

6. $\begin{cases} \left.\begin{array}{l}太公钓鱼\\王祥卧冰\end{array}\right\}以人设喻 \\ \left.\begin{array}{l}三顾茅庐\\四面楚歌\end{array}\right\}以事设喻 \\ \left.\begin{array}{l}东山再起\\垓下闻歌\end{array}\right\}以地名设喻 \\ \left.\begin{array}{l}杞人忧天\\女娲补天\end{array}\right\}以传说设喻 \end{cases}$

However Chinese allusions are to certain extent different from English allusions in some aspects, such as in tenor and vehicle, especially in national tint even if they have something in common in the implied meanings such as "Kill the goose that lays the golden eggs" and "杀鸡取卵", "Meet one's Waterloo" and "败走麦城", "paint(gild) the lily" and "画蛇添足", "rob Peter to pay Paul" and "挖肉补疮", to name but a few. These allusions have similar implications, yet they are different in some aspects, national tint in particular which is the focus of translating allusions.

In translation of allusions from English into Chinese or vice versa, the above-mentioned aspects are supposed to be taken into consideration and translation should be done flexibly. If the equivalent allusion can be found in the TL, translation can be done by means of substitution as follows:

7. "That's done it," said Manby, tearing up the agreement, "now we've burned our boats behind us and we've no option but to go forward with the project".

孟拜把协议撕了说:"就这样了,我们现在是破釜沉舟,别无选择,必须把计划进行下去。"

8. 你按部就班的干,做到老也是穷死。只有大胆的破釜沉舟地跟他们拼,还许有翻身的那一天!

If you work conscientiously you'll die a pauper. All you can do is to burn your boats and fight them in the hope that one day you'll come out on top!

Some English allusions seem similar to Chinese allusion on the surface, such as "in the same boat" and "同舟共济", "lock the stable door after the horse is stolen" and "亡羊补牢", to name but a few, with thorough analysis the difference will reveal itself to us in some aspects, especially in the implied meaning. The English allusion "in the same boat" means "in the same situation or circumstances" which is similar to "同舟" in image and "metaphor" but lacks the "meaning" of "共济" (in times of trouble) which is emphasized by Chinese allusion "同舟共济;" the English allusion "lock the stable door after the horse is stolen" and Chinese allusion "亡羊补牢" overlap in meaning to certain degree, but difference lies in that the former places its focus on "taking precautions when it is too late" (为时已晚), the latter places its focus on "it is not too late to mend" (犹未为晚). Hence translation of such allusions must be based on careful analysis of their implied meanings and the concrete context. Examples are as follows:

9. "There are thousands of young men like you, all in the same boat, because of the war."
"They are not parasites, I am".
"有成千上万像你这样的年轻人,由于战争的缘故处境都一样"。
"我是寄生虫,他们却不是"。

10. If we are called up to explain the loss of those documents, we are all in the same boat since every one of us handled them on the day they disappeared.
如果让我交代文件是怎样丢的,我们谁也脱不了干系,因为丢文件那天我们每个人都经过手。

11. After Tommy had shot Miss Watson's cat, his father took the air gun away from him. Miss Watson said, "It is too late to lock the stable door when the horse has been stolen".
汤米用气枪把华逊小姐的猫打死了,她爸才把枪收走。华逊小姐说:"马后炮,太晚了。"

Some allusions are directly translated into TL by means of literal translation as they are well-known to readers. Some examples:

12. Richard of Gloucestter: And that I love the tree from whence thou sprang'st,
Witness the loving kiss I give the fruit.
(He kisses the infant prince)
(Aside) To say the truth, So Judas Kissed his master, And cried "All hail!" whereas he meant all harm.
葛罗斯特:看我亲亲热热地吻着果子,由此来表示我对产生果子的大树有多么深挚的爱(亲王子)。(旁白)说老实话,我这一吻,好比犹大吻耶稣。口里喊"祝福",心里说"叫你遭殃"。

13. This small country had long been regarded as a Trojan horse placed in Southeast Asia by its master.
很久以来,人们一直把这个小国家看作是被其主子安置在东南亚的一具特洛伊木马。

14. 项庄舞剑,意在沛公。
Xiang Zhang performed the sword dance as a cover for his attempt on Liu Bang's life.

15. 只因薛蟠是"得陇望蜀"的,如今取了金桂又见金桂的丫头宝蟾有三分姿色,举止轻浮可爱,便时常要茶要水的,故意撩逗他。
Now Hsueh Pan was a living example of the saying "To covet the land of Shu after getting the

region of Lung." After marrying Chin-Kuei, he was struck by her maid Pao-chan's charms. As she seemed approachable as well as alluring, he often flirted with her when asking her to fetch him tea or water.

Some allusions are translated by means of liberal translation as literal translation or loan translation is not well-known to readers of TLT. Examples are as follows:

16. John is ashamed of his humble background. That is his Achilles heel.

约翰因出身卑贱而自惭形秽,这是他的致命弱点。

17. It is unfair that historians always attribute the fall of kingdoms to Helen of Troy.

历史学家仍常把王国的倾覆归咎于红颜祸水,这是不公平的。

18. 助着薛蟠图些银钱酒肉,一任薛蟠横行霸道。他不但不去管约,反"助纣为虐"讨好儿。

In return for money, drinks, and dinners, he had lately given Xue Pan a free hand in his nefarious activities—had, indeed, not only refrained from interfering with him, but even "aided the tyrant in his tyranny".

19. 先生大名,如雷贯耳。小弟献丑,真是"弄斧班门"了。

Your great fame long since reached my ears like thunder. I am ashamed to display my incompetence before a connoisseur like yourself.

Sometimes the same allusion can be and should be translated into different versions according to different contexts where it is placed. Flexibility is the focus on translation of such allusions, literal translation or liberal translation, it depends what context it is in and whether the allusion is tinged with strong national colour. If it is, literal translation plus annotation or hermeneutic translation is necessary. Examples are as follows:

20. Nobody will believe he is in trouble because he has cried wolf so many times.

因为他多次虚发警报,谁也不会再相信他遭了难。

21. Time and again the economists and forecaster had cried wolf, and the wolf had made only the most fleeting of visits. Time and again the Reserve Board had expressed fear of inflation, and inflation had failed to bring hard times.

经济学家和预报者们一再喊狼来了,狼只打了个照面,一闪便过去了。储备局一再表示害怕通货膨胀,通货膨胀却未造成艰难时世。

22. "难道这也是个痴丫头,又像颦儿来葬花不成?"因又自笑道:"若真也葬花,可谓东施效颦了;不但不为新奇,而且更是可厌。"

"Can this be another absurd maid come to bury flowers like Taiyu? He wondered in some amusement. If so, she's Tung Shih imitating His shih, which isn't original but rather tiresome."

His Shih was a famous beauty in the ancient Kingdom of Yueh. Tung Shih was an ugly girl who tried to imitate her ways.

译文(2) "Can this be some silly maid come here to bury flowers like Frowner?" he wondered. He was reminded of Zhuang-zi's story of the beautiful Xi-shi's ugly neighbour, whose endeavours to imitate the little frown that made Xi-shi captivating produced an aspect so hideous that people ran from her in terror. The recollection of it made him smile. "This is 'imitating the

Frowner"with a vengeance," he thought, "—if that is really what she is doing. Not merely unoriginal, but downright disgusting!"

All in all translation of traditional allusions is supposed to done flexibly. Surface translation and mechanical translation should be avoided. All factors and elements above-mentioned are supposed to be taken into consideration.

3.8.2 New Allusions

New allusions, as the term suggests, just refer to allusions that freshly come into being. It has not been accepted as a lexical entry by any dictionary, but as a new rhetorieal device it has been mentioned in a few books. In "Aesthetics of Chinese Rhetorical Figures" Tan Yongxiang defines new allusions as "话语中引用的现代特别是'文化大革命'中所流行的词语或句子,旨在幽默或嘲谑,这种修辞手法叫做'新典',也就是新的典故"。(谭永祥:《汉语修辞美学》) In *A Dictionary of English Figures of Speech* by Wen Jun, the author pointed out "英语典故除了常引用历史神话以及前人的文献、作品外,同代作家往往也相互引用,当代的重大事件和当代作家作品中的人物、故事等都可以入典"。(文军:《英语修辞格词典》)The contemporary epoch-making events and the heroes and stories in the contemporary works used as allusions are actually new allusions. Therefore we can say that new allusion is a fact that is well-established, yet not well defined from the perspective of time. The author believes that new allusions refer to the great events, historical figures, stories, heroes and words from the literary works since the May Fourth Movement, which are frequently cited by men of letters and writers. This definition is based on historical segmentation of history of China.

The followings are the sources from which new allusions mainly derive.

3.8.2.1 Great Events

Many epoch-making events frequently cited as allusions for illustration of something important by writers, the same is true of the great events in contemporary history. During the World War II the Pearl Harbor was suddenly bombed by Japanese planes, which resulted in heavy losses to American Navy. Hence a new allusion "pull a Pearl Harbor on sb./sth" came into being which means "to attack by surprise". Another sudden attack on Poland by Luftwaffe during the World War II was named "blitz" which shares the similar meaning with "pull a Pearl Harbor on sb./sth." For example, "He made a blitz tour of Asia."("他对亚洲作了一次闪电式访问。") "An army of doctors blitzed the disease". ("一大批医生对这种疾病发起猛攻。") Similar to traditional allusions, some new allusions are metaphorically based on historical spots, such as "Dunkirk"(敦刻尔克大败退) which is used figuratively to denote a forced military evacuation by sea to avoid disaster, a speedy and complete withdrawal, an entire abandonment of a position, is used to refer to "utter defeat" or "rout" or "a knotty situation". Watergate is another typical example which means "a scandal that involves officials violating public trust through subterfuge, bribery, burglary, and other abuses of power in order to maintain their positions of authority". If it is used as a verb, it means "to deal with in a covert or criminal manner". The word "gate" has since become a suffix that means "a political scandal", such as

Billygate　　　　　(比利门事件)

debategate　　　　（辩论门事件）
Irangate　　　　　（伊朗门事件）
Johannesburggate　（约翰内斯堡门事件）
intelligencegate　　（情报门事件）

During the "Cultural Revolution" in the 1960s a lot of new terms came into being, some of them have been cited frequently as allusions by writers in their works since the fall of the "Gang of Four". Some examples are as follows:

1. 别人说了什么事儿,您赶紧接着话茬儿来一句:"敢情!"这就等于说:"没错儿! 那还用说吗?"甚至可以说有那么点儿"句句是真理"的意思。

2. 精神生产究竟不同于物质生产,引进一种新技术便可以放到生产流程中去立见效应的。文化上的吸收,拿来主义,并不等于现炒热卖,可以收"急用先学,立竿见影"之效。

3. 蟋蟀一科,种类繁庶,最著名的当数油葫芦和棺材头……油葫芦打架,互相抱头乱咬,咬颈,咬胸,咬腿,野蛮之至。棺材头打架,互相抵头角力,显得稍为文明,基本上符合"要文斗,不要武斗"的原则。

4. 小时候也冻得尿过裤。"触及灵魂"的时候他冻得把唯一供给他热能的高粱米饭吐了一地。

It can thus be seen that new allusions are brimming with vitality and their rhetorical effect is remarkably visible.

3.8.2.2　Influential Figures

Since time immemorial many people have been crowned with eternal glory, but many infamous crooks have stamped their names on the pages of history. However famous or infamous they are, they may become allusions cited frequently by writers. Hitler, Quisling (Vidkun Quisling, 1887-1945) are the examples of infamous crooks; Ritz (Cesar Ritz, 1850-1919), Disney (Walt Disney, 1901.12.5-1996.12.15), Jordon (Michael Jordon) are the examples of famous figures. (For further information about Hitler and Jordon please see 3.1.5) Quisling was the Norwegian army officer and diplomat during the Second World War, who ruled Norway on behalf of the German occupying forces (1940-1945). Hence his name Quisling has since become a noun which means a traitor who collaborates with an enemy force occupying their country. Cesar Ritz, originally a waiter, gradually gained fame and fortune, now luxury hotels named after Ritz are all over the world. Ritz is now a synonym to luxury hotel. For example, "The outhouse was fusty, but for fifty pence who would expect the Ritz?"(这间外房有霉味,可是只花50便士谁还能指望住上豪华旅馆呢?) Disneyland founded by Walt Disney (American animator) is now a substitution for a fantastic or a fanciful place, or a never-never land, which can be illustrated by the example as "That is a delicious Disneyland, where everything is syrup and technicolor, cuteness and schalmz". ("好一个奇妙的梦幻世界,到处是明丽的色彩,旖旎的风光,温馨的情调和甜美的音乐。")

3.8.2.3　Literary Works

Literary works are one of the major sources of traditional allusions. There are also quite a few of new allusions that derive from literary works composed at the end of 19th century or in 20th century, such as "Uncle Tom" (from *Uncle Tom's Cabin*, further information please see 3.1.5), "Aunt Tom"(汤姆大婶;漠不关心妇女解放运动的女人,逆来顺受的妇女;from *Uncle Tom's Cabin*), "Shangri-La"(香格里拉;世外桃源,理想乐园;from *Lost Horizon*), "Catch-22" which means a paradox in a law, regulation or practice that makes one a victim of its provisions no matter what one does (from *Catch-22* by Joseph Heller in 1961, further information please see 3.1.5), James Bond(詹姆斯·邦德;神通广大,高手), Jay Gatsby (盖茨彼;热情好客、款待;豪华 from *The Great Gatsby* by Scott Fitzgerald), to name but a few here.

3.8.2.4 Business, Trade, Science and Technology

20th century witnesses the rapid development of science and technology, which results in the economic boom and many new products coming into being. The brand name effect causes some trade marks of name brand products to be more famous than the products themselves, and some famous trade marks are well-known to all. Coca-Cola is now the synonym to famous drinks in the world; Kodak is now the substitution for famous mini-cameras; Cadillac, as the trade mark of a name brand car, is so famous that it is loaded with the extended meaning of the first-class product, such as "the Cadillac of Chinese tea"(中国一流名茶), the Cadillac of German beers(德国啤酒中的名牌产品). Yo-Yo is the trade mark of a toy(悠悠球), but now it can be figuratively used to refer to a thing that repeatedly falls and rises again, or a stupid, insane person; it can also be used as a verb which means move up and down; or manipulate. Some examples:

1. Weight-watchers and manufacturers of diet food in the United States may perhaps be excused if they have had the feeling this past year of being treated like yoyos.

   如果美国的减肥者和减肥食品制造商仍在过去的一年中觉得别人视他们为忽冷忽热摇摆不定的人,那么或许他们是情有可原的。

2. Yet even embarked on a literary career of sort and with a straight job, Brady continued to play the human Yo-Yo, all the time wondering miserably why he couldn't stay out of prison.

   即便布莱迪开始了所谓的文学生涯,谋得一份可靠的工作,可他依然扮演着一个傻瓜的角色,始终不明白为何他摆脱不了身陷囹圄的困境。

3. The price will yo-yo.

   价格会上下波动。

4. The court has yo-yoed on this issue.

   法院对这个问题的态度摇摆不定。

5. I don't want the job if it means he gets to yo-yo me around.

   如果接受这份工作就意味着要受他的摆布,我宁肯放弃。

In the above examples, the same allusion is translated into five different versions as it is placed in various contexts which turn out to be the determining factor by which a new allusion is translated.

Translation Exercises

I. Translate the following sentences into Chinese with enough attention to the implied meanings of allusions in various contexts.

1. They received no sudden revelation of Watergate's wider dimensions, used no James Bond wiles to score their scoops.

2. Most of the applicants were weeded out early, including one 13-year-old aspiring James Bond.

3. The father of four sons, Lance lives with his family in a Gatsby-like mansion in Atlanta.

4. I didn't sell out or Uncle Tom when I became famous.

5. Some of them are regular Uncle Toms.

6. The junior Woodsteins have notched some impressive small coups.

7. Actually, the Woodstein of Koreagate is no stranger to "Page One".

8. There is no question that foreign TV producers have blitzed the U. S..

9. He ritzed the reporters and got a bad press.

10. A group of militant ladies are agitating to forbid U. S. newspapers from running separate Male and Female want ads. Borrowing their rhetoric from the negro civil rights movement, they call the practice segregation by sex, describing it as "Jane Crow" treatment, and call any ladies who tolerate it "Aunt Tom".

II. *Translate the following sentences into English with enough attention to the implied meanings of Chinese allusions.*

1. 而且这规则是不像现在那样朝三暮四的。

2. 猛地醒来,乃是南柯一梦。

3. 否则,袖手旁观,守株待兔,就变成了长期不抗不战了。

4. 他向来是惯叫农民来钻他的圈套的,真不料这回演了一套"请君入瓮"的把戏。

5. 从古以来,只有"杞人忧天",就是那个河南人怕天塌下来。

6. 小人"有眼不识泰山"！一时冒渎兄长,望乞恕罪。

3.9 Translation of Culture-loaded Words

Juri Lotman, a Russian semiotician, pointed out: "No language exist unless it is steeped in the context of culture; and no culture can exist which does not have at its centre the structure of natural language". The relationship between language and culture leads to a close relationship between translation and culture. If translation means decoding the meaning of a text in one language and encoding it into a different language, a translator is both the reader of the source language and the writer of the translated text in the target language. Then he (or she) is facing two different cultures, two different cultural systems to which the source and target languages respectively belong, and a cultural clash becomes an inevitable problem that confronts him (or her). If a translation is done between English and Chinese, cultural clash will be obvious and acute.

Generally speaking, anything that can be said in one language can certainly be said in another language. But it does not mean that the corresponding concepts can be formulated with the same degree of efficiency or precision. Different cultural sources lead to various kinds of ethnical customs and psychological dispositions. Dean C. Barnlund, an American anthropologist, pointed out: "Every society had its way of viewing the universe, and each developed from its premises of a coherent set of rules of behavior. Each tended to be blindly committed to its own style of life and regarded all others as evil". Thus a translator who uses a cultural approach is simply recognizing that each language contains elements which are derived from its culture (such as greetings, fixed expressions and especially the culture-loaded words), that every text is anchored in a specific culture that is specifically shown in culture-loaded words, and that conventions of text production and reception vary from culture to culture. An awareness of such issues can at times make it more appropriate to think of translation as a process which occurs between cultures rather than simply between languages.

Differences between English and Chinese cultures are typically reflected in culture-loaded words which refer to words, besides their conceptional meanings, invested with some connotations based on their accretion of culture and history through semantic change. Thus we say that culture-loaded words are semiotic entities with great message capacity, such as"诸葛亮","华佗","蓝桥","东风"in Chinese; and "Helen", "Judas", "Waterloo" and "West Wind" in English.

3.9.1 Similarity and Difference of Cultural Connotations between English and Chinese Culture-loaded words

There are many words in English whose conceptual meanings are similar or corresponding to their Chinese equivalents, but their cultural connotations are totally different or absent from each other. Chinese words such as"猫","牛","兔","蟾蜍","蝙蝠","猫头鹰"and so on are corresponding to "cat", "bull", "hare", "toad", "bat"and "owl" in conceptual meanings, but their cultural connotations are very much different. We can easily find out the conceptual meanings corresponding to Chinese characters such as"龟","鹤","雁", but their equivalents "turtle", "crane", "wild goose" have cultural connotations different from their Chinese counterparts. "杜鹃"in Chinese is a kind of bird and also a flower. Both the bird and the flower are loaded with profound cultural connotations. It is said that at the end of the Chou Dynasty the monarch of Shu State DuYu passed away immediately after he abdicated the throne to another person, and his state perished. After his death, Du Yu's soul turned into a bird that was named cuckoo(杜鹃). The bird cried day and night without stop, it seemed that it was weeping with tears and blood, and the blood turned into red flowers—azaleas. Thus the bird is always on a par with the flowers in the literary works by men of letters, as a Chinese poem goes"杜鹃花与鸟,怨艳两相赊,疑是口中血,滴成枝上花". In the classic Chinese poems both the bird cuckoo(杜鹃)and the flower azalea(杜鹃花) are invested with vivid imaginations and implications. Some examples:

1.

宣城见杜鹃花

——李白

蜀国曾闻子规鸟,

宣城又见杜鹃花;

一叫一回肠一断,

三春三月忆三巴。

2. 锦　瑟
　　——李商隐

锦瑟无端五十弦，
一弦一柱思华年。
庄生晓梦迷蝴蝶，
望帝春心托杜鹃。
沧海月明珠有泪，
蓝田日暖玉生烟。
此情可待成追忆，
只是当时已惘然。

3. 其间旦暮闻何物，
杜鹃啼血猿哀鸣。

（白居易:《琵琶行》）

4. 杜　鹃
　　——杜甫

杜鹃暮春至，
哀哀叫其间。
我见常再拜，
重是古帝魂。
生子百鸟巢，
百鸟不敢嗔。
仍为喂其子，
礼若奉至尊。

5. 绿遍山野白满川，
子规声里雨如烟。

（范成大:《村居即事》）

In the above examples, "杜鹃" is invested with various cultural connotations respectively: with "nostalgia" in Example 1, with "grief and sorrow" in Example 2, with "sob" in Example 3, with "king" in Example 4, and with "spring in the air" in Example 5, which are absent from its English equivalent "cuckoo".

In Chinese there are many plant terms symbolic of something beyond the plants themselves, such as "松" is the symbol of firmness; "竹" the symbol of straightness; "柳" the symbol of sentiment; "梅" the symbol of nobility; "菊" the symbol of elegance. But in English it is "oak" that is symbolic of firmness, lily symbolic of elegance. The equivalent words of the above Chinese plant terms (pine, bamboo, willow, plum and chrysanthemum) have no cultural connotations. Some Chinese plant terms, when used in different context, may have different cultural connotations. "荷花" is symbolic of "beauty" in the poem "归来池苑皆依旧,太液芙蓉未央柳"(白居易:《长恨歌》); symbolic of "slim foot" (feet) in the poem "明眸剪出玉为肌,凤鞋弓小金莲衬"(卢烟:《踏莎行》); symbolic of "gracefulness" in the prose "予独爱莲之出淤泥而不染,濯清涟而不妖"(周敦颐:《爱莲说》); symbolic of "romantic love" in the couplet "并蒂莲开莲蒂并,双飞燕侣燕飞双。" "杏", when used in the different contexts, may be symbolic of different connotations, such as "杏坛" stands for "forum", "杏林" refers to "medical circle", "红杏出墙" means "thought of love", "杏梁" denotes "boudoir" and "杏花" is symbol of "spring".

In English there are also a lot of plant terms that are loaded with cultural connotations. Examples are listed as follows:

bud—少女,少年
blossom—繁荣兴旺
flora—花神
lily—完美,高贵
laurel—荣誉,声望
narcissus—自恋的美少年
rose—爱情,安乐
apple—宝贝,宠物
cherry—童男,童女,新兵
nut—怪人,疯子
peach—迷人的美女,出色的事物
tomato—漂亮的美女
cypress—哀悼
oak—伟岸,长寿,坚实
olive—和平
root—根源,祖先
trunk—主流
branch—支脉,分科
flower—精华

Some of the plant terms in the above-listed examples have something in common with their Chinese equivalents so far as their connotations are concerned, such as flower and 花, rose and 玫瑰, laurel and 月桂, root and 根, olive and 橄榄 have the similar connotations, the same is true of some animal terms, such as fox and 狐狸, lamb and 羔羊, wolf and 狼, snake and 蛇, to name but a few.

To sum up in a few words, we can say that similarity and difference are characteristic of cultural connotations of English-Chinese culture-loaded words, difference is the main feature that is supposed to be taken into consideration in translation.

3.9.2 Cognitive Schema Theory Applied to Translation of Culture-loaded Words
3.9.2.1 Introduction to Schema

What is schema? Different people present different definitions. Some people believe that schema is the pre-existed knowledge in one's mind or what is called background knowledge, namely, the understanding of the world that is stored in the long-term memory of human mind. Some think that schema is the knowledge structure of the known things and the given information in human mind, which make it possible for information to be stored systematically in one's long-term memory. D. H. Rumelhart believes that schema is the sum total of one's general knowledge while schema theory, the theory of one's knowledge, concerns about how knowledge is represented and also how this kind of representation is realized in a specific manner so as to be helpful to the application of knowledge. According to the schema theory, all kinds of knowledge stored in one's mind could be divided into different units and could be established as "structures" and "systems". It is the very "structure" and "system" that are regarded as schema. *Routledge Dictionary of Language and Linguistics* defines schema as "Generalized knowledge about the sequence of events in particular sociocultural contexts, for example, going to a restaurant, purchasing a ticket, borrowing a book. Such structured everyday knowledge forms an essential basis for human language comprehension since it simplifies the interpretation of incomplete or ambiguous information. In this way the processing of stories is directed according to conventionalized knowledge about how stories are usually told, which sequences of occurrences are permissible and logical. Schema information is stored in one's long-term memory and can be quickly recalled in the course of processing information". *Shorter Oxford English Dictionary* (P. 2692) defines schema as "An (unconscious) organized mental model of something in terms of which new information can be interpreted or an appropriate response made".

Different as the definitions are, schema, on the whole, is the pre-existed knowledge stored in one's mind by which the new information can be quickly processed and consequently the relevant response will be made. This is the function of cognitive schema. Such being the case, we may come across three cases in translation of culture-loaded words.

3.9.2.2 Three Cases
Case A

1. In this case the new information overlaps the established schema, and then the schemata are further strengthened, which occurs in translation of the first kind of culture-loaded words—the words of the same conceptual meanings with the same or similar cultural connotations, such as fox, wolf, lamb, dove, ass, flower, rose, straw and their Chinese equivalents 狐狸、狼、羔羊、鸽子、驴子、花、玫瑰和稻草, to name but a few. Some examples：

(1) Every life has its roses and thorns.

人生之旅,有鲜花,亦有荆棘。

(2) 子系中山狼,得志便猖狂。

① Paired with a brute like the wolf in the old fable,

Who on his saviour turned when he was able.

② For husband she will have a mountain wolf,

His object gained he ruthlessly berates her.

Since "rose" and "wolf" in the SLT, and "玫瑰" and "狼" in the TLT share the same conceptual meanings, and what is more, they are loaded with similar connotations, thus the message capacity of "rose" and "wolf" in the SLT and that of "玫瑰" and "狼" in the TLT is approximately equal to each other. Therefore the cognitive schemata of the culture-loaded words in the SLT overlap those of the culture-loaded words in the TLT, so the new information can be easily and quickly processed by the established schema even by means of literal translation, and the same aesthetic effect can be reproduced in the translation, with the result that the cognitive schema is strengthened.

Case B

2. In this case the new information is different from the pre-existed schema in one way or another. Such being the case, the reader or the translator is supposed to modify the relevant pre-existed schema or add something new to the relevant schema so as to adapt it to the new information. This is the case in which the second kind of culture-loaded words—the words of the same conceptual meanings but with different cultural connotations are translated. West wind and "西风", for example, share the same conceptual meaning, but the cultural connotation of "west wind" is totally different from that of "西风". "龙" and "dragon" are of the same conceptual meaning, but their connotations are opposite to each other: for the Chinese people, "龙" is the largest divine creature in Chinese mythology as well as the major mascot, thus it is the symbol of Chinese emperors and there are so many words and idioms collocated with "龙" such as "龙颜", "龙袍", "龙床", "望子成龙", "龙腾虎跃", "龙飞凤舞", to name but a few. But in English, dragon is typically fire-breathing and tends to symbolize chaos and evil, and it is the symbol of fierce person, especially a woman. For example, "The woman in charge of the accounts department is an absolute dragon!" (会计科那个女科长是个十足的母夜叉!) In translation of such kind of culture-specific words, literal translation plus notes or annotation turns out to be of some help, which can be seen as follows:

我失骄杨君失柳,

杨柳轻飏直上重霄九。

(1) I lost my proud Poplar and you your Willow,

Poplar and Willow soar to the Ninth Heaven.

(2) You lost your darling willow and I my Poplar proud.

Both Poplar and Willow soar gracefully far above the cloud.

(Translator's notes: Your darling Willow: Li Shuyi's husband, Liu Zhixun. In Chinese, willow is pronounced as [liu], the same as the pronunciation of the family name Liu. The subtlety here is that willow(Liu) can also suggest willow catkin just as Poplar(Yang) can suggest poplar flowers; and we know the word Poplar (Yang) indicates the family name of Mao's wife, Yang Kaihui. Poplar and Yang in Chinese are the same both in sound and meaning. Thus we feel no difficult to understand the second line "Both Poplar and Willow soar gracefully far above the cloud"; it suggests the souls of Yang Kaihui and Liu Zhixun fly above the cloud to the moon like wafting the Willow catkins and poplar flowers.)

"柳"and its English equivalent "willow" are of the same conceptual meaning, but their cultural connotations are different. Chinese character "柳" has as many as 47 connotations, some of them refer to beautiful scenery, some beautiful women, and still some brothels; since"柳"is read similarly to "留", it is also the symbol of "to urge sb to stay", especially in classical Chinese poetry. Willow in English, however, has only two connotations: one is the symbol of a failure in love, the other implies "to grieve for the loss of a loved one" when collocated with wear (wear the willow). Therefore their connotations are different and what is more, most of connotations of the Chinese character"柳"are absent from the cognitive schemata of the TLT readers. Thus literal translation plus note in Example 8 can help readers of TLT modify their pre-existed schemata or add new content to them. By doing so, the translation, on the one hand, can make the pre-existed schema adapted to the new information, on the other hand, the pre-existed schema will be thus extended.

Case C

3. In this case, there is simply no established schema in the mind of the TLT reader that is relevant to the new information, that is to say, the implied meaning of the culture-loaded word of the SLT is entirely new to and absent from the pre-existed knowledge of the TLT reader. The translator has to help the TLT reader establish the new schema relevant to the new information from the TLT. This is the case in which the third kind of culture-loaded words—the words with the same conceptual meanings, but their cultural connotations are absent from each other—are translated. There are many words in English whose cultural connotations are absent from their Chinese equivalents, such as lily, narcissus, cherry, potato, tomato, oak, olive, stork and ostrich, to name but a few (cf their Chinese equivalents:百合,水仙,樱桃,土豆,蕃茄,橡树,橄榄,鹳,鸵鸟), the same is true of some Chinese words, such as"松"、"竹"、"梅"、"杏"、"雁"、"鹤"、"龟"and so on. In translation of such kind of culture-loaded words, liberal translation or literal translation plus further explanation is of great help for TLT readers to establish the new cognitive schema to process the new information from the TLT. Examples are as follows:

(1) He's such an ostrich—he doesn't want to know about his wife's love affair.

他真是自己骗自己——对妻子有外遇不闻不问。

(2) The idea that such a luscious tomato might be mixed up in murder was terrible.

如此甜美的女人居然会参与谋杀,想想真是太可怕了。

(3) 可知我"井底之蛙",成日家只说现在的这几个人是有一无二的;谁知不必远寻,就是本地风光,一个赛似一个。

I've been like the frog living at the bottom of the well who thought the world was little round pool of water. Up to now I've always believed that the girls in this household were without equals anywhere; but now, even without my needing to go outside, here they come, each one more beautiful than the last!

(4) 兴儿随将柳湘莲的事说了一遍。凤姐道:"这个人还算造化高,省了当那出名儿的忘八!"

Joker told her the whole story of San-jie and Liu Xianglian. "He was a lucky man," said Xi-feng when he had finished telling it. "I've no doubt that if he'd married her she would have made him a most notorious cuckold."

In the above examples, some culture-loaded words are liberally translated, some are translated literally with further explanation, both approaches are beneficial for TLT readers to their establishment of the new cognitive schema relevant to the new information.

It can thus be seen that connotations of some SLT culture-loaded words overlap those of TLT culture-loaded words, some are different from each other, and still some are absent from each other. In view of the various cases different approaches are supposed to be taken respectively in order to have the cultural connotations of the SLT appropriately conveyed to the readers of the TLT.

Translation Exercises

Ⅰ. *Translate the following phrases into Chinese with enough attention to the cultural connotations of colour terms.*

1. red rag
2. make sb to see red
3. a red-carpet reception
4. mark one's name white again
5. the white slave trade
6. white elephant
7. white moments of life
8. black sheep
9. a black lie
10. greenhorn
11. a yellow dog
12. blue films
13. blue revolution
14. make a blue joke
15. be born in the purple

Ⅱ. *Translate the following poem into Chinese with enough attention to the connotation of underlined words*

The West Wind

—John Masefield

It's warm wind, <u>the west wind</u>, full of birds cries,

I never hear <u>the west wind</u> but tears are in my eyes,

For it comes from the west lands, the old brown hill,

And April's in the west wind, and daffodils.

II. *Translate the following poems into English with enough attention to cultural connotations of the underlined words.*

1. 相见时难别亦难。
   东风无力百花残。

2. 碧云天,黄叶地,
   西风紧,寒雁南飞,
   晓来谁染霜林醉,
   尽是离人泪。

Chapter Four

Translation of Sentences

4.1 Differences and Similarities between English and Chinese in Syntax

English is a phonographic language and Chinese, an ideographic language. Differences between the two are reflected in various aspects, such as pronunciation, grammar, word formation, sentence formation, syntax and so on. But in sentence order there are some similarities. Differences and similarities, especially the former, are the important factors that should be taken into consideration in translation.

4.1.1 Difference and Similarity in Sentence Order

In *Cambridge Encyclopedia of Language* (D. Crystal, 1994), seven sentence patterns are listed as follows.

1. S + V
2. S + V + O
3. S + V + C
4. S + V + A
5. S + V + O_1 + O_2
6. S + V + O + C
7. S + V + O + A

(S = Subject; V = Verb; C = Complement; O = Object; A = Adverbial)

Seven examples attached to the above patterns for illustration are as follows:

1. The dog + is running.
2. The man + saw + a cow.
3. The car + is + ready.
4. A picture + lay + on the ground.
5. I + gave + John + a book.
6. He + called + John + a fool.
7. Mary + saw + John + yesterday.

If we have the seven examples translated into Chinese we can find similarity between the SLT

(Examples 1,2,3,5,6) and the TLT in sentence order; two possibilities for Example 4 as it can be translated into "地上放着一张照片", or "一张照片放在地上", the first version is different from the original in sentence order, and the second one is similar to the original. Example 7 is typically different from its translation (玛丽昨天见到了约翰) as the original adverbial is changed from the end position to the middle position which is the basic sentence pattern(主语+状语+谓语+宾语)that is mainly determined by the thinking mode of Chinese people. Through analysis of the above examples differences and similarities between English and Chinese in sentence order can be clearly seen. However, the difference in attributes must be the focus of translation between English and Chinese.

Difference and similarity mentioned above are only the characteristics reflected in normal position, namely the usual order. But in reality, in order to arrive at a specific goal or for achieving a special pragmatic purpose, an unusual order is also possible (for example:古木鸣寒乌,空山啼夜猿). The shift from usual order to unusual order (from the unmarked to the marked) often means the change of information focus, which is of common occurrence both in English and in Chinese.

4.1.1.1 The Marked Predicate (主谓殊位)

The predicate preceded by the subject is the usual order both in English and in Chinese. But if the information focus changes, the unusual order occurs, and then there will be the marked predicate as follows.

1. In came a man of about forty.
2. Roar, the mountains, thunders all the ground.
3. 房子中间放着一张桌子,桌后立着一面浅蓝色的屏风。

Since Chinese predicate and subject can be arranged similarly, so the translation is usually done in the same way.

1. 走进来一位四十岁左右的男子。
2. 怒吼吧,群山;咆哮吧,大地。
3. In the middle of the room was a table, behind it stood a screen of a light blue colour.

The subjects and predicates of the above examples are organized similarly in the TLT as they are in the SLT. However, the marked predicate sometimes is used not for emphasis on action, but for a prominence to the state of the subject, or for balance of a sentence. Such being the case, the translation should be flexible, the position of the subject and predicate should be placed according to the concrete condition. Some examples:

1. So out of tune with the world of nation-states was China that it did not even possess a ministry of foreign affairs until as late as 1858.

当时的中国与其他国家隔膜甚深,竟迟至1858年才建立一个主管外交事务的机构。

2. It is a truth universally acknowledged that a single man in possession of a good fortune must be in want of a wife.

大凡富有的单身男士总想娶位太太,这是一条举世公认的真理。

The unusual order is shifted to usual order in the TLT of Example 1 for the sake of Chinese syntax on the one hand, and on the other, for the prominence to the information focus of the SLT. The sentence pattern of Example 2 is absent from the TLT. If it is translated into "有一条举世公认的真理,即凡富有的单身男士总想娶位太太", which is in conformity with the original syntax, the translation will be not in conformity with the usual order of the beginning of a novel, especially a Chinese novel.

4.1.1.2　The Marked Object（宾语殊位）

Generally speaking, the usual order of an English object is similar to that of a Chinese one which is placed after the predicate. Sometimes, out of rhetorical purpose, the information focus is on the object, which will result in the unusual order of an object which is of common occurrence both in English and in Chinese.

1. His learning I admire, but his character I despise.
2. All these complaints Molly had to listen to.
3. 顶风,我敢!
   踏沙,我敢!
4. "钱我不要",我说,"困难可以克服……"

The sentence order of TLT can be placed in the same way as follows:

1. 他的学识,我佩服;但他的人格,我鄙视。
2. 所有的牢骚怨言,莫莉都只能听着。
3. To brave the wind, I dare!
   To cross the desert, I dare!
4. "The money I don't need," I said, "and the difficulty I can overcome..."

Sometimes there is the case in which the marked object can be placed flexibly in the TLT.

5. 孟子曰:"鱼,我所欲也,熊掌亦我所欲也;二者不可得兼,舍鱼而取熊掌者也。生亦我所欲也,义亦我所欲也;二者不可得兼,舍生而取义者也。"

Mencius, "I like fish and I also like bear's paws. If I cannot have the two together, I will let the fish go, and take the bear's paws. So, I like life, and I also like righteousness. If I cannot keep the two together, I will let life go and choose righteousness."

4.1.1.3　The Marked Adverbial（状语殊位）

The adverbial in Chinese is usually placed between the subject and the predicate; the adverbial in English is usually at the end of a sentence, but in reality its position is very flexible, sometimes taking the front position, sometimes the middle position, and sometimes the end position.

1. Seated on a stone beside the stream, she wiped her perspiring face with the edge of her tunic.

   她坐在小溪边的石头上,撩起衣角,揩去脸上的汗水。

2. I want by understanding myself, to understand others, I want to be all that I am capable of becoming.

   我要通过了解自己去了解他人;我希望要成为什么人就能成为什么人。

3. He battled at full speed from the start.

比赛一开始,他便全速力争。

In contrast with Chinese, there are more pile-up adverbials in English. The front position, middle position and end position may meet in a set of pile-up adverbials. Such being the case, they must be well arranged.

4. In two visits to the United States, Jamaica's Prime Minister, in response to the world Bank's repeated urges, suggested the message to the US policy makers for the good of both countries, particularly in the matter of bilateral monetary affair.

在世界银行的多次督促下,为牙买加和美国的共同利益,特别是双边金融事务方面的共同利益,牙买加总理在最近的两次访美中,向美国的决策者表示了上述意见。

Sometimes an adverbial is used as the modifier of a word, or a phrase, sometimes as the modifier of a whole sentence. Only by taking both cases into consideration can the translation arrive at the similar rhetorical effect.

5. Traditionally, Italian presidents have been seen and not heard.

译文①从传统来看,意大利的历届总统都是无实权的名义上的首领。

译文②意大利的总统都是无实权的名义上的首领,历来如此。

6. Not for a day has he neglected his duty.

7. 如果我能够,我要写下我的悔恨和悲哀,为子君,为自己。

I want, if I can, to describe my remorse and grief for Tzechun's sake as well as for my own.

8. 子曰:"甚矣吾衰也!久矣吾不复梦见周公!"

The Master said, "Extreme is my decay. For a long time, I have not dreamed, as I was wont to do, that I saw the duke of Zhou".

4.1.1.4 The Marked Attribute(定语殊位)

An attribute in Chinese is usually placed before the head word it modifies even if the pile-up attributes as in the example of "我国唐代开元年间宫廷内部的一场激烈的政治斗争". Sometimes, however, in order to emphasize the effect of attribute, or to have the sentence structure well balanced, or to give a prominence to the information focus of an attribute, the usual order of an attribute may be changed to unusual order, for example,"昏鸦数点傍林飞"(周敦颐:《题春晚》);"渔舟一叶江吞天"(苏轼:《书王定国所藏烟江叠嶂图》). Attributes in English are greatly different from those in Chinese. Prepositional phrases or infinitive phrases are always placed after the head words when they are used as attributes. A single word used as an attribute is usually placed before the head word. but exceptions are of common occurrence. Some examples:

1. the Attorney General　　（司法部长）
    ambassador extraordinary and plenipotentiary　　（特命全权大使）
    investment available　　（可用投资）
    time immemorial　　（远古）

    It can thus be seen that attributes in English can be more flexibly placed than those in Chinese, hence they can be flexibly translated.

2. O listen! For the vale profound

Is overflowing with the sound.

哦,听吧!这空谷幽幽,

久久回荡着她的歌喉。

3. They were staunch to the end against odds uncounted,
They fell with their faces to the foe.

他们坚持到底,抗拒了数不清的灾难。

他们是阵亡在敌人的面前。

4. 她一手提着竹篮,内中一个破碗,空的;一手挂着一支比她更长的竹竿,下端开了裂,她分明纯乎是一个乞丐了。

In one hand she carried a wicker basket, in which was a broken bowl, empty; in the other she had a bamboo pole longer than herself, split at the bottom: it was clear she had become a beggar.

"Profound" in Example 2 is placed after the head word "vale" for a prominence to the information focus on the one hand, and for rhyming with "sound" in the following line on the other hand. Having "profound" translated into "幽幽" and with its position intact, the translated text produces the similar aesthetic effect. In translation of Example 3 the unusual order of the attribute is changed to usual order for conformity with the syntax of Chinese attribute on the one hand, and for rhyme on the other hand. In translation of Example 4 the translator has the unusual order of the original attributes well preserved, and what is more, has another usual order "一支比她更长的" changed to unusual order. By doing so, the translation is faithful to the original not only in meaning, but also in style.

4.1.1.5 The Marked Clause(偏正殊位与主从殊位)

In Chinese, the main clause generally goes after the subordinate clause, which is the usual order of complex sentence. (e. g. 其身正,不令而行;其身不正,虽令不从。)(《论语·子路篇第十三》)The unusual order of a complex sentence will be arranged the other way round, for example,"总之,倘是咬人之狗,我觉得都在可打之列,无论它在岸上或在水中。"(鲁迅:《论"费厄泼赖"应该缓行》)Theoretically speaking, the usual order of an English complex sentence is just opposite to that of a Chinese complex sentence, yet in reality exceptions are of common occurrence. Hence the usual order of an English complex sentence is not remarkably different from the unusual order so far as its essential information is concerned. Comparatively speaking, the marked clause in Chinese is not so frequently used as it is in English, hence in translation from English into Chinese, both the marked and unmarked clauses are translated into unmarked clauses.

Examples are listed as follows:

1. Though they each, like Elizabeth, meant to dance half the evening with Mr. Wickham, he was by no means the only partner who could satisfy them.

虽然她们俩也跟伊丽莎白一样,想要和韦翰先生跳上个大半夜,可是跳舞会上能够使她们跳个痛快的决不止他一个人。

2. When tea was over, Mr. Hurst reminded his sister-in-law of the card-table.

喝过早茶以后,赫斯先生提醒他的小姨子把牌桌摆好。

There is no remarkable difference between the marked and unmarked clauses in English, hence the marked clause in Chinese is usually kept intact in English translation.

3. 今晚却很好,虽然月光也还是淡淡的。

But on this particular evening, it had a cheerful outlook, though the moon was pale.

4. 她久已不和人们交口,因为阿毛的故事是早被大家厌弃了的。

She had long since given up talking to people, because Ah Mao's story was received with such contempt.

Through the comparative study of difference and similarity between English and Chinese in sentence order we can see that the marked or unmarked elements reflect not only the syntactic form from the perspective of grammar, but also the writer's intention of utterance, the various thematic meanings and information focuses are thus emphasized. Since there are different aspects as well as similar ones between the SL and the TL, absolute formal correspondence can be hardly achieved in translation. When the contradiction between the SL and TL in sentence order can't be avoided, the focus of translation should be placed on the expression of writer's intention, manifestation of the thematic meaning and prominence to the information focus.

4.1.2　Difference and Similarity in Syntax

The fundamental difference between English and Chinese in syntax lies in that the former is mainly characterized by hypotaxis(形合), and the latter by parataxis(意合). Because of the difference between the two, English syntax is not so flexible and elastic as Chinese syntax is; and Chinese syntax is less compact, which is supposed to be the focus of trauslation between English and Chinese.

The difference between the two can be analysed from the three aspects as follows.

Syntagmas of words and phrases

In English, hypotaxis means "the dependent relation of a clause or construction on another"; parataxis refers to "the placing of related clauses, etc, in a series without the use of connecting words". It can be seen that generally the syntagma of an English sentence is dependent on connectives (connecting words), and the syntagma of a Chinese sentence is generally independent of connectives. As a matter of fact, even the formation of a phrase in English is dependent on connectives. The formation of a word is dependent on inflection which is absent from Chinese. Comparatively speaking, the syntagma of a Chinese word or phrase is free from the yoke of connectives. Consider the following examples:

花灯——festive lantern

花纹——decorative pattern

花鞋——embroidered shoes

花茶——scented tea

花甲——a cycle of sixty years

花魁——the queen of flowers

花心——two-timing(two-time)

花烛—candles with dragon and phoenix patterns used in the bridal chamber on the wedding night

Make a contrastive study of the Chinese phrases and their English versions, one can clearly see the difference between English and Chinese in syntagma of words or phrases and the difference will be more remarkable in syntagma of sentence.

Syntagmas of sentences

Consider the following examples, please.

1. 虚心使人进步,骄傲使人落后。
2. 子曰:"其身正,不令而行;其身不正,虽令不从。"
3. 晨起动征铎,
    客行悲故乡。
    鸡声茅店月,
    人迹板桥霜。

If we have the above examples compared with their English versions, the flexibility and elasticity of Chinese syntax will be remarkably visible.

4. Modesty helps one to go forward, <u>whereas</u> conceit makes one lag behind.

5. The Master said, "<u>When</u> a prince's personal conduct is correct, his government is effective without the issuing of orders. <u>If</u> his personal conduct is not correct, he may issue orders, <u>but</u> they will not be followed."

6. MORNING ON THE ROAD OF MT. SHANG
    　　　　　by Wen Ting yun
Journeying forth <u>with</u> tender thoughts of home,
<u>At</u> break of day the travellers, bell are heard.
<u>Behind</u> the thatched inn, crowing cock <u>and</u> setting moon;
<u>Upon</u> the planked bridge, footprints <u>in</u> the frost.

In contrast with the SLT, we can easily find that there are a lot of connectives used in the TLT, such as "whereas" in Example 4, "when" "if" and "but" in Example 5, "with", "at", "behind", "and", "upon" and "in" in Example 6, but no equivalents can be found corresponding to these connectives in the SLT with the exception for "but" (corresponding to "虽" in Example 5). So far as formal correspondence is concerned, this kind of translation is attributed to over-loaded translation(超额翻译), which is, however, in conformity with the overt syntagma and hypotaxis of English syntax, hence they are indispensable and therefore the translation is by no means over-loaded translation so far as its function is concerned. This is the distinction between overt syntagma and covert syntagma, the former characterizes English syntax, and the latter Chinese syntax, which results in simplification that is mainly used in translation from English into Chinese. Examples are as follows:

7. There is no month in the whole year, in which nature wears a more beautiful appearance than in the month of August!

四时之美,八月为最。

Each age has its pleasures and its pains, and the happiest person is the one who enjoys what each age gives him without wasting his time in useless regrets.

人生的不同时代有其不同的甘苦,最幸福之人当属尽享每个时代所赐而又终生无悔者。

All the connectives between clauses and words in the SLT are omitted in the TLT. In contrast with the SLT the covert syntagma of Chinese syntax is remarkably visible.

Syntagmas of discourse

Routledge Dictionary of Language and Linguistics defines "discourse" as "Generic term for various types of text", and "text" is defined as "Theoretical term of formally limited, mainly written expressions that include more than one sentence". It is obvious that discourse is composed of sentences and discourse is more complex than a single sentence semantically and syntactically. In an English discourse, the various relationships, such as causality, condition, logic, concession, presupposition and so on are mainly expressed by means of hypotaxis which is overt. The relationships in a Chinese discourse however, are mainly reflected by means of parataxis that is covert. The advantage of covert syntagma is pointed out by Liu Xie(刘勰) as "隐也者,文外之重旨也……夫隐之为体,义生文外,秘响旁通,伏采潜发,譬爻象之变互体,川渎之韫珠玉也。"(《文心雕龙》) which is clearly shown in the following examples.

1. 子曰:"由!诲女知之乎!知之为知之,不知为不知,是知也。"

2. 知彼知已,百战不殆;不知彼而知已,一胜一负;不知彼不知已,每战必殆。

3. 名不正,则言不顺;言不顺,则事不成;事不成,则礼乐不兴;礼乐不兴,则刑罚不中;刑罚不中,则民无所措手足,故君子名之必可言也,言之必可行也。

In the above examples, there are no connecting words used for the sake of various relationships which are yet well connected and integrated by means of covert syntagma. When translated into English, the covert relationship come to be overt.

4. The Master said, "You, shall I teach you what knowledge is? <u>When</u> you know a thing, to hold <u>that</u> you know it, <u>and when</u> you do not know a thing, to allow <u>that</u> you do not know it, —this is knowledge."

5. You can fight a hundred battles without defeat <u>if you</u> know the enemy <u>as well as</u> yourself. You will win one battle and lose one battle <u>if you</u> know yourself but leave yourself in the dark about the enemy. You will lose every battle <u>if you</u> leave both the enemy and yourself in the dark.②

6. <u>If</u> names be not correct, language is not in accordance with the truth of things. <u>If</u> language be not in accordance with the truth of things, affairs cannot be carried on to success. <u>When affairs</u> cannot be carried on to success, proprieties and music will not flourish. <u>When</u> proprieties and music do not flourish, punishments will not be properly awarded. <u>When</u> punishments are not properly awarded, the people do not know how to move hand or foot. <u>Therefore</u> a superior man considers it necessary that the names he uses may be spoken appropriately, and <u>also that what</u> he speaks may be carried out appropriately.

The same is true of the translation of contemporary Chinese even though its syntagma is not so concise as classic Chinese syntagma. The relationships involved in these words in the SLT have to be read between the lines, which is the difference between hypotaxis and parataxis, and actually the distinction between overt syntagma and covert syntagma. However the exception proves the rule, sometimes in translation from English into Chinese some connecting words are indispensable for a smooth TLT. Just consider the following example, please.

DUSK
by Saki

Norman Gortsby sat on a seat in the park. Hyde Park Corner, with its noise of traffic, lay immediately to the right. It was about thirty minutes past six on an early March evening, and dusk had fallen heavily over the scene, dusk with some faint moonlight and many street lamps. There was a wide emptiness over road and pavement, <u>and yet</u> there were many figures moving silently through the half-light, or sitting on seats and chairs.

The scene pleased Gortsby and suited his mood. Dusk, in his opinion, was the hour of the defeated. Men and women, <u>who</u> had fought the battle of life and lost, <u>who</u> hid their dead hopes from the eyes of the curious, came out in this hour, <u>when</u> their old clothes and bent shoulders and unhappy eyes might pass unnoticed.

On the seat by Gortsby's side sat a rather old gentleman with a look of <u>defiance that</u> was probably the last sign of self-respect in a man who had stopped defying successfully anybody or anything. As he rose to go Gortsby imagined him returning to a home <u>where</u> he was of no importance, or to some uncomfortable lodging <u>where</u> his ability to pay his weekly rent was the beginning and end of the interest which he caused.

黄 昏
（萨基）

诺曼·高茨彼坐在公园的一条凳子上，右边就是海德公园角，周围车水马龙、喧嚣嘈杂。时值早春三月的一个傍晚，六点半钟光景，暮色沉沉、月光朦胧，街灯初上。马路和人行道上一片空旷，瞑瞑暮色中但见许多身影在默默地徘徊，还有些人在椅凳上端坐。

此时此景正合高茨彼的心境，他感到惬意。黄昏，在他看来，是属于失意者的；那些在人生的激流中奋争而又败下阵来的男男女女，此时走出家门，他们将破灭的希望深藏心底，以逃避世人好奇的目光。也正是此时，他们那褴褛的衣衫、佝偻的身躯、忧郁的神情才不致引起路人的注目。

高茨彼旁边坐着一位神情孤傲的老者。那神色或许是一位强者难以再与世抗争时留下的最后一丝自尊。老人起身离去时，高茨彼心想，老头是要回家了吧，在家里恐怕也是个多余的人；或许是去一个简陋的寓所，在那里，除了房东向他催要房租外，没人会对他感兴趣。

Readers can easily find the underlined words in the SLT corresponding to those in the TLT, which are logically necessary and syntactically necessary as well.

Translation Exercises

Ⅰ. *Translate the following sentences into Chinese, having the multiple adverbials well arranged.*

1. I leave Beijing tonight, hearted with the agreement we have reached, cheered by the frankness and fullness of our discussions, grateful for the hospitality you have accorded our party.

2. Recently, Prime Minister Tanake of Japan paid a visit to China, and the two sides have reached an important agreement on the normalization of the relations between China and Japan, thus realizing the long standing aspirations of the two peoples and opening up a new chapter in the relations between the two countries.

3. For some, especially state universities, institutional autonomy and academic freedom should be strengthened by federal and state support in lieu of their domination, in order to ensure quality education.

4. In that same village and in one of these very houses (which, to tell the precise truth, was sadly time-worn and weather-beaten), there lived many years since, while the country was yet a province of Great Britain, a simple good-natured fellow, of the name of Rip Van Winkle.

Ⅱ. *Translate the following essay into Chinese with enough attention to difference between overt syntagma and covert syntagma.*

How Should One Read a Book?
Virginia Woolf

It is simple enough to say that since books have classes—fiction, biography, poetry—we should separate them and take from each what it is right that each should give us. Yet few people ask from books what books can give us. Most commonly we come to books with blurred and divided minds, asking of fiction that it shall be true, of poetry that it shall be false, of biography that it shall be flattering, of history that it shall enforce our own prejudices. If we could banish all such preconceptions when we read, that would be an admirable beginning. Do not dictate to your author: try to become him. Be his fellow-worker and accomplice. If you hang back, and reserve and criticise at first, you are preventing yourself from getting the fullest possible value from what you read. But if you open your mind as widely as possible, then signs and hints of almost imperceptible fineness, from the twist and turn of the first sentences, will bring you into the presence of a human being unlike any other. Steep yourself in this, acquaint yourself with this, and soon you will find that your author is giving you, or attempting to give you, something far more definite. The thirty-two chapters of a novel—if we consider how to read a novel first—are an attempt to make something as formed and controlled as a building, but words are more impalpable than bricks; reading is a longer and more complicated process than seeing. Perhaps the quickest way to understand the elements of what a novelist is doing is not to read, but to write; to make your own experiment with the dangers and difficulties of words. Recall, then, some event that has left a distinct impression on you—how at the corner of the street, perhaps, you passed two people talking. A tree shook; an electric light danced; the tone of the talk was comic, but also tragic; a whole vision, an entire conception, seemed contained in that moment.

But when you attempt to reconstruct it in words, you will find that it breaks into a thousand conflicting impressions. Some must be subdued; others emphasized; in the process you will lose, probably, all grasp upon the emotion itself. Then turn from your blurred and littered pages to the opening pages of some great novelist—Defoe, Jane Austen, Hardy. Now you will be better able to appreciate their mastery. It is not merely that we are in the presence of a different person—Defoe, Jane Austen, or Thomas Hardy—but that we are living in a different world. Here, in Robinson Crusoe, we are trudging a plain high road; one thing happens after another; the fact and the order of the fact is enough. But if the open air and adventure mean everything to Defoe they mean nothing to Jane Austen. Hers is the drawing-room, and people talking, and by the many mirrors of their talk revealing their characters. And if, when we have accustomed ourselves to the drawing-room and its reflections, we turn to Hardy, we are once more spun around. The moors are round us and the stars are above our heads. The other side of the mind is now exposed—the dark side that comes uppermost in solitude, not the light side that shows in company. Our relations are not towards people, but towards Nature and destiny. Yet different as these worlds are, each is consistent with itself. The maker of each is careful to observe the laws of his own perspective, and however great a strain they may put upon us they will never confuse us, as lesser writers so frequently do, by introducing two different kinds of reality into the same book. Thus to go from one great novelist to another—from Jane Austen to Hardy, from Peacock to Trollope, from Scott to Meredith—is to be wrenched and uprooted; to be thrown this way and then that. To read a novel is a difficult and complex art. You must be capable not only of great finesse of perception, but of great boldness of imagination if you are going to make use of all that the novelist—the great artist—gives you.

Ⅲ. *Translate the following prose into English with enough attention to the proper use of connectives in the process of the shift from parataxis to hypotaxis.*

泡菜坛子
李汉荣

母亲从乡下来,住了十天。临走时,她老人家想为我们添置一件东西,留个纪念。

母亲说:"你们什么都有,又好像什么都没有。电视机是你们的,里面走来走去都是些陌生的人,有时候,杀人犯、贼、贪官、小偷也在里面出出进进;收录机是你们的,可尽是人家在唱歌;书架的书是你们的,可那都是别人写的字;电冰箱是你们的,一年四季都装一箱不知从哪里落下的霜。方便是方便,可就是没有一样是你们自己的。"

走的那天,母亲起了个早,从街上抱回一个泡菜坛子。她说:"在坛子里腌一些菜吧,调调自家的口味。"

我们的家里,从此有了泡菜,有了自己的味道。朋友上门,我们时常以泡菜佐酒,微醺中,大家就会说:"乡下的味道,不错;不错,乡下的味道!"

于是我们大家都有了自己的味道。再看那泡菜坛子,静静地守在那里,在喧嚣的日子,在钢筋混凝土的单元里,守着一坛平静的心情,酝酿着古老而纯朴的乡下味道。

4.2　Translation of Attributive Clauses

　　To speak of translation of subordinate clauses, attributive clause turns out to be the knottiest one of all. In order to have it done skillfully, we have to have a marked classification of attribute and attributive clauses and their positions.

　　In the Chinese language, a single word, when used as an attribute, is generally placed before the Head Word (中心词 or antecedent) and so is an English attribute with the exception of a few cases, such as the examples mentioned in 4.1.1.4. A phrase when used as an attribute is generally placed after the head word with the exception of the following examples.

　　a well-to-do family

　　a happy-go-lucky life

　　a good-for-nothing professor

　　In nine cases out of ten, English phrases (instead of a single word) when used as attributes, are placed after the head words. But a Chinese head word is normally placed after its modifier, even it is modified by many modifiers (pile-up attributes). For example, 北京四中一位有30年教龄的优秀语文教师。

　　But every rule has its exceptions which can be found in the sentences as follows:

　　1. 行李略已齐集,木器不便搬运的,也小半卖去了。
　　2. 先找着了凤姐的通房大丫头,名唤平儿的。
　　3. 一个人走向铜像下边的台阶,高高的颧骨,犀牛嘴。
　　4. 再将我妹一人,乳名兼美,表字可卿者,许配于你。
　　5. 红火照着他的两只脚,一前一后地走。
　　6. 火生起来,炉子烧得通红,上头坐着一饭盒饭,盒盖上刻着禹龙大字样。
　　7. 海边的沙地都种着一望无际的碧绿的西瓜,其间有个十一二岁的少年。项戴银圈,手捏一柄叉向一匹猹尽力地刺去。

　　This kind of structure is called the unusual position of attribute which is placed after the head word (antecedent). This provides to some extent a pattern to follow in translating some attributive clauses, especially long ones.

　　Pile-up attributes can be classified as follows:

　　1. Restrictive premodifier　　　　　　(限定性前置定语)
　　2. Descriptive premodifier　　　　　　(描述性前置定语)
　　3. Classified premodifier　　　　　　　(分类性前置定语)

　　Restrictive premodifiers refer to articles, demonstrative pronouns, indefinite pronouns, the possessive case of a noun, and ordinal numbers when used as attributes; descriptive premodifiers refer to attributes used for judgement (e.g. good, bad, dull, interesting, wise, stupid, etc.) and that for description (e.g. shape, colour, smell, etc.) and classified premodifiers refer to nationality, material and function words when used as attributes. When a head word is modified by a lot of attributes of which the most essential one should be placed nearest to the head word.

For example:
1. the famous oval meeting office
   著名的椭圆形会议室
2. a splendid white marble arch
   一座雄伟壮观的白色大理石拱门
3. two skillful English-speaking diplomats
   两位讲英语的老练的外交官

By comparison between the above-mentioned examples and their Chinese versions, we can see that the word order of the Chinese versions is similar to that of the original but for the last one, and that the classified premodifiers of both English and Chinese are usually connected closely with head words. The arrangement of pile-up attributes of English is different from that of Chinese in that the latter is arranged from "the big to the small", from "the strong to the weak", from "the specific to the general": the former seems opposite to the latter. But this is not a rule unchangeable to follow in translation of attributes and attributive clauses. Polishing of sentence structure and whetting of diction lead to smoothness and a good readability comes from a careful reading in which the sense of language counts a great deal.

In English, attributive phrases and clauses are ususlly placed after the antecedent (We call this kind of modifier postmodifier)(后置修饰语). Relation between the head word and the postmodifier (attributive phrases or clauses) is of great importance to us in the comprehension of the original and the expression in Chinese. An attribute may modify a word, a phrase (sometimes more than one), even a whole sentence. Accurately ascertaining the antecedent is the key point which a translator must look into very cautiously. The original would be otherwise misunderstood and translation unfaithful.

Compare the following versions with their original and make sure whether there is something wrong in comprehension and expression.

1. Some of our most skilled people don't get the salaries of maids in U. S.
我们有些很有技术的人才在美国还比不上女佣人的工资高。

2. Needs Vary. We met women in their late thirties with grown children who want to return to school on a part-time basis.

有各种各样的要求,我们遇到过一些年近40岁的妇女,她们的孩子已经长大,而这些孩子则要求以半工半读的方式再度入学。

In translation from English into Chinese, the complex attributes or attributive clauses we may come across are as follows:
The head word is separated far away from the postmodifier (the remote headword) and there are two or even more words which may be taken as head words.

1. We must tear down the walls of isolation, confusion and confrontation which separate us from each other.

The key point here is to ascertain what the attributive clause modifies. If the head word is mistaken, the translation will be a misrepresentation of the original.

2. And everywhere you could see signs of vandalism and general neglect, litter and graffiti that disfigured many British urban estates.

Instead of modifying one element of a sentence, the attributive clause modifies the whole sentence. The word near the attributive clause might be mistaken for the head word.

3. Nevertheless the problem was solved successfully, which showed that the computations were accurate.

4. The war that ignited the whole area took two years to reach this wonderful land, which was beyond the reach of everybody's imagination.

Ambiguity of relation between attributive clause and its antecedent will cause misunderstanding which gives rise to mistranslation as follows:

- **Confuse the head word with others**

1. The thought is surely not enounced (express in a systematic way) in those lines of the famous poem, which both we and the critic would agree.

（1）这一思想毫无疑问地没有体现在这首名诗的这几行中,而这是一首名诗。这一点我们与批评家之间并无分歧。

（2）毫无疑问,这首名诗的这几行诗句没有体现诗人的这一思想。对此,我们与批评家之间不会有什么分歧。

Judge by yourself which of the two versions is correct.

2. What was it that nature would say? Was there no meaning in the live repose of the valley behind the mill, and which Homer or Shakespeare could not re-from for me in words?

（1）大自然有什么话要对我说呢? 磨坊后面的山谷,安闲中有无限生机。虽荷马或莎士比亚重生,也不能将它化为文字——这里面难道没有意义吗?

（2）……这一切,即便是荷马与莎翁再生,也只能望景生叹。

3. The succession of native plants in the pastures and roadsides, which makes the silent clock by which time tells the summer hours, will make even the divisions of the day sensible to a keen observer.

牧场下,官道旁,野草杂树,四季代谢,宛然替大自然摆下一架无言的大钟,假如观察的人目光锐利(敏锐),非但可以看见四时更替,而且还可以看出一天的朝夕变化,十二时辰的运行呢。

If one fails to make an overall analysis of the context (cannot see the wood for the trees) and confuses the prepositional phrases with head words he will surely misunderstand the original.

- **Miss some head words when there are two or even more ones**

1. This is the danger of large scale conflicts breaking out between peoples and cultures of widely different origin, which were formerly safely separated.

（1）这样,就存在着各国人民之间爆发大规模冲突的危险,以及在原先是互不相干而又相安无事的几种渊源很不相同的文化之间爆发大规模冲突的危险。

（2）这样,就存在着在起源极不相同而原先是相安无事,互不联系的各民族和各种文化之间爆发大规模冲突的危险。

2. He was said to suffer poor memory and self-admitted lack of good judgement, which in his

last years went only from bad to worse.

（1）据说他苦于健忘,到了晚年他那自己也供认不讳的昏庸,又发展得愈趋严重。

（2）据说他苦于记忆衰退,而且连他自己也承认拙于健全的判断,到了晚年,痼疾又复加剧。

（poor memory 应与 lack of good judgement 并列）

- **Some words that are not modified by attributive clauses (or attributive phrases) might be mistaken for head words**

3. He summarizes impending issues and possible choices which have already been filtered through his aids.

（1）他将阻碍事态进展的问题以及可能的办法加以汇总,这类问题和办法都已经过他的助手们过滤了。

（2）他将阻碍事态发展的问题以及可供选择的解决办法加以综述,而所谓解决办法则都是经过他手下的人筛选过的。

4. Their basic fear is of the slack up protectionism and above all, American capital outflows which to them mean job outflows.

（1）他们感到是恐慌的是不坚持保护主义,尤其是美国资本的外流。因为对他们说来,这样就意味着工作机会的外流。

（2）他们感到最恐慌的是放松了保护主义,尤其是美国资本的外流。因为资本外流等于工作机会的外流。

Attributive clauses are usually placed after the head words (antecedents). But the immediately preceding noun（紧靠定语从句的先行词）should not be mechanically taken as the head word. Sometimes there are phrases (prepositional phrases or other phrases) between the attributive clause and its antecedent (headword). The immediately preceding noun may be a part of the phrase between the attributive clause and its antecedent. This construction is called "The Split Structure" shown as follows:

(Antecedent)　　　　　　　(modifier)
The Head Word + (prep.) Phrase + Attributive Clause

Therefore, translators must be cautious enough of the surface structure as not to mistake the immediately preceding noun in the prepositional phrase for the head word.

Be careful of the grammatical relation of syntax, especially the coherence between subject and predicate and number which count a great deal in ascertaining the head word that is modified by attributive clause.

Besides, it's necessary to take the logic relation of the context into consideration. Make sure with which word the relation between the modifier (the attributive clause) and head word will be more reasonably formed. Be free from ambiguity in diction and phrase of your version and avoid contradiction in expression.

We have mentioned the variety, position of attribute and attributive clause, and the importance of relation between modifier and its antecedent in translation. Now let's take up the methods used in translating attributive clauses.

● **As a premodifier**（前置）

The attributive clause is translated into Chinese as a premodifier by placing it before the head word, which is in accordance with the normal order of Chinese syntax.

1. The General Assembly may call the attention of the Security Council to situations which are likely to endanger international peace and security.

大会对足以危及国际和平与安全之形势,需提请安理会注意。

2. In 1582, Richard Mulcaster, one of the earliest English grammarians who paid attention to this problem, wrote "the English tongue is of small reach, stretching no further than this island of ours (England), nay, not there over all."

最早注意到这一问题的英语语法学家之一理查德·迈尔卡斯特在1582年写道:"英语的流行范围很小,充其量只在英格兰,而且没有遍及全岛。"

3. This is no class war, but a war in which the whole British Empire and Commonwealth of Nations are engaged, without distinction of race, creed, or party.

这决不是一场阶级之间的战争,而是一场不分种族,不分信仰,不分党派,整个大英帝国及英联邦全体成员国无不参加的战争。

The attributive clause in this sentence is rather long, but it is still translated as a premodifier as it is closely connected with its antecedent. By doing so, the Chinese version is compact, well-knit and terse, with good coherence in thinking logic. But if the attributive clause is too long and loosely connected with the main clause in thinking logic coherence, the attributive clause as a premodifier would be too long, which would result in sluggishness, monotonousness and poor readability of the Chinese version. Such being the case, it can be translated (by cutting and splitting) as a postmodifier.

● **As a postmodifier**（后置）

The Chinese connectives between main clause and subordinate clause are often omitted as the main clause and subordinate one are connected by means of parataxis. The English connectives, however, can't be so frequently omitted as those of Chinese, as English main clause and subordinate one are connected by means of hypotaxis. Cutting and splitting used in translation mean taking a long sentence apart at the joint where the main clause and subordinate one are connected, then piece together the short sentences by means of parataxis. The original attributive clause is rearranged as a postmodifier or as the further explanation to the head word (antecedent).

1. The Security Council shall hold periodic meetings at which each of its members may, if it so desires, be represented by a member of the government or by some other specially designated representative.

安理会应举行定期会议,每一理事国认为合宜时,得派政府大员或其他特别指定之代表出席。

2. A small unit was set up in the association to prepare for an international conference on the problems already mentioned, which is to take place in Rome, in September 1981.

本协会曾成立了一个小组以便筹备一次国际会议,讨论上述各个问题,会议拟于1981年9月在罗马召开。

3. This land, which once barred the way of weary travellers, now has become a land for winter and summer vacations, a land of magic and wonder.

这个地方现在已经成了冬夏两季的休假胜地,风光景物,蔚为奇观;而从前精疲力竭的旅游者都只能到此止步。

4. The total expenditures of the U. S. government for the so-called Fiscal Year 1970, that is the period from July 1, 1969 to June 10, 1970, were about 195 billion dollars, of which about 80 billion was for national defence.

美国政府1970财政年度的总支出约为1950亿美元,其中800亿左右为国防开支,所谓1970年财政年度系指1969年7月1日至1970年6月10日这段时间。

5. The very important oil industry, which has done much to rejuvenate the economy of the South since the end of World War II, made considerable headway especially in the five states of Arkansas, Louisiana, Mississippi, Oklahoma and Texas.

第二次世界大战以后,石油工业对振兴南部经济起了很大的作用。这一重要的工业(部门)已取得了重大进展,尤其是在阿肯色、路易斯安娜、密西西比、俄克拉荷马和得克萨斯五个州。

cf.(战后,石油工业作为一门重要的工业对振兴南部经济起了重要作用,取得了长足的进展,尤其是在阿肯色、路易斯安娜、密西西比、俄克拉荷马和得克萨斯五个州。)

6. They (men) vanish from a world where they were of no consequence; where they achieved nothing where they were a mistake and a failure and foolishness; where they have left no sign that they had existed—a world which will lament them a day and forget them forever.

(1)他们从世间消失了,在那个世界里,他们无足轻重,一事无成;在那个世界里,他们存在的本身就是一个错误,就是一大错误,就是一件愚蠢的事;在那个世界里,他们没有留下任何表明他们曾经存在过的踪迹,那个世界将为他们哀悼一时,然后永远将他们忘却。

(基本保留原文的句法结构)

(2)他们无足轻重,一无所成,对他们来说,人世的周遭原本就是一桩谬误的蠢行;世间不会留下他们的踪迹:他们将从这个世界上消逝,得到的只是世人旦夕的哀思,但却是永恒的忘却。

Translating attributive clauses into Chinese premodifiers or postmodifiers by means of cutting or splitting is actually an essential technique used in translation of long sentences. The question whether we ought to translate an attributive clause by cutting or by splitting, whether it should be a premodifier or postmodifier all depends on whether or not our version can convey the original meaning faithfully and smoothly. Practical translation calls for flexibility.

Translation Exercises

I. *Translate the following passage into Chinese, with enough attention to the translation of attributive clauses.*

On Beauty

A young man sees a sunset and, unable to understand or to express the emotion that it rouses in him, concludes that it must be the gateway to a world that lies beyond. It is difficult for any of us in moments of intense aesthetic experience to resist the suggestion that we are catching a glimpse of a light that shines down to us from a different realm of existence different and, because the experience is intensely moving, in some way higher. And, though the gleams blind and dazzle, yet do they convey a hint of beauty and serenity greater than we have known or imagined. Greater too than we can describe; for language, which was invented to convey the meanings of this world, cannot readily be fitted to the uses of another.

That all great art has this power of suggesting a world beyond is undeniable. In some moods Nature shares it. There is no sky in June so blue that it does not point forward to a bluer, no sunset so beautiful that it does not waken the vision of a greater beauty, a vision which passes before it is fully glimpsed, and in passing leaves an indefinable longing and regret. But, if this world is not merely a bad joke, life a vulgar flare amid the cool radiance of the stars, and existence an empty laugh braying across the mysteries: if these intimations of something behind and beyond are not evil humour born of indigestion, or whimsies sent by the devil to mock and madden us; if, in a word, beauty means something, yet we must not seek to interpret the meaning. If we glimpse the unutterable, it is unwise to try to utter it, nor should we seek to invest with significance that which we cannot grasp. Beauty in terms of our human meanings is meaningless.

Ⅱ. *Polish the following translation of Chinese.*

Without doubt, Stowe aimed "Uncle Tom's Cabin" at the women on both sides of the Mason Dixon line, and particularly the mothers. Her strategy, startling at the time, was simply to portray black people with the same needs, feelings, and religious convictions as white people. In this regard, it is no coincidence that the novel's two most lingeringly memorable scenes form a parallel structure. One portrays the tragic death of a white child—little Eva St. Claire—and the other portrays a mother's heroic flight over the ice, in order to save her infant from the living death of slavery. Stowe knew that women would identify with and weep over the forced separation of families, the death of loved ones, a mother's driven instinct to protect her child, the sale of pure young girls, the sexual violation of families and the use of women as "breeders," whether the victims of these travesties of the family were white or black. Even the novel's detractors (and there were many; fourteen proslavery novels almost immediately challenged Uncle Tom's Cabin) admitted that "a nation's sympathy has been awakened."

Just as Uncle Tom's Cabin brought visibility and sympathy to the victims of slavery, the nineteenth-century domestic novels, taken as a whole, gave middle-class housewives a sense of shared destiny and common, if difficult, alternatives to that destiny. For one thing, these novels argued that life was more interesting than it might seem. The carefully detailed and often sensual descriptions of such tasks as cooking and gardening argued inherently for the pleasure involved in these domestic chores. Furthermore, the novels suggested that self-improvement or ministering to the needs of others were always options for the woman whose present life bored her. For the desperate or very courageous, there was even paid employment.

Still, the dominant metaphors in the novels suggested powerlessness and isolation. Although kinship tie abound—sometimes discovered only at the novel's end—they are often abstract relationships of blood only, since feelings of love and loyalty must often be won. Husbands and guardians are the arbiters of authority, but they rarely exercise their power lovingly and most often they outright abuse it.

You are supposed to polish the following Version.

无疑,斯托将《汤姆叔叔的小屋》瞄准了梅森—狄克逊线的父母亲双方,特别是母亲这一方。开始时,她的战术中是描述与白人具有同样的需要、情感和宗教信仰的黑人。因此,小说的两个最长的令人难忘的场景构成了平行的结构并非巧合。一个是叙述了一个白人孩子小伊娃·金·克莱尔的悲惨死亡;另一是母亲勇敢地飞跑过冰河,为的是从活死人的奴隶制里救出她的婴儿。斯托知道女人会认同,活活拆散了一家骨肉,爱人的早亡,母亲本能地保护自己的孩子,拍卖纯洁的少女,女人的性的狂暴,女人用作"哺育者",不管这些模仿的家庭的牺牲者是白人还是黑人,即使这本小说的反对者(有很多,十四本崇尚奴隶制的小说几乎立即对《汤姆叔叔的小屋》群起而攻之)也承认"一个民族的同情心被唤醒了"。

正如《汤姆叔叔的小屋》对奴隶制的牺牲者带来了能见与同情,十九世纪的家庭小说总的来说,给中产阶级的家庭主妇一种共同的命运与通向这种命运的共同的,如果困难的话,选择的感觉。有一点,这些小说争论该生活比它显示的更有趣得多,对于诸如烹调、园艺这类的活的精细通常是感官的描写,遗传性地争辩说为了包含在这些家务琐事中的愉悦。此外,这些小说建议自我完善或者照顾别人的需要永远是当前生活使她厌倦的女人的选择。对于那些勇气十足的人,其中有着偿报的职业。

仍然,小说中占主导地位的隐喻暗示无权力和孤独,虽然亲属的纽带紧系着——有时只在故事的结尾才发现——它们常常只是抽象的血缘关系。因为必须赢得爱和忠诚的感觉,丈夫和监护人是权威和仲裁者,但是他们很少可爱地行使他们的权力,他们经常错误地滥用它。

Ⅲ. *Appreciation and analysis.*

Beauty

There is still another aspect under which the beauty of the world may be viewed, namely, as it becomes an object of the intellect. Beside the relation of things to virtue, they have a relation to thought. The intellect searches out the absolute order of things as they stand in the mind of God, and without the colors of affection. The intellectual and the active powers seem to succeed each other, and the exclusive activity of the one generates the exclusive activity of the other. There is something unfriendly in each to the other, but they are like the alternate periods of feeding and working in animals; each prepares and will be followed by the other. Therefore does beauty, which, in relation to actions, as we have seen, comes unsought, and comes because it is unsought, remain for the apprehension and pursuit of the intellect; and then again, in its turn, of the active power. Nothing divine dies. All good is eternally reproductive. The beauty of nature reforms itself in the mind, and not for barren contemplation, but for new creation.

All men are in some degree impressed by the face of the world; some men even to delight.

This love of beauty is Taste. Others have the same love in such excess, that, not content with admiring, they seek to embody it in new forms. The creation of beauty is Art.

The production of a work of art throws a light upon the mystery of humanity. A work of art is an abstract or epitome of the world. It is the result or expression of nature, in miniature. For although the works of nature are innumerable and all different, the result or the expression of them all is similar and single. Nature is a sea of forms radically alike and even unique. A leaf, a sunbeam, a landscape, the ocean, make an analogous impression on the mind. What is common to them all—that perfectness and harmony, is beauty. The standard of beauty is the entire circuit of natural forms—the totality of nature; which the Italians expressed by defining beauty "il piu nell'... uno." Nothing is quite beautiful alone; nothing but is beautiful in the whole. A single object is only so far beautiful as it suggests this universal grace. The poet, the painter, the sculptor, the musician, the architect, seek each to concentrate this radiance of the world on one point, and each in his several work to satisfy the love of beauty which stimulates him to produce. Thus is Art a nature passed through the alembic of man. Thus in art does Nature work through the will of a man filled with the beauty of her first works.

The world thus exists to the soul to satisfy the desire of beauty. This element I call an ultimate end. No reason can be asked or given why the soul seeks beauty. Beauty, in its largest and profoundest sense, is one expression for the universe. God is the all-fair. Truth, and goodness, and beauty, are but different faces of the same All. But beauty in nature is not ultimate. It is the herald of inward and eternal beauty, and is not alone a solid and satisfactory good. It must stand as a part, and not as yet the last or highest expression of the final cause of Nature.

自然界之美还可以从另外一个角度来看,那就是它可以用理智来研究自然界万物同道德固然有关系,但是同思想也是结了不解之缘的。万物在上帝的心灵中自有其固定的秩序。人可以抛弃了情感上的好恶,直接用理智来探讨。人的思考能力和活动能力似乎是互相交替的,纯然的思考产生纯然的活动,纯然的活动也产生纯然的思考,两者微有抵触之处,但是它们同动物的进食和工作两段时间互相交替一样,后者接续前者,但是前者也为后者做准备。我们前面已经讨论过,美同行动的关系是不求而自生,惟其因为不求而自生,行动过后,美仍保留,作为理智方面思考和研究的对象,思考和研究过后,美仍旧可以激发行动。凡是神圣的东西决不死亡。善一定是生生不息的,自然界的美在人心中转化为思想,但是思想不是徒然的冥想,思想必有结果——思想是新创造的准备。

自然界的美,人类多少都是感受的,有些人不仅感受而已,还可以大有喜悦之感。爱美之情,是谓"趣味"。还有些人受之不已,觉得单是欣慕,犹有不足。进而创造新的形式,把美纳入其中。美之创造,是谓"艺术"。

美术品的创造,实可解释人生之一谜。美术品是宇宙的精华,也是世界的缩影,它是自然界所产,也是自然界具体而细微的表现。自然万物,虽然品类众多,参差不一,但是根据它们而产生艺术,或者它们在艺术上面的表现,却是单纯齐一。自然界形形式式,根本上别无二致,实际上可以说只是一种形式。一片树叶,一道阳光,山水海洋,虽景物不同,然而它们在我们心灵上并没有造成不同的印象。它们的共同之处,是完整,是和谐,也就是美。美的标准是自然的全体,也是自然界各种形式的总汇。意大利人替"美"所下的一个定义,最富哲理,他们说"美"就是"一中见多"。单独而论,没有一样东西可算是美,就全体观之,没有一样东西是不美的。一件物体如能称得上美,一定是小中见大:它可以反映宇宙全体的美。诗人、画家、雕刻家、音乐家、建筑师其道各有不同,但是他们只是用不同的方式,将宇宙的光采集中于一点,他们的创造,是受爱美之情的激发,他们的作品,就是要满足心灵上的爱好,所以艺术者,是自然之美经过人心提炼后的产物。人心有感于万物之美,自然界仍藉艺术家的灵魂,作第二步的创造,是为艺术。

所以宇宙的存在,是要满足灵魂上爱美的欲望。这是宇宙终极的目的。因为无人能问也无人能解释:灵魂为什么要追求美。从最广和最深的意义上说来,美是宇宙的一种表现。上帝是至美,真善美三者,只是一个本体的三个方面的表现而已。可是自然界的美并非无上法门,它本身并不是充实圆满的"善",它只是为内在的永恒"美"作先导而已。我们可以把它看作是全体中的一个部分,宇宙另有其根本原因,其表现的方式众多,自然界的美也不是它终极的或是最高的表现。

4.3 Comparison and Contrast

When one thing is compared or contrasted with another in respect of a certain attribute, we use an inflection called comparison. Comparison can express quality, superiority; that is to say, it can state whether two people or things possess some quality in the same degree (equality) or in different degrees (superiority or inferiority). It can also express supremacy of one person or thing in respect of an attribute.

There are three degrees of comparison as follows:

1. the Positive Degree
2. the Comparative Degree
3. the Superlative Degree

Equality is expressed by the Positive Degree, e. g. Mary is as careful as Margaret.

It is just as hot today as it was yesterday.

Superiority is expressed by the Comparative Degree, e. g. Tom is more careful than John.

It is hotter today than it was yesterday.

Inferiority is expressed by using "less than".

John is less careful than Tom.

It is less hot today than it was yesterday. But this construction is rarely used; the following construction is more frequently used today.

John is not so (as) careful as Tom.

It is not so (as) hot today as it was yesterday. However there is no remarkable difference between the two constructions in translation.

Supremacy is expressed by the Superlative Degree, e. g. That was the happiest day of his life.

I think "Hamlet" is the most sublime of Shakespeare's plays.

The superlative degree often expresses the same thing as the comparative but from a different point of view. e. g.

"Richard is the tallest of the three brothers and is the oldest boy in the school" is actually the same as "Richard is taller than his two brothers and is older than any other boys in the school", which is worth our attention in translation. We can translate it into "理查在兄弟三人中身材最高,在学校也是年龄最大的男学生。"or"理查比其他兄弟二人身材都高,在学校他比任何男同学年龄都大"。

Comparison if in detail, can be classified as follows:

1. the Equal Comparison   同等比较
2. the Differential Comparison   差等比较
3. the Ultimate Comparison   终极比较
4. the Alternative Comparison   选择比较
5. the Progressive Comparison   累进比较
6. the Antithetic Comparison   对立比较
7. the Interrelated Comparison   关联比较
8. other kinds of comparison   其他比较

Equal comparison is used when equality is expressed but sometimes we may come across sentences with equal comparison that requires attention in translation, e. g.

1. As I would not be a slave, so I would not be a master.
2. He hurried away without so much as leaving an address.
3. I have not so much as heard of him much less know him.
4. Thousands of enemy soldiers were killed and quite as many captured.
5. If they can finish it in three hours, we should have no difficulty in accomplishing it in as few.

When two people or things possess quality in different degrees (superiority or inferiority), differential comparison is used; more often than not differential comparison can be used instead of ultimate comparison in expressing supremacy.

Differential comparison is the most common of English comparisons, it is also easy to master its use. But comparative degree is sometimes ambiguous in meaning, e. g.

汤姆比约翰高明。

There are probably three possibilities involved in this simple sentence:

(1) Both Tom and John are wise.
(2) Neither of them is wise.
(3) Tom is wise and John is foolish.

If we say "汤姆比约翰更高明":

There is no alternative meaning but for "Both Tom and John are wise", but the former is much cleverer than the latter. However, in English, "more" shares the meaning of "较"and that of"更"as well in Chinese. Thus when translated into Chinese, the Chinese version of "more" is worth our special attention instead of a simple expression as"比较……好(坏,差……),比……更好(坏,差……)"。

1. What the Chinese people are altogether unprepared for, however, is the death of Mao without the comforting presence of Chou En-lai as chief mourner. If Mao has been China's spiritual guide these many years, Chou has been its security blanket.

然而,中国人民心理上最没有准备的是周先毛而逝,因为如果在毛逝世后有周做主祭人可以起安抚人心的作用。假如说毛多年来是中国的精神引路人,那么周恩来则是中国的安全保障。

2. Douglas-Home: Mr. Khrushchev said that the Russian brand of communism puts education and goulash first. That is good; goulash-communism is better than war-communism, and I am glad to have this confirmation of our view that fat and comfortable communists are better than lean and hungry.

道格拉斯—霍姆:"赫鲁晓夫先生说过,俄国牌的共产主义是把教育和土豆烧牛肉放在第一位的。这很好,土豆烧牛肉的共产主义比军事共产主义好,而且我高兴的是,这证明了我们的观点:肥胖和享福的共产党人要比瘦弱和饥饿的共产党人好些。"

Here we put comparative degree in Sentence (1) into "更"不可缺少的人物 instead of "较为"不可缺少的人物, and that in Sentence (2) into "比……好" instead of "比……好些", which is based on the concrete contexts of the sentences mentioned above.

The ultimate comparison is usually expressed by means of the superlative degree of an adjective or adverb. Sometimes, however, we can come across some exceptions, e. g.

3. I couldn't agree with you more.

我和你的意见完全一致。

4. I've never had a better or a more comfortable dinner.

我还没有出席过比这更丰盛更令人惬意的宴会。

5. There could have been no better man in charge of the evacuation from Dunkirk than 57-year-old Vice-Admiral Romsay.

五十七岁的海军中将拉姆齐是负责敦刻尔克撤退的最理想人选。

6. I could not care less about money.

7. More than anything else I ever wanted, I want to marry Hannah Ward.

我最大的心愿是和罕娜·华德结婚。

The above-mentioned five sentences all express the ultimate comparison, but in a round about way instead of a direct superlative degree of adjectives or adverbs. Translation of this kind of ultimate comparison should be whetted carefully according to the manner of speaking.

By alternative comparison we mean that alternative is involved in the form of comparison with comparison as its prerequisite.

8. She was more a protegee than a friend.

与其说她是朋友,不如说是门徒。

9. It is more a poem than a picture.

10. Better to light one candle than to curse the darkness.

与其诅咒黑暗,毋如燃起蜡烛。

11. "I'd rather get the chair than spend another 15 years in jail!"

This kind of comparison is usually present at the construction of differential comparison in which the meaning of negation is obvious. In translation, we must be sure that which of the two is negated and which is affirmed, it will be, otherwise, misunderstood.

There are two common forms of comparison used in English: "the more... the more"; "more and more". The former expresses "corresponding increase" (or parallel increase) and the latter "progressive increase". This kind of comparison is named "the Progressive Comparison" by some grammarians. The corresponding Chinese version is"愈……愈","越……越";越来越,愈来愈 e. g.

12. More haste, less speed.

欲速则不达。(愈急愈慢)

13. And my more-having would be as a sauce.

To make me hunger more...

我拥有的财富越多,

我的贪心就越不满足……

14. "There is corruption here," conceded a Venezuelan journalist last week. The closer to the government you are, the more chance you have of getting something.

一位委内瑞拉记者上星期承认:"这儿贪污舞弊成风,谁越接近政府,就越有捞一把的机会(就越有机会捞一把)。"

15. The more the Curies talked about this discovery, the more determined they become to find out the how and the why of these queer rays.

There is a paralleled construction in the English Language from appearance of which no comparative form is obvious, but from context you can find the two parts of the construction are closely connected by means of striking contrast. This is called the Antithetic Comparison with the characteristic of parallel use of a pair of antonyms or antonymous phrases which are forcefully expressive, e. g.

16. Man proposes, God disposes.

谋事在人,成事在天。

17. Not that I loved Casear less, but that I loved Rome more.

不是我不爱凯撒,而是我更爱罗马。

This construction, which is called antithesis, can also be found in Chinese, e. g.

野火烧不尽,春风吹又生。

朱门酒肉臭,路有冻死骨。

先天下之忧而忧,后天下之乐而乐。

横眉冷对千夫指,俯首甘为孺子牛。

This kind of antithesis is called "opposite antithesis" (or "理殊趣合的对偶"by Liu Xie) which means the two parts are opposite in appearance but supplement each other in essence. (反对) Unlike opposite antithesis, the parallel parts of analogous antithesis "(正对) express the similar idea by means of different examples."(Liu Xie called it"事异义同"的对偶).

e. g.

青楼含日光,绿池起风色。

春蚕到死丝方尽,蜡炬成灰泪始干。

四海翻腾云水怒,五洲震荡风雷激。

English and Chinese antithetic comparisons are similar to each other both in construction and form. So it is not difficult in translating this kind of comparison from English into Chinese, e. g.

18. As the touchstone tries gold, so gold tries man.

试金石可以试金,金子则可以试人。

19. And so, my fellow Americans, ask not what your country can do for you; ask what you can do for your country.

因此,我的美国同胞们,你们不要问你们的国家能够为你们做什么,而要问你们能为自己的国家做些什么。

20. If there is an irresistible force, there can be no immovable object. If there is an immovable object, there can be no irresistible force.

如果有不可抵制的力量,就不可能有搬不动的东西。如果有搬不动的东西,就不可能有不可抵制的力量。

21. The strong economies have to be kept strong and vigorous at the same time as the weak economies are being strengthened. We can all swim well together, but we can also all sink together.

在贫弱的经济得到发展的同时,强大的经济也必须保持强大而有活力。我们可能一起顺利地破浪前进,我们也可能一起葬身水底。

The very beginning of the famous novel *A Tale of Two Cities* by Dickens has seven antitheses well used, which made a strong impression on readers.

22. It was the best of times, it was the worst of times, it was the age of wisdom, it was the age of foolishness, it was the epoch of belief, it was the epoch of incredulity, it was the season of Light, it was the season of Darkness, it was the spring of hope, it was the winter of despair, we had everything before us, we had nothing before us, we were all going direct to Heaven, we were all going direct the other way.

这是最美好的时期,又是最恶劣的时期;这是智慧的年代,又是愚蠢的年代;这是有信仰的时代,又是令人怀疑的时代;这是光明的季节,又是黑暗的季节;这是富有希望的春天,又是充满绝望的寒冬;我们拥有一切,而又一无所有;人们笔直地走向天堂,也会笔直地走向地狱。

In English there is a kind of comparison with only the comparative form of adjectives or adverbs but without the corresponding part that can be compared with in appearance. With careful analysis, however, you can imagine the corresponding words or phrases that can be compared with. In fact, the corresponding part for comparison is involved in the omitted part. This comparison is called the Interrelated Comparison. The words and phrases correlated with comparison should be retained and carefully weighed in translation from English into Chinese, e. g.

23. They are fighting for a better life.

他们正在为改善生活而斗争。

24. They strive for lower birth rate.

他们力争降低出生率。

25. Their increasing strength made them less dependent on the United States.

随着力量的不断增长,他们对美国的依赖减少了。

26. Soon the sky began to grow lighter and the shadows in the city less dark.

不久,天空渐渐发白,城里的阴暗之处也渐渐明亮起来。

Sometimes we may come across some other comparisons, e. g.

What you have said is most interesting.

你所说的真是太有意思啦。

Here "most" + an adjective may express the presence of a quality in a very high degree, but without thought of a direct comparison. Some more examples:

She is a most beautiful girl.

He showed the greatest (the utmost) patience.

And still some idiomatic constructions, e. g.

If he will help us, so much the better.

If he doesn't work, so much the worse for him.

I like him none the worse for being outspoken.

他说话虽然不客气,但我依然喜欢他。

If the worst comes to the worst we can always walk home.

This kind of idiomatic constructions composed of the comparative or the superlative should be translated according to the fixed meanings given by dictionaries, or on the basis of the contextual clues involved.

Translation Exercises

Ⅰ. *Translate the following sentences into Chinese with enough attention to the expression of comparison.*

1. The moon shone bright and silver, insects hummed, and the fireflies were numerous dots of glittering light in the shrubbery. However, I was absolutely not in the mood to appreciate this masterpiece of nature. My heart, which seemed to be pulled downward by a piece of hanging lead, sinking lower and lower...

2. Japan is already on the verge of becoming the world's second greatest industrial power and China has nine times the population of Japan, and an incomparably greater wealth of natural resources.

Ⅱ. *Translate the following passage into Chinese with proper approaches to translation of comparison.*

The United States no longer regarded itself as the policeman of the world; those long, frustrating war in Indochina had altered America's image of itself, but, even more important, the lopsided strategic advantage that America had once enjoyed was lost. The Soviet Union and China were now more hostile to each other than to the United States, what was once thought by many analysts to be pure gospel—monolithic unity among the communist countries, with Moscow calling the signals—had proved to be a misreading of history. What is more, the conflict between Moscow and Beijing, coupled with their domestic problems, had prodded Russia into softening its policy of blunt confrontation with the West, and China into re-examining its policy of lofty isolation. Europe and Japan had more than regained their economic vitality; they were now capable of playing a greater role in international affairs. Some Arab leaders were beginning to recognize that war with Israel was not the only policy option open to them. The new countries had emerged from their first outbursts of nationalism and now seemed eager for more profitable dealings with the rest of the world. There were tensions, but not all were threatening. The world seemed to be rumbling its way toward new relationships.

4.4 Translation of Long Sentences

English sentences, generally speaking, are longer than Chinese sentences. Just take the following sentences for instance:

1. 世有伯乐,然后有千里马。千里马常有,而伯乐不常有。
2. 山不在高,有仙则名,水不在深,有龙则灵。
3. "I wish either my father or my mother, or indeed both of them, as they were in duty both equally bound to it, had minded what they were about when they begot me; had they dully considered how much depended upon what they were then doing—that not only the production of a rational being was concerned in it, but that possibly the happy formation had temperature of his body, perhaps his genius and the very cast of his mind—and, for aught they knew to the contrary, ever the fortune of his whole house might take their turn from the humours and dispositions which were then uppermost—had they dully weighed and considered all this, and proceeded accordingly, I am verily persuaded I should have made a quite different figure in the world, from that in which the reader is likely to see me".

The first Chinese sentence, which deals with two things, is made up of only 21 characters, and the second one only composed of 16 characters, also mentions two things. The English sentence, however, is made up of 145 words, which is 7 times as along as the first Chinese sentence and 9 times the length of the second one. To have a correct understanding of this English sentence is by no means easy, let alone translate it into good Chinese. That's the difference between the two languages in length. The factors that result in a long English sentence are:(1) multiple modifiers,(2) parallel elements,(3) complicated syntax. The key point that marks the difference between English and Chinese is syntax. Hypotaxis characterizes the English syntax which is described by some grammarians as "a big tree with a mass of branches and foliage", as a long sentence is usually composed of many clauses and modifiers just like a big tree with many branches and a mass of foliage. The Chinese syntax, stressed on parataxis, is described by some people as "waves surging forward at the vast sea". To make a distinction between two languages is of great help to us in translating a long sentence from English into Chinese. The whole process of translation can be divided into two steps: Comprehension and expression which go through the complete process of thinking in translation and they can be illustrated as follows:

Comprehension
1. Find out the trunk through condensing the whole sentence, be sure of SV/SVO/SVIO-DO
2. Be sure of the main and subordinate clauses, modifiers and the elements they modify.
3. Sort out the arrangement of ideas, judging the train of logic thinking.

Expression
4. Discriminate meanings of words, be sure of the fixed meaning of every word.
5. Marshal the arrangement in conformity with Chinese syntax.
6. Polish words and phrases, having every word carefully weighed in consideration of the style of the original.

This six-step-method can be used in translating any complicated sentences from English into Chinese. The time allotment to each of the six steps depends on concrete circumstances. An intelligent translator never gives equal amount of time to various steps.

Different sentences can be translated into Chinese by means of the following techniques.

Now let's try the six-step method in translation of the following sentence.

I am quite convinced that a new situation would arise if the United States, which has manifested its wish for pacification, as reaffirmed most recently by Ambassador Goldbury, were to stop the bombing of North Vietnam, without conditions or limitations and while this session of the General Assembly is in progress.

Three steps in the process of comprehension come first. As there is no clear line between any two steps one can draw, the first step and the second one are usually carried out simultaneously. But the third step is worth great care on the basis of a good job of the fourth step which will contribute a great deal to discriminating meanings of words. On the basis of a clear idea of the original syntax, the fixed meaning of every word, you can start the process of expression: adjusting and reorganizing the original syntax according to Chinese syntax, during which you can decide which one of the six techniques (including three techniques mentioned in translation of attributive clause) can be used.

Now analyse the following version:

我深信新的局面就会出现,如果美国政府,它已经表明它希望讲和,正如戈德堡大使重申的那样,停止轰炸北越,无条件地无限制地于本届大会正在进行期间。

This kind of expression is the very beginning of expression which is entirely in agreement with the original syntax only. It may be necessary for a beginner who can not get such a long sentence translated at one go, but not necessary for an experienced translator who can have his version roughly organized in mind while analysing the original. What is needed is enough effort on three steps of expression. But a beginner has to have each step taken carefully. As the old saying goes: "Clumsy birds have to start flying early". The very beginning of expression to a beginner of translation is just like an early flying to a clumsy bird. And afterwards, he has to have the rough version reorganized in syntax and weighed in diction.

The following version is a little better in syntax but there is still much to be desired in syntax from a satisfactory version. Have it analysed and further polished, please.

我确信如果美国无条件、无限制地放弃炸北越,并且这届大会能取得进展,一个新的局势就会诞生。美国已正式宣布了和谈的想法,正如戈德堡大使再三断言的那样。

Now, let's take up translation of long sentences by means of "reversing", "inserting" and "recasting".

Reversing

Unlike inversion which means to have one or two of the sentence elements placed in inverted order, reversing, however, means to change or adjust the sentence structure thoroughly or partly in order to have translation arranged in harmony with the Chinese syntax. Let's take the following sentences for instance.

1. The original members of United Nations shall be the states which, having participated in the United Nations Conference on International Organization at San Francisco, or having previously signed the Declaration by United Nations of 1 January 1942, sign the present Charter and ratify it in accordance with Article 110.

凡曾经参加旧金山联合国国家组织会议或此前曾签字于1942年1月1日联合国宣言之国家,签署本宪章,并依本宪章第110条规定而予以批准者,均是联合国之创始会员国。

2. Then, most Americans had little interest in 1 500 000 square km. of icebergs and polar bears—beyond Canada's western borders, far from the settled areas of the United States.

对(阿拉斯加)这个毗连加拿大西部边境,远离美国已开发地区的150万平方公里满山是冰山和北极熊的地方,当时大多数美国人根本不感兴趣。

Try to translate this sentence by arranging the syntax in conformity with the original and compare the different versions with each other.

3. I felt a trifle shy at the thought of presenting myself to a total stranger with the announcement that I was going to sleep under his roof, eat his food and drink his whisky, till another boat came in to take me to the port for which I was bound.

我要去见一个素不相识的陌生人,向他宣布我得住在他家,吃他的,喝他的,一直等到下一班船到来把我带到我要去的港口为止,一想到这儿,我真有点不好意思了。

4. And he knew how ashamed he would have been if she had known his mother and the kind of place in which he was horn, and the kind of people among whom he was born.

他出生这一类人中间,出生在这种地方,他还有这样的母亲;这些要是让她知道的话,他会多么丢人。

5. There were no sounds but that of the booming wind upon the stretch of tawny herbage around them, the crackling wheels, the tread of men, and the foot steps of the two shaggy ponies which drew the van.

那时,只听见辚辚的车轮声,沙沙的脚步声,拉车的鬃毛蓬松的小马嘚嘚的蹄声,除此之外,再也听不到别的声音了。

Inserting

By inserting, we mean the use of dash, bracket and comma to insert the difficult part in translation. Correct use of dash, bracket or comma to insert the difficult part will keep the original style untouched and it is convenient to do so, in the meanwhile, it can avoid careless omission.

Give enough attention to the following points in the use of dash, bracket and comma for inserting.

(1) What's inserted shouldn't be too long, otherwise the elements of the trunk of the sentence will be isolated too far away from each other, and the sentence structure will be too loose. If the inserted part is too long, it should be translated by means of splitting.

(2) Note the position of the inserted part which is usually placed between the subject and predicate; or between predicate and object.

(3) Do not use inserting unless absolutely necessary, e. g.

1. The snow falls on every wood and field, and no crevice is forgotten; by the river and the pond, on the hill and in the valley.

雪,在四处飘落着。雪花撒在树上,撒在田野,撒在河边、湖畔、山上、谷底——没有一条岩缝墙隙里不飘满雪花。

(雪花撒落在树上,撒落在田野,撒落在河边、湖畔、谷底、大雪纷飞,连小小的岩缝中都飘进了雪花。)

2. There is in fact a strong likelihood that the administration will preside over a $ 100 billion—plus budget deficit in the current fiscal year, putting its promise to balance the budget by fiscal 1983—which begins in only twenty months—firmly out of reach.

(美国)政府将要在本财政年度应付 1 000 亿美元以上的预算赤字,这样就使其诺言——平衡1983 年财政年度(再过 20 个月才开始的年度)的预算根本无法实现。这是极有可能的事。

(美国政府将要在本财政年度应付 1 000 亿美元以上的预算赤字,这样就使它提出的平衡1983 年财政预算的诺言根本无法实现。而1983 年财政年度要再过20 个月才开始,遭致这种结局是极有可能的。)

3. On this and succeeding days, during which our anti-craft guns were doubled in numbers, very hard and continuous air fighting took place over the capital, and the Luftweffe were still confident through their overestimation of our losses.

在当天和随后的几天(我们的高射炮在这几天增加了一倍),首都上空发生了连续不断的激烈空战,德国空军由于过高地估计了我们的损失,因而仍然信心十足。

So far as expression is concerned, the key point lies in the organization and arrangement of the Chinese version. If you are not very sure of your own version, better have more than one compared with each other and sort out the most natural, faithful one as the final version.

Recasting

By recasting, we mean breaking the crust structure of original sentence on the basis of complete digestion, having the original reorganized and rearranged according to the original meaning. The recast version is surely free from the yoke of the original crust, but must be in harmony with the original in essence (in deep structure) and with the Chinese syntax as well. e. g.

1. What the New Yorker would find missing is what many outsiders find oppressive and distasteful about New York—its rawness, tension, urgency; its bracing competitiveness; the rigor of its judgments; and the congested, democratic presence of so many other New Yorkers encased in their own world.

纽约的粗犷、紧张,那种急迫感和催人奋发的竞争性,它的是非观念之严酷无情;纽约市的那种各色人等熙熙攘攘,兼容并蓄于各自的天地之中的格局;这一切都使些非纽约人感到厌恶和窒息;而这一切,又正是纽约人所眷恋的。

2. Decision must be made very rapidly; physical endurance is tested as much as perception, because an enormous amount of time must be spent making certain that the key figures act on the basis of the same information and purpose.

必须把大量时间花在确保关键人物均已根据同一情报和目的行事,而这一切对身体的耐力和思维能力都是一大考验。因此一旦考虑成熟,决策者就应迅速作出决策。

3. They (the poor) are the first to experience technological progress as a curse which destroys the old muscle power jobs that previous generations used as a means to fight their way out of poverty.

对于以往的几代人来说,旧式的体力劳动是一种用以摆脱贫困的手段,而技术的进步则摧毁了穷人赖以为生的体力劳动。因此,首先体验到技术进步之害的是穷人。

4. Complaints of poverty of poets are as old as their art, but I never heard that they wrote the worse verses for it. It is enough, probably, to call forth their most vigorous efforts, that poetry is admired and honoured by their countrymen.

自古以来,诗人即以贫困而怨拆不绝。但因贫而不功于艺者,于我则闻所未闻。盖天下爱诗而敬之,则诗人虽尽其才力仍因以自慰。这大概就是原因之所在吧。

The surface structure of the original is changed to a great extent, and the Chinese version is rearranged according to the original meaning.

5. He was indefatigable. When he fitted his eye on his prey he hunted it with the persistence of a botanist who will expose himself to dangers of flood, earthquake, fever and hostile natives to find an orchid of peculiar rarity.

他那种锲而不舍的精神倒很像一位植物学家,精微观察,四处寻觅,只要看到奇花异草,任什么险阻——洪水、地震、瘟疫、杀气腾腾的土人……一切不在话下。

The following Chinese versions are completely recast ones.

6. Learning is, in too many cases, but a foil to common sense, a substitute for true knowledge. Books are less often made use of as spectacles to look at nature with, than as blinds to keep out its strong light and shifting scenery from weak eyes and indolent disposition.

书本理应是观察自然的透镜,却常常被视力不够和生性懒惰的人用来遮光护眼,好使他们对自然的光芒和变幻的景色视而不见。那种把学识当作常识的陪衬,以学识代替真知的人真是太多了。

7. The great difficulty of introducing radically new computer architectures which requires customers to rewrite most of their software excluded the possibility for these techniques to find their way to the commercial marketplace.

采用全新的计算机体系结构，势必要求用户改写其大部分软件，因此难以付诸实现，这就排除了这种技术进入商品市场的可能性。

It is very difficult to have the Chinese version arranged according the original syntax as it is well knitted, thus we have to recast it according to the Chinese syntax.

Sometimes we may come across some long sentences which can not be translated with only one technique, such being the case, we have to apply two techniques simultaneously, or more techniques comprehensively. Let's take the following sentence for instance.

8. This spirit of fair-play, which in the public schools, at any rate, is absorbed as the most inviolable of traditions, had stood out race in good stead in the professions, and especially in the administration of dependencies, where the obvious desire of the officials to deal justly and see fair-play in disputes between natives and European has partly compensated for a want to sympathetic understanding, which has kept the English strangers in lands of alien culture.

这种公正的精神，至少在私立学校中是当作最为神圣不可侵犯的传统而加以全盘灌输的。这种精神在人们的供职上，尤其在属地统治上，对于不列颠民族是很有用的。当统治属地时，英国的官员抱有一种愿望，显然想要公正地处理土人和欧洲人间的争执，而得到公平的解决，使英国人因处在海外的异族文化中，缺乏同情的谅解而格格不入的情形，多少获得一点补偿。

Translation of long sentences is by no means easy, but by means of being patient and careful on the one hand, and having six-step method skillfully used on the other, you will be surely capable enough of translating any complicated long sentences into proper Chinese ones.

Translation Exercises

I. *Translate the following sentences into Chinese, making comprehensive use of methods and techniques in your translation.*

1. Miss Temple had always something of serenity in her air, of state in her mien, of refined prosperity in her language, which precluded deviation into the ardent, the excited, the eager—something which chastened the pleasure of those who looked on her and listened to her, by a controlling sense of awe; and such was my feeling now, but as to Helen Burns, I was struck with wonder.

2. When Miss Sharp had performed the heroical act mentioned in the last chapter, and had seen the Dixonary, flying over the pavement of the little garden, fall at length at the feet of the astonished Miss Jemima, the young lady's countenance, which had before worn an almost livid look of hatred, assumed a smile that perhaps was scarcely more agreeable, and she sank back in the carriage in an easy frame of mind, saying, "So múch for the Dixonary; and thank God, I am out of Chiswick."

3. If she had long lost the blue-eyed, flower-like charm, the cool slim purity of face and

form, the appleblossom colouring which had so swiftly and oddly affected Ashurst twenty-six years ago, she was still at forty-three a comely and faithful companion, whose cheeks were faintly mottled, and whose grey-blue eyes had acquired a certain fullness.

4. However, even the prescient Tocqueville(托克维尔), who predicted 150 years ago that the United States and Russia would emerge as two great contending world powers, could not have foreseen that the nation that potentially could decide the world balance of power in the last decades of the twentieth century, and that could become the most powerful nation on earth during the twenty-first century, would be China.

5. I feel that this award was not made to me as a man, but to my work—a life's work in the agony and sweat of the human spirit, not for glory and least of all for profit, but to create out of the materials of the human spirit something which did not exist before.

6. Set along the blue Danube beneath the wooded hills of the Wienerwald, which were studded with yellow-green vineyards, it was a place of natural beauty that captivated the visitor and made the Viennese believe that providence had been especially kind to them. Music filled the air, the towering music of gifted native sons, the greatest Europe had known, Haydn, Mozart, Beethoven and Schubert, and, in the last Indian-Summer years, the gay haunting waltzes of Vienna's own beloved Johann Strauss. To a people blessed and so imprinted with the baroque style of living, life itself was something of a dream and the good folk of the city passed the pleasant days and nights of their lives waltzing and wining, in light talk in the congenial coffee houses, listening to music and viewing the make-believe of theater and opera and operetta, in flirting and making love, abandoning a large part of their lives to pleasure and to dreams.

II. *Translate the following passage into Chinese with enough attention to the arrangement of long sentences.*

The Fall of the Third Reich(An Excerpt)
by William L. Shirer

The guns in Europe ceased firing and the bombs ceased dropping at midnight on May 8-9, 1945, and a strange but welcome silence settled over the Continent for the first time since September 1, 1939. In the intervening five years, eight months and seven days millions of men and women had been slaughtered on a hundred battlefields and in a thousand bombed towns, and millions more done to death in the Nazi gas chambers or on the edge of the S. S. Einsatzgruppen pits in Russia and Poland—as the result of Adolf Hitler's lust for German conquest. A greater part of most of Europe's ancient cities lay in ruins, and from their rubble, as the weather warmed, there was the stench of the countless unburied dead.

No more would the streets of Germany echo to the jack boots of the goose-stepping storm troopers or the lusty yells of the brownshirted masses or the shouts of the Fuehrer blaring from the loudspeakers.

After twelve years, four months and eight days, an Age of Darkness to all but a multitude of Germans and now ending in a bleak night for them too, the Thousand-Year Reich had come to an end. It had raised, as we have seen, this great nation and this resourceful but so easily misled people to heights of power and conquest they had never before experienced and now it had never before experienced and now it had dissolved with a suddenness and a completeness that had few, if any, parallels in history.

The people were there, and the land—the first dazed and bleeding and hungry, and, when winter came, shivering in their rags in the hovels which the bombing had made of their homes; the second a vast wasteland of rubble. The German people had not been destroyed, as Hitler, who had tried to destroy so many other peoples and, in the end, when the war was lost, themselves, had wished.

But the Third Reich had passed into history.

4.5 Conversion between the Passive Voice and the Active Voice

4.5.1 Introduction

Grammatically speaking, the form of a verb, both in English and in Chinese, can be classified into the active voice and the passive voice. If the person or thing denoted by the subject of a sentence is the doer(or agent) of the action, then that form of the verb is the active voice, e.g.

The boy kicked the football. (active voice)

If the person or thing denoted by the subject of a sentence is the receiver or sufferer of the action (or object), then that form of the verb is the passive voice, e.g.

The football was kicked by the boy. (passive voice)

We must note that the passive voice may have the same form as "be + past participle" (used adjectively), e.g.

The tree was uprooted by the wind. (passive voice)

The tree was uprooted when we saw it. (be + past participle)

It can be seen from the above examples that the passive voice is not merely a formal variant of the active voice, able to replace it without any change of meaning, there is a difference of emphasis. Generally speaking, the subject of the sentence is the main point of interest, the passive voice is the grammatical device that gives the object of a transitive verb prominence by making it the subject (the information focus). So when we want to place the emphasis on the performer of the action, we generally use the active voice, when we want to place the emphasis on the action, or the receiver of the action, we use the passive voice. Thus, in the following sentence: "Tom is cleaning the car." (active voice) The focus of our interest is primarily "Tom". The sentence is the answer to some question like: "What is Tom doing?" But in the sentence: "The car is being cleaned by Tom." (passive voice) The information focus is on "the car" and the emphasis on the fact that "it is being cleaned". This sentence is perhaps the answer to the question "What is happening to the car?" We are so little concerned with "who" is cleaning it that quite often we should omit all reference to the agent and simply say: "The car is being cleaned". This is particularly the case where the agent is vague or unimportant or unknown, which is of common occurrence both in English and in Chinese, e.g.

1. Portuguese is spoken in Brazil.

巴西讲葡萄牙语。

2. Books in the Reference Library must not be taken away.

阅览室的图书不得带出。(or 仅供阅览,不得带出。)

3. Have the chicken been fed yet?

鸡喂了吗?

4. The cotton goods are made in China.

这些棉织品是中国产的。

5. 这台机床已20年没用过了。

This machine tool hasn't been used for twenty years.

6. 问题已经解决。

The problem has been solved.

7. 据说,事故是因玩忽职守所致。

It is said that the accident was due to negligence.

8. 众所周知,中国人在四千年前就发明了指南针。

It is well known that the compass was invented in China four thousand years ago.

Since the agents of the above examples are either vague or unimportant or unknown, so the construction "by + agent" would be unnatural and unnecessary in sentences like these, and in translation of this kind of the passive voice, the agent with "by" is always omitted. Some of the expressions have become the fixed patterns as follows:

It is alleged that... 人们断言……

It is hoped that... 希望……

It is reported that... 据报……

It is said that... 据说……

It is supposed that... 据推测……

It must be admitted that... 必须承认……

It must be pointed out that... 必须指出……

It is asserted that... 有人主张……

It is believed that... 据信……

It is well known that... 众所周知……

It will be said that... 人们会说……

It was told that... 人们曾说……

It was told that... 听说……

Since, in the change from active to passive voice, the subject of passive construction is formed by the object of the active one, only transitive verbs can be used in the passive voice. So verbs of Incomplete Predication, e.g. "seem", "be", "become", etc, can never be used in the passive, e.g. "He became King" could never have a passive form such as "A king was become by him". However, certain intransitive verbs can be made into transitive ones by the addition of a preposition. These verbs can be used in the passive voice as follows:

1. His plan was laughed at by everyone who heard it.

2. That is a famous bed, it was slept in by the first emperor of the Tang Dynasty.

3. The children will be cared for while she is away.

4. Such success was never dreamed of when we first started.

Though all transitive verbs can theoretically be made passive there are cases where, in practice, the passive would not be used. For example:

"He had a good breakfast before he went to work" would not be used passively as:

"A good breakfast was had by him."

Some verbs such as give, tell, show, lend, bring, teach in English, and "送", "给", "问", "教" in Chinese, take two objects, one usually standing for a person, the other a thing. The word for the person is the Indirect Object and is the first of the two objects, the word for the thing is the Direct Object[e.g. He sold us (indirect) his house (direct). Here, "us" means "to us"]. If a sentence contains two objects and it is expressed in the passive voice, either of those objects may become the subject, though it is perhaps more usual to make the personal object the subject of the passive voice. Some examples:

Active: The boss offered him a fat job in the company.

Passive: { (A) He was offered a fat job in the company.
         { (B) A fat job in the company was offered him.

Active: They awarded him the Nobel Peace Prize in 2006.

Passive: { (A) He was awarded the Nobel Peace Prize in 2006.
         { (B) The Nobel Peace Prize was awarded him in 2006.

In the above examples the omission of the agent with "by" is noticeable as the "doer" is either clear from the meaning of the sentence, or is not of interest to us. This kind of the passive voice is called the covert passive voice (隐性被动句, the passive voice in a broad sense) that is different from the overt passive voice (显性被动句, the passive voice in a narrow sense) which is usually formed by means of the construction "by + agent".

4.5.2 Conversion between the Passive Voice and the Active Voice

The passive voice is more frequently used in English than in Chinese, especially in journalistic texts and scientific and technical writings. The passive voice is the first choice when the news or the receiver of the action is more important than the agent, especially when casualties of the disaster become the focus of the news. Examples:

1. DALLAS, NOV. 22—President John Fitzgerald Kennedy was shot and killed by an assassin today.

2. Two children at play were killed and 12 others injured today when a speeding sports car jumped the curb outside Prospect Park and ran them down.

3. MOSCOW (Reuters)—Chechnya's Moscow-backed president and the commander of Russian forces in the restive region have been killed by a bomb blast in packed stadium during annual celebrations of "Victory Day", the Interfax news agency reports.

4. He added that 108 people have been killed in six weeks of conflict in this impoverished former Soviet republic.

The passive voice is of common occurrence in the scientific and technical writings. According to statistics, there are a third of English verbs in scientific and technical writings which are used in the form of the passive voice. The same is true of the case in Chinese, but more verbs are used in the form of the covert passive voice.

Some examples:

5. The coolant is circulated through the annular spaces between the fuel elements and the moderator, absorbing heat as it passes, and the heat so absorbed is conveyed out of the core to the heat exchanger. Very large quantities of heat are generated by fission, and in order that these may be rapidly dissipated, a large volume of coolant is required. It is therefore frequently pressurized, especially where a gaseous coolant is used, to increase its density. A number of different coolants have been employed, including water, carbon dioxide and liquid metals.

冷却剂在释热元件和缓和剂之间作环形循环,循环时吸收热量,并把吸收过来的热量从反应器中心向热交换器传递。裂变产生大量的热量。为使这些热量快速消散,需要大量的冷却剂。因此,要不停地加压(尤其使用气体冷却剂时),以便增加其密度。现已使用的冷却剂有若干种,其中包括水,二氧化碳和液态金属等。

6. As oil is found deep in the ground, its presence cannot be determined by a study of the surface. Consequently, a geological survey of the underground rock structure must be carried out. If it is thought that the rocks in a certain area contain oil, a "drilling rig" is assembled. The most obvious part of a drilling rig is called "a derrick". It is used to lift sections of pipe, which are lowered into the hole made by the drill. As the hole is being drilled, a steel pipe is pushed down to prevent the sides from falling in. If oil is struck a cover is firmly fixed to the top of the pipe and the oil is allowed to escape through a series of valves.

石油埋藏于地层深处。因此,仅仅靠研究地层表面,无法确定有无石油,必须对地下的岩石结构进行地质勘测。如果确定了某一区域的岩石蕴藏着石油,就在此安装钻机。钻机最明显的部分是机架,用以提举一节一节的钢管。这些钢管被压入井孔。一边钻井,一边下钢管。以防周围土层塌陷。一旦出油,就紧固管盖,让油从各个阀门喷出。

7. 这些机器应在正常状态下测试。

These machines should be tested under normal working condition.

8. 我院二十年来共收治急性阑尾炎8 000余例,总死亡率低于0.2%。

In the past 20 years, more than 8 000 cases of acute appendicitis were treated in the Beijing Children's Hospital. The overall case mortality-rate was lower than 0.2%.

9. 自从第一颗原子弹试验以来,全世界都已知道,原子可分裂,原子能可利用。

Since the first test of the atomic bomb the world has learnt the atom can be split and its power can be used.

In Example 5 and 6, 21 of 23 verbs in all are used in the form of the passive voice, which speaks volumes for the great frequency of the passive voice in scientific and technical writings.

4.5.2.1 Translation of the Overt Passive Voice

In English, the construction "by + agent" would be natural and necessary if it is a sentence of the overt passive voice. The preposition "by" is followed by the "doer" (agent), which, at the same time, suggests that the subject of the overt-passive-voice sentence is the "receiver of the action." The same is true of the case where a Chinese verb is used in the form of the overt passive voice. Hence in translation from Englis into Chinese, the constructions such as "被……", "受……", "为……所", "把……", "由……", "让……", "叫……", "遭……" are often used, whereas in translation from Chinese into English the construction "by + agent" is usually used.

Examples:

1. The radioactive material should be kept safely to protect the surrounding areas from being polluted by radiation.

放射性材料应该安全储藏,以保护周围环境不受辐射污染。

2. This level is somewhere between that created by very heavy street traffic and that caused by the arrival of an underground train in a station.

这个声压级别大约介乎交通极为繁忙的街道上的噪声和地铁到站时所引起的噪音之间。

3. This kind of steel is not corroded by air and water.

这种钢不会被空气和水腐蚀。

4. The metric system is now used by almost all the countries in the world.

米制现在几乎被全世界所有国家采用。

5. Our foreign policy is supported by people all over the world.

我们的对外政策受到全世界人民的支持。

6. I was seized with sadness as I thought of how the ancient city had been spared during the Second World War and now might be destroyed by an impending riot.

想到这座古城在二次大战或得以幸免,而现在却要遭到即将来临的暴乱的破坏,我内心便感到悲伤。

7. These views of Marx and Engels have now been adopted by all proletarians who are fighting for their emancipation.

马克思和恩格斯的这种观点,现在已为正在争取解放的全体无产阶级所采纳。

8. By evening the occupation was complete, and the people were chased off the street by an eight o'clock curfew.

时至傍晚,占领已完成。八点钟开始的宵禁把人们从街道赶走。

9. Most letters from his wife are read to him by the nurse in the hospital.

他妻子给他的信件,大多数是由医院里的护士念给他听的。

10. 艾滋病病毒只能通过血液或其他体液传播。

The AIDS virus is only transmitted by blood and other body fluids.

11. 疟疾是由蚊子携带的寄生虫传播的。

Malaria is caused by a tiny parasite carried by mosquitoes.

12. 环滁皆山也。

The district of Chu is entirely surrounded by hills.

13. 过往客人不计其数,都被这畜生吃了!

As for the travelers, it is not known how many have been eaten by this beast.

14. 贾政遂命开门进去,只见一带翠嶂,挡住面前。

Well content, Mr. Cheng moved on. Just inside the gateway the eye was met by a green hill.

4.5.2.2 Translation of the Covert Passive Voice

Both in English and in Chinese, if the "doer", or the "receiver" of the action is visible from the meaning of the sentence, or is not of interest to us, the construction "by + agent" would be omitted, this kind of passive voice is called the covert passive voice. In translation of the covert passive voice from English into Chinese, the construction "被……" and the likes of it are generally not necessary, neither is the construction "by + agent" in translation from Chinese into English. Examples:

1. The oil of the world will have been used up, and man will be using the more convenient power obtained from the splitting of the atom.

全世界的石油将会用尽,人们将使用从原子分裂获得的更为方便的动力。

2. A national link-up of computers could mean that a large amount of information will be supplied to anyone who uses the system.

把全国的电脑连接起来意味着可以向任何使用该系统的人提供大量信息。

3. The Premier and his entourage are scheduled to tour Tokyo, Kobe, Osaka, Nara and Kyoto during their stay.

这位总理及随行人员在逗留期间,将访问东京、神户、大阪、奈良和京都等地。

4. Agreement on most of the agenda items had already been reached in an exhaustive series of presummit talks between foreign ministers of the two countries.

为高峰会议作准备的两国外长经过一系列深入细致的前期会谈之后,已就所讨论的大多数问题取得了一致意见。

5. Most of the serious political differences were kept out of sight in a joint statement that diplomats said was made deliberately vague on a number of points to avoid disagreement.

许多严重的政治分歧没有在联合声明中提及,外交官们认为,联合声明为了避免分歧而故意在一系列观点上措辞含糊。

6. 说话时,已摆了茶果上来。

Meanwhile refreshments had been served.

7. 林如海已葬入祖坟了,诸事停妥,贾琏方进京的。

Lin Ruhai had been buried in the ancestral graveyard and, his obsequies completed, Jia Lian was able to start back for the capital.

8. 叔叔两下里住着,过个一年半载,即或闹出来,不过挨上老爷一顿骂……就是婶子,见生米已做成熟饭,也只得罢了。

Then you'll have two homes, uncle. After a year or so, if word does get out, at most you'll get reprimanded by your father... When Aunt Hsi-feng sees that the rice is already cooked, she'll have to put up with it.

There are the cases in translation where the covert passive voice can be changed to active voice by adding the "agent" or the logical subject of the sentence. Some examples:

9. She hadn't been told Bette's other name, or she'd forgotten it.

人家没告诉过她蓓蒂姓什么,要不然也许是她忘了。

10. His successes were so repeated that no wonder the envious and the vanquished spoke sometimes with bitterness regarding them.

他赢钱的次数那么多,无怪乎眼红的人,赌输的人,有时说起这事便要发牢骚。

11. Cuff's fight with Dobbin, and the unexpected issue of that contest, will long be remembered by every man who was educated at Dr. Swishtail's famous school.

凡是在斯威希泰尔博士那有名的学校里念过书的学生,决不能忘记克甫和都宾两人打架的经过和后来意想不到的结局。

12. It has been mentioned that Rebecca, soon after her arrival in Paris, took a very smart and leading position in society of that capital, and was welcomed at some of the most distinguished houses of the restored French nobility.

我曾经说过,利蓓加到达法国首都巴黎不久之后,便在上流社会出入,又时髦,又出风头,连好些光复后的王亲国戚都和她来往。

13. Early in the spring of 1750, in the village of Juffure, four days upriver from the coast of the Gambia, West Africa, a manchild was born to Omoro and Binta Kinte.

1750年初春时节,在距西非冈比亚海岸溯河而上四天路程的朱富雷村,奥摩罗·肯特和宾塔·肯特夫妇生下一个男孩。

14. He said he was assured by the State Department that the U. S. is willing to normalize relations with his country.

他说,国务院向他担保美国愿意同他的国家恢复正常关系。

To sum up in a few words, in translation of the overt passive voice from English into Chinese, the constructions such as "被……","受……","为……所","由……","叫……","遭……" are generally used, whereas in translation of the overt passive voice from Chinese into English, the construction "by + agent" is usually necessary. However, in translation of the covert passive voice from English into Chinese the construction "被……" and its likes are generally omitted, and in translation from Chinese into English, the construction "by + agent" is not necessary in most cases.

Translation Exercises

I. *Translate the following prose into Chinese, please see to it that the passive voice is properly approached.*

Love Is Not Like Merchandise
Sydney J. Harris

A reader in Florida, apparently bruised by some personal experience, writes in to complain, "If I steal a nickle's worth of merchandise, I am a thief and punished; but if I steal the love of another's wife, I am free."

This is a prevalent misconception in many people's mind—that love, like merchandise, can be "stolen." Numerous states, in fact, have enacted laws allowing damages for "alienation of affections."

But love is not a commodity; the real thing cannot be bought, sold, traded or stolen. It is an act of the will, a turning of the emotions, a change in the climate of the personality.

When a husband or wife is "stolen" by another person, that husband or wife was already ripe for the stealing, was already predisposed toward a new partner. The "love bandit" was only taking what was waiting to be taken.

We tend to treat persons like goods. We even speak of children "belonging" to their parents. But nobody "belongs" to anyone else. Each person belongs to himself, and to God. Children are entrusted to their parents, and if their parents, do not treat them properly, the state has a right to remove them from their parents' trusteeship.

Most of us, when young, had the experience of a sweetheart being taken from us by somebody more attractive and more appealing. At the time, we may have resented this intruder—but as we grew older, we recognized that the sweetheart had never been ours to begin with. It was not the intruder that "cause" the break, but the lack of a real relationship.

On the surface, many marriages seem to break up because of a "third party." This is, however, a psychological illusion. The other woman or the other man merely serves as a pretext for dissolving a marriage that had already lost its essential integrity.

Nothing is more futile and more self-defeating than the bitterness of spurned love, the vengeful feeling that someone else has "come between" oneself and a beloved. This is always a distortion of reality, for people are not the captives or victims of others—they are free agents, working out their own destinies for good or for ill.

But the rejected lover or mate cannot afford to believe that his beloved has freely turned away from him—and so he ascribes sinister or magical properties to the interloper. He calls him a hypnotist or a thief or a home-breaker. In the vast majority of cases, however, when a home is broken, the breaking has begun long before any "third party" has appeared on the scene.

II. *Translate the following passage into English, with enough attention to the proper use of the passive voice in your translation.*

邓小平谈"一国两制"

在中国某些地区,如香港和台湾,虽然允许资本主义存在,但社会主义依然是中国的主体。在解决香港问题上已经证明行之有效的"一国两制"构想也可用于解决国际问题。……

(该杂志)引用邓和外宾及港澳人士的一系列谈话,追述了这类构想在1978年中国共产党"十一届三中全会"上首次讨论以来的形成过程。

引用邓的话说,如果资本主义制度在港台得不到保障,那里的繁荣与稳定就不能维持,和平解决问题也就不可能了。

邓说,之所以提出自1997年起维持香港的资本主义制度50年不变的构想,是因为中国需要50到60年才能实现现代化。

据邓所说,采取"一国两制"适合中国国情,并非权宜之计。文章引用邓的话说,统一中国是全民族的愿望,即使一千年也是要实现统一的。

邓说:"'一国两制'构想并非我个人的想法,而是由全国人民代表大会通过的原则与法律,因此是不会改变的。"

杂志还引用邓的话说,其他国家亦可使用这一构想解决困难问题。解决难题有两种方法:和平的与非和平的。由于许多问题无法用传统办法解决,他说就不得不去寻求新的办法。

Chapter Five

Translation of Various Types of Writings

5.1 Translation of Advertisements

With the development of the market-oriented economy and economic globalization, advertising finds its way in the four corners of the earth, and becomes indispensable to our life. Advertisements follow us like shadows.

There are advertisements and advertisements. They can be classified into a great variety of forms, such as press advertisement, TV advertisement, radio advertisement, outdoor and transport advertisement, direct mail advertisement, etc. The purpose of advertising (no matter what sort of advertisement it may be) is to persuade, persuade people to believe and persuade people to do something. It serves as: information; persuasion; maintenance of demand; creating mass market and; quality. To attain this target, businessmen and advertisers spare no efforts to make their advertisements convincing, appealing and impressive. Gradually, language of advertising forms its own unique style: simple form, vivid language, terse syntax and implicative context. Advertising language involves many factors concerning literature, psychology, economics, marketing, sociology, aesthetics and so on. It is therefore of great value in commerce, but to some extent worth our appreciation and linguistic study. A study of linguistic features of advertising is to be made in three aspects as follows:

5.1.1 Lexical Level

Difference between advertising language and other types of writing lies first of all in words. In order to solicit more customers, promote the sale of more goods and save more money, advertisement agents try to provide customers with the greatest possible quantity of information in the shortest possible passage. Thus, words used in advertising are generally concise, vivid and terse.

- **Monosyllables and Midget Words are Frequently Used**

G.N. Leech lists in his book "English in Advertising" the most frequently-used words as follows:

make, come, love, get, go, use, know, feel, have, keep, take, see, look, start, buy, need, give, taste.

In addition to the verbs mentioned above, Leech also lists some adjectives frequently used in advertising:

crip, good, better, best, rich, fine, free, new, fresh, special, great, delicious, real, full, big, sure, easy, clean, extra, bright, safe.

Of the 40 words mentioned above by Leech, there are 36 monosyllables, making up 90%; there are no more than 1/4 of the words with more than 4 letters, making up only 22.5%, which shows that commonly-used words in advertising are monosyllables and midget words.

Now the examples:

Only Carvers can do a job like this.

Because only Carvers have the new Supa-Drive Electric Power-Pack.

Ordinary power-tools have ordinary motors.

But Carvers have a Power Pack.

And it's power that packs a punch.

See how they can saw. Power Saw. And Drill. Power drill.

And sand Power sand.

Carvers Power Pack power tools lend more power to your elbow.

Carvers. See them now. At your local Power pack stockist.

There are 71 words in the above advertisement, of which 41 words with no more than 4 letters, making up 58%; and there are 53 monosyllables, making up 74%; which shows that monosyllables and midget words enjoy great frequency in advertisement. The same is true of Chinese advertising. One can easily find the Chinese monosyllables such as "新","奇","帅","棒","强","快","香","甜","脆","鲜","艳","美". By using such words, one can kill two birds with one stone: on the one hand, making advertising language more concise and expressive, and on the other, saving more space or time, as a result, more money will be saved.

- **Commendatory Terms**

Frequent use of commendatory terms is another unique feature of advertising language, which is closely connected with its target. To solicit more customers, advertising must be appealing, convincing and impressive. Compared with other words, only commendatory words, especially commendatory adjectives can play the part. Of 21 adjectives mentioned above by Leech, 19 words are commendatory adjectives. Its proportion is larger than that of any other types of writing. Analysing the following example:

Bask in the warmth of the Philippines

Bask... indulge... luxuriate... in beautiful white-sand beaches. Breathtaking scenic wonders... world-class facilities and effcient service. But, best of all, back in special warmth and comfort that is uniquely, wonderfully Filipino.

On reading this advertisement, customers would be carried away by beautiful white-sand beach, breathtaking scenic wonder, world class facilities, efficient service and special warmth of the Philippines, which is the effect and function of commendatory words. In this advertisement there are 13 commendatory words which are greatly appealing to readers. In Chinese advertising, commendatory words are also frequently used. For example "英克莱自行车,新,奇,帅!","袭人鲜花,花香袭人". If without video and audio effect frequent use of commendatory words plays a special part in written advertising.

• Clever Use of Coinages

Without advertising, it is hard for a new product to develop market and have a foot in modern market no matter how good its quality is. Advertisers are well aware of importance of advertising, so they spare no pains to have diction well polished for attracting more customers. Cooking up new words and strange words is one of the techniques commonly used. Some examples of cooking up new words:

1. In Miami, it's no newelty.
2. Come to OUR fruice.
3. The Orangemostest Drink in the world.
4. Give a Timex to all, to all a good Timex.
5. Compucessories a new word? Yes... We've just coined it to describe those Data-Processing Accessories we at PCA delight in designing, and without which your computer cannot function well with full efficiency.

The underlined parts are coinages. In Example 1, newelty = new + novelty; in Example 2, fruice = fruit + juice; in Example 3, orangemostest = orange + most + est; in Example 4, Timex = time + excellent; and in Example 5, compucessories = computer + accessories. Coinages of this kind are nowhere to be found in dictionaries, but they seem familiar to readers in appearance. One can guess their meanings by means of context without the help of dictionaries. When you are attracted by the newly cooked-up words, you learn the information about the products, which is the very target of advertising. Thanks to the new coinages, customers are attracted and the target of advertising is attained. But coinages must be well based on aftertaste and implication, without which coinages can produce little effect and will be meaningless.

Misspelling some daily-used words is also a clever use of coinages, e. g.

6. Twogether.

The Ultimate All Inclusive One Price Sunkissed Holiday.

7. We know eggsactly how to tell eggs.

Example 6 is an advertisement for sightseeing and holiday taking. Twogether is the variation of "together","To" is misspelt as "two" on purpose by the author, which is to show that you can enjoy the bliss of the newly-married couple and dream again the sweet experience of your honeymoon. Why not go for sightseeing? In Example 7, the author makes clever use of a witty, strange and eye-catching word—"eggsactly" which is the homophony of "exactly", which is very attractive to customers. One can find a lot of Chinese advertisements similarly, e. g.

九华蚊香,默默无蚊的奉献。

常备不泻。

一贴见笑。

玉环牌沐浴水器让您随心所浴。

荣昌肛泰,痔在必得,有痔之士,好福气啊!

(Common Abbreviations in Help Wanted Advertisements)

ad	= advertisement, advertising	grd	= graduate
ads	= advertisements	hrs	= hours
adv	= advertising, advertisement	loc	= location
aft	= after	m	= month
AM, a.m.	= morning	mdtwn	= midtown
ave	= avenue	M/F, M-F	= Monday to Friday
Betw, btw, btwn	= between	mnth	= month
Bkkpg	= bookkeeping	No	= number
Bkkpr	= bookkeeper	ofc	= office
Bnfts	= benefits	P.A., pa	= per annum
co	= company	pdtn	= production
coop	= cooperation	PM, p.m.	= afternoon
CV	= curriculum vitae(简历)	p.m.	= per month
Dept	= department	p/t	= part time
Dsgn	= design	ref(s)	= reference(s)
eng	= engineer, engineering	req'd	= required
Equiv	= equivalent	sal	= salary
exp	= experience, experienced	secty	= secretary
exp'd	= experienced	st.	= street
exper	= experience	temp	= temporary
f	= female, feet(英尺)	w	= women
f/t	= full time	W/, w/	= with
gd	= good		

(Common Abbreviations in House Selling/Renting Ads)

apts	= apartments	fin	= finished
blks	= blocks	furn	= furnished
br	= bedroom	gar	= garage
brk	= brick	hse	= house
bths	= bath rooms	ht	= heating
c/a	= central air conditioning	incl	= including
conv	= convenient or convenience	kits	= kitchens
clpe	= couple	lg	= large
dng	= dining	lge	= large
dsh-wahrs	= dish washers	loc	= location
fam	= family	lrg	= large

mo	= month	st	= street
nr	= near	transp	= transportation
occup	= occupancy	unfurn	= unfurnished
rd	= road	w/fpl	= with fireplace
rm	= room	yr(s)	= year(s)
schl	= school		

5.1.2 Syntactic Level

Advertising is characterized by three remarkable features in syntax as follows:

- **Simple and Elliptical Sentences**

No matter what kind of advertisement it may be, its length is limited to a great extent for the sake of time and money. An advertiser must make great effort to convey the greatest quantity of information in the shortest possible message, which calls for simple syntax and terse diction instead of superfluity. Therefore simple, brief and elliptical sentences are a frequent occurrence. The example on page 180 is the typical one that contains 71 words in 15 sentences, each of which contains only 4.7 words, shorter than usual sentences, and what is more, even shorter than daily-used colloquial sentences. Shakespeare pointed out "Brevity is the soul of wit", which can be best shown by advertising. More terse, easier to memorize, simpler the syntax is, more appealing (it is) to customers and it is much more like a motto. Some examples:

1. Love in your heart—peace in your mind—lifeguard in your home—the disinfectant you trust completely.

2. Make it a Mild Smoke.

Mild Seven

Smooth, rich, rewarding(Japanese Mild Seven Brand Cigarette)

Subjects and predicates of advertisements can be omitted (e. g. 1. 2), sometimes one can come across verbless sentences with all verbs omitted, e. g.

1. More than a timepice. An acquisition(A watch ads).

2. Safe, Easy. Quick and With Fun!

(KITCHEN WONDER Vegetable Processor)

Simple and elliptical sentences are also frequently used in Chinese advertising, e. g. "一册在手,纵览全球"(a magazine ads),"今年二十,明年十八"(a cosmetics ads). Compared with simple and elliptical sentences in English advertising, the similarities of Chinese advertising are only different in approach, but can produce equally satisfactory effect.

- **Frequent Use of Imperative Sentences**

Advertising is an agitating language with the purpose to persuade people into accepting its propaganda, to convince people to take action, which is in conformity with the function of imperative sentences. Imperative sentences thus are of importance in advertising. For example:

Is her skin really this beautiful?

Not without a little help, it isn't.

Max Factor Foundations are too sheer, too light, to be seen. But the results can't be missed. Choose from: Velvet Balanced Make-up a pH balanced, oil-free liquid to maintain your skin's natural acid balance.

Velvet Touch. A gossamer light, basic foundation to give your skin a fresh radiant look.

Ultra Moisturized foundation that's especially kind to drier skins.

Use one of these foundations from Max Factor and they could be asking it of you. Is her skin really that beautiful!

DON'T YOU LOVE BEING A WOMAN?
MAX FACTOR

Some more examples:

1. Go well. Go Shell. (Shell—an oil company)
2. Stop in at any Ford or Lincoln. (—Mercury dealer)
3. Put it all behind you. (—Honda Civic Wagon)
4. Buy one pair. Get one free. (—Pearle Vision Center)
5. So come into Mcdonald's and enjoy a Big Mac Sandwich. (—Mac Sandwich)

Imperative sentences are also a frequent occurrence in Chinese advertising, e. g. "东奔西走，要喝宋河好酒！","与其道听途说，不如亲身体验。"(a cosmetics ads)

• **Frequent Use of the Simple Present Tense**

In English, the simple present tense is used for a habitual, permanent, or repeated action, or for a general statement. In customers' eyes, all the products of high quality enjoy good durability. Advertisers, making use of their need and taking advantage of their psychological activity, frequently use simple present tense in advertising, which seems likely to add something to eternity and durability of their products. For example:

The Older Way to blend away gray.

The Better way.

Clairol Men's Choice vs. Just For Men.

They both blend away gray in only 5 minutes. But that's where the similarity ends.

Clairol Men's Choice gives you an exclusive conditioning system Just For Men just doesn't have. Clairol Men's Choice has a thick rich gel-Just For Men doesn't. Clairol Men's Choice is gentler to your skin than Just For Men and is as gentle to your hair as water. And now only Clairol Men's Choice comes with the convenience of one product specially packaged for both your hair and your beard or mustache.

Clairol Men's Choice. All the know-how of the haircolor experts... Clairol, of course. It's the better way to blend away gray.

CLAIROL
MEN'S CHOICE

Some more examples:

1. Persil washes whiter and it shows:

Persil takes care of whiteness (a washing powder ads)

2. Arthritis pains? All you need is Bayer Aspirin. (a medicine ads)

The simple present tense is used both in Examples 1 and 2. In the former it shows that "Persil" enables your dress to be clean and stainless, together with the comparative degree of adjective "white", it means that fact speaks louder: Persil can have our dress washed cleaner than any other. In the latter, the simple present tense indicates to customers that they are now in need of Aspirin produced in Bayer, it seems to customers that they can get rid of arthritis pain as soon as they take the medicine, the earlier you take, the sooner you'll be free from suffering. It seems to be urging people to take action without any delay.

5.1.3 Rhetorical Devices

Advertising language is a comprehensive artistic language, a mixture of literature, aesthetics, psychology, marketing and rhetoric. A good advertisement is a great success that is easy for people to recite and deeply impresses them, which owes much to rhetorical devices. In order to have their advertising unique and eye-catching, advertisers try to polish and whet their advertising by hook or by crook. Frequently-used rhetorical devices are as follows:

- **Repetition**

Most frequently repeated words in advertising are adjectives, especially, commendatory words. "Power" in the above-mentioned sentence is repeated for 11 times just to show that the electric device is powerful enough to do anything for you. A clever use of repetition will surely enhance the effect of advertising. Some examples:

1. Incredible sale; beautiful, beautiful, beautiful lynx and mink, top quality, latest style for garments.

2. Call it Wrigleys.

Call it Spearmint

Call it Gum   (a gum ads)

Repetition of adjectives is for advertising quality of products; syntactic repetition is to enhance the rhythm of the advertising language which enjoys good readability and smoothness and on the other hand pleasant to ear.

- **Pun**

Pun is to take advantage of phonetic and semantic condition to make a sentence have double meanings (ambiguous). People have to read between, beyond and behind the lines. Pun is classified to homophonic pun and semantic pun. Implication and overtones in advertising are mainly emphasized in a roundabout way for attaining commercial target, e. g.

1. Make your every hello a real good-buy. (a telephone ads)

2. A Deal With Us Means A Good Deal To You.

3. Coke refreshes you like no other can.

In Example 1, the author makes good use of homophone between good-buy and good-bye for attracting customers, promoting the sale of goods. Example 2 is a neon advertising hung from the building of a department store, the ingenuity and originality of which are that the basic meaning of the phrase "a good deal" (很多,许多) is in harmony with the implication of advertising (一笔好买卖). It is humorous enough to amuse the dead. "Can" in Example 3 can be regarded as a model verb of the elliptical sentence of "Coke refreshes you like no other (drinks) can (refresh) you." It can be also considered as a container (can = tin) containing drink or beer. Thus "can" in this advertisement shares double meanings, which is witty, humorous and impressing.

- **Classical Allusions and Idioms**

Most of classical allusions are the concentration of vivid historical stories, some of them are words, some phrases, still some sentences. Classical allusions set readers thinking and share remarkable rhetoric effect as they are terse, implicative and profound in meaning.

Idioms are established set phrases used throughout generations. Most of idioms are fixed in form and terse in meaning, like classical allusions, they also share remarkable rhetoric effect. Because of this, classical allusions and idioms are frequently used in advertising. Some examples:

1. Ask for More. (a cigarette ads)
2. Not all cars are created equal. (a car ads)
3. Better late than the late. (a traffic safety ads)

In Example 1, "More" is a trademark of a cigarette, going together with "ask for", the phrase "Ask for More" reminds readers of the novel "Oliver Twist" by Charles Dickens. The hero of the novel Oliver often asked for more when he was begging. "Ask for More" as an advertisement is derived from the famous phrase in the novel. In the novel it means asking for more food to eat, but as an advertisement its meaning is obvious without explanation. Example 2 is an advertising for promotion of the sale of cars in U.S by a Japanese Company. Americans are clear enough about the origin, "Declaration of Independence". Lincoln the late president of U.S. once said in the famous Gettysburg Address "all men are created equal", the Japanese are clever enough to make a good use of quotation by changing "all men are created equal" into "Not all cars are created equal", which on the one hand, gives prominence to the superiority of their products, and on the other hand, deeply impresses the Americans by means of originality. The effect of the advertising is a great success. Example 3 is also a great success as it makes a clever use of "late" in the idiom "Better late than never" as a semantic pun. "Better late than never", as a traffic advertisement for safety, is striking enough to warn the drivers against carelessness. However, the advertiser is so wise that he changes "never" in the original idiom into "the late", which enhances the rhetoric effect of advertising, what is more, makes advertising more implicative as "the late" means "the dead" or "loss of life". On reading this advertisement, no driver dares to drive carelessly any more.

In addition to above-mentioned rhetorical devices, also frequently used are metaphor, hyperbole, personification, rhyme and rhythm, etc. In order to attain commercial target, advertisers spare no efforts to make full use of various rhetorical devices for more vivid language, for more effective approach that will convince customers of the quality of their products and buy them without any doubt.

• **Translation of Advertising**

Advertising, as mentioned above, can be classified into a variety of forms. Different approaches should be taken to translation of different sorts of advertisements. For convenience sake, they are classified into picture advertising and written advertising in this book, and the following discussion is mainly stressed on translation of these two forms.

The so-called picture advertising consists of TV advertising, the press and magazine advertising and outdoor picture-poster advertising. By means of paralinguistic situation such as sound, light, image, picture and colour, which add a great deal to the situation, the video-audio effect is greatly enhanced, as a result, the products are made known to the public. Video effect comes first, words are only attached to picture and image. Thus language of picture advertising is as terse as a slogan. Translation of picture advertising must be accurate, terse and flexible. For example, a Chinese picture advertising "美味水饺,味道鲜美", in the picture a customer is putting a fresh dumpling between his lips and he seems greatly intoxicated. In translating this advertising, one word—"delicious" will be enough. Any more words would be like painting the lily, as paralinguistic situation adds a great deal to the translation. Some examples:

1. Wonder where the yellow went.

黄牙锈哪里去了?

2. Things go better with Coca-Cola.

可口可乐,可口又欢乐。

3. This is what the best people use. (a cosmetics ads)

名士佳丽,当用名优产品。

4. When your anger becomes a volcano. (a sedative medicine)

纵然您七窍生烟,也让您烟消云散。

5. In Miami, it's no newelty. (a tour ads)

到了迈阿密,才知天下奇。

In translating Chinese advertising, flexibility of syntax should be greatly stressed instead of surface meaning, the key point of which is to have the semantic core well expressed, to have the key words accurately translated. Some examples:

6. 袭人鲜花,花香袭人.

Flowers by Aroma, Aromatic indeed!

7. 寿星喝了矿泉水,扔了拐杖比健美。

From a champion of age to

A champion of callisthenics game

You need no stick but

Health Mineral Water

8. 抹上一点爱萝丽,呀,你的脸上就是一幅世界名画。

With some Iroli, aha, you are a Mona Lisa!

9. 与其道听途说,不如亲身体验。(a cosmetic ads)

Billi Slimming cream—

Using is believing.

10. 城乡路万条,路路有航天。

East, west, Hangtian is best.

The above-mentioned 4(7-10) advertisements are all translated into English by means of liberal translation. Some are translated with stress on key words(e.g. 7,8,9),some with enough attention to conveying the essence of the deep structure(e.g. 8,10),some by means of imitating the syntax of English idioms and classical allusions(e.g. 7,10). Translations are terse in diction, flexible and faithful to the original in form and in essence, making possible effort to take the original syntax into consideration.

Without the help of sound, light, image and picture, without the advantage of paralinguistic situation, written advertising can be translated with the emphasis only on written introduction which is thus longer in length, not so terse in diction and flexible in syntax as picture advertising. In translating written advertising, morphology, syntax and rhetorical devices should be taken into consideration and if possible, linguistic features of the original should be preserved. Now take the following as example:

GILLETTE Sensor

The only razor that senses and adjusts to the individual needs of your face.

Gillette Sensor: the shave personalized to every man. It starts with twin blades, individually and independently mounted on highly responsive springs. So they continuously sense and automatically adjust to the individual curves and unique needs of your face.

Innovation is everywhere. You can feel it in the textured ridges and the balance of the Sensor razor. You appreciate it in the easy loading system and the convenient shaving organizer.

Even rinsing is innovative. The new blades are 50% narrower than any others—allowing water to flow freely around and through them, for effortless cleaning and rinsing.

All these Sensor technologies combine to give our individual face a personalized—shave the closest, smoothest, safest, most comfortable.

The best shave a man can get

Gillette

吉列传感剃须刀

唯一能够感知并随您脸形调整的剃须刀。

吉列传感剃须刀:适于每一个男人特性的剃刀。它内含双层刀片,各自与高度灵敏弹簧相连。能够连续地感受并根据您的面部不同曲线和独特需要自动调整。

革新比比皆是。其精致的脊背、匀称的造型足以使你能体会至深。简单的装卸系统与方便的剃刮功能皆能任您享用。

创新还在于剃刀的清洗。其新型刀片的宽度仅为一般刀片的一半,可用水自动冲涤、毫不费力。

诸多传感技术的融合,给您富有个性的脸颊一把特制的剃刀——最贴切、最滑顺、最安全、最舒适。

男人所能享用的最佳剃刀!
吉列

Compared with picture advertising, this advertisement is not only longer in length but complicated in syntax. The above-mentioned features are taken into full consideration: repetition of the superlative degree of adjectives completely preserved in translation, the linguistic characteristics of the original are well expressed in translation, which is the key point of translation of advertising language.

Commonly-used terms for advertising are listed as follows:
a complete range of specifications　规格齐全
aesthetic appearance　式样美观
a great variety of models　款式多样
agreeable sweetness　甜而不腻
ample supply and prompt delivery　货源充足,供应及时
A plastic case is compartmentalized for safe storage.　塑盒分装,便于保存
aromatic character and agreeable taste　香味可口
aromatic flavor　香味浓郁
as effectively as a fairy does　功效神奇
attractive and durable　美观耐用
attractive appearance　造型美观
attractive designs　款式新颖
attractive fashion　式样新颖
available in various designs and specifications for your selection
　　　　备有各种款式的现货,任君选择
a wide selection of colors and designs　花色繁多
beautiful and charming　华丽臻美
beautiful in color　色泽艳丽
bright and translucent in appearance　外观美泽艳丽
bright in color　色泽鲜艳
bright luster　色泽光润
by scientific process　科学精致
can be repeatedly remoulded　能多次翻新
carefully-selected materials　用料精选
catalogs will be sent upon request　备有详细目录,惠索即寄
choice materials　选料考究
clear and distinctive　清晰突出
clear-cut texture　条纹清晰
colors are striking, yet not vulgar　色彩夺目,迥然不同
comfortable and easy to wear　穿着舒适轻便

comfortable feel　手感舒适
complete in specifications　规格齐全
complete range of articles　品种齐全
complete range of specifications　规格齐全
convenient to cook　烹制简便
cool in summer and warm in winter　冬暖夏凉
courteous service　服务周到
crease-resistance　防皱
Customers from various countries and regions are welcome to establish and develop business contacts.　欢迎与世界各地客商进一步加强合作,建立和发展贸易关系。
delicacies loved by all　大众所喜爱品尝之佳品
delicious in taste　口味鲜美
dependable performance　性能可靠
distinctive for its traditional properties　具有传统风味特色
diversified in packaging　包装多样
diversified latest designs　款世新颖众多
diversified practices and efficient services　方式灵活,方便客商
drip-dry　快干
durable in use　经久耐用
durable-modelling　定型耐久
durable service　经久耐用
easy and simple to handle　操作简便
easy contacts and flexible trading methods　业务联系方便,贸易做法灵活
easy to lubricate　易于润滑
easy to repair　维修简易
easy to use　使用方便
economy and durability　经济耐用
elegant and graceful　典雅大方
elegant and sturdy package　包装美观牢固
elegant appearance　美观大方
elegant in smell　香气高雅
elegant in style　式样雅致
elegant (in) shape　外型大方
excellent in cushion effect　缓冲性能好
excellent (in) quality　品质优良
exquisite craftsmanship　技艺精湛
exquisite traditional embroidery　传统刺绣工艺
exquisite in workmanship　做工讲究
extremely efficient in preserving heat　耐热性强

183

fashionable and attractive packages　包装新颖美观
fashionable patterns　花式入时
fashionable (in) style　款式新颖
fashionable styles, rich varieties　花色新颖,品种多样
fast color　永不褪色
fine craftsmanship　技艺精湛
fine quality　质地优良
fine (in) workmanship　做工精细
firm in structure　结构坚固
fragrant aroma　香气馥郁
fragrant (in) flavor　香味浓郁
general wholesale　百货批发
good companions for children as well as adults　老少良友
good heat preservation　保温性强
good taste　味道纯正
great varieties　种类繁多
handsome appearance　造型美观
harmonious colors　颜色调和
highly polished　光洁度高
high quality materials　选料讲究
high resilience　富有弹性
high safety　保险性强
high standard in quality and hygiene　质量高,又卫生
ideal gift for occasions　节日送礼之佳品
in many styles　式样众多
in plain, fancy color　色彩奇异大方
inquiries and orders are warmly welcome　竭诚欢迎客户惠购
inquiries are cordially welcome　欢迎洽购
inquiries are welcome　欢迎洽询订购
intense coverage　覆盖率高
jade white　洁白如玉
latest technology　最新工艺
limpid in sight　色泽清澈
long and rich experience　历史悠久,经验丰富
long performance life　使用寿命长久
lovely luster　色泽鲜艳可爱
low noise level, low power consumption　低噪音,耗电省
lustrous, soft and anti-slippery　色泽光洁,柔软防滑
lustrous surface　表面光泽

luxuriant (in) design　设计华丽
luxurious in design　设计华丽富贵
matching in color　色彩协调
meticulous dyeing processes　染制精良
mild and mellow　口感和醇
moderate cost　价格适中
moderate price　价格公道
modern and elegant in fashion　式样新颖大方
modern design　设计新颖
modern techniques　技术先进
neither too hard, nor too soft　软硬适中
new varieties are introduced one after another　新品迭出
non-ironing　免烫
novel (in) design　款式新颖
numerous in variety　品种多样
orders are welcome　欢迎惠订
outstanding features　优点出众
packing of nominated brand　定牌包装
perfect in workmanship　制作精巧
pleasant after taste　回味隽厚
pleasant to the palate　清香爽口
please order now　欲购从速
popular both at home and abroad　驰名中外
possessing Chinese flavor　具有中国风味
prestige first　声誉至上
pretty and colorful　瑰丽多彩
professional design　专业设计
promoting health and curing diseases　保健治病
prompt delivery　即时交货
punctual timing　走时准确
pure and mild flavor　香味纯和
pure white and translucent　洁白透明
pure whiteness　洁白纯正
quality and quantity assured　保质保量
quality first, customers first　质量第一,用户第一
rapid heat dissipation　散热迅速
reasonable price　价格公道
reliable performance　性能可靠
rich and magnificent　雍容华丽

rich experience and strict scientific management　丰富的生产经验及严格的科学管理
rich in poetic and pictorial splendor　富有浓厚诗情画意
round-the-clock business (service)　昼夜营业
selected materials　用料考究
selling well all over the world　畅销全球
shrink-proof　不缩水
sincerely wish to strengthen business relations with counterparts both at home and abroad　竭诚欢迎国内外同行加强业务联系
skillful manufacture　制作精巧
smooth run　运转平稳
soft and full　柔软丰满
sophisticated technologies　工艺精良
Stocks are always available in large quantities for prompt delivery.　备有现货，交货及时。
strict quality control　严格的质量管理
strong packing　包装牢固
strong resistance to heat and hard wearing　抗热耐磨
structural durabilities　经久耐磨
sturdy construction　结构坚固
sufficient supplies　货源充足
suitable for men, women and children　男女老少皆宜
superior materials　选料精良
superior performance　性能优越
superior (in) quality　质地优良
The branch is ready to provide excellent service to customers.　本公司乐意提供优质服务。
timely delivery guaranteed　交货及时
to adopt advanced technology　采用先进技术和工艺
to assure years of trouble-free service　多年使用，不出故障
to attain and surpass advanced world level　赶超世界先进水平
to be awarded a silver medal　荣获银质奖
to clear out of annoyance and quench thirst　除烦止渴
to be distinguished for high quality　以质量上乘著称
to be distributed all over the world　行销世界
to be highly praised and appreciated by consuming public　深爱国内外消费者的称赞与青睐
to be specially designed for women　专为妇女所设计
to catch up with and surpass advanced world level　赶超世界先进水平
to enjoy high reputation at home and abroad　誉满全球
to enjoy high reputation in the world market　在国际上享有声誉
to ensure smooth transmission　传送灵活
to have a long historical standing　历史悠久

to have a long history in production and marketing　产销历史悠久
to have a long history, rich experience and reliable reputation
　　历史悠久,经验丰富,信誉可靠
to have a unique national style　具有独特的民族风格
to have both the quality of tenacity and hardness　韧硬性能好
to help digest greasy food　助消化,除油腻
to improve management and administration　改善经营管理
to insure a like-new appearance indefinitely　外型永保如新
to invigorate health effectively　促进体质
to keep you fit all the time　保君健康
to make one feel at ease and energetic　安心益气
to offer you the best convenience　方便诸君
to produce an effect against clear vision, refreshment, and digestion helping
　　　　　　　　　　　　清火祛热,怡神醒脑,帮助消化
to promote a diversified economy　发展多种经济
to provide clients with excellent service　向客户提供优质服务
to rank first among similar products　领先于同类产品
to reduce body weight and prolong life　轻身延寿
to satisfy the demands of consumers　满足消费者需要
to win a high reputation and is widely trusted at home and abroad
　　　　　　　　深受国内外用户的信赖与称赞
to win high admiration　享有声誉
to win warm praises from customers　深受顾客欢迎
unequal in performance　性能无与伦比
up-to-date styling　款式新颖
utmost in convenience　使用方便
various styles　款式齐全
vivid and great in style　款式活泼大方
warm and windproof　保暖防风
waterproof, shock-resistant and anti-magnetic　防水,防震,防磁
We accept orders according to customers' requirements as well as processing on giving materials and compensation trade.　欢迎按需订货,来料加工和补偿贸易。
well-known for its fine quality　以优质著称
Wholesale and retail are welcome.　欢迎批发零售。
wide varieties　品种多样
with most up-to-date equipments and techniques　拥有最新设备及工艺水平
with traditional methods　沿用传统的生产方式

Translation Exercises

Ⅰ. *Translate the following advertisement for house renting into Chinese*

Southgate Area

Brand new luxury 1 and 2 bedroom apts. At Heatherdowns and Green Streets. Convenient to Southgate Shopping Center. Close to bus route 22. Rentals from ﹩250 include heat, air, shag carpet, appliances, dishwashers. Patio, laundry room, pool. 1 year lease. Security deposit.

One pre-school-aged child considered in 2 bedroom. Absolutely no pets.

Model open weekdays 1-6. Sat., Sun. 1-5 or by appointment. 241-7721. Managed by Sands Corporation. An equal housing opportunity.

Ⅱ. *Translate the following advertisement for food into English with enough attention to the linguistic features of advertising.*

北京烤鸭

北京烤鸭是一种风味独特的中国传统名菜,已有三百多年历史。最早是从金陵(南京)王府膳房流传出来的。

北京烤鸭以北京填鸭为原料,经特殊加工而成。烤鸭色枣红、鲜艳、油亮、肉嫩、味美适口,别有其香中,久吃不腻,营养丰富。

北京烤鸭店第一分店

地址:北京前门大街 24 号

5.2　Translation of Journalistic Texts

5.2.1　Definition

News is "the reporting of anything timely which has importance, use or interest to a considerable number of persons in a publication audience." As is shown in the following sentence: "If a dog bites a man, it is not news; if a man bites a dog, it's big news.", news must be a report that is timely, important, prominent, unusual, interesting, and close to the public.

Journalistic style may be defined as follows: "The style of writing characteristic of material in newspapers and magazines, consisting of direct presentation of facts or occurrences with little attempt at analysis or interpretation."

5.2.2　Classification

Journalistic writing can be classified according to means of dissemination as follows: newspaper coverage; magazine coverage; radio news; TV news; news agency dispatches.

According to the nature of news, it can be classified into hard news which is information-oriented and soft news which is entertainment-oriented. A detailed classification can be done according to news style:

1. News reporting.
2. Features.
   (1) News stories
   (2) Interviews

(3) Personal Profiles

3. Opinion Writing

(1) Editorials

(2) Columns

(3) Reviews

5.2.3 Stylistic Features

5.2.3.1 Lexical Features of Journalistic English

1. Midget words are frequently used.

Bid(attempt), ban(forbid), probe(investigation), pact(treaty)

2. Nonce words (coinages).

(1) Affixation

Anti-corruption: fight against corruption

Disinformation: distortion of information

Moggigate: scandal concerning Juventus' manager Moggi

Oilwise: in the aspect of oil

(2) Compounding & Blending

kingmaker: the assistants for the presidential candidate

hardliner: those adopting uncompromising attitude

Reagonomics: Reagon + economics

Ameritocracy: American + aristocracy

(3) Acronym

SIM: Subscriber Identity Module

ABM: Anti-Ballistic Missile

HIV: Human Immunodeficiency Virus

NATO: North Atlantic Treaty Organization

(4) Clipping

flu: influenza; rep: representative; demo: demonstration

3. Borrowed terms.

(1) From other fields

Mafia: any clique, esp. underground

Catalyst: stimulus

Backlash: counterforce

Showdown: the concluding confrontation

(2) Loan words from other languages

coup d'etat: military rebellion

Apartheid: racial segregation

Translate the following sentences with your attention to the underlined part.

1. At the state level, deciding who is going to clean up (the waste) and who's going to pay (for the pollution) often becomes a jurisdictional black hole of *fingerpointing* and *buckpassing*.

2. Manned lunar exploration for purely scientific reasons probably will not resume for many years. And when it does, it most likely will use a more low-keyed, cost-effective approach than the use-"em-up-throw-"em-away Apollo program.

3. Opponents of the bill said they feared it would lead to government repression and fuel the civil war that has plagued the country for the past decades.

4. US president Bill Clinton acted tough by expelling a persona non grata. Russians huffily brand the whole spy case a "propaganda counteroffensive".

5. No matter what his personal eccentricities, the films starring this Kungfu master have made a lucrative hit in Hong Kong and Taiwan, and now its rock- "n"-rolling its way to new audience round the mainland.

6. Bonn has also told Damascus it did not intend to impound the tanks and expressed a desire to settle the issue cordially.

5.2.3.2 Syntactic features of Journalistic English

The following part is an abridged and adapted excerpt from Newsweek (Sept. 10, 2007 issue):

Bridging the Gap
After a stormy break with the U.S.,
European leaders are forging a new Atlantic alliance.

Forty-four years ago, John F. Kennedy traveled to then divided Berlin and gave a round of historic speeches. "Americans may be far away," he said, "but ... this is where we want to be today. When I leave tonight, I leave—and the United States stays."

Over the decades, America floated in and out of Europe's graces. Probably Washington's darkest hour in Europe since Vietnam was the 2003 invasion of Iraq and its grim aftermath. Iraq split the continent in two—into "old" and "new" Europe. In Britain, Spain, Italy and elsewhere, governments fell or were wounded by their association with George W. Bush.

Now the tables have turned again. European governments are rebuilding transatlantic bridges. Remarkably, the continent's political elites are embracing pro-Americanism when people on the street are as anti-American as they've been since Coalition forces rolled across Iraq. By going against the public grain at obvious political risk, Europe's leaders are demonstrating just how determined they are to bury anti-Americanism. French President Nicolas Sarkozy told a meeting of his ambassadors in Paris, "I am among those who believe that the friendship between the United States and France is as important today as it has been over the course of the past two centuries."

Secretary of State Condoleezza Rice has traveled extensively in and around Europe—about 128 000 kilometers in 2007—to get European leaders back onside. "Secretary Rice's intense travel schedule and the strategic outreach to Europe that it represents have had an obvious impact," Assistant Secretary of State Daniel Fried told NEWSWEEK. "She has made clear that we—the core democratic nations of the world—are better off tackling key issues together than on our own. And she has made clear that multilateral approaches—the U. N. where possible, NATO, and the U. S. with the EU—are options of choice, not last resort."

Sarkozy and German Chancellor Angela Merkel are on the leading edge of the New Atlanticism. The two of them behave as if Chancellor Gerhard Schroder and President Jacques Chirac belonged to another era, with Sarkozy attempting to revive an alliance that dates back to the American War of Independence and Merkel, as the leader of the world's largest exporter, championing what her officials call "a larger common market" with the United States.

America could hardly have asked for better advocates than Merkel and Sarkozy, especially since Bush's chief European ally, Tony Blair, was being nudged into retirement because of his closeness to the president and to U. S. Iraq policy. Merkel, an East German physicist who grew up under Soviet domination and became politically active after the fall of the Berlin wall in 1989, looks as much west as she does east. When she speaks of "the power of freedom," she can sound positively Kennedyesque. As for Sarkozy, a sometimes fawning French press compares him and his young, attractive family to the Kennedys. He has never disguised his admiration for America.

Britain, having been shoulder to shoulder with America for so long, is now something of an exception. Brown is trying so hard not to be Blair that he's sending out mixed signals to Washington—the Menwith Hill decision on the one hand, the suggestion that he's slowly disengaging from Iraq on the other. To reinforce his Britishness, he went to the English seaside. No one would accuse Brown of anti-Americanism. But it says something when he is out-Americanized by his German and French counterparts: the Continental drift toward America is very real.

From the passage above, the major syntactic features of journalism can be exemplified as follows:

1. Expanded Simple Sentence.

Simple sentence is expanded into long and complicated sentences, by supplementing attributes, adverbials and appositives.

"The two of them behave as if Chancellor Gerhard Schroder and President Jacques Chirac belonged to another era, with Sarkozy attempting to revive an alliance that dates back to the American War of Independence and Merkel, as the leader of the world's largest exporter, championing what her officials call 'a larger common market' with the United States."

In the paragraph above, the sentence frame is "The two of them behave"; there are two major adverbials: one is led by "as if"; the other is "with Sarkozy and Merkel" in essence. "Sarkozy" is further explained by supplying an adverbial led by "attempting to"; and "Merkel" further illustrated by supplying an adverbial led by "championing". Within the adverbial, there are one that-clause and a prepositional phrase led by "as", both serving as a postmodifier.

2. Direct and indirect speech are frequently used.

"Secretary Rice's intense travel schedule and the strategic outreach to Europe that it represents have had an obvious impact," Assistant Secretary of State Daniel Fried told

NEWSWEEK.

3. Parenthetical elements are frequently used.

"She has made clear that we—*the core democratic nations of the world*—are better off tackling key issues together than on our own. And she has made clear that multilateral approaches—*the U. N. where possible*, *NATO*, *and the U. S. with the EU*—are options of choice, not last resort."

4. The simple present tense is always used to replace the past tense to achieve freshness, a sense of reality and immediacy.

Merkel, an East German physicist who grew up under Soviet domination and became politically active after the fall of the Berlin wall in 1989, looks as much west as she does east. When she *speaks* of "the power of freedom," she can sound positively Kennedyesque.

5.2.4 Major Components

The major components of journalistic English are headline, lead, and body, which will be discussed as follows:

Headline

Headline is the eye-catching title of the passage. From the perspective of journalism, the function of Headlines can be classified as follows by George Mott:

1. Advertising the story.
2. Summarizing the story.
3. Beautifying the newspaper page.

Three ways of arrangement can be seen in headlines:

1. Flush-left head(垂直式)

How Apple's iPhone

Ate The New iPods?

2. Indented head/dropped-line.(缩进式)

Sleet Storm

    Breaks State

        Power Lines

3. Centered head.(中心式)

        Rice vows support for

        Russian rights activists

Ellipsis

There will be phrases as well as complete sentences in headlines to save space and make it eye-catching:

China's Secret Growth Engine

Skinny and the City

Searching For The Best Engine

Golden weeks or silver days?

Three types of words are frequently omitted:
1. Be.
2. Articles.
3. Conjunction. (and)

Nokia (is) to acquire digital mapping firm Navteq

Three Gorges Dam (is) to create eco-refugees

Capello (is) eager to start (the) "dream" job

Milicic (is) trying to jump-start career in Memphis

7-footer picked before Wade, (and) Anthony in 2003 draft

Rhetorical devices

In headline writing various rhetorical devices can be used such as simile/metaphor, pun and personification.

Rhyme and allusions may also be used to attract the reader's attention. Identify the rhetorical devices employed in the following examples:

1. Middle East: A Cradle of Terror.
2. Genes Get Lonely Too.
3. Narcissists in Neverland.
4. Small City, Big Impact.
5. The Old Man and the Economic Sea.
6. New Stalin, Old Stalin, Same Stalin.
7. Make Your Bed, Save Your Brain.
8. Soccer Kicks off with Violence.

Lead

Lead is the first paragraph or leading paragraphs of a passage summarizing the basic ideas from the following aspects: Who, What, When, Where, Why/How. Let's look at the following example:

TRIMDON, England-Prime Minister Tony Blair said Thursday that he will step down as prime minister on June 27, after a decade in office in which he brokered peace in Northern Ireland and followed the United States to war in Afghanistan and Iraq.

After a careful analysis of the above-mentioned lead, the six elements abbreviated as "5W" and "1H" can be clarified as follows:

Who—Tony Blair

What—step down as prime minister on June 27

When—Thursday

Where—TRIMDON, England

Why/How—he brokered peace in Northern Ireland and followed the United States to war in Afghanistan and Iraq

In order to attract the reader's attention, the format of the lead varies according to the content and the effect the reporter wants to create. There are different versions of subclassification. Zhang Jian(张健) makes a detailed classification of lead into 12 major types, among which the following three types are more often adopted than others:

1. Summary lead.

Summary lead contains a succinct account of the major elements in a news report, including the 5W and 1H, by which the reader may grasp the essential information. For example:

BEIJING—Delegates to a pivotal Communist Party congress whittled down a list of candidates for senior committee assignments on Saturday, a prelude to selecting China's new leadership.

2. Descriptive lead.

Descriptive lead is another major type of lead which introduces some interesting details or concrete experiences to enhance the atmosphere and provides a sense of involvement. Quotations can often be found to substantiate the validity of the report.

Tui Stark is searching for a vacation paradise and can't find it. Googling "snorkeling beaches" turns up listings for scuba diving, real-estate firms. So Stark, turns to Quintura, one of many upstart search engines, which allows her to focus the results on snorkeling. "The **Google** results just had too much stuff I wasn't looking for," she says. "I wanted to zoom in on the best snorkeling beaches." And within seconds, Quintura delivers.

3. Delayed lead.

Delayed lead is also termed as multi-paragraph lead, in which the essential information is placed in the latter paragraphs rather than the leading ones. Those seemingly irrelevant details in the leading paragraphs create a climatic effect with a strong sense of suspense. Suspense stimulates the reader to further explore what the news is really about.

Queens are meant to be looked at, not touched. Early in the new film *Elizabeth: The Golden Age*, England's Elizabeth I, is bored by a bad date. Watching, at close range, is a flock of curious courtiers; her suitor, a stuttering continental royal, is clearly terrified by the mob. Ever gracious, the queen offers some advice. Her secret for life in the public eye, she tells her companion, is to pretend she lives behind "a pane of glass."

Elizabeth is worth watching in the midst of this election season even if it offers us little escape. The Virgin Queen's world, after all, is in many ways our own. A nation is in peril. Bitterly divided at home, it vacillates between two warring dynasties. Threatened by dark forces abroad, it worries that a decisive moment is coming when one great empire will rise and another will fall.

And a female leader is struggling to maintain her femininity while proving she can rule as well as any man. Watching it, I couldn't help thinking of **Hillary Clinton**, quite possibly the next president of the United States, a woman who often seems to live behind her own plate of glass.

Body

Body refers to paragraphs after the Lead containing less important detailed information, which may be exhibited in the following styles:

Inverted Pyramid Style

In the inverted pyramid style, the information of the news report is arranged in descending sequence of importance.

Chinese Leader Gives President a Mixed Message

BEIJING, Nov. 20—In a day of polite but tense encounters, President Hu Jintao of China told President Bush on Sunday that he was willing to move more quickly to ease economic differences with the United States.

Although American officials described the leaders as more comfortable with each other on Sunday than in any previous encounter, Mr. Hu made clear, by his words and his government's actions, that he had no intention of giving in to American pressure.

Meeting with reporters in the evening, Mr. Bush said his talks had amounted to a "good, frank discussion," but he seemed unsatisfied. He chose his words about Mr. Hu carefully and repeated that the relationship with China was "complex," though later he added that it is "good, vibrant, strong."

On economic issues that are of major concern to American businesses—letting market forces set the value of the undervalued Chinese currency and protecting intellectual property from rampant piracy in China—Mr. Bush made marginal progress. He secured a public statement from Mr. Hu that he would "unswervingly press ahead" to ease a $200 billion annual trade surplus that wildly outstrips anything Mr. Bush's father faced with Japan in the late 1980's.

After a day of talks that began with a 90-minute meeting inside the Great Hall of the People, Mr. Bush emerged with little progress to report beyond a $4 billion deal for China to buy 70 Boeing aircraft.

On Sunday, Mr. Hu and Prime Minister Wen Jiabao detailed for Mr. Bush steps they were taking to curb the theft of movies, software and similar goods, emphasizing that they believed that those moves were necessary to develop the Chinese economy.

Mr. Bush said that he and Mr. Hu had also discussed strategies for handling the potential outbreak of avian flu and the long-running talks on nuclear disarmament for North Korea.

The first paragraph is a summary lead, providing basic facts about the news. While in the latter two paragraphs, the general reaction of the two presidents are stated. In the fourth and fifth paragraph, the information focuses on the economic issues. The last two paragraphs are mainly concerned with domestic and international issues which are of interest to both China and U.S. The information is arranged in the order of importance, thus makes the above-mentioned passage a typical example of a body written in inverted pyramid style. Inverted pyramid style is most often adopted by news writer, for it will be more convenient for editors to make abridgement and necessary deletion.

Pyramid Style

Pyramid style, sometimes called chronological style, arrange the news in sequence of time in order to create a sense of suspense. The above-mentioned passage entitled "Bridging the Gap" is a typical example, with time adverbial in the beginning of the first three paragraphs as marks: "Forty-four years ago", "Over the decades" and "Now".

Hourglass Style

Hourglass style is also called mixed forms of inverted pyramid and pyramid styles. It is composed of a summary lead, detailed information arranged in chronological order, and a consequential ending as a conclusion. The ending and the lead are equally important and attractive.

5.2.5 Translation Strategies

For journalistic coinages, word formation analysis with context as the frame of reference will be beneficial to the proper choice of words. Take the passage entitled "Bridging the Gap" as an example:

Remarkably, the continent's political elites are embracing *pro-Americanism* when people on the street are as *anti-American* as they've been since Coalition forces rolled across Iraq.

值得一提的是，欧洲大陆的政治领袖们都采取亲美政策，而参与游行的民众们的反美情绪，在联合国军横扫伊拉克之后却丝毫未减。

When she speaks of "the power of freedom," she can sound positively *Kennedyesque*.

当她说起"自由的力量"的时候，听上去和当年肯尼迪总统如出一辙。

To reinforce his *Britishness*, he went to the English seaside.

为了证明自己捍卫英国利益的决心，他去了英国的海滩。

But it says something when he is *out-Americanized* by his German and French counterparts: the Continental drift toward America is very real.

德国总理和法国总统比他和美国的关系还要亲近，这说明，欧洲大陆如今渐渐地倒向美国一边。

On the syntactic level, adjustment in sentence structure is inevitable, mainly exhibited in the following two aspects: 1) the adjustment of adverbials and attributes; 2) splitting and providing cohesive devices:

The two of them behave as if Chancellor Gerhard Schroder and President Jacques Chirac belonged to another era, with Sarkozy attempting to revive an alliance that dates back to the American War of Independence and Merkel, as the leader of the world's largest exporter, championing what her officials call "a larger common market" with the United States.

萨克奇和默克尔的举动使得他们和其前任施罗德和希拉克看上去根本生活在两个世纪，萨克奇试图恢复美法两国自从美国独立战争就建立起的友谊，而默克尔，作为世界第一出口大国的领导人，也支持和美国一起实施德国官员所谓的"更大规模的共同市场。"

Merkel, an East German physicist who grew up under Soviet domination and became politically active after the fall of the Berlin wall in 1989, looks as much west as she does east.

默克尔，原本是东德的一名物理学家，成长于苏联统治之下，在1989年柏林墙被推倒后在政治上崭露头角,她兼有西方和东方的思想特征。

Concerning the use of rhetoric devices, preservation or substitution are always preferable, which is especially the case in the translation of headlines:

Genes Get Lonely Too

基因也孤独

Small City, Big Impact

城市虽小,影响空前

New Stalin, Old Stalin, Same Stalin

斯大林的旧事新闻

Make Your Bed, Save Your Brain

每日铺床,大脑无恙

Soccer Kicks off with Violence

足球开踢,拳打脚踢

An Eye High in the Sky (satellite)

九重天外千里眼

Maker and Breaker of Peace in the Middle East. (Palestinian Liberation Army)

中东和平,成也巴解,毁也巴解。

The Great White Wait

大雪铺天盖地,民航频频告急。

Cannes: Orgy of Glitz?

群星璀璨戛纳夜,盛事狂欢电影节

Translation Exercises

Translate the following passage into Chinese.

Northern Europe among most competitive economies

Northern Europe and key east Asian countries and regions are the most competitive economies in the world, retaining their positions in the top 10 of a survey released Wednesday by the World Economic Forum.

For the third straight year, Finland has the most competitive economy, followed by the United States, according to a survey of almost 11,000 business leaders in the "Global Competitiveness Report." The poll was conducted for a 26th consecutive year.

Rounding out the top 10 in the survey—expanded this year to include 117 countries and regions—were Sweden, Denmark, Taiwan, Singapore, Iceland, Switzerland, Norway.

The success of the Nordics is based on their "very healthy macroeconomic environments and public institutions that are highly transparent and efficient," said Augusto Lopez-Claros, chief economist and director of the Geneva-based institute's global competitiveness program.

Japan slipped to No. 12 from No. 9 last year as a result of poor management of its public finances, but reforms proposed by Prime Minister Junichiro Koizumi to privatize the sprawling postal service could help turn things around, the study said.

China dropped for the second straight year to No. 49 from No. 44 in 2003, as the survey said it continues "to suffer from institutional weaknesses which, unless addressed, are likely to slow down their ascension to the top tier of the most competitive economies in the world." India rose three places to come in just behind at No. 50.

The aim of the survey, the World Economic Forum says, is to examine the range of factors that can affect an economy's business environment and development—including levels of judicial independence, protection of property rights, government favoritism and corruption.

Lopez-Claros said the Nordic nations were disproving the common belief that high taxes hinder competitiveness.

Finland, home of mobile phone giant Nokia Corp., topped the study because of its swiftness in adapting to new technology and the quality of its public institutions, the report said.

The United States ranked second because it "demonstrates overall technological supremacy, with a very powerful culture of innovation," the World Economic Forum said. But it suggested the United States might have been kept from the top spot because of its low scores for contractual law and macroeconomic management.

5.3 Translation of English for Tourism

5.3.1 Definition

According to Cambridge International Dictionary of English, tourism is "the business of providing services such as transport, places to stay or entertainment, for people who are on holiday." Tourism texts include the following major types: tourist guidebook, introduction to scenic spots, publicity brochures, tour guide's interpretation and tourist advertisement. It may cover a large range of topics, concerning politics, economy, culture, history, geography, religion, etc.

5.3.2 Stylistic Features

5.3.2.1 Lexical Features

1. Informative and vocative language.

Text in tourism is function-oriented in nature, which dwells on the appealing effect to the reader. In other words, the major purpose is to attract the tourists' attention, and persuade them to actually make the tour. Therefore, the language has to be informative and vocative at the same time.

In order to achieve the informative effect, plain language is adopted in tourism to make it readily accessible to the largest number of potential tourists. The words are usually common language in terms of levels of formality, as is shown in the following example:

The canyons of the American Southwest are a true national treasure. Bryce Canyon bristles with whimsical red spires; hanging gardens cascade down the time-sculpted walls of Zion; and the Grand Canyon stands as a majestic tribute to the power of nature. Hike into canyons, raft the Colorado River, and discover the geological and natural wonders of these unique national parks.

The vocative effect is realized by the use of commenta... rms, to make the place enticing in the readers' eye.

Within the mountains of Peru lies a wealth of Spanish colonial cathedrals, majestic Inca temples, and breathtaking Andean vistas. Discover the magnificent ancient capital of Cusco, hike to ruins in the Urubamba Valley, examine pre-Columbian treasures at the renowned Larco Herrera Museum, and encounter incomparable Machu Picchu.

2. Frequent use of proper nouns and specialized terminology.

Proper nouns, such as names for places and persons frequently appear. Specialized terminologies are no rare occurrence, for example:

Namibia's wild landscapes have no parallel. The rippled *sand dunes of Sossusvlei* soar into the sky, turning from crimson to gold in the shifting light. *Oryx* and *zebra* congregate on lunar-like *salt pans*, and the austere beauty of the *Kaokoveld* is accented by the colorful traditions of its *Himba* nomads. Discover incredible wildlife on game drives, meet local tribespeople, and explore mystical *deserts*.

The italicized words can be classified into four categories: "Namibia", "Sossusvlei" and "Kaokoveld" are names for places; "Himba" is a name for a tribe. All of them are proper nouns. "Sand dunes", "salt pans" and "deserts" are geographical terms; "oryx" and "zebra" are names for animals. They belong to specialized terminologies.

3. Words rich in cultural connotation.

黄山古名黟山,唐代时,传说古代轩辕黄帝曾在这里修真炼丹,得道升天,于是在天宝六年(公元747年),由唐玄宗亲自下令,改名为黄山。

In the above-mentioned example, "轩辕黄帝", "天宝六年", "唐玄宗" are closely connected with Chinese history; while "修真炼丹" and "得道升天" are superstitious practice of ancient emperors. All those words are culture-specific.

5.3.2.2 Syntactic Features

1. Simple present tense.

Simple present tense is often used to present a matter-of-fact description of the scenery.

Great Smoky Mountains National Park is one of the largest protected land areas east of the Rocky Mountains. With over 500 000 acres of forest, the Smoky Mountains contain an enormous variety of plants and animals. In terms of biological diversity, a walk from mountain base to peak is often compared to the 2 000 mile hike on the Appalachian Trail from Georgia to Maine.

2. Mixed use of perspectives.

In most cases, tourism text adopts third person perspective to describe the natural scenery objectively. But in order to increase the sense of involvement, second person perspective is also employed.

Canyonlands National Park, a unique destination full of spires, buttes, arches, rivers and most spectacular of all, vast canyons. This park is home to The Needles, Maze and Island of the Sky districts. Each area offers its own unique scenery and vastness that provide feelings of solitude. Canyonlands is sliced into these three areas by the Green and Colorado rivers. Beautiful vistas and overlooks have kept park visitors in awe for many years. Canyonlands is still an untrammeled and quiet mass of canyons that often appeal to the more rugged of hikers, 4 wheel drivers and mountain bikers.

If you plan to visit Canyonlands National Park, summers are hot and winters cool, if not sometimes very cold. Any time of year it is best to travel with layers and as water is not available in most parts of the park, plan ahead by picking up water in the nearby towns such as Moab.

If you have time, don't forget to visit the nearby park, Arches National Park. These two parks compliment each other beautifully with two very different types of scenery. If a desert and canyon area is something you have not yet seen, Canyonlands National Park is a must see!

5.3.2.3 Rhetorical Features

In English tourism text, the description is often objective; however, in Chinese tourism text, parallel structure and four-character structure may be used in order to strike the reader's ear as well as his eye.

这里三千座奇峰拔地而起,形态各异,有的似玉柱神鞭,立地顶天;有的像铜墙铁壁,巍然屹立;有的如晃板垒卵,摇摇欲坠;有的若盆景古董,玲珑剔透——神奇而又真实,迷离而又实在,不是艺术创造胜似艺术创造,令人叹为观止。

Those phrases with "似", "像", "如" and "若" are four-character structure in parallel, which makes the scenery all the more intriguing.

5.3.3 Translation Strategies

While the tourism text in English and in Chinese share the common features mentioned above, difference also exists.

In diction, English tourism text is plain and straightforward, Chinese tourism text is refined and elaborated. Four-character structures are often used. In addition, Chinese tourism text may resort to allusions and quotations from poems to enhance the atmosphere.

黄山巍峨挺拔,雄奇瑰丽。古人评为"具有泰岱之雄伟、华山之险峻、衡岳之烟云、匡庐之飞瀑、雁荡之巧石、峨嵋之清秀","集天下奇景于一体"。明代大旅行家徐霞客二游黄山,叹曰:"薄海内外无如徽之黄山,登黄山天下无山,观止矣。"黄山有如天造的画境,她没有富丽堂皇的庙宇,也没有宏伟壮观的禅院宫观,全凭自己毫不雕饰的天姿国色。

1. Amplification.

In translation process, proper amplification is needed for rhetorical effect, to make it more enticing to the tourists.

One of the most popular destinations is the Grand Canyon. Its dramatic scenery enthralls even the most jaded visitors and leaves all who witness it somehow changed.

Its dimensions are mind-blowing. The Grand Canyon is a mile deep and averages 10 miles wide. Snaking along its floor are 277 miles of the Colorado River, which has carved the canyon over the past six million years.

大峡谷国家公园是最受欢迎的景点之一。景色之壮观让人乐此不疲,游客至此有震慑心神之感。

巍峨的群山让人兴奋不已。大峡谷深达一英里,平均宽度为10英里。6百万年间,长达 277 英里的科罗拉多河蜿蜒其间,将峡谷一分为二。

In the translation above,"乐此不疲","震慑心神","兴奋不已","蜿蜒其间","一分为二" are four-character structures, which enhances the vividness in the Chinese version.

Graced with glacial mountains, dramatic fjords, cascading waterfalls, and sky-blue lakes, New Zealand is a paradise for those who love the outdoors. Explore lush rain forests, cruise the stunning Milford Sound, float on a subterranean river, search for whales and other sea mammals, and kayak in secluded bays on New Zealand's exotic South Island.

晶莹的冰山,壮美的海湾,飞泻而下的瀑布,碧蓝澄澈的湖水,诸多胜景让新西兰成为了户外旅行者的天堂。在这片土地上,你可以探寻郁郁葱葱的雨林,徜徉于美不胜收的米尔福德峡湾,在地下河上漂流,与鲸鱼及众多海洋生物为伴,乘坐皮艇在极具异域风情的南岛享受远离尘嚣的日子。

2. Omission.

Omission is also needed for the purpose of accessibility. In order to make the passage more comprehensible, specialized terminologies and repetitious expressions may be omitted. For example:

满树金花,芳香四溢的金桂;花白如雪,香气扑鼻的银桂;红里透黄,花朵味浓的紫砂桂;花色似银,季季有花的四季桂,竞相开放,争妍媲美,进入桂林公园,阵阵桂香扑鼻而来。

The Park of Sweet Osmanthus is noted for its profusion of Osmanthus trees. Flowers from these trees in different colors are in full bloom which pervade the whole garden with the fragrance of their blossom.

In this passage, the writer uses four specialized terminology, namely, "金桂", "银桂", "紫砂桂" and "四季桂". Even if translators may find the corresponding English version, the terms in botany will be incomprehensible to a tourist. For the sake of clarity, the four proper nouns are summarized as "Profusion of Osmanthus trees". The premodifiers can be classified into two major categories:"满树金花","花白如雪","红里透黄","花色似银" are used to describe the colour;"芳香四溢","香气扑鼻","花朵味浓" are used to describe the fragrance. In the given version, the essential information concerning color and fragrance is highlighted.

3. Annotation.

Annotation technique is frequently used to clarify those culture-specific expressions, by providing detailed explanation of the origin.

路左有一巨石,石上原有苏东坡手书"云外流苏"四个大字。

To the left is another rock formerly engraved with four big Chinese characters, Yun Wai Liu Chun, meaning "Beyond clouds flows spring", written by Su Dongpo (1037-1101), the most versatile poet of the Northern Song Dynasty (960-1127).

4. Analogy.

Analogy, as a technique, conveys the original meaning by finding a rough equivalent in the source language as a comparison.

银川是宁夏回族自治区的首府,位于自治区中心,从明清以来,她就是伊斯兰教在西北部的居住地和传播中心。

Honoured as a smaller Mecca, Yingchuan, the capital of Ninxia Hui Autonomous Region, is located in the centre of the Autonomous Region. Since the Ming and Qing dynasties, Yingchuan has been a place for Moslems to live and a center for Islamic education in the Northwest.

In this example, Yingchuan is compared to Mecca, which is comparable in religious significance as "the spiritual center of Islam".

Exercises

Yellowstone National Park contains some of the strangest and most interesting geological features found anywhere in the world. This vast caldera or volcanic basin is the remnant of a giant volcano that blew its top many millennia ago. The area still sits atop a hot spot in the earth's crust and provides us with a unique opportunity to view a fascinating assortment of highly active geothermal phenomena. It is one of the few places on our planet where hot water and steam come bubbling, fizzing, gurgling, hissing and even exploding out of the earth at thousands of colorful mineral-encrusted hot springs and vents. Cauldrons of mud bubble and splat their colorful liquid plasters to form large volcanic cones. Hundreds of geysers sleep in placid hot springs for hours or days, then at semi-regular intervals erupt into great plumes of hot water and steam rising hundreds of feet overhead before retiring to their tepid hibernation. You can find geysers in a few other locations around the world, but there are more active geysers in Yellowstone National Park than there are in every other location combined.

Yellowstone was the first National Park created by the US government in 1876 to preserve the natural beauty of this strange and beautiful place. In addition to preserving its multitude of geothermal attractions, Yellowstone National Park serves as a refuge for a wide variety of native American wildlife. The last remaining herd of wild bison (buffalo) in the USA still peacefully roams the meadows of Yellowstone along with vast herds of wild elk, deer, moose, coyotes, eagles, bears and wolves. You can easily spot many of these wild creatures from your car as you drive through the gorgeous scenery of Yellowstone.

5.4 Translation of Scientific and Technical Writings

"Knowledge explosion" and "information explosion" are two popular terms prevailing in the world today. Whether a country can acquire valuable knowledge and the latest information would doubtlessly matter greatly to its advance of science and technology and development of economy. But how to acquire them, translation plays a very important part in disseminating information on international scale. A UNESCO study (1957) estimated that something between 1 and 2 million scientific and technical articles, reports, patents and books were published annually, but about half of them were in English, and the rest were in German (14%), French (13%), Spanish (5%), Italian(4%), Japanese and some other languages other than Chinese. That is to say more than 90% scientific and technical works were published in languages other than Chinese, which helps to explain the demand for technical translation which is bound to increase, perhaps by leaps and bounds.

Scientific and technical translation is in many ways simpler to understand than literary translation. In the latter, emotive elements such as rhythm and assonance are important, whereas they play no part in technical works. We can provisionally distinguish technical writing by three main characteristics: subject matter, type of language and purpose. The subject matter is always technical. The language displays a greater frequency of technical terms than ordinary language and the purpose is always a practical one. The guiding motive of technical texts is the communication of information. It is always a means and never an end in itself. Technical translation is not as exciting as literary translation which is a creative, artistic activity. It does not offer the most glamorous of careers. This is one reason why there is a shortage of properly qualified technical translation. Another reason is the misconception of translating prevalent among the general public, which tends to lower the status of technical translator. In fact technical translating demands high qualifications if it is to be done properly. It does have a creative element; it demands intelligence, ingenuity and a great deal of knowledge. While it involves much routine work, it does have its moments of "appealingness". Since it is primarily concerned with the transference of information, it goes without saying that any specialized knowledge is a great advantage for translating in that field and perhaps in related field. Naturally one must also have a good knowledge of one's own language and the foreign language, and possess a flair for translation, though this is hard to define. The relatively high proportion of standardized terms in technical texts is a great advantage to the technical translator. Against this we must set off the inadequacy of other aids, particularly, technical dictionaries.

5.4.1 Linguistic Features of Scientific and Technical Writings

Lexical features

Scientific and technical translation is composed of three principal types of document that are classified as follows:

1. the results of pure science intended as a contribution to knowledge, without regard to possible practical applications;

2. the results of applied scientific research carried out in order to solve a particular problem;

3. the work of the technologist, which is intended to result in an industrial product or process that can be sold on the market. These three types overlap. The most significant linguistic feature they share is its vocabulary, the specialized terminology of the particular discipline, e. g.

electron	电子
neutron	中子
proton	质子
nuclear fission	原子核裂变
sunspots	太阳黑子
space suit	太空服
lunar dust	月球尘埃
ozone layer	臭氧层

Some of them can also be used as general words but when they appear in the technical texts they turn into specialized words with rigorous scientific meaning of the particular discipline. Such as "sunspots", "space suit", "lunar dust".

Many scientific and technical words are formed by means of word formation such as "prefix":

mini-	小型,微型
minicomputer	微型计算机
minicam	小型照相机
minilaser	微型激光器
minicab	微型出租汽车
sub-	在……下;超小型,次,亚,半,付,分
subzero	零下的
subcompact	超小型汽车
subequal	几乎相等的
subtransparent	半透明的
subsystem	子系统
subclinical	亚临床型的
substandard	付标准的
tele-	远(距离)遥(控)电报电视;电话传真、照相
teleautomatics	遥控自动学
telecar	收发报汽车
telecon	电话会议、电传、电报会议
teletype	电传打字机
telewriter	传真电报机
telemicroscope	望远显微镜
telephoto	传真相片
telectroscope	电传照相机
telefax	光波传讯法
telemechanics (telemechanism)	遥控机械学,遥控力学

Besides, abbreviations are frequently used in the technical text, e. g.

MIRV—multiple independently targeted re-entry vehicle	多弹头分导重返大气层运载工具
SLBM—satellite launched ballistic missile	从人造卫星发射的弹道导弹
RAM—random access memory	电子计算机随机存取储存器
MDR—memory-data register	存储数据寄存器
ATS—application technology satellite	应用技术卫星
ECG/EKG—electrocardiogram	心电图
PCG—phonocardiogram	心音图
ECG and PCG data automatic analyser	心电心音数据自动分析装置
EEG—electroencephalogram	脑电图
EMG—electromyogram	肌电图
BSP—brain stem potential	脑干电位

In translating a technical text from English into Chinese, every word, especially technical terms must be clearly and accurately expressed with the help of a dictionary of technology, especially a dictionary of particular discipline. Some specific terms should be expressed in idiomatic phrases established through common practice. A technical term, once rendered, should be expressed with consistency throughout the whole passage. The original technical term, if with a concrete meaning, should be translated according to its meaning instead of transliteration, for examples:

laser　激光　　　　　　　instead of　莱赛
vitamin　维生素　　　　　instead of　维他命
telephone　电话　　　　　instead of　德律风
penicillin　青霉素　　　　instead of　盘尼西林
philosophy　哲学　　　　instead of　菲洛索菲
bourgeoisie　资产阶级　　instead of　布尔乔亚

The name given to the original technical term must match the reality, must be the most suitable choice that is in harmony with the essential meaning of the original.

Technical terms can also be translated into Chinese by means of transliteration, e.g.

nylon　尼龙
sonar　声纳
opium　鸦片
copy　拷贝
lymph　淋巴
brandy　白兰地
trust　托拉斯
pound　磅

Transliteration should be done according to pronunciation of respective languages, a French technical term should be transliterated according to French pronunciation, and a Russian term should be equally rendered according to Russian pronunciation.

Abbreviations are more frequently used in technical texts than in other texts as they are very convenient and concise. Most of them should be translated completely according to the exact meaning of each word such as SAMOS—satellite antimissile observation system 卫星反导弹观察系统, EWRS—early-warning radar screen 预警雷达网

Some of them can be transliterated if they are easy to pronounce, such as

Radar—雷达, AIDS—艾滋病, KGB—克格勃, OPEC—欧派克　and so on.

Some are not necessary to render, especially those that are familiar to the public, such as BBC, VOA, Ph. D. MA. and so on.

The grammar of technical writing does not differ very sharply from that of other kinds of writing. They all share the common grammar of the language, though there are some striking peculiarities and tendencies in the morphology and syntax of technical prose. The great frequency in the use of the passive in technical English comes readily to mind. In many ways the features of technical language are also those of officialese—it is a highly stylized language and would sound stilted and pompous if used in everyday speech. The normal rules of clarity of expression do not always apply to technical texts. Thus the high frequency of the passive, which some have condemned, serves the informative purpose of technical writing with the suppression of emotion and individual personality.

Besides, the Simple Present Tense is frequently used in expressing the timeless general statement (无时间性的一般叙述) such as natural phenomena, natural law, definition, theorem, formula and so on. Non-finite Verbs are also frequently used. Take the following passage for instance.

These added quantities of inert gas have an important characteristic. The relative abundance of their isotopes, which are elements having the same atomic number but different atomic weight's, is characteristic of the process that produces them. For example, helium that originates as alpha particles consists only of the isotope helium-4. Argon from the radioactive decay of potassium exists only as the isotope argon-40, and xenon from spontaneous fission consists primarily of xenon-134 and xenon-136.

Consequently, the inert gases found in the various rocks, minerals, and waters of the earth and its atmosphere are "tagged" with unique isotopic "signatures." These isotopic patterns enable earth scientists to utilize the inert gases as tracers in a number of natural geochemical processes.

Some of these characteristic isotopic signatures for the inert gases have been known and used for a long time. For example, argon-40 is the basis for the potassium-argon method used to date rocks and minerals.

Because inert gases occur in such small quantities in the earth adding even a little inert gas to terrestrial material represents a significant increase in the total. In May 1978, geochemists Ichiro Kanecka and Nobuo Takaoka of the Geophysical Institute of the University of Tokyo reported that they found excess quantities of a xenon isotope. xenon-129 in minerals from recent lava flows in Hawaii. Xenon-129 is produced by radioactive decay. Any radioactive isotope decays into the isotope of another element—in the case, iodine-129—decays into xenon-129.

Iodine-129 has a very short half-life of 17 million years, compared with the age of the earth. A half-life is the length of time it takes for one-half of a radioactive element to decay. Because of this short half-life, any iodine-129 that was present when the earth was formed disintegrated very early in the earth's history. The fact that there is excess xenon-129 in the earth today indicates that iodine-129 was present in the earth when it was formed. It also indicates that some of the xenon-129 into which the iodine-129 decayed has been trapped within rocks in the earth throughout its history.

The characteristics of syntax of technical writings.

The latter half of 20th century has witnessed an epoch-making advance in the field of sciences and technology. New ramifications of sciences such as space science, life science, environmental science, computer science, etc. have risen in succession to the occasion. A series of new theories, hypotheses are contending in a duel of wits for academic sphere of influence. The specialists have been conducting experiments of top sciences, invoking the aid of advanced contrivances and techniques. This has ushered in an era of "intellectual explosion." Nowadays, the outdated and outmoded means of expression can hardly present the up-to-date technical information as it actually is.

Necessity is the mother of invention. That is why the newly devised technical syntax comes into existence. To further the mutual transference of alien languages in the domain of neoteric sciences, it is of vital magnitude to initiate some counter-devices of translation accordingly.

1. A distant separation between the subject and the predicate.

The robot a man so subtle that he seems to be not one but the incarnation of a winged angel, who can fly up to the skyscraper and hand in person the milk bottles to users, really a superman comes into being on the earth—*Robot*.

In the above-cited example there exists between the subject and the predicate an insular wall built of thirty-seven words. The segregating constituents range from the appositive "a man" as an inception to another appositive "a superman" as a terminus with "so...that" clause and "who" clause straggling between them. In translating this type of sentence it is imperative to employ the knack of "following syntactical sequence". For emphasis' sake, "be not one but..." is transferred into its Chinese counterpart "简直是", while "它" supplied to form a clause wherewith to protrude the second appositive "superman".

Chinese version:

机器人如此精巧,简直是长着翅膀的安琪儿的化身,能够飞上摩天大楼,亲手把牛奶交给用户。它的确是出生于地球上的超人。

2. A cross network of subordinate clauses.

The theory that bacteria are serviceable in devouring contaminants, that repeated experiments have proved true and that air may be artificially purified through dissociation, that has so far been in embryo, an advanced one, prevail widely in the domain of environmental science.

The first "that" clause is appositive; the second, attributive; the third, appositive with its antecedent "the theory" omitted; and the fourth, attributive, qualifying the elliptical element "the theory", whereto "one" in "an awkward one" is the appositive. The predicate "prevail" brings up the rear in the sentence. In rendering this type of sentence with alternate presence of appositive and attributive clauses, it is advisable to conjure up the following magic weapons:

(1) Initial decomposition and subsequent combination

① decomposition

A "细菌……这一理论"

B "可以通过……这一先进理论"

② combination

"上述两种理论"

(2) Translation of attributive clauses preceded by rendition of appositive ones

Chinese version:

细菌可用于吞噬污染物,这一理论通过反复实验之后业经证实。人们又可以通过离解的方法人工地净化空气,这一先进理论迄今处于萌芽阶段。上述两种理论在环境科学领域中流行甚广。

3. Frequent occurrence of parenthetical elements.

As a last resort, conditions permitting, we may seek at home medical service, namely, diagnosis and treatment from abroad, to use a professional terminology, telesatdiag, as compared with vis-a-vis consultation, say, in an ill-equipped, poorly staffed hospital, particularly, on an acute, severe or, in physician's view, unidentified case, undoubtedly a most effective therapeutic device available.

This lengthy sentence is set with seven interconnected parenthetical elements—"conditions permitting", "namely", "to use a professional terminology", "say", "particularly", "in physician's view", "as compared with vis-a-vis consultation". The author's dexterity at their utilization is crowned with rhetorical charms of compactness, succinctness, smoothness and naturalness. Three elements are interlaced with appositives such as "medical service", "diagnosis and treatment", "telesatdiag" and "therapeutic device". It is noteworthy that four parenthetical elements sever apart the third and the fourth appositives. However, with the word "undoubtedly" as a medium, the said two appositives coexist as if in vicinity without engendering a feeling of remoteness on the part of the readers.

It is judicious to appeal to the following translating devices:

(1) Commencing with the rendition of parenthetical elements

The initiative step is to translate "condition permitting".

(2) Conformity with the original sequence of parenthetical elements

This method can hardly dispense with the insertion of connectives.

(3) Punctuating parenthetical elements with "dash"

The version of the source language from "say" to "hospital" is justifiably placed after the mark of dash.

(4) Punctuating parenthetical elements with round brackets

The version of the source language from "particularly" to "case" is enclosed in round brackets.

Chinese version:

如果条件许可的话,我们还可以采取最后的手段,那就是居国内而向国外求医——诊断和治疗,用专业术语来说,也就是电视卫星诊断。与面诊——比如说在一个设备不良,医务人员水平不高的医院里进行诊断(特别是诊断那种急性,重症或是医师认为病因不明的病例)——相比,电视卫星诊断无疑是一种可以利用的非常有效的医疗手段。

4. Inversion of principal clause and subordinate clause.

Such a spick-and-span branch of science that human creature might survive untimely age, being proof against diseases through immunization, and which serves to lengthen longevity and rejuvenate man from decrepit senility to vital youth, a so-claimed "age-proof science", we have been devoting our uttermost efforts to the pursuit of, that it wins a leading role in the sphere of life science.

A grammatical analysis of syntactical structure will help towards perceptual and conceptual comprehension of this example.

(1) principal clause—"We have been devoting our uttermost efforts to the pursuit of such a spick-and-span branch of science."

(2) Adverbial clause—"Such... that it wins a leading role in the sphere of life science."

(3) Appositive clause—"that it wins a leading role in the sphere of life science."

(4) Attributive clause—"which serves to lengthen longevity and rejuvenize man from decrepit senility to vital youth."

(5) Appositive phrase—"a so-claimed 'age-proof science'" appositive to "... branch of science."

To emphasize age-proof science as a neoteric creation of human intelligence, "such a spick-and-span branch of science" is inversely put in the foremost part of the sentence.

The striking features of this sentence find their manifestation in the following:

(1) The subject and predicate are placed between "such..." and "that it wins..." human creature might survive untimely age, being proof against diseases through immunization, and which serves.

(2) "Such..." is widely separated from "that it wins..." by appositive and attributive clauses and appositive phrase.

(3) "Such..." bears the brunt and "that it wins..." takes the rear.

(4) "To the pursuit of" is closely followed by a comma wherewith to keep "of" apart from its object "... branch of science". Since its object is shifted to the head of the sentence and heeled by an adverbial clause "that human creature..." it is indispensably necessary to punctuate "to the pursuit of" with a comma in order to dissociate "of" from the said adverbial clause.

Chinese version:

我们一直在致力于钻研一项所谓"防老科学",它足以延年益寿,返老还童,使人脱离龙钟衰老而恢复生机勃勃的青春。该项科学旨在通过免疫使人类具有抵抗疾病的能力,从而有可能不至于因早衰而死亡。它是一门如此崭新的科学,所以在生命领域中赢得了主导地位。

5. Frequent use of formal subjects.

Since it is beyond doubt that a part of the free phosphates formed by the above method forms phosphoric esters with hydroxyl radicals or causes a weak ionic bonding with nitrogen-containing radicals, these bonds being relatively weak, it follows that if the ambient PH value is made to be somewhat acidic, for example, equivalent to about the acidity of citric acid, hydrolysis occurs readily whereby phosphoric acid in a free state is again formed and passes into the solution, thus converting, the water or citric acid insoluble phosphates into those that are soluble and enabling this reaction to occur repeatedly.

In the most up-to-date English of scientific information prevails a sentence pattern with "it" as formal subject. For example, "It is authentic that..." "It remains to be proved that..." etc.

In the above-mentioned example, two clauses are written after the said pattern: "It is beyond doubt that..." and "It follows that..." The translator is well advised to render the first subordinate clause with the aid of amplified expressions("上述","这一点") for eliciting the principal clause, the version of which(由此可以推定) punctuated with colon, elicits in turn other subordinate clauses.

Chinese version:

用上述方法生成的游离磷酸的一部分与羟基形成磷酸酯,或与含氮基因产生弱离子键(相对地来说,这些键是较弱的)由于这一点是肯定无疑的,因此可以推定:如果使周围的PH值呈微酸性(比如说,大致相当于柠檬酸的酸度),就很容易发生水解,又生成游离状态的磷酸进入溶液中,从而把不溶于水或柠檬酸的磷酸盐溶化成为可溶于水或柠檬酸的磷酸盐并使这种反应能够反复地进行。

5.4.2 Increase or Decrease in Quantity

Increase or decrease in quantity is a knotty problem over which controversies are going on up to the present. Various opinions mentioned in different books on this problem affect greatly the correct translation of English for science and technology. Any error in translation of a certain figure would cause a great loss, so we must acquaint ourselves with the system of numeral unit, which includes thousand system (大陆制 mainly used in U.S. and Russia) and million system(英国制 mainly used in Britain and Germany). But they are different from Chinese unit which changes when increased by 10^4 time. For example: We express "ten thousand" by means of "万" instead of "十千", "hundred thousand" by means of "十万" instead of "百千" "ten million" by means of "千万" instead of "十百万". Thousand system, however, is frequently used in expression of scientific and technological data in English. Let's take the following sentence for instance.

In just one drop of water there are about 3 300 billion billion atoms.

仅在一滴水里就有大约33万亿亿(33×10^{20})个原子。

Increase

Expression of increase is closely connected with the expression of multiple. Including the base or not is the most essential point in expression of multiple. English is different greatly from Chinese in the expression of multiple. In Chinese, including the base in the expression of multiple is very much different from the expression of multiple without the base included. But in English, the base is always included. Translation from English into Chinese must be an accurate expression of multiple, whether or not your version includes the base can never be ambiguous, e.g.

  (1) 甲比乙多 n 倍   Not including base
  (2) 甲是乙的 n 倍   Including base
  (3) 甲比乙增加了 n 倍 Not including base
  (4) 甲增加到乙的 n 倍 Including base

The base is always included in the expression of the above-mentioned circumstances in English. Thus when translated from English into Chinese, expression of multiple must be "n-1" in Chinese, e. g.

"A is 3 times more than B." should be expressed in Chinese as

(1) 甲是乙的 3 倍

(2) 甲比乙多 2 倍

(3) "甲 3 倍于乙"instead of "甲比乙多 3 倍"

Some examples:

1. This country has doubled her annual output of steel during the post-war year.

战后,这个国家钢的年产量翻了一番。

2. This box is three times as that one.

这个箱子是那个箱子重量的 3 倍。

3. Output of strip steel this year was three-fold up on that before liberation.

全年的带钢产量比解放前增加 2 倍。

Some people argue that "increase by n times" should be expressed by means of 净增加, which is actually wrong as "by n times" means "multiplying by n"(用 n 数乘), e. g. 15 increased by 4 times = 15 × 4 = 60. The net increase should be three times instead of four times. Thus, "increase by n times" should be expressed in Chinese as "增加倍(n-1)"instead of "n 倍", e. g.

1. The particles on the surface layer are three times more than those beneath the crust.

表层的粒子比表壳下的粒子数多 2 倍。

2. The distance is eight times as long as the previous one.

(1) 这一距离为前者的 8 倍。

(2) 这一距离 8 倍于前者。

(3) 这一距离比前者长 7 倍。

3. Auto accidents increased by 2.5 times compared with late 1960s.

汽车事故比六十年代末期增加了 1.5 倍。

This is to say, "N + times + more than" = "N + times + as much as", as both "more than" and "as much as" include the base. Of course, there are some people who don't think "N + times + more than" = "N + times + as much as". Traditionally, however, British and American scientists express multiple with the base included. Consult English dictionaries as Concise Oxford Dictionary, (Sixth edition) Oxford English Dictionary or Webster's New Collegiate Dictionary, you will find "times" means "multiplied by" "n times" means "multiplied by n", ten times easier = ten times as easy.

Therefore we can say "the volume of the earth is 49 times larger than that of the moon" = "The volume of the earth is 49 times as large as that of the moon"(地球的体积为月球的四十九倍)。

Now translate the following sentences into Chinese.

1. The grain output in this country was two times over that of 1957.

2. By comparison with 1948, the foreign trade turn-over of that country in 1957 increased 3.5 times.

3. With the result of automation productivity has increased sixty-sixfold in that factory.

4. A temperature rise of 100℃ increases the conductivity of a semiconductor by 50 times.

5. The speed exceeds the average speed by a factor of 3.5.

6. The peak power is as great again as the carrier power.

7. Mercury weighs 13.5 times as much as an equal volume of water.

8. Water conducts heat about 20 times better than air does.

Decrease

Decrease in quantity is generally expressed as follows:

(1) decrease N times expressed in Chinese as 减少了 $\dfrac{n-1}{n}$

(2) decrease by N times(减少 $\dfrac{N-1}{N}$ 或减少到 $\dfrac{1}{N}$)

(3) decrease to N times(减少到 $\dfrac{1}{N}$)

(4) be(reduced, cut, shortened, to N times decrease)(减少了 $\dfrac{N-1}{N}$ 或减少到 $\dfrac{1}{N}$)

The above-mentioned methods are more or less the same with decrease in quantity expressed in Chinese, e.g.

The antenna height is reduced by 60% because the new designed antenna system uses a retarded wave principle.

由于新设计的天线系统采用延长迟波原理,所以天线高度降低了60%。

Decrease in multiple must be expressed by conversion of multiple into fraction(将倍数换算成分数). The result in Chinese can be expressed as "减少了 $\dfrac{N-1}{N}$ 或减少到 $\dfrac{1}{N}$", e.g.

1. If you double the distance between two objects, their gravitational attraction decreases "two times two".

若把两个物体之间的距离增大一倍,则它们的万有引力就减少3/4。

2. The leads of the new capacitor are shortened twofold as those of the old, yet the functions are the same.

新型电容器的导线比旧式电容器的导线短了一半,但作用相同。

3. This box is three times as light as that one.

这个箱子比那个箱子轻2/3。

4. The equipment developed three months ago has reduced the error probability by a factor of 6.

这台新设备是3个月前研制成的,它使误差概率降低了5/6。

5. The hydrogen atom is nearly 16 times lighter than the oxygen atom.

氢原子比氧原子大约轻15/16。

6. With the new programming technique, the error rate of the programs written in the same language has decreased one order of magnitude.

使用这种新编程方法,以同一种语言编写的程序,其出错率减少了一个数量级。

In a word, decrease in quantity can't be expressed in Chinese as "减少多少倍" as it is ambiguous in concept, e. g "A rope shortened by 5 times" expressed correctly in Chinese should be "一段绳子短了 4/5", suppose the original rope is 20m in length, the shortened rope should be 4m. long. If expressed "缩短了 5 倍或 4 倍", then, what's the exact length of the shortened rope? It's too ambiguous to know.

Translation Exercises

Ⅰ. *Translate the following sentences into Chinese.*

1. The principal advantage over the old-fashioned machine is a four-fold reduction in weight.

2. An increase in RE from 150 to 900Ω is roughly equivalent to a decrease in power by a factor of 5.

3. The switching time of the new type transistor is shortened by three times.

4. The power output of the machine is twice less than its input.

5. This weight is three times lighter than that one.

6. 只要把这些方法稍作修改,就可以确定太阳系的范围。

7. 喷射器的作用是增加再生空气的压力。在环路中,此压力低于干燥空气压力,以免湿气漏泄到干空气中。

8. 早期设计的车床有导螺丝杆,这种丝杆有双重用途:作为标准螺旋和作为进给轴。

9. 即使把可能发现的新油田考虑进去,到本世纪末,石油也可能全部用尽或所剩无几。

10. 由于实物模型具有局限性,因此,在工程领域中,人们研制出了数学模型来表示各种机械结构。自从采用大型数字模拟计算机装置后,用这种解析方法研制数学模型有了长足的发展。

Ⅱ. *Translate the following essay into Chinese.*

The Living Seas

The ocean covers three quarters of the earth's surface, produces 90 percent of all its life-supporting oxygen, and is the driving force behind the entire weather system. There are over 450 million cubic miles of sea water on the earth; and each cubic mile contains over 150 million tons of minerals.

So vast and so pervasive is the sea that if the earth's crust were made level, ocean water would form a blanket over 8 000 feet deep.

The oceans contribute immeasurably to the earth's life support system as well as provide an untapped storehouse of food, minerals, energy, and archaeological treasure.

Advanced atmospheric diving suits permit researchers to descend to depths of 1 500 feet. Yet the ocean's average depth is greater than 12 000 feet. It is at these depths that remarkable discoveries are being made, discoveries which only a short time ago would have been impossible.

In that depth, where darkness is absolute and pressure exceeds eight tons per square inch, robotic submersibles have discovered enormous gorges, four times deeper than the Grand Canyon. Here, too, are volcanoes that vastly outnumber those on land. Landslides the size of Rhode Island have been recorded, as well as raging undersea storms that go completely unnoticed on the surface while dramatically rearranging the underwater landscapes.

And under these seas the largest single geological feature on earth has been found—a mountain range that dwarfs the Himalayas. It's a range that covers nearly one quarter of the earth's surface.

All these discoveries have come from the exploration of less than one-tenth of this undersea mountain range.

The earth is the only planet we know that has an ocean. The ocean is the largest feature on earth. Yet it's the one feature we know the least about. We know more about the moon 240 000 miles away than we know about the three-fourths of the earth covered with water. Man has set foot on the moon, but not on the most remote part of the earth, 35 000 feet under the sea.

Technology is changing all that. It's literally parting the waves for today's undersea explorers. And it's bringing about the opportunity to transform vision, curiosity, and wonder into practical knowledge.

Properly managed as a tool to serve society, technology is the best hope for overcoming economic and social problems facing people everywhere. It always has been. The earliest relics of human life are tools. And our ancient ancestors used these tools to understand and change the world around them and make it better. The same is true today.

The deep sea is the last frontier left to explore.

5.5 Translation of Diplomatic Literature

What is Diplomacy?

The Oxford Dictionary defines diplomacy as follows:

Diplomacy is the management of international relations by negotiation; the method by which these relations are adjusted and managed by ambassadors and envoys; the business or art of the diplomat. S. L. Roy writes: Diplomacy has always played a very great role in adjusting international policies. It is evident that very few problems in international relations can be completely erased. The majority of them have to be adjusted or settled through compromise. This can be done through diplomacy. In this respect Richard W. Sterling's observation deserves notice. He says, "Diplomacy is, indeed, the politics of international relations; it is international politics in the most precise sense of the term". (S. L. Roy: "Diplomacy")

Adam Watson and Eyre Methuen believe that "States which are aware that their domestic policies are affected by everything that happens" outside, are not content merely to observe one another at distance. They feel the need to enter into a dialogue with one another. This dialogue between independent states—the machinery by which their governments conduct, and the networks of promises, contracts, institutions and codes of conduct which develop out of it—is the substance of diplomacy. ("Diplomacy—the Dialogue between States")

A state is usually regarded as a member of the international society, its policies, both external and internal, are modified by international relations. Therefore, it is obliged to adjust its relationship with other states through diplomatic negotiations, which are supposed to be carried out by means of various languages. Hence language plays a very important role in diplomacy.

5.5.1 Features of Diplomatic Language

Due to the heavy influence of the rigid feudalist hierarchy of Europe and the culture of Latin Christendom, diplomatic activities have the characteristics of being conservative, formal and rigid in rank and precedence, which are remarkably reflected on diplomatic language.

Diplomatic language, in a broad sense, is the lingua franca between states, the common language used in diplomatic activities. Just as the standard language of a nation is usually a common language of a nation based on the dialect of the region which is most developed economically, culturally and politically, diplomatic language is generally the language of the nation which is most powerful and influential in a certain historical period of time. Before the middle of the 18th century, the diplomatic language of Europe was Latin, the common language of the Roman Empire whose territory covered parts of Europe, Asia and Africa and whose rule lasted for 15 centuries. After the middle of the 18th century, the diplomatic language of Europe was French, as France under Louis XIV and Napoleon was so developed that it became the model of European diplomacy. After the Paris Conference of 1918-1919, English became the most important diplomatic language, as Britain was the greatest colonial empire at the end of the 19th century and the beginning of the 20th century. Britain declined after the Second World War, but the United States rose to power and saved English as the major diplomatic language in the world. With the birth of the former Soviet Union, the first socialist country in the world, the founding of the People's Republic of China and the establishment of the national independent countries in Asia, Africa and Latin America, world diplomacy has undergone great changes. Nations in the world, big or small, are considered equal and therefore many of them use their own mother tongues in diplomatic activities. However, to facilitate their communication with each other, a few languages have been adopted as lingua franca. In the United Nations Organization, English, French, Chinese, Russian and Spanish are the official languages, and English and French are the two major working languages. For historical, political and other reasons, different languages are used as diplomatic language in different parts of the world. This is a reflection of the decentralization of world diplomacy. Europe is no longer the only political centre in the world. However, English is still the most widely used and most important diplomatic language in the present-day world.

Some of the commonly used terms are quoted as follows:

ad referendum (Latin)	尚需考虑
agre'ment (French)	同意
aide-memoire (F.)	备忘录
casus foederis (L.)	参战理由
charge d'affaires (F.)	代办

续表

communique (F. L.)	公报
demarche (F.)	交涉
donner acte (F.)	予以承认
donner la main (F.)	让席
detente (F.)	缓和
de facto (L.)	事实上
de jure (L.)	据权利的,法律上的
fin de non-recevoir (F.)	拒绝接受
note verbale (F.)	普通照会
ne varietur (L.)	不得更改
paraphe (F.)	缩写签名
placement (F.)	安排位次
status quo (L.)	现状,原状
sine qua non (L.)	必要条件
ultimatum (L.)	最后通牒

Diplomatic language is on the whole rather formal although it varies in degree of formality according to its use. All varieties have a greater or less degree of formality and share to some extent the linguistic features of formal written language. The most formal of all are legal diplomatic documents which make up a considerable part of diplomatic language.

The formality of diplomatic language is shown on various levels of diplomatic language according to "Diplomatic English" by Guo Hong and Peng Xiaodong.

Syntactic Level

(1) Long and complicated sentences are often used.

(2) Participial phrases are often used as attributives or adverbials.

(3) Formal phrasal prepositions are often used, e. g. "in accordance with" (according to), "in contravention of" (violating), "in (with) regard to" (regarding) etc.

(4) Existential "there" is often used, e. g.

There are established as the principal organs of the United Nations: a General Assembly, a Security Council, and Economic and Social Council, a Trusteeship Council, an International Court of Justice, and a Secretariat (Chapter III, Charter of the United Nations). (cf. The principal organs of the United Nations are...)

(5) Independent structure is often used, e. g.

Members of the United Nations also agree that their policy in respect of the territories to which this chapter applies, not less than (in respect of their metropolitan areas), must be based on the general principle of good-neighborliness, due account being taken of the interest and well-being of the rest of the world, in social, economic, and commercial matters. (Article 74, Charter of the United Nations)

Lexical Level

(1) Words of Latin, French or Middle English origin are often used such as "allay" (lessen)- ME < Fr < L, "foil" (frustrate)-ME < Ofr, "comply" (to act in accordance)- ME < Ofr < L, "residence"-ME < MF < ML.

(2) Latin and French words remain in wide use. Latin: "ipsofacto", "inter alia", "persona non grata", etc. French: "force majeure", "charge d"affaires ad interim".

(3) Words of legal language are often used, e. g. "thereof", "thereon", "threrunder", "thereto", "therefrom", "hereby", "hereinafter", "hitherto", "the foregoing objectives (categories)", etc.

1. Diplomatic language is a persuasive and precise language.

Language has always assumed great importance in diplomacy. In ancient times, kings appointed people skilful in using language to be their envoys. In modern diplomacy, great importance has also been attached to the use of language. Diplomatic language is a language to which lawyers bring a sense a legal precision and is at the same time persuasive. On significant international issues, words spoken by diplomats concern the vital interests on their states, and once delivered, can never be retrieved. Therefore, diplomats must use their language in a very discreet and precise way.

2. Diplomatic language is a polite and tactful language.

Politeness tends to increase to the extent that the addressed is more senior in a status and less intimate. This phenomenon is all the more prominent in diplomatic language, because in diplomacy seniority means difference in the position and prestige of the states concerned, and there is little intimacy between diplomats as they are complete strangers to each other. Even if they know each other, they are first of all representatives of different states. For example, complimentary phrases are used at the end of a formal note:

"I avail myself of this opportunity to express to Your Excellency (or to you) the assurances of my highest consideration." or "Please accept, Your Excellency, the assurances of my highest consideration."

Polite formulae are used at the beginning and the end of verbal note, what is more, politeness prevails in diplomatic language and behaviour as a whole. Diplomats are supposed to have decent manners and not to resort to personal attacks on any occasion.

3. Diplomatic language is a language in which impersonality is often used.

Language becomes impersonal when it avoids direct reference to the addresser and the addressee. In legal documents, impersonality is pervasively used to show their equal validity regardless of the person concerned. And legal diplomatic documents, such as treaties, agreements, protocols, conventions make up a great part of diplomatic documents. Besides, impersonality is often employed to avoid mentioning the party or person concerned to make the language polite and tactful, the root cause for the impersonality of diplomatic language is that the relationship between diplomats is impersonal.

The manifestations of impersonality in diplomatic language are as follows:

(1) Use of expressions of indirect reference.

In drafting and signing a treaty, an agreement, a protocol or other diplomatic document, the mentioning of the names of the signatory states or their representatives is usually avoided to show that the document is valid independently of the state or person who participates in drafting and signing it. They are generally mentioned in the text as "the contracting parties", "the other contracting party", "either contracting party", "each party", "Party A", "Party B", etc.

"In the Charter of the United Nations", terms like "the Organization", "All Members", "each Member" are used.

In "Vienna Convention on Diplomatic Relations", terms like "the state Parties to the Present Convention", "the sending State", "receiving State", "a third State" are used.

(2) The use of passive voice.

The passive voice is often used to avoid mentioning the addresser or the addressee to make the language polite and tactful.

4. Diplomatic language is fairly accessible.

Language tends to be inaccessible if it is formal, polite and impersonal. But diplomatic language is an exception for the following reasons:

Diplomatic language is meant for foreigners to read and listen to intelligibly, so especially long and involved sentences or extremely difficult words are generally avoided. Besides, diplomatic language, as stated above, is a precise language, and no ambiguity unless intended, is allowed. Furthermore, diplomatic language is a formal standard language.

5.5.2 Translation of Diplomatic Literature

In translation of diplomatic documents, the linguistic features of diplomatic documents must be taken into careful consideration.

Consider the translation of the following documents.

1. 　　　　　　　递交国书时所致颂词

阁下,我荣幸地向您递交××共和国总统任命我为驻贵国特命全权大使的国书。

××国总统嘱咐我向阁下转达他的崇高敬意和诚挚友谊,并祝贺您的伟大国家的人民获得成就和进步。同时,请允许我向阁下、您的政府和伟大的贵国人民表示我个人的深切敬慕之意。

阁下,我们是邻国,在远古的历史上,就有着我们密切和良好联系的记载……我谨向阁下保证,我以我国派驻在伟大贵国的代表身份,将为加强我们两国之间的友好关系和积极合作而不断努力。

我相信,我在这种努力方面将会得到贵国政府的全力的诚挚合作。

Speech Upon Presenting the Letter of Credence

Your Excellency, I have the honour to present to you the Letter of Credence by which the President of the Republic of ×× has accredited me as Ambassador Extraordinary and Plenipotentiary to ×× Country.

The President of ×× Country has charged me to convey to Your Excellency the assurances of his high esteem and sincere friendship and greetings for the success and progress of the people of your great country. At the same time, let me add the expression of my profound respect and admiration for Your Excellency's Government and the great people of your country.

Your Excellency, we are neighbours and have a record of close and fruitful association which dates back to the distant past of history... I avail myself of this opportunity to extend to Your Excellency the assurances that in the capacity of our country's accredited representative to your great county, I shall work unceasingly for strengthening the friendly relations and active cooperation between our two countries.

I am confident that I shall receive the unfailing and sincerest cooperation of the Government of your country in my efforts in this direction.

2. **Reply Upon Receiving the Letter of Credence**

Your Excellency Mr. Ambassador.

I am very happy to have received the Letter of Credence from you as Ambassador Extraordinary and Plenipotentiary to ×× Country. And I thank his Excellency Mr. ××, President of ×× Country, for his good wishes for the happiness and prosperity of my country and its people conveyed by you. Allow me to avail myself of this opportunity to renew to you the assurances of our constant friendship and earnest wishes for the welfare and prosperity of your country.

Your Excellency Mr. Ambassador, as you are a great friend to us and you have always had profound respect for my country, we warmly welcome you to reside with us in the character of your country's supreme representative. Please rest assured that in your glorious mission to strengthen the friendly relations between our two countries, you can always rely upon our active support and assistance.

接受国书时所作的答词

大使阁下：

我非常高兴地接受了您作为××国派驻我国的特命全权大使递交的国书。我感谢贵国总统××先生阁下通过您转达的对我和我国人民的祝福。请允许我乘此机会再次表示我对我们两国之间的永恒友谊和贵国的幸福与繁荣的良好祝愿。

大使先生阁下,您是我们的伟大朋友,您一向尊重我的国家,我们热诚地欢迎您作为贵国的最高代表留驻我国。请您相信,在您完成加强我们两国之间的友好关系的光荣使命中,永远都能指望得到我们的积极支持和帮助。

In the above-mentioned examples, the translator attaches great importance to the linguistic features of diplomatic documents such as "formality", "conservativeness", "politeness", "preciseness", "impersonality", etc, which are clearly reflected in the translated texts.

On April 1, 2001, a U.S military surveillance plane bumped into and damaged a Chinese military jet over the South China Sea, when reporting the incident, the two sides are quite different from each other in wording as follows：

3. 朱邦造说,4月1日上午,美国一架军用侦察机抵中国海南岛海域上空活动,中方两架军用飞机对其进行跟踪监视。9时07分,当中方飞机在海南岛东南104公里处正常飞行时,美机突然向中方飞机转向(其机头和左翼与中方一架飞机相碰)致使中方飞机坠毁。中方正在搜寻飞行员下落。我们对这名飞行员的状况十分关心。美机未经中方允许,进入中方领空;并于9时33分降落在海南岛陵水机场。

中国军用飞机在中国沿海对美国军用侦察机实施跟踪监视,属于正当的飞行活动,符合国际惯例。

中方飞机坠毁的直接原因,是美机违反飞行规则突然向中方飞机转向、接近造成的。发生这一事件的责任完全在美方,中方已就此向美方提出严厉交涉和抗议,对美方给中方造成的损失问题,中方保留进一步交涉的权利。

目前,中方已对美方飞机上的24名机组人员做出妥善安排。中方对美机未经允许进入中国领空并降落中方机场一事保留进一步向美方交涉的权利。

U. S. military plane bumps Chinese jet.

A U. S. military surveillance plane bumped into and damaged a Chinese military jet over the South China Sea on April 1, according to the Chinese Foreign Ministry.

The U. S. plane approached China's Hainan Island, and two Chinese military jets were scrambled to track it, Foreign Ministry spokesman Zhu Bangzao said.

At 9:07a. m., 104km southeast of Hainan Island, the U. S. plane suddenly turned towards the Chinese jets, bumping into and damaging one of them.

China is very much concerned about the missing Chinese pilot from the crashed jet and is searching for him, Zhu said.

Without permission from the Chinese side, the U. S. surveillance plane intruded into Chinese airspace and made an emergency landing at Lingshui Airport in Hainan at 9:33a. m. It was normal for Chinese military jets to track the U. S. surveillance plane over Chinese waters, said the spokesman.

The direct cause of the damage and crash of the Chinese jet was that the U. S. plane suddenly veered into the Chinese jet which is against flight rules. Therefore, the U. S. side should bear all responsibility arising therefrom, Zhu added.

The Chinese side has made solemn representations and protested to the U. S. side. China has made proper arrangements for all 24 crew members on board the U. S. plane, Zhu said, adding that China reserves the right to further negotiate with the U. S. side on the U. S. plane's intrusion into China's airspace and landing at the Chinese airport without permission.

What the U. S. claims is that the plane's collide, the Chinese pilot collides with the U. S. Navy EP-3E and crashes into the sea.

According to the fact mentioned by the Foreign Ministry Spokesman Zhu Bangzao and the English version of his speech, the United States should apologize to the Chinese for the incident and bear all responsibility. However, the U. S. plays with words (claiming that it is the Chinese pilot who collides with the U. S Navy EP-3E...) in order to evade responsibility, which is of common occurrence for the U. S. government. The statements on the Taiwan issue in the China-U. S. Shanghai Communique (February 28, 1972) provide a good example. China states her solemn posture on the issue of Taiwan as follows:

4. 中华人民共和国政府是中国的唯一合法政府,台湾是中国的一个省,早已归还祖国;解放台湾是中国内政,别国无权干涉;全部美国武装力量和军事设施必须从台湾撤走。中国政府坚决反对旨在制造"一中一台"、"一个中国,两个政府"、"两个中国"、"台湾独立"和鼓吹"台湾地位未定"的活动。

译文:The government of the People's Republic of China is the sole legal government of China, Taiwan is a province of China which has long been returned to the motherland; the liberation of Taiwan is China's internal affair in which no other country has the right to interfere; and all U. S. forces and military installations must be withdrawn from Taiwan. The Chinese Government firmly opposes any activities which aim at the creation of "one China, one Taiwan", "one China, two governments", "two Chinas", "independent Taiwan" and advocate that "the status of Taiwan remains to be determined".

In reply to the above statement, the U. S. makes the statement which is tactfully worded as follows:

The United States acknowledges that all Chinese on either side of the Taiwan Strait maintain there is but one China and that Taiwan is a part of China. The United States Government does not challenge that position. It reaffirms its interest in a peaceful settlement of the Taiwan question by the Chinese themselves. With this proposal in mind, it affirms the ultimate objective of the withdrawal of all U. S. forces and military installations from Taiwan. In the meantime, it will progressively reduce its forces and military installations on Taiwan as the tension in the area diminishes.

译文:美国认识到,在台湾海峡两边的所有中国人都认为只有一个中国,台湾是中国的一部分。美国政府对这一立场不提出异议。它重申它对由中国人自己和平解决台湾问题的关心。考虑到这一前景,它确认从台湾撤出全部美国武装力量和军事设施的最终目标。在此期间,它将随着这个地区紧张局势的缓和逐步减少它在台湾的武装力量和军事设施。

In order to avoid mentioning "the People's Republic of China" and "the Republic of China", "all Chinese on either side of the Taiwan Strait" is used which is indeed the common position of the two sides that there is but one China and that Taiwan is a part of China, and so the statement will not lead to the opposition of either side. By Sentence 3, 4 and 5 in the above statement, the U. S. feels justified in withdrawing or not withdrawing its forces and military installations on Taiwan depending on the rate at which the tension in the area diminishes. Therefore the statement of the U. S. serves its purpose and in principle, acceptable to China on the one hand, and it does not offend the Taiwan authorities excessively on the other hand, what is more, it leaves some leeway for itself.

Translation Exercises

Ⅰ. *Translate the following document into English, wording the diplomatic terms tactfully.*

中华人民共和国和美利坚合众国关于建立外交关系的联合公报

中华人民共和国和美利坚合众国商定自1979年1月1日起互相承认并建立外交关系。

221

美利坚合众国承认中华人民共和国政府是中国的唯一合法政府。在此范围内，美国人民将同台湾人民保持文化、商务和其他非官方关系。

中华人民共和国和美利坚合众国重申上海公报中双方一致同意的各项原则，并再次强调：

双方都希望减少国际军事冲突的危险。

任何一方都不应该在亚洲——太平洋地区以及世界上任何其他地区谋求霸权，每一方都反对任何其他国家或国家集团建立这种霸权的努力。

任何一方都不准备代表任何第三方进行谈判，也不准备同对方达成针对其他国家的协议或谅解。

美利坚合众国政府承认中国的立场，即只有一个中国，台湾是中国的一部分。

双方认为，中美关系正常化不仅符合中国人民和美国人民的利益，而且有助于亚洲和世界的和平事业。

中华人民共和国和美利坚合众国将于1979年3月1日互派大使并建立大使馆。

II. *Translate the following speech into Chinese with enough attention to the diction and linguistic features of diplomatic language.*

President Nixon's Toast at the Banquet Given by Premier Zhou Enlai (Feb. 21, 1972)

Mr. Prime Minister and all of your distinguished guests this evening:

On behalf of all of your American guests, I wish to thank you for the incomparable hospitality for which the Chinese people are justly famous throughout the world. I particularly want to pay tribute, not only to those who prepared the magnificent dinner, but also to those who have provided the splendid music. Never have I heard American music played better in a foreign land.

Mr. Prime Minister, I wish to thank you for your very gracious and eloquent remarks. At this very moment, through the wonder of telecommunications, more people are seeing and hearing what we say than on any other such occasion in the whole history of the world. Yet what we say here will not be long remembered. What we do here can change the world.

As you said in your toast, the Chinese people are a great people, the American people are a great people. If our two peoples are enemies the future of this world we share together is dark indeed. But if we can find common ground to work together, the chance for world peace is immeasurably increased.

In the spirit of frankness which I hope will characterize our talks this week, let us recognize at the outset these points: we have at times in the past been enemies. We have great differences today. What brings us together is that we have common interests which transcend those differences. As we discuss our differences, neither of us will compromise our principles. But while we cannot close the gulf between us, we can try to bridge it so that we may be able to talk across it.

So let us, in these next five days, start a long march together, not in lockstep, but on different roads leading to the same goal, the goal of building a world structure of peace and justice in which all men stand together with equal dignity and in which each nation, large or small, has a right to determine its own form of government, free of outside interference or domination. The world watches. The world listens. The world waits to see what we will do. What is the world? In a personal sense, I think of my eldest daughter whose birthday is today. As I think of her, I think of all the children in the world, in Asia, in Africa, in Europe, in the Americas, most of whom were born since the date of the foundation of the People's Republic of China.

What legacy shall we leave our children? Are they destined to die for the hatreds which have plagued the old world, or are they destined to live because we had the vision to build a new world?

There is no reason for us to be enemies. Neither of us seeks the territory of the other; neither of us seeks domination over the other; neither of us seeks to stretch out our hands and rule the world.

Chairman Mao has written, "So many deeds cry out to be done, and always urgently; the world rolls on, time presses. Ten thousand years are too long, seize the day, seize the hour!"

This is the hour. This is the day for our two peoples to rise to the heights of greatness which can build a new and a better world.

In that spirit, I ask all of you present to join me in raising your glasses to Chairman Mao, to Prime Minister Chou, and to the friendship of the Chinese and American people which can lead to friendship and peace for all peoples in the world.

Chapter Six

Translation of Literary Works

6.1 Introduction

What is literature?

Different people have different views of the definition of literature. The so-called New Critics, who flourished in the United States from the 1920s until the 1960s, believed that literature had certain properties that experts trained in the writing and studying of literature could identify—such things as imagery, metaphor, meter, rhyme, irony, and plot. The New Critics confidently identified and evaluated works of literature, elevating the "great" works of literature to high status. Literature for them consisted, with but few exceptions, of poetry, drama, and fiction. However, some theorists have challenged even the concept of literature. Some argue that literature is not definable by properties, such as rhyme, meter, plot, setting, and characterization. "Nonliterary" works often have such properties—advertisements, popular songs, jokes and graffiti. Some say that a work becomes literature when it is no longer "specifically relevant to the immediate context of its origin". If a physics textbook is no longer read for information about physics but instead is read for some other reason—say, the elegance of its prose style – then it transcends the "immediate context of its origin" and becomes literature.

Kelley Griffith, in his book *Writing Essays about Literature*, interprets literature as follows: "Literature is language." The word literature has traditionally meant written—as opposed to spoken—works. But today, given the broadened meaning of the word, it includes oral as well as written works. Most critics believe that language is a key aspect of literature and that there has to be enough language in a work for it to be considered literature. Writers of literature, in contrast, use language connotatively—to bring into play all the emotional associations words may have. Connotation is the meaning that words have in addition to their explicit referents. An example of connotation is the word "mother", whose denotation is simply "female parent", but whose connotations include such qualities as protection, warmth, unqualified love, tenderness, devotion, mercy, intercession, home, childhood, the happy past. Some kinds of literature (poetry, for example) rely more heavily on connotation than others.

Literature is fictional. In fantasy fiction, for example, human beings fly, perform magic, remain young, travel through time, metamorphose, and live happily ever after. But even historical fiction, which relies on actual events, is fictional. It includes characters, dialogue, events, and settings that never existed. Some novels, such as *The Romance of the Three Kingdoms* (《三国演义》) *The Pilgrimage West* (《西游记》) and *Creation of the Gods*. (《封神演义》) are typical examples. The fictional quality of literature is the second "place" to look for meaning in literature. The fantasy element in literature is fun in itself, but fiction grants authors the option to fill in gaps that always exist in historical events, to make connections that historians cannot.

Literature is true as it mirrors the social life. Even though works of literature are fictional, they have the capacity for being true. Authors have ideas they want to communicate to readers. They embed them in works of literature and "send" the works to readers. Sometimes they directly state their ideas as in the following poem by Henry Howard, Earl of Surrey, written in 1547:

MY FRIEND, THE THINGS DO ATTAIN

Henry Howard, Earl of Surrey

My friend, the things that do attain
The happy life be these, I find;
The riches left, not got with pain;
The fruitful ground; the quiet mind;

The equal friend; no grudge, no strife;
No charge of rule, nor governance;
Without disease, the healthy life;
The household of continuance;

The mean diet, no dainty fare;
Wisdom joined with simpleness;
The night discharged of all care,
Where wine the wit may not oppress;

The faithful wife, without debate;
Such sleeps as may beguile the night;
Content thyself with thine estate,
Neither wish death, nor fear his might.

Here the poet tells us straight out his ideas about how to live the "happy life." More typically, however, authors refrain from directly stating their ideas. Instead, they present them indirectly by means of literary conventions such as plot, metaphor, symbol, irony, musical language, and suspense. All the details of a work make up an imaginary "world" that is based on the author's ideas about the real world. You may have heard the phrase "strange than fiction", as if the characters and events in works of fiction are abnormal and bizarre. But, ironically, it is real life that gives us freakish events and inexplicable people. To do this, they represent characters who typify real people, and they recount actions that would probably happen in real life. The characters and actions in *The Scholars* (《儒林外史》) by Wu Jingzi are typical examples.

Allegory is a kind of literature in which concrete things—characters, events and objects are meant as symbols of purity, truth, patience, etc. Here is an example:

Fear knocked at the door.

Faith answered.

There was no one there.

In this story, the character "Fear" is equivalent to the idea of faith. The setting of the story is a house, which symbolizes our psychological selves. Fear's knocking at the door shows an emotion that everyone experiences. Faith's opening the door shows a possible response to fear. The "moral" of the story, implied in the conclusion, is that we should all have faith because faith makes fear disappear.

So prominent in literature are typical characters and probable actions that most works of literature are to some extent allegorical. In English literature, some characters could be given names to represent ideas: Hamlet could be named "Melancholy", Othello could be called "Jealous", Ophelia "Innocent", Romeo "Love Sick", Iago "Sinister", and so forth; In *A Dream of Red Mansions*(《红楼梦》) "贾雨村" stands for "fiction in rustic language", "卜世仁" stands for "not a human being", "贾化" stands for "false talk", "甄世隐" stands for "true facts concealed", and so forth. We can infer authors' worldviews from the "allegorical" qualities of their works—typical characters, suggestive places, probable actions, even titles and epigraphs such as *Grapes of Wrath*, *Pride and Prejudice*, *Great Expectations*, *Measure for Measure* and *Vanity Fair*. Truth of literature is the most important place to look for meaning in literature.

Literature is "aesthetic"; it gives pleasure. The aesthetic quality of literature—it's "beauty"—is hard to define. However, like various other art forms—music, patterns of colour in paintings, photographs of sunsets, dance, its beauty can be sensed and perceived by readers. The pleasure of literature rests in the way authors use literary conventions, such as metaphor, plot, symbolism, irony, suspense, themes, and poetic language, which, taken together, constitute the form of the work that causes readers to feel empathy for the author and the characters portrayed by the author. The aesthetic quality of literature can lead readers while reading into the artistic mood in which they seem to be present at the very spot, involved in the very occurrence, witnessing the very parties concerned, iterating the very utterances, experiencing the very joy and sorrow, sharing the very weal and woe, partaking of the glee and grief. In brief they seem experiencing everything in person while reading, and experiencing the beauty of literature evokes a strong echo in readers, which is the effect and value of the aesthetic quality of literature.

Literature is intertextual: It relates to other works of literature, it incorporates established literary conventions, and it belongs to at least one genre of literature. The intertextuality of literature is a rich source of meaning for interpretation of individual works. The following two poems are the typical examples of intertextuality.

THE PASSIONATE SHEPHERD TO HIS LOVE

Come live with me and be my love,
And we will all the pleasures prove,
That valleys, groves, hills, and fields,
Woods, or steepy mountain yields.

And we will sit upon the rocks,
Seeing the shepherds feed their flocks,
By shallow rivers to whose falls,
Melodious birds sing madrigals.

And I will make thee beds of roses
And a thousand fragrant posies,
A cap of flowers, and a kirtle
Embroidered all with leaves of myrtle;

A gown made of the finest wool
Which from our pretty lambs we pull;
Fair lined slippers for the cold,
With buckles of the purest gold;

A belt of straw and ivy buds,
With coral clasps and amber studs:
And if these pleasures may thee move,
Come live with me, and be my love.

The shepherds' swains shall dance and sing
For thy delight each May morning:
If these delights thy mind may move,
Then live with me and be my love.

    Christopher Marlowe (1600)

THE NYMPH'S REPLY TO THE SHEPHERD

If all the world and love were young,
And truth in every shepherd's tongue,
These pretty pleasures might me move
To live with thee and be thy love.

Time drives the flocks from field to fold,
When rivers rage and rocks grow cold,
And Philomel becometh dumb;
The rest complains of cares to come.

The flowers do fade, and wanton fields
To wayward winter reckoning yields;
A honey tongue, a heart of gall,
Is fancy's spring, but sorrow's fall.

Thy gowns, thy shoes, thy beds of roses,
Thy cap, thy kirtle, and thy posies
Soon break, soon wither, soon forgotten—
In folly ripe, in reason rotten.

Thy belt of straw and ivy buds,
Thy coral clasps and amber studs,
All these in me no means can move
To come to thee and be thy love.

But could youth last and love still breed,
Had joys no date nor age no need,
Then these delights my mind might move
To live with thee and be thy love.

    Sir Walter Raleigh (c. 1600)

These poems are intertextual in the three ways mentioned above. First, Raleigh's poem is an almost line-for-line response to Marlowe's. We can understand Marlowe's poem without knowing Raleigh's, but we would miss a lot in Raleigh's poem if we did not know Marlowe's. Second, Marlowe's poem belongs to a genre called pastoral poetry. Third, in composing his poem, Marlowe incorporated the conventions of the pastoral genre: a peaceful, simple rural setting; carefree shepherds (the word pastor means "shepherd"); a season of eternal spring; an absence of the difficulties of life—hard work, disease, harsh weather, betrayal; lovers who talk genially about love; and a playful, witty, charming poetic style. Raleigh knows the conventions of pastoral poetry so well that he can challenge their basic assumptions.

(Griffith, 25)

The same is true of Chinese literature, especially Chinese poetry. There are quite a few examples of intertextuality in the collection of poems by Mao Zedong, such as "Reply to Mr. Liu Yazi to the tune of Seven-Character Lü Shi"(《七律和柳亚子先生》), "Reply to Mr. Liu Yazi to the tune of Silk Washing Stream"(《浣溪沙·和柳亚子先生》). "Reply to Li Shuyi to the tune of Butterflies Love Flowers"(《蝶恋花·答李淑一》), "Reply to Comrade Guo Moruo to the tune of Seven-Character Lü Shi"(《七律·和郭沫若同志》), to name but a few. Consider the following Ci poems.

蝶恋花
答李淑一
一九五七年五月十一日

我失骄杨君失柳,
杨柳轻飏直上重霄九。
问讯吴刚何所有,
吴刚捧出桂花酒。

寂寞嫦娥舒广袖,
万里长空且为忠魂舞。
忽报人间曾伏虎,
泪飞顿作倾盆雨。

(李淑一原词)
菩萨蛮
惊 梦
兰闺索寞翻身早,
夜来触动离愁了。
底事太难堪,
惊侬晓梦残。

征人何处觅?
六载无消息,
醒忆别伊时,
满衫清泪滋。

The two Ci poems are intertextual in three ways: First, Mao's poem is a response to Li's poem. Second, Li's poem is composed in memory of Liu Zhixun, her husband, Mao's in memory of Yang Kaihui, his wife and her classmate as well as her good friend Liu Zhixun. So the themes of the two poems are the same. Third, the hero of Li's poem is one of the two characters mentioned by Mao in his poem. Therefore each one serves as the interpretation of the other.

The above-mentioned five points are actually the basic attributes possessed by literature. The definition of literature varies with individuals and books. It is defined as "用文字写下的作品的总称。常指凭作者的想象写成的诗和散文,可以按作者的意图及写作的完美程度而识别。文学有各种不同的分类法,可按语言和国别分,可按历史时期、体裁或题材分"(《简明不列颠百科全书》第 11 卷). It is defined as "文学是显现在语言蕴籍中的审美意识形态"(《文学理论教程》). M. Gorky (1868.3-1936.6) believes that literature is a human science (文学是人学). Analysis of the basic elements of literary activities can manifest the close relationship between literature and human beings. Frist, human beings are the subject of literary creation, novels are written by writers, poems are composed by poets. No subject of creation, no literary works. Second, the object of literary creation is social life which is the totality of all realms of superstructure, and the totality of material life and spiritual life of human beings in the realistic world. Literature is the mirror of social life without which literary creation will be a castle in Spain. Finally, literary activities include not only the literary creation by writers and poets but also reading and appreciation by readers, without which the literary process is incomplete as the true value of literature can't be realized without communication, cooperation and interaction between writers and readers. In brief, the proposition that literature is a human science can be verified from various perspectives.

Similar to literary reading, literary translation is also a process of communication, but it is more complicated than literary reading, which can be illustrated as follows:

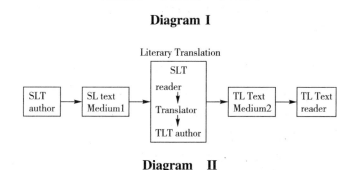

Diagram Ⅱ

From Diagram Ⅰ, it can be seen that the conversation and communication (in the indirect way) are carried out between the addresser (the author) and addressee (the reader) by means of literary work which is the only medium that makes the communication possible. The process of literary translation, however, is much more complicated as it is carried out in a bidirectional way. To the SL text, the translator is the reader, whereas to the TL text, he is the author, that is to say, a translator plays his dual role as the SLT reader and TLT author in literary translation. Therefore the communication between the SLT author and the TLT reader is carried out through two media—the source language text and the target language text. If the same literary text is used in the process of literary reading and that of literary translation, theoretically speaking, the same literary value should be achieved in both processes. However, the fact turns out otherwise. The literary work of a writer can only be regarded as "the first text" before being read by readers because it is only in a state of being-in-itself (being that lacks conscious awareness, being as potentiality). So long as it is read by readers, the literary work can free itself from the state of being-in-itself and become being-for-itself (conscious being, being as actuality). That is "the second text" that reflects the literary value. If we say the second text, based on the first text, results from the reading and appreciation of readers, and then the third text—translation is based on the process of deep-structure interpretation which is composed of empathy, sympathetic echo, purification and comprehension. This is the gap between the reading by an ordinary reader and that by a translator: the former can be done at the surface, shallow or the deep structure level, but the latter must be based on the thorough understanding, that is to say, a translator must show his insight into the deep structure of the SLT, otherwise there would be a big gap between the SLT and the TLT, and readers of the TLT would be much less informed than readers of the SLT.

6.2　Fidelity to SLT Literary Messages

Translation is the replacement of the information of the source language by its counterpart of the target language. The quality of translation is determined by the degree of fidelity to the SLT. Absolute fidelity to the SLT is impossible, but a good translation enjoys great fidelity. Compared with nonliterary works, the information of literary work is composed of much more complicated factors and elements, such as semantic information, grammatical information, rhetorical information, pragmatic information, cultural information, syntactic information and aesthetic information. A good translation with greatest fidelity to the SLT is supposed to involve all kinds of messages involved in the SLT.

6.2.1　Fidelity to Semantic Information

Semantic information is the most essential part of literary information that relates to and influences other kinds of information. The semantic information is usually shown at the surface level which is called the semiotic level by structuralists. Generally speaking, the whole meaning of literary discourse is involved at three levels—the surface level, the suggestive level and the symbolic level (or the semiotic level, figurative level and deep-structure level according to structuralism). The meaning at the surface level is usually the denotation of a word which can be easily perceived, but errors and misunderstanding lead to loss of semantic information and then loss of fidelity in translation. Consider the following examples:

1. 旺儿又打着千儿回道："奴才天天在二门上听差事,如何能知道二爷在外头的事呢?"
译文:(1) "I'm on duty all day long at the inner gate", stammered Lai Wang. "How could I know about the Second Master's business?"

(2) I spend all my time on call at the inner gate, Madam. I have no means of knowing what the master does outside.

(3) Little Wang bent one knee, "the slave performs his service at the second gateway day

after day. How can he know what the master does outside?"

"奴才", as a self-abasing term in Chinese clearly expresses the social status of the speaker who is in a lower-to-higher relationship with the hearer, which is, however, lost in Version 1 and Version 2. "Slave" is not the equivalent corresponding to "奴才", what is more, it is by no means a social deictic expression in English. "Slave" in Version (3), without specific explanation, would probably be mistaken as the third one mentioned by the speaker as the translator changes the first person to the third person. Thus Version (3) is not faithful to the original either. Henry Fielding(1707-1754), contemporary with Cao Xueqin (曹雪芹,? -1763) has many expressions like "your humble servant," "we servants," "us servants," "us poor servants"and "such a rascal as I" used in his famous novel "History of Tom Jones," so "奴才" can be translated into "as your humble servant I," which is semantically faithful to the original and in conformity with the principle of conventionality then. Thus Example 1 can be translated as follows:

(4) Lai Wang bent one knee and replied:"As your humble servant, I'm on duty all day long at the inner gate. How can I know about the Second Master's business?"

2. "你在家时,谁敢来放个屁?"

译文:(1) "When you were at home, who dared to come and pass his wind?"

(2) "When you were at home. who dared to come and insult me?"

3. 武行者心中要吃,哪里听他分说,一片喝声道:放屁! 放屁!

Now Wu the priest longed much in his heart to eat, and how could he be willing to listen to his explanation? He bellowed forth:" Pass your wind! pass your wind!"

In Example 2, the essential information of "放个屁" is contained at the suggestive level (or the figurative level) of the literary text. The translator of Version 1 only expresses the meaning of the surface level, which is the misrepresentation of the original, and will lead to misreading among the readers of the TLT. The same is true of the translation of Example 3, which can be polished as "... Nonsense, no more nonsense!"

6.2.2 Fidelity to Grammatical Information

Grammatical information is attributed to the system of expression which is the prime condition of correct understanding of the SLT, Though the TLT is different from the SLT in grammar, the message involved in the SLT grammar must be properly conveyed to readers of the TLT by all means possible. Otherwise intention of the SLT author would be misrepresented. Consider the following examples:

1. 那宝玉才合上眼睛便恍恍惚惚地睡去,犹似秦氏在前,悠悠荡荡,跟着秦氏到了一处。

As soon as Bao-yu closed his eyes he sank into a confused sleep in which Qin-shi was still there yet at the same time seemed to be drifting along weightlessly in front of him. He followed her until they came to place of marble terraces and vermilion balustrades...

The idiom "悠悠荡荡" in the original is used as the modifier to "宝玉"(即:"宝玉觉得自己悠悠荡荡地跟着秦氏到了一处"),but it is mistaken by the translator as the modifier to "秦

氏", which leads to the loss of grammatical information in the TLT. Translation by Yang Xianyi has the grammatical information properly conveyed to readers of the TLT as follows:

Bao-yu fell asleep as soon as he closed his eyes and dreamed that Ko-ching was before him. Absent-mindedly he followed her a long way to some crimson balustrades and white marble steps among green trees and clear streams...

2. Tom's new job started yesterday week.

汤姆的新工作是八天前开始的。

"Yesterday week", without being placed in a context, may refer to "8 days ago" or "in 6 days", its contextual meaning is determined by the tense of the verb "start". If the future tense is used in Example 2, the Chinese version should be "汤姆的新工作将于6天之后开始". In addition, the difference between the SL and the TL in number, gender, person, voice, tense and aspect should also be taken into consideration.

6.2.3 Fidelity to Rhetorical Information

There are many points of similarity between English and Chinese in rhetoric. There are 88 rhetorical figures in all in *A dictionary of English Figures of Speech*, only 2 of them are different from Chinese rhetorical figures. Yang Chunlin and Liu Fan have 103 rhetorical figures listed in *A Dictionary of Chinese Rhetoric*, only 10 figures of speech are absent from English, hence most of the rhetorical figures in English and Chinese can be translated interchangeablly. Some examples:

1. Icy distancing with Yuri Andropov would probably play better with the Reagan constituency.

同尤里·安德罗波夫拉开一段冰冷的距离会有利于里根在选区的竞选。

2. She possessed two false teeth and a sympathetic heart.

她有两颗假牙,一颗富于同情的心。

Transferred Epithet in Example 1 and Zeugma in Example 2 are faithfully shifted to their equivalent Chinese rhetorical figures by means of literal translation.

But, sometimes, the same rhetorical figures should be translated flexibly in a different way in order to keep fidelity to the SLT rhetoric. Consider the following examples:

3. 母亲不由地向后挪动一步,身上立时起了一层寒冷的鸡皮疙瘩。

Mother couldn't help starting back, her hands shivering nervously with chill, and with gooseflesh all over suddenly.

4. On his fishing trip, he caught three trout and a cold.

外出垂钓,他钓得鳟鱼三条,害了感冒一场。

If the SLT rhetorical figures are absent from the TLT, translation should be done carefully and flexibly by means of natural collocation, reasonable syntax, avoiding farfetched translation.

6.2.4 Fidelity to Pragmatic Information

Pragmatics is defined as "the study of how utterances have meanings in situation". (Leech, 1974) Participants in the communication can exchange ideas with each other just because they share the same cognitive environment that is mutually manifest to each side of the communication. The speaker or hearer during the communication, based on the mutually relevant context, can make ostensive inference and then get the optimal relevant information before he is sure of what the speaker intends to say, what the speaker intends to imply and his attitude to what's said and implied, or in other words, he is sure of the illocutionary force of the utterance. But in translation, the translator is not in the face-to-face relationship with the SL writer, so the cognitive environment is not mutually manifest to each other as that is to the speaker and hearer. Such being the case, the translator can only depend on the context to infer the illocutionary force of the utterance. Consider the following question:

Have you read this book?

To assert the illocutionary force of this example, the translator has to be aware that the example of utterances of "Have you read this book?" points up a necessary distinction between grammatical form and pragmatic use: all utterances of "Have you read this book?" are interrogative in grammatical form, but not all its utterances share the plain illocutionary function of eliciting information. On occasion it may be concluded that the "real" or ulterior aim of uttering such a question is to patronise and belittle even to embarrass the hearer. Thus the correct interpretation of the speaker-intended utterance depends very much on the context, paralinguistic context in particular. If it is to patronise or belittle the hearer, possible translations are as follows:
译文:(1)"你看过这本书吗?"言者语气中流露出蔑视。
(2)"你读过这本书吗?"言者流露出几分高人一等的神色。
(3)"你看过这本书?"言者语气中带有几分疑惑。

What is added to each translation serves as the compensation for the possible loss of pragmatic message of the utterance.

6.2.5 Fidelity to Cultural Information

In Chapter Three we have discussed the translation of culture-loaded words and learned that culture and language are closely correlated with each other. So we say cultural information is always embedded in language. However, some cultural messages, especially the relevant cultural background knowledge shared by the author and his/her intended readers, are often omitted by the author as he/she takes it for granted that readers are well acquainted with such cultural background knowledge. It may be true that the readers of the SLT are familiar with such cultural messages because they share the same language and culture with the SLT author who scarcely takes foreign readers into consideration. Such being the case, cultural default is of frequent occurrence in translation, especially in translation between English and Chinese. What is transparent to the SLT reader in the form of cultural default often is opaque to the TLT readers, sometimes the translator included. How to approach the cultural default in translation concerns very much the fidelity to the cultural information of the SLT.

Opinions on approaching cultural default in translation vary with translators, some foreigners prefer cultural translation, some cultural borrowing, some favour cultural substitution, still some prefer cultural transplantation. As for Chinese scholars, they have advanced the approaches as "compensation outside the TLT", "compensation inside the TLT", "domestication", "omission" and "literal translation".

"Compensation outside the TLT" means translating a cultural word literally, without any further explanation inside the body text, but with a footnote to the cultural word at the bottom of the page, or with an endnote at the end of the chapter or the TLT. Consider the following example:

宝玉心中想道:"难道这也是个痴丫头,又像颦儿来葬花不成?"因又自叹道:真也葬花,可谓"东施效颦",不但不为新奇,而且更是可厌了。

译文:(1) "Can this be another absurd maid come to bury flowers like Daiyu?" he wondered in some amusement. "If so, she is 'Dong Shi imitating Xi Shi', which isn't original but rather tiresome." (Translated by Yang Xianyi)

At the bottom of the very page there is a footnote attached to the above translated text which serves as a further explanation to "Dong Shi imitating Xi Shi" (东施效颦) as follows:

Xi Shi was a famous beauty in the ancient Kingdom of Yue. Dong Shi was an ugly girl who tried to imitate her ways.

By doing so, the translator retains the aesthetic effect of the original text—the covert cultural message leaves some room for readers to imagine. If the covert cultural message of "Dong Shi imitating Xi Shi" is opaque to readers of the TLT, the footnote can help them. Unlike "compensation outside the TLT," "compensation inside the TLT" means translating a cultural word with further explanation immediately after it within the very translated version. Translation of this example done by D. Hawkes is the typical example.

(2) "Can this be some silly maid come here to bury flowers like Frowner?" he wondered. He was reminded of Zhuang-zi's story of the beautiful Xi-shi's ugly neighbour, whose endeavours to imitate the little frown that made Xi-shi captivating produced an aspect so hideous that people ran from her in terror. The recollection of it made him smile.

This is "imitating the Frowner" with a vengeance, he thought, if that is really what she is doing. Not merely unoriginal, but downright disgusting!

Version (2) by D. Hawkes doubles the length of Version (1) by Yang Xianyi. The further explanation to the allusion "东施效颦" in Version (2) is even longer than the translation of the SLT itself. By doing so, Version (2) changes the covert message of the allusion into the overt message, and consequently what is opaque to the readers of the TLT becomes transparent. However, this kind of translation spoils the coherence of SLT as it adds too much within the TLT, as a result of this the imagination room left by the SLT author for readers disappears, and then the aesthetic effect of SLT is lost to a great extent. Comparatively speaking, Version (1) is more faithful to the SLT. So we say "compensation outside the TLT" is an effective approach to cultural default and it is the proper way to keep fidelity to the cultural information of SLT.

6.2.6 Fidelity to Syntactic Information

In Chapter Four, differences and similarities between English and Chinese in syntax are discussed. It is well known to us that "a sentence is not autonomous, it does not exist for its own sake but as part of a situation and a part of a text. And one of the most important functions of information dynamics is precisely to link a sentence to its environment in a manner which allows the information to flow through the text in the desired manner". (Enkvist, 1978) As a translator, one should be aware not only of the cognitive meanings and basic syntactic structures in his text, but also of its information dynamics, especially the interrelationship between meaning, choice and markedness. The three are interrelated closely. A linguistic element carries meaning to the extent that it is selected. Meaning is closely associated with choice, so that the more obligatory an element is, the less marked it will be and the weaker will be its meaning. The fact that adjectives have to be placed in front of nouns in English, for instance, means that their occurrence in this position has little or no significance because it is not the result of choice. If we change the position of an element from the unmarked into the marked one as follows:

(A) Her eyes were beautiful. (unmarked)

(B) Beautiful were her eyes. (marked)

The complement of (B) is therefore highly marked in this position and indicates a more conscious effort on part of the speaker/writer to highlight this particular element as his point of departure. Therefore (B) carries more meaning because it is the result of choice. The more marked a choice the greater the need for it to be motivated in translation. If we have (A) translated into "她的眼睛很美(迷人)", and then a faithful version in syntax should be "迷人的是她的眼睛". The marked element is thus highlighted in translation, and then fidelity to syntactic information is achieved.

According to transformational-generative grammar of Noam Chomsky, one kernel sentence can be transformed into quite a few derived sentences with various part marked as follows:

Unmarked: The book received a great deal of publicity in China.

Marked
(1) In China the book received a great deal of publicity.
(2) What the book received in China was a great deal of publicity.
(3) What was received by the book in China was a great deal of publicity.
(4) It was the book that received a great deal of publicity in China.
(5) It was a great deal of publicity that the book received in China.
(6) It was in China that the book received a great deal of publicity.

The above six marked sentences are derived from the unmarked one "The book received a great deal of publicity in China". In translation of the derived sentences above-mentioned (even the unmarked one) we can find that sometimes we can preserve the thematic patterning of the original without distorting the target text[such as Example (1) and Example (6)], sometimes we cannot preserve the thematic patterning of the original without distorting the target text[such as Examples (2),(3),(4) and (5)], which is caused by the differences in syntax and grammar between English and Chinese, and results in difficulty and even impossibility of keeping fidelity to syntactic information.

6.2.7 Fidelity to Aesthetic Information

Literature is aesthetic. The aesthetic information is composed of all the aspects mentioned above, including the semantic message, grammatical message, rhetorical message, pragmatic message, cultural message and syntactic message as beauty of literary works is reflected in the various aspects of language. So fidelity to aesthetic information is based on the faithful conveyance of the above six kinds of messages to the TLT. Take translation of poetry for example, fidelity to aesthetic information is concretely reflected in sound, diction, form, rhyme and rhythm. Consider the following example:

1. 　　　　　登　高
　　　　　　　——杜　甫
风急天高猿啸哀,渚清沙白鸟飞回。
无边落木萧萧下,不尽长江滚滚来。
　　　　　……

译文:(1) THE HEIGHTS

  The wind so fresh, the sky so high
  Awake the gibbons wailing cry.
  The isles clear-cut, the sand so white,
  Arrest the wheeling sea-gulls' flight.
  Through endless space with rustling sound
  The falling leaves are whirled around.
  Beyond my ken a yeasty sea
  The Yangtze's waves are rolling free.

(2) A LONG CLIMB

  In a sharp gale from the wide sky apes whimpering,
  Birds are flying homeward over the clear lake and white sand.
  Leaves are dropping down like the spray of a waterfall,
  While I watch the long river always rolling on.

(3) ON THE HEIGHT

  The wind so swift, the sky so wide, apes wail and cry;
  Water so clear and beach so white, birds wheel and fly.
  The boundless forest sheds its leaves shower by shower;
  The endless river rolls its waves hour after hour.

Version (1) is a good translation with well-knit parallelism and antithesis, its diction is well-whetted and the rhyme and rhythm sound natural and beautiful, the artistic mood of the original poem is re-established but for the only fly in the ointment—the form of the original poem is changed from 4 lines into 8 lines. The second version, even though the form is similar to the original, is not faithful because its diction is not well weighed, its rhyme and rhythm are unpleasant, and what is more, "飞回", which means "to hover", is mistranslated as "flying homeward". Hence the readers of Version (2) cannot experience the beauty of the SL poem because it can hardly lead them into the same artistic mood as the original poem does. Version (3) would be perfect if the translator changes "river" into "Yangtze". Comparatively speaking, Version (3) is of greater fidelity to the aesthetic information of the TL poem.

Consider and analyse the following translations, and then give your opinions on fidelity to the aesthetic information of the SL poems.

2.   TO SORROW

I bade good morrow
And thought to leave her far away behind;
But cheerly, cheerly,
She loves me dearly;
She is so constant to me, and so kind.
I would deceive her,
And so leave her,
But ah! She is so constant and so kind.

译文:(1)
我向悲痛告别了,
我要把她抛在远远的后面;
但她却欢欣地,欢欣地,
亲密地恋着我;
她对我是这样的忠实,这样的亲切呀。
我要欺瞒了她,
从此抛开了她,
但是,啊! 她对我是这样的忠实,
这样地亲切呀!

(2)
我向"愁烦",
说了声再见,
本打算,和他一别天样远;
谁知她,恋恋,
爱我似心肝;
意惹不自持,情牵割难断。
我想弄机关,
把她巧欺骗,
却又转念,她对我,情不断。

3.   **古诗十九首其一**

青青河畔草,郁郁园中柳
盈盈楼上女,皎皎当窗牖
娥娥红粉装,纤纤出素手
昔为娼家女,今为荡子妇
荡子行不归,空床难独守

译文:(1)
NEGLECTED

Green grows the grass upon the bank,
The willow-shoots are long and lank,
A lady in a glistening gown
Upon the casement and looks down.
The roses on her cheek blush bright,
Her rounded arm is dazzling white
A singing-girl in early life,
And now a careless roue's wife...
Ah, if he does not mind his own,
He'll find some day the bird has flown!

(2)
THE BEAUTIFUL TOILET

Blue, blue is the grass about the river
And the willows have overfilled the close garden.
And within, the mistress, in the midmost of her youth,
White, white of face, hesitates, passing the door,
Slender, she puts forth a slender hand.
And she was a courtezan in the old days.
And she has married a sot,
Who now goes drunkenly out
And leaves her too much alone.

(3)
Green, green,
The grass by the river-bank.
Thick, thick,
The willow trees in the garden.
Sad, sad,
The lady in the tower.
White, white,
At the casement window.
Fair, fair,
Her red-powdered face.
Small, small,
She puts out out her pale hand.
Once she was a dancing-house girl,
Now she is a wandering man's wife
The wandering man went, but did not return.
It is hard alone to keep an empty bed.

6.3 Translation of Fiction

6.3.1 Introduction

The "notion" of fiction is first used in a Chinese Taoist classic Zhuang Zi (《庄子外物》):"夫揭竿累,趣灌渎,守鲵鲋,其于得大鱼难矣! 饰小说以干县令,其于大达亦远矣". But it originally meant trivial utterance which is different from the conception of "小说" in "New Doctrine" by Huan Tan (桓谭):"小说家合丛残小语,近取譬论,以作短书,治身理家,有可观之辞"。Huan Tan's definition to "小说" is very much similar to the definition of fiction today:"Literature consisting of the narration of imaginary events and the portrayal of imaginary characters". (*Shorter Oxford English Dictionary*). Fiction, one of the three major genres of literature (fiction, drama, and poetry) belongs to a large category of communication called narrative. Narrative is the telling of a story, a recounting of events in time. In contrast to nonfiction narrative (biography, memoir, autobiography, history), narrative fiction, whether written in poetry or prose, features a telling of made-up events. The following elements typify narrative fiction:

Theme

Themes are ideas about human condition that we draw from works of literature—not just from fiction but from literature in all genres. Although the terms "subject" and "theme" are often used interchangeably, they are different. The subject is what the work is about. You can state the subject in a word or phrase: "The subject of Shakespeare's Sonnet 116 is love". In contrast, theme is what the work says about the subject. Stating a theme requires a complete sentence, sometimes several sentences: "A theme of sonnet 116 is 'Love remains constant even when assaulted by tempestuous events or by time.'"

In some literary works, especially complex ones, there may be several, even contradictory themes. A subject of Tolstoy's Anna Karenina is sacred love. But another, equally important subject is social entrapment. One theme of Anna Karenina seems to be that people should not abandon "sacred" commitments, such as marriage and parenthood, for extramarital "loves", no matter how passionate and deeply felt they may be. This theme emerges from Anna's desertion of her husband and child for Count Vronsky. An alternate theme is that people, through little fault of their own, can become trapped in painful, long-lasting, and destructive relationships that they want desperately to escape. This theme emerges from Anna's marriage. When she was very young, Anna married an older man whom she now realizes is too petty, prim, and self-absorbed to satisfy her generous and passionate nature. So discordant is her relationship with her husband that it seems no less "immoral" than her affair with Vronsky. Tolstoy, in other words, draws complex, even contradictory lessons from Anna's adultery. She is not simply the sinful person; she is also the driven person. This combination of traits characterizes the condition of many people. (Griffith, 2006) Some literary works, however, have no clear themes. They may display images, actions, atmosphere, and characters that have no apparent relationship to the world outside the works.

Plot

Plot consists of three things. First, it is the work itself, the author's arrangement of events from the first page to the last. By reading the work, we experience the events as the author has arranged them. Second, plot includes the linkage of events by cause and effect. An inevitable byproduct of cause and effect is conflict. Third, plot is the author's presentation of events so as to engage readers intellectually and emotionally. Authors do this through such devices as pacing, intense conflict, surprise, rising action, climax, withheld information, and foreshadowing of later events.

Characters

Characters are the people in narratives, and characterization is the author's presentation and development of the traits of characters. Sometimes, as in fantasy fiction, the characters are not people. They may be animals, robots, or creatures from outer space, but the author endows them with human abilities and human psychological traits. They really are people in all but outward form.

Setting

Setting includes several closely related aspects of a work of fiction. First, setting is the physical, sensuous world of the work. Second, it is the time in which the action of the work takes place. And third, it is the social environment of the characters: the manners, customs, and moral values that govern the characters society. A fourth aspect—"atmosphere"—is largely, but not entirely, an effect of setting.

6.3.2 Translation of Titles

A title is the name of a novel which usually embodies the theme of the literary work as it is highly condensed by the author. A title may be overt or covert, whatever it may be, it should be the focus of translation as it concerns very much about the success of translation. An overt title usually expresses the subject of the novel or is just the name of the protagonist, so most of them are translated literally as follows:

Lady Chatterley's Lover—《查太莱夫人的情人》

Women in Love—《恋爱中的女人》

Tess of the D'urbervilles—《德伯家的苔丝》

Jane Eyre—《简爱》

Gimpel, the Fool—《傻瓜吉姆佩尔》

A Tale of Two Cities—《双城记》

War and Peace—《战争与和平》

Treasure Island—《金银岛》/《宝岛》

《三国演义》—The Three Kingdoms

《西厢记》—The Story of the West Pavilion

《牡丹亭》—The Peony Pavilion

《浮生六记》—Six Chapters of A Floating Life

A covert title usually reflects the theme of a novel in a symbolic way. Thus a covert title is usually translated into a covert one as follows:

Vanity Fair—《名利场》

The Rainbow—《虹》

Gone with the Wind—《飘》

《红楼梦》—A Dream of Red Mansions

Gone with the Wind as the title of a novel, is based on Chapter 24 of the novel, which means the protagonist's hometown is gone with the wind. It was translated into《随风而去》by Shanghai Film Studio which is in conformity with its original title as the name of a film. But it is not suitable for the title of a novel. Later, it was translated into《乱世佳人》which is very much appealing to audience as the title of a film. Fu Donghua had the title of the novel translated into《飘》which is very much appropriate for the novel as it on the one hand reflects symbolically the essence of the work, and on the other, directly expresses the denotations as well as the connotations of the key words "gone" and "wind".

6.3.3 The Stylistic Features Reproduced in Translation

Just as each writer has his own style, a successful translator has also his own style of translation. But the latter is not entirely independent of the former, it is based on the former instead. An experienced translator usually has his own style naturally reflected in his translation on the basis of being harmonious with the original style and never let the secondary supersede the primary. The following elements are supposed to be taken into consideration in translation.

Traits of Times

The classical Chinese literary works are very much different from the modern literary works in spelling, diction, syntax and style. Similarly, the Old English is very much different from the Modern English in spelling, diction and grammar. Shakespeare is different from Thackeray, from Hemingway in artistic quality as their works are written against certain historical periods, so they possess their own traits of times. Features of times should be taken into consideration in translation, and besides, each writer has his (or her) own style apart from the features of times, which must be also taken into account in translation. Some examples:

1. Madam—After her six years' residence at the Mall, I have the honour and happiness of presenting Miss Amilia Sedley to her parents, as a young lady not unworthy to occupy a fitting position in their polished and refined circle. Those virtues which characterize the young English gentlewoman, those accomplishments which become her birth and station, will not be found wanting in the amiable Miss Sedley whose industry and obedience have endeared her to instructors, and whose delightful sweetness of temper has charmed her age and her youthful companions.

夫人—爱米丽亚·赛特笠小姐在林荫道(女校)已经修业六年,此后尽堪至府上高雅的环境中占一个与她身份相称的地位,我因此感到万分荣幸和欣喜。英国大家闺秀所特有的品德,在她家世和地位上所应有的才学,温良的赛特笠小姐已经具备。她学习勤勉,性情和顺,博得师长们的赞扬,而且她为人温柔可亲,因此校内无论长幼,一致喜爱她。

The original is taken from a letter presented to Mrs. Sedley, Miss Amelia's mother, by the school mistress Pinkerton. The letter, with excessive attention to wording is prolix deliberately. The two negative structures "not unworthy to occupy" and "will not be found wanting" are used for the purpose of striking a pose to impress people, which showed the author's style of ornamental writing. This style is largely expressed in the target language.

2. 闺房记乐

余生乾隆癸未冬十一月二十有二日,正值太平盛,且在衣冠之家,居苏州沧浪亭畔,天之厚我,可谓至矣。东坡云:"事如春梦了无痕,"苟不记之笔墨,未免有辜彼苍之厚。

因思关雎冠三百篇之道,故列夫妇于首卷;余以次递及焉。所愧少年失学,稍识之无,不过记其实情实事而已。若必考订其文法,是责明于垢鉴矣。

Wedded Bliss

I was born in 1763, under the reign of Ch'ienlung, on the twenty-second day of the eleventh moon. The country was then in the heyday of peace and, moreover, I was born in a scholar's family, living by the side of the Ts'anglang Pavilion in Soochow. So altogether I may say the gods have been unusually kind to me. Su Tungpo said, "Life is like a spring dream which vanishes without a trace." I should be ungrateful to the gods if I did not try to put my life down on record. Since the Book of Poems begins with a poem on wedded love, I thought I would begin this book by speaking of my marital relations and then let other matters follow. My only regret is that I was not properly educated in childhood; all I know is a simple language and I shall try only to record the real facts and real sentiments. I hope the reader will be kind enough not to scrutinize my grammar, which would be like looking for brilliance in a tarnished mirror.

From the above-mentioned examples, we can see that the original style is composed of two aspects: spiritual factor and material form, the former refers to the writer's figure and his mental attitude, the latter means diction, syntax, rhetoric devices and artistic quality of the writer expressed in his works. Only by expressing the two aspects completely, can we have the original style conveyed to the readers of the target language.

Traits of Various Characters

Characters in a novel are different from each other in identity, personality and many other aspects. Characterization is mainly shown by words of various levels of formality and sentences of different structures, which are supposed to be reproduced in the target language. Consider the following examples:

3. I am Gimpel the fool. I don't think myself a fool. On the contrary. But that's what folks call me. They gave me the name while I was still in school. I had seven names in all: imbecile, donkey, flax-head, dope, grump, ninny, and fool. The last name struck. What did my foolishness consist of? I was easy to take in. They said, "Gimpel, you know the rabbi's wife has been brought to childbed?" So I skipped school. Well, it turned out to be a lie. How was I supposed to know? She hadn't had a big belly. But I never looked at her belly. Was that really so foolish? The gang laughed and heehawed, stomped and danced and changed a goodnight prayer. And instead of the raisings they give when a woman's lying in, they stuffed my hand full of goat turds. I was no weakling. If I slapped someone he'd see all the way to Cracow. But I'm really not a slugger by

nature. I think to myself. Let it pass. So they take advantage of me.

俺叫吉姆佩尔,人家叫俺傻瓜。可俺自己并不觉俺傻,而正好相反。还在上学时,他们就这么叫俺。拢共有七个外号哩:什么憨子、蠢驴、木头人、白痴、笨蛋、呆子、傻瓜。倒霉的就是这最后一个外号,一叫就叫开了。俺哪儿傻呢? 就是好上当呗。那伙人说:"吉姆佩尔,你知道吗,拉比夫人坐月子啦!"俺连学没有上,跑去一打听,嘿! 根本没影子的事。她坐不坐月子俺咋知道,俺没见她大肚子,也从来没瞧过她的肚子。这真的能叫傻吗? 那帮人连嚷带笑,连蹦带跳地蹓了,末了还丢下两个字"晚安!"要是谁家的老婆真的坐了月子,他们便塞给俺一包羊屎蛋当是葡萄干,叫俺送去。俺可不是稀松蛋,要扇谁一巴掌,准把他扇到爪哇国去。不过,说真的,俺本来就不是什么拳击手。想一想,算了吧,就让他们讨回巧吧。

The above example is the very beginning of the novel *Gimpel the Fool* by I. B. Singer, which is charaterized by two remarkable features: ①words of low level of formality ②loose sentence structure. These two features function effectively in characterization of the protagonist—Gimpel—an illiterate simpleton. The translator takes these traits into consideration and has them vividly represented in the target language. Hence the original image of the protagonist is vividly conveyed to readers of the TLT. If the protagonist is a person of different identity who enjoys high social status, the case will be quite otherwise as follows.

4. 北静王见他语言清朗,谈吐有致,一面又向贾政笑道:"令郎真乃龙驹凤雏,非小王在世翁前唐突,将来'雏凤清于老凤声',未可量也。"贾政陪笑道:"犬子岂敢谬承金奖,赖藩郡余恩,果如所言,亦荫生辈之幸矣。"北静王又道:"只有一件:令郎如此资质,想老太夫人自然钟爱;但吾辈后生,甚不宜溺爱,溺爱则未免荒失了学业。昔小王曾蹈此辙,想令郎亦未必不是如是也。若令郎在家难以用功,不妨常到寒邸,小王虽不才,却多蒙海内众名士凡至都者,未有不垂青目的。是以寒邸高人颇聚,令郎常去谈谈会会,则学问可以日进矣。"贾政忙躬身答道:"是"。

译文:(1) The clarity and fluency of Pao-yu's answers made the prince turn to observe to Chia Cheng, "Your son is truly a dragon's colt or young phoenix. May I venture to predict that in time to come this young phoenix may even surpass the old one ?" "My worthless son does not deserve such high praise, "rejoined Chia Cheng hurriedly with a courteous smile. "If thanks to the grace of Your Highness such proves the case, that will be our good fortune."

"There is one thing, however, "cautioned the prince. "Because your son is so talented his grandmother and mother must have doted on him; but over-indulgence is very bad for young people like ourselves as it makes us neglect our studies. I went astray in this way myself and suspect your honourable son may do the same. If he finds it difficult to study at home, he is very welcome to come as often as he likes to my humble house. For although untalented myself, I am honoured by visits from scholars of note from all parts of the empire when they come to the capital. Hence my poor abode is frequented by eminent men and conversation with them should improve his knowledge."Chia Cheng bowed and assented to this without hesitation.

(2) Delighted that everything Bao-yu said was so clear and to the point, the prince observed to Jia Zheng that "the young phoenix was worthy of his sire".

"I trust I shall not offend you by saying so to your face," he said, "but I venture to prophesy that this fledgling of yours will one day sing sweeter than the parent bird".

Jia Zheng smiled politely.

"My son is doubtless unworthy of the compliment. Your Highness is good enough to pay him. If, thanks to your encouragement, he turns out as you say, we shall count ourselves truly fortunate."

"There is only one drawback in possessing such charm," said the prince, "I am sure it must make his grandmother dote upon him; and, unfortunately, being the object of too much affection is very bad for people of our years. It leads us to neglect our studies. This used at one time to be the case with me, and I suspect is now the case with your son. If he does find difficulty in working at home, he would be very welcome to come round to my palace. I do not pretend to be a gifted person myself, but I am fortunate in counting distinguished writers from all over the empire among my acquaintances, and my palace is a rendezvous for them when they are in the capital, so that I never want for intellectual company. By constantly mixing and conversing with such people at my palace your son could do much to improve his education."

"Yes." Jia Zheng bowed deferentially.

A lot of social deictic terms such as "令郎", "龙驹凤雏", "小王", "犬子" and "寒邸" are used in order to indicate the identities and social status of the prince and Jia Zheng. Comparatively speaking, Version (1) is more faithful than Version (2) as it has social deictic terms and words of high level of formality more accurately expressed in the TLT. Thus the linguistic features of the characters are manifest to readers of the TLT.

Translation Exercises

Ⅰ. Translate the following passages into English with enough attention to the irony directed at the protagonist of the source language text.

1. 平儿听了,便作了主意:"叫他们进来。先在这里坐着就是了。"周瑞家的听了,方出去领了他们进入院来。上了正房台矶,小丫头打起了猩红毡帘,才入堂屋,只闻一阵香味扑了脸来,竟不辩是何气味,身子如在云端里一般。满屋之物都是耀眼争光的,使人头悬目眩。刘姥姥此时惟点头咂嘴念佛而已。

2. 次日,面谋之如海。如海道:"天缘凑巧,因贱荆去世,都中家岳母念及小女无人依傍教育,前已遣了男女船只来接,因小女未曾大痊,故未及行。此刻正思向蒙训教之恩,未经酬报,遇此机会,岂有不尽心图报之理? 但请放心。弟已预为筹画至此,已修下荐书一封,转托内兄,务为周旋协佐,方可稍尽弟之鄙诚,即有所费用之例,弟于内兄信中,已注明白,亦不劳尊兄多虑矣。

Ⅱ. *Translate the following passage into Chinese with enough attention to the author's intention and the linguistic style of the source language text.*

Sir Pitt went and expostulated with his sister-in-law upon the subject of the dismissal of Briggs, and other matters of delicate family interest. In vain she pointed out to him how necessary was the protection of Lord Steyne for her poor husband; how cruel it would be on their part to deprive Brigges of the position offered to her. Cajolements, coaxings, smiles, tears could not satisfy Sir Pitt, and he had something very like a quarrel with his once admired Becky. He spoke of the honour of the family; the unsullied reputation of the Crawleys; expressed himself in indignant tones about her receiving those young Frenchmen—those wild youngmen of fashion, my Lord Steyne himself, whose carriage was always at her door, who passed hours daily in her company, and whose constant presence made the world talk about her, as the head of the house he implored her to be more prudent. Society was already speaking lightly of her. Lord Steyne, though a nobleman of the greatest station and talents, was a man whose attentions would compromise any woman; he besought, he implored, he commanded his sister-in-law to be watchful in her intercourse with that nobleman.

6.4 Translation of Prose

Prose, as a literary form, is distinct from poetry or verse. It is the ordinary form of spoken or written language without metrical structure. A prose can function as narrating story, portraying characters, painting scenery, picturing objects or commenting current affairs. The syntax of prose is elastic, sometimes loose, sometimes compact, sometimes simple, sometimes complex. The style of prose is characterized by clarity, brevity, and sincerity. Specifically, it can be categorized as follows:

Noun style

Consider the following example.

1. The connection between behaviour in the socially real world and dramatic performance is a double link. Much of everyday social behaviour and socially consequential action is itself composed, and often in a fashion which is recognised at the time as "theatrical" or is revealed as such afterwards. When we construct special buildings or settings for ritual occasions of many kinds, from judicial proceedings to love-making, when we set scenes and dress up or dress down for a social occasion there is a resemblance, which may not be admitted even to ourselves, to the enactment of composed theatrical performances by professional actors. Tacitly or explicitly we constantly draw on symbolic references and typifications shared by playwright, actors and audience. This is the basis of the adoption of dramaturgic terminology by social scientists and of elaboration in the mere analogy of the analysis of social behaviour as more or less skilled performance, by Erving Goffman, and as "symbolic interaction" by Blumer, Becker and others.

The second connection runs, so to speak, the other way. Drama is a presentation of interpretations of everyday social behaviour and of consequential action which are, or are offered for good currency. Moreover, because, as the audience, people can be shown more of the course, causes and consequences of action than they can ever know in the socially real world, the theatre provides usable paradigms for conduct. The excellence of the playwright as composer of theatrical action lies in this. The emergence of modern drama from religious ritual by way of Miracle plays and Moralities is not simply a fact of inconsequential chronology. First, in the Miracles there was the presentation in "ideal types" of conduct, good, evil, wayward, mundane or spiritual, in confrontation, and eventually representation of stereotype figures working out recognisable or plausible strategies of action in order to engage themselves in or disengage themselves from recognisable or plausible social relationships of situations; all these constitute an evolutionary or epigenetic pattern familiar enough in the interpretation of contemporaneous historical changes.

All social structures maintain themselves by means of an apparatus of institutional forms which provide individual members of the society with codes of behaviour and grammatical rules for reading the behaviour of others.

The basic pattern used in the above prose is : "noun + is + prepositional phrase". It can be illustrated as follows:

The connection between behaviour

in the socially real world

and dramatic performance

is a double link.

Sometimes prepositional phrases precede "is ", as follows:

Drama is a presentation

of interpretations

of everyday social behaviour and

of consequential action which are, or are offered

for good currency.

Through the analysis of the above example it can be seen that the prose of noun style is characterized by long sentences and compact syntax. Just opposite to the prose of noun style is the prose of verb style.

Verb style

Compare the style of the following two examples.

2. Posit the two extremes of our spectrum. Both are unliterary. At the extreme left, childish babble, nursery rhymes, pure pleasure in words. Words here are things. You play with them. They have shape, sound, corporeality. At the other end, a mathematical equation, pure significance, all sign. Pleasure flows from concepts. Nonsense rhyme presents a perfectly opaque surface, equations a perfectly transparent one.

Noun style

3. A perception of the two extreme poles of this spectrum of language is derived from a conception of the range of language under consideration. The unliterary quality of the kinds of discourse found on each pole of the spectrum must first be understood, however. The left pole of this spectrum is characterized by the presence of the babble associated with children and the presence of children's nursery rhymes; in terms of the attitudes associated with this pole of the spectrum, there is a general preference for the derivation of pleasure from language. Language on the left pole of the spectrum is characterized by the reification of words; in other words, words are given a tangible quality.

In accordance with this theory, words are found by the reader to be the objects of play. A categorization of the properties of this kind of language reveals in it the existence of a principle of contour, an audible quality, and a sense of physical corporeality. On the pole to the extreme right of the spectrum, there is an abundance of symbols, notably the equations associated with the practice of mathematical inquiry, which appear to exist for the sake of their denotative quality; transparent signifiers and their readily comprehensible signifiers are to be found on this pole of the spectrum. On this pole, concepts constitute the body of ideas from which pleasure is derived. From this discussion it is apparent that the verbal surface of types of prose like nonsense rhymes is characterized by opacity; transparency is more characteristic of the surface texture of mathematical equations, however.

The above two examples convey basically the same message to readers. However, Example 3 is 3.6 times longer than the textual material of Example 2, which is due to the distinction between verb style and noun style. Therefore it is supposed to be taken into consideration in translation from English into Chinese. English syntax is generally characterized by hypotaxis. But sometimes you may come across a passage of paratactic style.

Paratactic style

4. Now in the fall the trees were all bare and the roads were muddy. I rode to Gorizia from Udine on a camion. We passed other camions on the road and I looked at the country. The mulberry trees were bare and the fields were brown. There were wet dead leaves on the road from the rows of bare trees and men were working on the road, tamping stone in the ruts from piles of crushed stone along the side of the road between the trees. We saw the town with a mist over it that cut off the mountains. We crossed the river and I saw that it was running high. It had been raining in the mountains. We came into the town past the factories and then the houses and villas and I saw that many more houses had been hit. On a narrow street we passed a British Red Cross ambulance. The driver wore a cap and his face was thin and very tanned. I did not know him. I got down from the camion in the big square in front of the Town Mayor's house, the driver handed down my rucksack and I put it on and swung on the two musettes and walked to our villa. It did not feel like a homecoming.

On the basis of a thorough analysis of the structure of Example 4, we can find that there are three basic patterns as follows:

Pattern 1   I + verb

I rode to Gorizia

I looked at the country

I saw that it was running high

I saw that many more houses

I did not know him

I got down from the camion

I put it on

Pattern 2   We + verb

We passed other camions

We saw the town

We crossed the river

　　We came into the town

　　We passed a British Red Cross ambulance

　　Pattern 3　　Noun + was/were

　　The trees were all bare

　　The roads were muddy

　　The mulberry trees were bare

　　The fields were brown

　　There were wet dead leaves

　　Men were working

　　It was running high

　　It had been raining

　　His face was thin

　　It did not feel like a homecoming.

　The specific patterns add a great deal to this Hemingway hero who does not reflect on the world he passes through; he notes and endures it, which is the author's intention that is supposed to be reproduced in translation.

　　Opposite to paratactic style is the hypotactic style as follows:

Hypotactic Style

　　5. If you have been in line, ordered simply to wait and to do nothing, and have watched the enemy bring their guns to bear upon you down a gentle slope, have seen the puff of the firing, have felt the burst of the spherical case-shot as it came toward you, have heard and seen the shrieking fragments go tearing through your company, and have known that the next or the next shot carries your fate; if you have advanced in line and have seen ahead of you the spot which you must pass where the rifle bullets are striking; if you have ridden by night at a walk toward the blue line of fire at the dead angle of Spottsylvania, where for twenty-four hours the soldiers were fighting on the two sides of an earthwork, and in the morning the dead and dying lay piled in a row six deep, and as you rode have heard the bullets splashing in the mud and earth about you; if you have been on the picket-line at night in a black and unknown wood have heard the spat of the bullets upon the trees, and as you moved, have felt your foot slip upon a dead man's body; if you have had a blind fierce gallop against the enemy, with your blood up and a pace that left no time for fear—, if in short, as some, I hope many, who hear me, have known, you have known the vicissitudes of terror and of triumph in war, you know that there is such a thing as the faith I spoke of.

　　(The Soldier's Faith. An Address Delivered on Memorial Day, May 30, 1895, at a Meeting Called by the Graduating Class of Harvard University)

　　The apodosis is preceded by so many "if" clauses (the protasis) that we have to pass one-by-one before reaching the "then" clause, which is one of the syntactic features of hypotactic arrangement that should be taken into consideration in translation from English into Chinese.

The syntactic style is the key factor that should be considered in translation. Consider the following prose.

6.   **THE FIRST SNOW**

The first snow came. How beautiful it was, falling so silently all day long, all night long, on the mountains, on the meadows, on the roofs of the living, on the graves of the dead! All white save the river, that marked its course by a winding black line across the landscape; and the leafless trees, that against the leaden sky now revealed more fully the wonderful beauty and intricacies of their branches. What silence, too, came with the snow, and what seclusion! Every sound was muffled, every noise changed to something soft and musical. No more tramping hoofs, no more rattling wheels! Only the chiming of sleigh-bells, beating as swift and merrily as the hearts of children.

Example 6 is a very short prose composed of only seven sentences. But readers are deeply impressed by its terse style, smooth rhythm and flexible syntax which add up to a vivid picture of snow landscape. If we have the similar structures listed as follows, the syntactic style of the prose will be manifest to all of us.

(1) Prepositional phrases

on the mountains

on the meadows

on the roofs of the living

on the graves of the dead

(2) Adverbial phrases

all day long

all night long

(3) Clauses

What silence

What seclusion

Every sound was muffled

Every noise changed to something soft and musical

No more tramping hoofs

No more rattling wheels

The translator is supposed to have these features represented in his translation. Consider the following versions:

译文:(1)

第一场雪

第一场雪飘落,多么美啊! 昼夜不停地下着,落在山岗,落在草场,落在世人的房顶,落在死人的墓地。遍地皆白,只有河流像一条黑色的曲线穿过大地;落光叶子的大树映衬在铅灰色的天幕下,越发显得奇特壮观,还有那错落有序的树枝。下雪时多么寂寥,多么幽静! 所有的声音都变得浑浊了,所有的噪声都变得轻柔而富有乐感。没有得得的马蹄声,没有辚辚的车轮声,只能听到雪橇那欢快的铃声如童心在跳动。

(2)

初雪

初雪飘临,如万花纷谢,整日整夜,纷纷扬扬,真美极了。雪花儿无声无息,飞上山巅,撒向草原,飘至世人的房脊,落在死者的坟茔。莽莽原野,银装素裹,惟有长河逶迤,像一条黑色的长龙蜿蜒爬行于皑皑雪原。枯藤老树,枝丫盘错,光秃秃地直刺灰蒙蒙的天宇,此刻越发显得苍古遒劲,奇特壮观。

白絮飞舞,大自然静谧寂寥,超然幽远。所有的声音响都趋于沉寂,一切喧嚣都化作了轻柔的乐曲。得得的马蹄声听不到了,辚辚的车轮声也消逝了,惟有雪橇的铃声回荡在空中,那欢快的节奏犹如童心在跳动。

(3)

初雪

瑞雪飘临,无声无息。
纷纷扬扬,壮观之极!
飞上山巅,撒向草原,
飘至房顶,落在墓地。
茫茫大地,银装素裹。
蜿蜒远去,长河逶迤。
老树虬枝,枝丫盘错。
直刺苍穹,愈发壮丽。
白絮蹁跹,超然幽寂,
喧嚣之声,化作乐曲。
看不见辚辚车轮,
听不见得得马蹄,
惟闻雪橇的铃儿,丁零,丁零……
如童心跳动,永不停息。

Based on a comparison with the original prose one can find that Version 1 is not so flexible in syntax, not so smooth in expression and its rhythm is far from lucid and sprightly. Version 3 goes too far away from the target text as the type of writing of the original is altered from prose to poem. Version 2 compared with the other two versions, is terse in style, well-knit in syntax, smooth in rhythm and well-selected in diction. All in all Version 2 is a success. The same is true of prose translation from Chinese into English, but the conversion of syntax is just opposite to that of English-Chinese translation, it is the conversion from parataxis into hypotaxis. Hence connectives are often added to the translation. Consider the following example:

夕幕
郭沫若

　　我携着3个孩子在屋后草场中嬉戏着的时候,夕阳正烧着海上的天壁,眉痕的新月已经出现在鲜红的云缝里了。

　　草场中放牧着的几条黄牛,不时曳着悠长的鸣声,好像在叫它们的主人快来牵它们回去。

　　我们的两匹母鸡和几只鸡雏,先先后后地从邻寺的墓地里跑回来了。

　　立在厨房门内的孩子们的母亲向门外的沙地上撒了一把米粒出来。

　　母鸡们咯咯地叫起来了,鸡雏们啁啁地争食起来了。

　　——"今年的成绩真好呢,竟养大了10只。"

　　欢愉的音波,在金色的暮霭中游泳。

DUSK
Guo Moruo

While my three kids, accompanied by myself, were frolicing about on the meadow behind our house, the sky above the distant edge of the sea was aglow with the setting sun and the crescent new moon was already peeping out from behind the scarlet clouds.

A few cows grazing on the pasture let out a long drawn-out moo now and then as if urging their master to lead them home as quickly as possible.

Our two mother hens and their baby chicks were scurrying homewards one after another from the graveyard of the nearby monastery.

The kids' mother, standing by the kitchen door, sprinkled a handful of rice onto the sandy ground in the open.

At the clucking of the hens, the chicks scrambled for the feed, chirping.

"We've done quite well this year, with ten chicks growing fast," beamed my wife.

The joyous sound wave drifted through the golden evening mist.

From the underlined parts of the translation, one can find that the translator attaches great importance to choice of words, the syntactic features and style of the original are also taken into consideration by the translator so the translation is a great success.

Translation Exercises

Ⅰ. *Translate the following prose into Chinese with enough attention to the syntactic features and diction of the original, and have them reproduced in translation.*

Spring
James J. Kilpatrick

Springs are not always the same. In some years, April bursts upon our Virginia hills in one prodigious leap—and all the stage is filled at once, whole choruses of tulips, arabesques of forsythia, cadenzas of flowering plum. The trees grow leaves overnight.

In other years, spring tiptoes in. It pauses, overcome by shyness, like my grandchild at the door, peeping in, ducking out of sight, giggling in the hallway. "I know you're out there," I cry, "Come in!" And slips into our arms.

The dogwood bud, pale green, is inlaid with russet markings. Within the perfect cup a score of clustered seeds are nestled. One examines the bud in awe: Where were those seeds a month ago? The apples display their milliner's scraps of ivory silk, rose-tinged. All the sleeping things wake up primrose, baby iris, blue phlox. The earth warms—you can smell it, feel it, crumble April in your hands.

The dark Blue Ridge Mountains in which I dwell, great-hipped, big-breasted, slumber on the western sky. And then they stretch and gradually awaken. A warm wind, soft as a girl's hair, moves sailboat clouds in gentle skies. The rains come—good rains to sleep by—and fields that were dun as oatmeal turn to pale green, then to kelly green.

All this reminds me of a theme that runs through my head like a line of music. Its message is profoundly simple and profoundly mysterious also: Life goes on. That is all there is to it. Everything that is, was; and everything that is, will be.

I am a newspaperman, not a preacher. I am embarrassed to write of "God's presence". God is off my beat. But one afternoon I was walking across the yard and stopped to pick up an acorn—one acorn, nut brown, glossy, cool to the touch; the crested top was milled and knurled like the knob on a safe. There was nothing unique about it. Thousands littered the grass.

I could not tell you what Paul of Tarsus encountered on that famous road to Damascus when the light shone suddenly around him, but I know what he felt. He was trembling, and filled with astonishment and so was I that afternoon. The great chestnut oak that towered above me had sprung from such an insignificant thing as this; and the oak contained within itself the generating power to seed whole forests. All was locked in this tiny, ingenious safe—the mystery, the glory, the grand design.

The overwhelming moment passed, but it returns. Once in February we were down on the hillside pulling up briars and honeysuckle roots. I dug with my hands through rotted leaves and crumbling moldy bark. And behold: at the bottom of the dead, decaying mass a wild rhizome was raising a green, impertinent shaft toward the unseen winter sun. I am not saying I found Divine Revelation. What I found, I think, was a wild iris.

The iris was doing something more than surviving. It was growing, exactly according to plan, responding to rhythms and forces that were old before man was young. And it was drawing its life from the dead leaves of long-gone winters. I covered this unquenchable rhizome, patted it with a spade, and told it to be patient: spring would come.

And that is part of this same, unremarkable theme: spring does come. In the garden the rue anemones come marching out, bright as toy soldiers on their parapets of stone. The dogwoods float in casual clouds among the hills.

This is the Resurrection time. That which was dead, or so it seemed, has come to life again—the stiff branch, supple; the brown earth, green. This is the miracle; There is no death; There is in truth eternal life.

So, in spring, we plunge shovels into the garden plot, turn under the dark compost, rake fine the crumbling clods, and press the inert seeds into orderly rows. These are the commonest routines. Who could find excitement here?

But look! The rain falls, and the sun warms, and something happens. It is the germination process. Germ of what? Germ of life, germ in explicable, germ of wonder. The dry seed ruptures and the green leaf uncurls. Here is a message that transcends the rites of any church or creed or organized religion. I would challenge any doubting Thomas in my pea patch.

Everywhere, spring brings the blessed reassurance that life goes on, that death, is no more than a passing season. The plan never falters; the design never changes. It is all ordered. It has all been always ordered.

Look to the rue anemone, if you will, or to the pea patch, or to the stubborn weed that thrusts its shoulders through a city street. This is how it was, is now, and ever shall be, the world without end. In the serene certainty of spring recurring, who can fear the distant fall?

II. *Translate the following prose into English, having the style of the orginal reproduced in translation.*

中国人的饮茶习俗

中国是茶的故乡,茶是中国的国饮。中国人最懂茶趣,也最讲究饮茶艺术。

在中国大部分地区,沿袭明清传统,以清饮雅赏的冲泡茶为主。但各地区所好仍有不同。一般说,北方(包括华北、东北与四川等地区),喜欢喝花茶;南方,尤其是江浙皖等地喜欢喝绿茶;东南沿海则喜欢乌龙茶。有趣的是,湖南人喝茶,不仅饮其汁,而且连茶叶一并咀嚼吞服。

如果再加上各地特殊嗜好,少数民族的异风奇俗,那么,中国的饮茶方式,可说是繁花似锦了。

6.5 Translation of Poetry

6.5.1 Opposite Opinions on Translation of Poetry

What is poem?

The New Oxford Dictionary of English says: It is a piece of writing in which the expression of thoughts and feelings or the description of places and event is given intensity by particular attention to diction (sometimes involving rhyme), rhythm (sometimes involving metrical composition), and imagery. (O. E. D. 1430) We Chinese say that a poem is the picture of poet's inspiration and aspiration (诗言志). But Robert Frost, American poet, pointed out: "Poetry is what gets lost in translation." His remark seems to be the definition of poetry, it actually highlights the difficulty or impossibility of translating poetry.

What on earth is lost in translation of poetry, the artistic mood, style or the rhyme and rhythm? Soame Jenyns(索姆·詹宁斯), the translator of "the Selected Tang Poems", believes that to certain degree translation of poetry is in vain, because the essential beauty of a poem is not only manifested in its content, but rather in the way it is manifested (or how it is manifested). The personality of a poet and his style like a tender flower that is too tender to be grafted onto another language. Hence in the course of translation, even if the basic meaning of the poem can be preserved, its rhyme and rhythm, and the beauty of sound must be lost to some extent. John Denham(约翰·德纳姆) believes that a poem has a kind of subtle soul which will disappear in translation from one language into another. If the translator does not put anything new (new spirit) into his translation, the TLT would be nothing but a pile of language dregs. These are the opinions of some representative scholars abroad on translation of poetry. In China, some scholars have the same opinions on translation of poetry. Lu Xun(鲁迅) believed that translation of poetry was a kind of arduous work which would result in nothing; Zhu Guangqian(朱光潜) believed that translation of poetry was impossible.

The above-mentioned are representative scholars who think that translation of poetry is impossible. However, some of them have contributed a lot to translation of poetry. Shelley is the typical example. He, too, believed essentially in the impossibility of poetical translation, and yet he produced several verse translations from Greek, Latin, Spanish and Italian poetry and is a good representative of early writers on the subject, who tended to emphasize the futility of the undertaking whilst undertaking it none the less! A contemporary translator, William Trask, perhaps sums up this attitude succinctly when he says: "impossible, of course, that's why I do it" (in Honig 1985: 7), and what is more, there are many scholars who think differently. They have devoted themselves to translation of poetry even though their work is perhaps regarded as a futile effort, or may have very few alter egos in another country, they have yet made their contribution to extending the literary domain of the world. Thanks to their efforts, those who know nothing about Chinese get to learn Li Bai and Du Fu, and those who know nothing about English get to learn about Shakespeare.

The author of this book believes that poetry is translatable; translation of poetry is actually a kind of literary resurrection, which is determined by the nature of the task, and is based on reception theory and the hermeneutic motion.

Any translation of a poem will require attention to each of the various levels on which a poem functions. On the semantic level, a poem carries some message or statement about the real world or the author's reaction to it, and this is often considered the core which any translation must reproduce. However, the message of a poem is often implicit and connotative rather than explicit and denotative, the poet's intention is rarely obvious or inferable with any degree of certainty. Hence a poem often gives rise to different readings and multiple interpretations. One might suppose that semantic problems of interpretation could be dealt with by simply consulting the poet if he or she is still alive, but, as Socrates relates in The Apology, readers are often more informed than authors, and the meaning of a poem lies not with the author but within the text itself and the reader's interpretation of it.

According to reception theory, understanding of a poem varies from reader to reader as the original text is like an empty basket into which each reader can put his interpretation by reading. A translator is first a reader, which justifies the various translations of the same poem, even if its message is explicit and denotative as follows:

静 夜 思
——李白

床前明月光，
疑是地上霜。
举头望明月，
低头思故乡。

译文:(1) by Witter Bynner

In the Quiet Night

So bright a gleam on the foot of my bed—
Could there have been a frost already?
Lifting up my head to look, I found that it was moonlight.
Sinking back again, I thought suddenly of home.

(2) by Arthur Cooper

Before my bed
/there is bright moonlight
So that it seems
/like frost on the ground;
Lifting my head
I watch the bright moon,
Lowering my head
I dream that I'm home.

(3) by L. Cranmer-Byng

Athwart the bed
I watch the moonbeams cast a trail
So bright, so cold, so frail,
That for a space it gleams
Like hoar-frost on the margin of my dreams.
I raise my head—
The splendid moon I see;
Then droop my head,
And sink to dreams of thee—
My fatherland, of thee!

(4) by W. J. Fletcher

Seeing the Moon before my couch so bright
I though hoar frost had fallen from the night.

On her clear face I gaze with lifted eyes;

Then hide them full of Youth's sweet memories.

(5) by Herbert A. Giles

I wake, and moonbeams play around my bed,

Glittering like hoar-frost to my wandering eyes;

Up towards the glorious moon I raise my head.

Then lay me down—and thoughts of home arise.

(6) by 黄新渠

Thoughts on a Silent Night

A gleam of light streams down over my bed,

Could it be the real frost on the ground.

Raising my eyes, I gaze at the bright moon,

Lowering my head, my sweet home comes around.

(7) by Amy Lowell

In front of my bed the moonlight is very bright.

I wonder if that can be frost on the floor?

I lift up my head and look at the full moon, the dazzling moon.

I drop my head, and think of the home of old days.

(8) by 刘军平

Homesick at a Still Night

A sliver moon hangs by the balustrade,

I fancy moonlight as frost on the ground.

Gazing up of the bright moon I'm looking,

Lowering my head of my native land I'm missing.

(9) by 马红军

Before my bed the moon gleams bright,

And frosts the floor with a hoary light.

My eyes to the fair moon o'erhead roam—

Head bent, I'm lost in dreams of home.

(10) by S. Obata

I saw the moonlight before my couch,

And wondered if it were not the frost on the ground.

I raised my head and looked out on the mountain moon,

I bowed my head and thought of my far-off home.

(11) by 孙大雨

Thoughts in a Still Night

The luminous moonshine before my bed,

Is thought to be the frost fallen on the ground.

I lift my head to gaze at the cliff moon,

And then bow down to muse on my distant home.

(12) by 屠笛,屠岸

   Homesickness in a Silent Night

Before my bed the silver moonbeams spread—

I wonder if it is the frost upon the ground.

I see the moon so bright when raising my head,

Withdrawing my eyes my nostalgia comes around.

(13) by 王大濂

   Homesickness in a Quiet, Moonlit Night

What bright beams are bedside my bed in room!

Could on the ground there be the frost so soon?

Lifting my head, I see a big, full moon,

Only to bend to think of my sweet home.

(14) by 万昌盛,王僴中

   Reflections on a Quiet Night

Before my bed shine bright the silver beams,

It seems the autumn frost on the ground so gleams.

I gaze upwards toward the moon in the skies,

And downwards look when a nostalgia does arise.

(15) by Burton Watson

   Still Night Thoughts

Moonlight in front of my bed—

I took it for frost on the ground!

I lift my eyes to watch the mountain moon,

Lower them and dream of home.

(16) by 翁显良

   Nostalgia

A splash of white on my bedroom floor. Hoarfrost?

I raise my eyes to the moon, the same moon.

As scenes long past come to mind, my eyes fall again on the splash of white, and my heart aches of home.

(17) by 许渊冲

   Thoughts on a Tranquil Night

Before my bed a pool of light—

Can it be hoar-frost on the ground?

Looking up, I find the moon bright;

Bowing, in homesickness I'm drowned.

(18) by 徐忠杰

I descry bright moonlight in front of my bed.

I suspect it to be hoary frost on the floor.

I watch the bright moon, as I tilt back my head.

I yearn, while stooping, for my homeland more.

(19) by 赵甄陶

Quiet Night Thought

Moonlight before my bed,

Could it be frost instead?

Head up, I watch the moon;

Head down, I think of home.

(20) by 张炳星

Longing in the Night

Before the bed shone the bright moonlight at hand,

I fancied it was frost on the ground.

I raised my head to look at the bright moon,

And lowered my head to think of my native land.

(21) by 卓振英

In the Quiet of the Night

The ground before my bed presents a stretch of light,

Which seems to be a track of frost that's pure and bright.

I raise mind head: a lonely moon in what I see;

I stoop, and homesickness is crying loud in me!

(22) by Wong Man

Night Thoughts

On bed bright moon shone,

Thought frost on ground formed.

Raised head faced bright moon,

Lowered head dreamed of home.

(23) by John Turner

Night Thoughts

As by my bed

The moon did beam,

It seemed as if with frost the earth were spread.

But soft I raise

My head, to gaze

At the fair moon, and now,

With head bent low,

Of home I dream.

(24) by 黄龙

Still Night's Muse

Affront the bed the Luna beams bright,
Wearing a look of seemingly rime white.
Eyes upcast toward the Luna,
Eyes downcast, engenders my nostalgia.

(25) by 周方珠

               Homesick at Night

Before my bed a pool of moonlight,
It seems to me the rime white;
Raising my head I see the moon so bright,
Lowering my head I'm homesick at night.

Of the 25 versions above-mentioned, each one is different from others either in diction, syntax, rhyme and rhythm or in some other aspects, which justifies that appreciation and translation of poetry are closely tied to TAO (translation aesthetic object 翻译审美客体) and TAS (translation aesthetic subject 翻译审美主体), and then the interpretation and translation of poetry are open-ended to ①cognition of TAS, ②TAS' attitude towards TAO, ③time span of aesthetic action and ④perspective of aesthetic action. James Joyce pointed out in "A Portrait of the Artist as a Young Man" that: "The mystery of aesthetic like that of material creation is accomplished. The artist, like the God of the creation, remains within or behind or beyond or above his handiwork, invisible, refined out of existence, indifferent, paring his fingernails." In the process of composing a poem, the poet is the artist who observes, appreciates and describes the objective world from various perspectives, hence Mount Lushang is pictured by Su Shi as: "横看成岭侧成峰,/远近高低各不同。/不识庐山真面目,/只缘身在此山中 。"Similarly, in the process of translating a poem, the translator is the artist. (Many writers have claimed that one must be a poet to translate poetry) Composing a poem is a creative work in which the self-awareness is manifested, that is the reflection of the subjectivity of the SLT writer, translating a poem is also a creative work in which the self-awareness is manifested, that is the representation of translator's subjectivity [for example Version (3) by L. Cranmer-Byng, Version 16 by 翁显良]. In poetry translation, who should be visible, the poet or the translator? Who should be invisible, the poet or the translator? There is no consensus on this issue up till now.

6.5.2 Different Opinions on Subjectivity

Up to this day, literary criticism has gone through three stages: the writer-centred theory, the text-centred theory and the reader-centred theory, which exercise great influence on translation theory. There are three different opinions on the subject of translation: Some people think that the SLT writer should be taken as the subject of translation, some believe that the SL text should be taken as the subject of translation, still some prefer that a translator is supposed to be the subject of translation. The first opinion claims that the translator should leave the writer in peace as much as possible and bring the reader to writer because he is the only one who is authorized to interpret his own intention involved in his writings, hence the SLT writer should be 100% visible in the TLT. The second opinion asserts that the SL text is the translation aesthetic object that is indispensable to translator and translation, so the translated text is supposed to be absolutely faithful to the SL text. The third opinion states clearly that a translator can do whatever he wants to the SL text as he is, on the one hand, the writer of the translated text, and on the other hand, the reader of SL text, to whom the interpretation of the SL text is open-ended. Hence the translator can leave the reader in peace as much as possible and bring the writer to the reader, and then translator's subjectivity is always visible.

The author of this book believes that the SL writer is beyond question the subject of the SL text which reflects his style. If the translator takes the style (diction, syntax, rhyme and rhythm, and rhetorical figures) of the SL text into consideration, he is, at the same time, taking the SL writer into consideration. It is known to all that no one can enjoy boundless longevity, so the view that the SL writer is the only one who is authorized to interpret the SL text and the intention involved in it is not tenable. A translator, as the reader of the SL text, can interpret it at his own will as the writer of the TL text, however, his translation must be based on the SL text and his subjectivity should be limited to proper degree that well matches the subjectivity of the SL writer. The intersubjectivity between the SL writer and the translator should be a harmonious one, in short, both the SL writer and the translator should be visible in poetry translation. In the above 25 versions to Li Bai's poem, most translators manifest their subjectivity to the appropriate degree, only two of them [Version(3) by L. Granmer-Byng and Version(16) by 翁显良, have the original poem translated into prose] have their subjectivity manifested to the greatest possible degree so that the SLT writer (the poet) is invisible in the TL text.

6.5.3 Translation of Poetry between English and Chinese

So far as strategies employed for the translation of verse forms are concerned, scholars have different opinions on the issue. Andre Lefevere catalogues seven different strategies as follows: (Susan Bassnett, 2004)

1. Phonemic translation, which attempts to reproduce the SL sound in the TL while at the same time producing an acceptable paraphrase of the sense. Lefevere comes to the conclusion that although this works moderately well in the translation of onomatopoeia, the overall result is clumsy and often devoid of sense altogether.

2. Literal translation, where the emphasis on word-for-word translation distorts the sense and the syntax of the original.

3. Metrical translation, where the dominant criterion is the reproduction of the SL metre. Lefevere concludes that, like literal translation, this method concentrates on one aspect of the SL text at the expense or the text as a whole.

4. Poetry into prose. Here Lefevere concludes that distortion of the sense, communicative value and syntax of the SL text results from this method, although not to the same extent as with the literal or metrical types of translation.

5. Rhymed translation, where the translator "enters into a double bondage" of metre and rhyme. Lefevere's conclusions here are particularly harsh, since he feels that the end product is merely a "caricature" of Catullus.

6. Blank verse translation. Again the restrictions imposed on the translator by the choice of structure are emphasized, although the greater accuracy and higher degree of literalness obtained are also noted.

7. Interpretation. Under this heading, Lefevere discusses what he calls versions where the substance of the SL text is retained but the form is changed, and imitations where the translator produces a poem of his own which has only title and point of departure, if those, in common with the source text.

Holmes (1988:25) identifies four strategies as follows:

(1) mimetic, where the original form is retained;

(2) analogical, where a culturally corresponding form is used;

(3) organic, where the semantic material is allowed to "take on its own unique poetic shape as the translation develops";

(4) deviant or extraneous, where the form adopted is in no way implicit in either the form or content of the original.

Among Chinese scholars who believe poetry is translatable, there is no consensus on strategies employed for translation of poetry. But in translation practice some scholars employed some of the above strategies, such as poetry translation by Weng Xianliang is mainly based on the strategy of translating Chinese poetry into prose; poetry translation by Xu Yuanchong is based on the strategies of metrical translation, rhymed translation and mimetic translation; English poetry translation by Chinese scholars on rhymed translation and mimetic translation. The choice of strategy, of course, is itself a reflection of target language norms and the preferences of a particular cultural community at a particular point in time.

There is no consensus up to now as regards what criteria should be adopted for translation of poetry. Some scholars favours beauty in three aspects ("三美": "意美" logopoeia, "形美" phanopoeia, "音美" melopoeia by Xu Yuanchong); some prefer beauty in eight aspects(顾正阳, 2006) ("意境美", "动静美", "流动美", "别趣美", "形象美", "以小见大美", "空白美" and "声音美"). The author of this book believes that translator of poetry should strive for the greatest possible degree of convergence between the SLT and the TLT in five aspects: diction; rhyme and rhythm; syntax; tropes; artistic mood.

Diction

Diction refers to the poet's choice of words. Poets like unusual words. They are sensitive to the subtle shades of meanings of words, to the possible double meanings of words, and to the denotative and connotative meanings of words. The denotation of a word is its core meaning, its dictionary meaning. Connotation is the the subjective, emotional association that a word has for one person or group of people. Poets often choose words that contribute to the poem's meaning on both a denotational and a connotational level. "但愿人长久,千里共婵娟" are the perfect acme of poetical lines read through all ages. If we have "婵娟" replaced with "明月" the meaning might be unchanged, yet the quality of music sound, the lingering charm and aromatic appeal of the poem are lost; if we have "烽火连三月,家书抵万金" changed into "家信抵万金", it is by no means a poetical line even through only one word is changed. Words chosen by poets have to be read between the lines, beyond the lines and behind the lines if a reader(a translator is first the reader of the poem) wants to have a correct understanding of their denotative and connotative meaning, and at the same time to be aware of the formality levels of words. Consider the following examples and their translations.

1. 草枯鹰眼疾,
   雪尽马蹄轻。
   Keen are falcon's eyes above the withered grasses,
   And light the horse's hoofbeats in the melted snow.

2. 车辚辚,马萧萧,
   行人弓箭各在腰。
   Chariot rumbles, horses neigh,
   As they who must depart strap on their weapons.

3. 乱花渐欲迷人眼,
   浅草才能没马蹄。
   Riotous flowers more and more dazzle the eyes,
   The short grass barely covers the horses' hooves.

The above three examples are translated by Zhang Tingchen and Brue M. Wilson. The Chinese character "马" is chosen by the poet in the three poems respectively. They may have similar denotation, but their connotations are different from each other: in Example 1, it refers to the horse for hunting(a hunter); in Example 2, it refers to the cavalry horse(a charger); in Example 3, it refers to a steed. Unfortunately the three words are all translated into "horse" which is different from the "hunter", "charger" and "steed" in subtle shades of meanings and the levels of formality. The word "horse" is a superordinate, whereas "hunter", "charger" and "steed" are hyponyms. The meaning of a hyponym is more specific than that of a superordinate. The original poems are classic poems of the Tang Dynasty, which are of the formal style, thus the words chosen should be formal and specific. If "马" in the above examples was translated into "horse", the style and the level of formality of diction would be lost, and then the TLT would be underloaded to certain degree. Hence "马" in the above examples should be respectively rendered into "hunter", "charger" and "steed", and then the greater degree of convergence between the SLT and the TLT in diction would be realized. The same is true of the case in which English poetry is translated into Chinese. Consider the diction, especially the denotations and connotations of the words underlined.

4.
THE SICK ROSE
William Blake
O Rose, thou art sick.
The invisible worm
That flies in the night
In the howling storm

　　　　　　　Has found out thy bed
　　　　　　　Of crimson joy,
　　　　　　　And his dark secret love
　　　　　　　Does thy life destroy.

　　This poem might be understandable as a literal treatment of horticulture: a real rose beset by an insect that preys on roses. But Blake probably means for us to see the rose, the worm, and the action of the worm as symbolic. For one thing, the poem occurs in Blake's collection of poems *Songs of Experience*, suggesting that it has to do with ominous aspects of human life. For another, much of the poem makes little sense unless it can be taken symbolically. What can we otherwise make of the "howling storm," the bed of "crimson joy," the worm's "dark secret love"?

　　Blake's diction, furthermore, links to symbolic Christian literature, which he knew well. The archaic meaning of "worm" is dragon, an image of evil that harks back to the devil's appearance to Eve as a snake. In Christian romances the rose represented female beauty and purity and sometimes the Virgin Mary, Blake, then, may symbolize here the destruction of purity by evil. The poem may have sexual implications, since the worm (a phallic image) comes at "night" to the rose's "bed". More generally, the poem may show the destruction of all earthly health, innocence, and beauty by mysterious forces.

　　The point is that although we get the drift of Blake's meaning, we do not know precisely what the symbolic equivalents are. Yet the symbols are so sensuous and the action so dramatic that the poem mesmerizes. (Griffith, 2006)

　　Based on the analysis made by Griffith, the author has Example 4 translated as follows:

　　　　　　　病玫瑰
　　　　　　嗟,玫瑰,你一副病容。
　　　　　　只怪那看不见的小虫
　　　　　　它乘夜幕
　　　　　　驾恶风

　　　　　　寻觅到你的宝床
　　　　　　床上的喜悦绯红,
　　　　　　然而,他那隐秘的恋情
　　　　　　却毁掉了你的一生。

Rhyme and Rhythm

　　Rhyme refers to correspondence of sound between words, especially when these are used at the ends of lines of poetry. Rhyme can be classified into subcategories as follows:

　　(1) masculine rhyme (the rhymed words end with a stressed syllable: "man—ran," "detect—correct").

　　(2) Feminine rhyme (the rhymed words end with one or more unaccented syllables: "subtle—rebuttal," "deceptively—perceptively").

(3) Internal rhyme(the rhymed words are within the line).

(4) End rhyme(the rhymed words appear at the ends of lines).

(5) Approximate rhyme (the words are close to rhyming: "book—buck," "watch—match," "man—in"). (Griffith, 2006)

Rhythm refers to pattern produced by emphasis and duration of notes in music or by stressed and unstressed syllables in word. All human speech has rhythm, but poetry regularizes rhythm into recognizable patterns which are called meters. The most utilized metrical pattern in English poetry is accentual-syllabic, a pattern based on the number of stresses and the number of syllables per line. The best known such pattern is iambic pentameter, which consists of five stresses (iambs) and ten syllables (Griffith, 2006). The following are the names of accentual syllabic line lengths:

monometer	(one foot)
dimeter	(two feet)
trimeter	(three feet)
tetrameter	(four feet)
pentameter	(five feet)
hexameter	(six feet)
heptameter	(seven feet)
octameter	(eight feet)

There are similarities and differences between English poetry and Chinese poetry in many aspects: sonnet is a type of English poetry, there are also sonnets in Chinese poetry; alliteration, end rhyme and approximate rhyme are of frequence occurrence in English poetry, the same is true of Chinese poetry; English metrical patterns are different from Chinese tonal patterns, but pause (顿) can be used instead of meter in translation of English poetry into Chinese. The following translation by Yang Deyu (杨德豫) is the typical example:

5.   **SHE WALKS IN BEAUTY**

> She walks in beauty, like the night
> Of cloudless climes and starry skies,
> And all that's best of dark and bright
> Meet in her aspect and her eyes,
> Thus mellow'd to that tender light
> Which heaven to gaudy day denies.
>
> One shade the more, one ray the less,
> Had half impair'd the nameless grace
> Which waves in every raven tress,
> Or softly lightens o'er her face,
> Where thoughts serenely sweet express
> How pure, how dear their dwelling-place.

And on that cheek, and o'er that brow
So soft, so calm, yet eloquent,
The smiles that win, the tints that glow
But tell of days in goodness spent,
A mind at peace with all below,
A heart whose love is innocent.

她走在美的光影里

她走在美的光影里,好像
无云的夜空,繁星闪烁;
明与暗的最美的形相
交会于她的容颜和眼波,
融成一片恬淡的清光——
浓淡的白天得不到的恩泽。

多一道阴影,少一屡光芒,
都会损害那难言的优美;
美在她绺黑发上飘荡,
在她的脸颊上洒布柔辉,
愉悦的思想在那儿颂扬,
这神圣寓所的纯洁高贵。

那脸,那眉宇,悠闲沉静,
情意却胜似万语千言;
迷人的笑容,灼人的红晕,
显示温情伴送着芳年;
和平的、涵容一切的灵魂!
蕴蓄着纯真爱情的心田!

It can be seen from the above translation and the original poem that the number of pauses in each line of the translated poem is approximately similar to that of the feet of the original poem, which is of great importance to reproduction of the original rhythm. Sometimes the English poem can be translated by means of mimetic rhythm as follow:

6. **THE ROSE IN THE WIND**
James Stephens

Dip and swing,
Lift and sway;
Dream a life,

In a dream, away.

Like a dream
In a sleep
Is the rose
In the wind;

And a fish
In the deep;
And a man
In the mind;

Dreaming to lack
All that is his;
Dreaming to gain
All that he is.

Dreaming a life,
In a dream, away
Dip and swing,
Lift and sway.

风中蔷薇花

吉姆司·斯提芬司

颤颤巍巍,
颉之颃之;
睡梦生涯,
抑之扬之。

睡中之梦,
风中之花,
蔷薇颠倒,
睡梦生涯。

水中有鱼,
心中有君;
鱼难离水,
君是我心。

梦有所丧,
丧其所有;
梦有所得,
得其自由。

睡梦生涯,
抑之扬之,
颤颤巍巍,
颉之颃之。

As for translation of Chinese poetry into English, one can imitate the original rhyme and rhythm as follows:

7. <center>天净沙

秋

孤村落日残霞,
轻烟老树寒鸦,
一点飞鸿影下。
青山绿水,
白草红叶黄花。

Autumn

To the Tune of sky-clear Sand

Lonely hamlet, setting sun, evening glow,   (a)
Curling smoke, old tree, shivering crow,   (a)
A flying swan casts downwards its shadow.   (a)
Green mountains, limpid water,   (b)
Withered grass, red leaves, daisies are yellow.   (a)

One can also change the Chinese rhyme into English rhyme as follows:

8. <center>枫桥夜泊

(唐)张继

月落乌啼霜满天,
江枫渔火对愁眠。
姑苏城外寒山寺,
夜半钟声到客船。

译文:(1) **Anchored at Night by the Maple Bridge**

The moon is setting, rooks disturb the frosty air,   (a)
I watch by mapled banks the fishing-torches flare.   (a)
Outside the Suzhou wall, from Hanshan Temple's bell,   (b)
I hear its sound aboard and feel its midnight spell.   (b)

267

(2) Mooring by Maple Bridge at Night
> At moonset cry the crows, streaking the frosty sky; (a)
> Dimly lit fishing boats' neath maples sadly lie. (a)
> Beyond the city wall, from Temple of Cold Hill (b)
> Bells break the ship-borne roamer's dream and midnight still. (b)

Example 7 is translated into English with the rhyme pattern that corresponds with that of the original poem, and Example 8 is translated into English with the rhyme pattern that corresponds with the TLT, both patterns are acceptable.

Syntax

Syntax is sentence structure, the way words go together to make sentences. English syntax is remarkably different from Chinese syntax in that the former is characterized by hypotaxis and the latter parataxis. Syntax in poetry can be profoundly meaningful but also confusing both in English and in Chinese, especially when the syntax of a poem is arranged in a variant form as follows:

9.

(1)　　　　(2)

The unique typography of Example 9(1)(2) makes the poems meaningful and confusing as they can be re-arranged and read in various ways. The poet e. e. cummings for example, built visual elements into his poetry with verse and ingenuity. Unless we can see his quirky punctuation and arrangement of words on the page, we cannot make sense of his poems. Even his name (all lower case) partakes of the visual nature of his poetry. Consider the following example.

10.　　　　　　　　e. e. cummings　　　孤独
　　　　　　　　　　1(a　　　　　　　　荧
　　　　　　　　　　le　　　　　　　　　荧
　　　　　　　　　　af　　　　　　　　　一
　　　　　　　　　　fa　　　　　　　　　片
　　　　　　　　　　ll　　　　　　　　　叶
　　　　　　　　　　s)　　　　　　　　　子
　　　　　　　　　　one　　　　　　　　然
　　　　　　　　　　l　　　　　　　　　飘
　　　　　　　　　　iness　　　　　　　零

Syntax is perhaps the most stringent and least flexible of all the constraints translators must work under since it regulates the order of the words to be translated and because few liberties can be taken with that order before the text veers into the unintelligible. Hence the syntactic form of a poem should be retained in translation to the greatest possible degree. Consider the following examples:

11.
WHITECHAPEL
Richard Aldington

Noise;
Iron hoofs, iron wheels, iron din
Of drays and trams and feet passing;
Iron
Beaten to a vast mad cacophony.

In vain the shrill, far cry
Of swallows sweeping by;
In vain the silence and green
Of meadows Apriline;
In vain the clear white rain—

Soot; mud;
A nation maddened with labour;
Interminable collision of energies—
Iron beating upon iron;
Smoke whirling upwards,
Speechless, impotent.

In vain the shrill, far cry
Of kittiwakes that fly
Where the sea waves leap green.
The meadows Apriline—

Noise, iron, smoke;
Iron, iron, iron.

伦敦贫民区怀德洽陪尔
力却德·沃丁东

闹;
过路的货车、电车和脚下
铁的蹄,铁的轮,铁的喧嚣;
铁
打成了一片庞大的癫狂的不协调。

哪儿有掠过地面的燕子
尖锐地遥远地叫；
哪儿有四月的牧场
碧绿而静悄悄；
白净的雨也没有了——

烟碳；泥淖；
国民以劳动而癫狂了；
种种力能的无止境的混淆——
铁打上铁；
煤烟卷上云霄，
无语,无聊。

哪儿有海水的绿波跳跃，
飞着的小海鸥
在尖锐地、遥远地叫，
要找四月的牧场也徒劳——

铁,煤烟,闹；
铁的轮,铁的蹄,铁的喧闹。

12. **NIGHT**

　　　　　　　　　　Max Weber

Fainter,dimmer,stiller each moment,
Now night.

译文:(1)　　　　　　　夜

　　　　　　　　　麦克司·威伯
　　　　　　　愈近黄昏，
　　　　　　　暗愈暗，
　　　　　　　静愈静，
　　　　　　　每刻每分，
　　　　　　　已入夜境,

(2)　　　　　　　　夜

　　　　　　　　　麦克司·威伯
　　　　一刻比一刻缥缈、晦暗、安宁，
　　　　　　　夜,来了

(3) 夜

麦克司·威伯

暮色生,景朦胧,人初静,
入夜境。

The syntactic structure of Example 10 is well retained in the TLT from which the message of the translated poem benefits a great deal. Example 12 is provided with three versions. Consider the two lines of the original poem, one can find that the first line is much longer than the second, the first line expresses the gradual change from twilight into night, the second line that is very short expresses that night creeps unconsciously. The message of the SLT depends very much on the syntactic form of poem. Unfortunately the first version alters the syntactic shape of the SLT, which results in the loss of the syntactic message of the original poem. Comparatively speaking, Version 2 and Version 3 have the syntactic information better conveyed to readers of the TLT as translators have the syntactic form of the original poem well retained. The same is true of translation from Chinese into English.

13.   丑 奴 儿

(宋)辛弃疾

少年不识愁滋味,
爱上层楼。
爱上层楼,
为赋新词强说愁。

而今识尽愁滋味,
欲说还休。
欲说还休,
却道天凉好个秋。

To "The ugly slave"

译文:(1) In youth, not knowing the taste of sorrow,
I loved to ascend the storeyed towers,
I loved to ascend the storeyed towers,
And, to fashion new verses, I made myself speak of sorrow.

But now, having all the taste of sorrow,
I should speak of it but refrain,
I should speak of it but refrain,
Instead, I say: "A cool day, a fine Autumn."

(2) **Tune: "Song of Picking Mulberry"**
While young, I knew no grief I could not bear,

I'd like to go upstair.
I'd like to go upstair
To write new verses, with a false despair.

I know what grief is now that I am old.
I would not have it told.
I would not have it told
But only say I'm glad that autumn's cold.

14.   寿阳曲
洞庭秋月
——马致远

一阵风,
一阵雨,
满城中落花飞絮。
纱窗外蓦然闻杜宇,
一声声唤春回去。

Autumn Moon over Dongting River
To the Tune of Life-donating Sun
A gust of wind,
A spatter of rain,
Fallen petals and catkins over the city fly.
Cuckoos outside the screen window suddenly cry,
Cuckoo, cuckoo, calling the spring to return from high.

The translators of the above-mentioned two examples take the syntactic form of the original into serious consideration, which adds a great deal to the convergence between the SLT message and the TLT message, hence the translated poems work effectively as the original poems do.

Tropes

Tropes refer to rhetorical figures. Tropes in poetry refer to figures of speech most commonly used in poetry; they are simile, metaphor, personification and so on. These rhetorical figures are frequently used both in English poetry and in Chinese poetry, and function similarly so they can be translated interchangeably with one another as follows:

15.   Passions are liken'd best to floods and streams:
The shallow murmur, but the deep are dumb
激情如洪水,似溪流:
水面喧声淙淙,水底无语无声……

16.   White butterflies in the air;

White daisies prank the ground;
The cherry and hoary pear
Scatter their snow around.
粉蝶空中时蹁跹;
延命菊花饰郊原;
樱桃梨树共争妍,
四处飞花如雪片。

17. Rough wind, that moanest loud
Grief too sad for song;
Wild wind, when sullen cloud
Knells all the night long;
Sad storm, whose tears are vain
Bare woods, whose braches strain,
Deep caves and dreary main,
Wail, for the world's wrong.
嚎啕大哭的粗鲁的风,
悲痛得失去了声音;
横扫阴云的狂野的风,
彻夜将丧钟打个不停;
暴风雨把泪水流,
树林里枯枝摇个不休。
洞深,海冷,处处愁——
嚎哭吧,来为天下鸣不平!

Simile in Example 15, metaphor (a covert metaphor; the falling petals are covert) in Example 16 and personification in Example 17 are respectively rendered into "明喻""隐喻" and "拟人", which fulfill the functions of the original figures of speech. The same is true of translation of rhetorical figures in Chinese poetry. Consider the following example:

18. 竹枝词
——刘禹锡

山桃红花满山头,
蜀江春水拍山流。
花红易衰似郎意,
水流无限似侬愁。

Tune:" Bamboo Branch Song"

Liu Yuxi (772-842)

The mountain's red with peach blossoms above;
The shore is washed by spring water below,

Red blossoms will fade as my gallant's love;
The river as my sorrow will e'er flow.

19.
卜算子
送鲍浩然之浙东
——王 观

水是眼波横,山是眉峰聚。
欲向行人去哪边？眉眼盈盈处。
才始送春归,又送君归去。
君到江南赶上春,千万和春住。

Tune:"Song of Divination"
Parting with Bao Hao-ran
Wang Guan

A stretch of rippling water is beaming eye;
The arched brows around are mountains high.
If you ask where the wayfarer is bound,
Just see where beaming eyes and arched brow are found.
I've just seen spring depart,
And now again with you I'll part.
If in the South you o'er take the spring,
Be sure not to let it slip away.

20.
泪眼向花花不语,
乱花飞过秋千去。
（欧阳修:《蝶恋花》）

My tearful eyes ask flowers but they fail to bring
An answer. I see blossoms fall beyond the swing.

(Translated by Xu Yuanchong)

  The same rhetorical figures corresponding to the original ones are used in translation of the above Chinese poems and they function similarly in the TLT. In most cases, tropes can be approached in the same way in translation of poetry between English and Chinese. Sometimes, however, some of the tropes, reduplicated words for example must be approached with great care and flexibility.

  Reduplicated words, as a kind of tropes, are frequently employed in Japanese, Chinese and some other languages. There are also reduplicated words in English, such as talkee-talkee(喋喋不休), bubble-bubble(汩汩起泡) and frou-frou(沙沙声). But in Chinese, reduplicated words due to their unique rhetorical function are far more frequently employed in poetry (22% in the poetry of the Tang Dynasty); 35.6% in the Ci poetry of the Song Dynasty and 26% in the Sanqu poetry of the Yuan Dynasty Reduplicated words in Chinese poetry reflect their values and tastes in two aspects: the music aesthetic effect and the expressiveness, the former is composed of harmonious sound and melodious rhythm, the latter is reflected in their effect of depicting and portraying. Some examples:

21. 翠翠红红,处处莺莺燕燕;
     风风雨雨,年年暮暮朝朝。

22. 大弦嘈嘈如急雨,
     小弦切切如私语。
     嘈嘈切切错杂弹,
     大珠小珠落玉盘。

23. 无边落木萧萧下,不尽长江滚滚来。

Example 21 is a couplet composed of 10 pairs of reduplicated words. Some of them are adjectives, some are nouns, the collocation of them presents a vivid picture of spring to readers, and in the meanwhile reflects the truth: fallen petals are carried away as years flow on. The words themselves are soundless, but the poet of Example 22 made the readers hear the melodious notes of pipa by means of clever use of reduplicated words. By reading Example 23 readers will feel deep empathy for the poet and what he had been through. The reduplicated words "萧萧" and "滚滚" add so much to the artistic mood of the poem that readers would be naturally ushered into and then carried away by the vast and powerful mood. Translation of reduplicated words is by no means easy, but possible to certain extent. Some examples are as follows:

24.
Spring
Thomas Nash

Spring, the sweet Spring, is the year's pleasant king;
The blooms each thing, then maids dance in a ring,
Cold doth not sting, the pretty birds do sing.
Cuckoo, jug-jug, pu-we, to-witta-woo!

春
安默斯·讷余

春,甘美之春,一年之中的尧舜,
处处都有花树,都有女儿环舞。
微寒但觉清和,佳禽争着唱歌,
嗝嗝,啾啾,哥哥,割麦,插一禾。

25. **A Red Red Rose**
Robert Burns

O my Luve's like a red, red rose
That's newly sprung in June:
O my Luve's like the melodie
That's sweetly play'd in tune.
...

红红的玫瑰
罗伯特·彭斯

我爱人像一朵红红的玫瑰,
在六月迎风初放;
我爱人像一支美妙的乐曲,
听起来甜润而悠扬。
……

Translation of reduplicated words in Chinese poetry is comparatively difficult due to the difference between Chinese and English in formation of words. Hence translation should be flexibly approached as follows:

26. **杳杳寒山道**
——寒山

杳杳寒山道,
落落冷涧滨。
啾啾常有鸟,
寂寂更无人。
淅淅风吹面,
纷纷雪积身。
朝朝不见日,
岁岁不知春。

译文:(1) **Dim, Dim, the Path across Cold Hill**

Dim, dim, the path across Cold Hill,
Bleak, bleak, the canyon ford so chill.
Cheep, cheep, a few chattering birds,
Lone, lone, no sound of human words.
Sough, sough, the face-assailing blow,
Swirl, swirl, the body-wrapping snow,
Day in day out, no trace of Sol,

Year in year out, no spring at all.

(2) LONG, LONG THE PATHWAY TO COLD HILL

Long, long the pathway to Cold Hill;
Drear, drear the waterside so chill.
Chirp, chirp, I often hear the bird;
Mute, mute, nobody says a word.
Gust by gust winds caress my face;
Flake on flake snow covers all trace.
From day to day the sun won't swing;
From year to year I know no spring.

27.

迢迢牵牛星

无名氏

迢迢牵牛星,
皎皎河汉女。
纤纤擢素手,
扎扎弄机杼。
终日不成章,
泣涕零如雨。
河汉清且浅,
相去复几许?
盈盈一水间,
脉脉不得语。

Altair
Anonymous

Far, far, so dim looms Altair,
Bright, bright glitters Vega fair.
Slim, slim, fingers reach out sleeves,
Click, click, on the loom she weaves.
She can't weave one roll a day,
Like rain, her tears drop away.
The Silvern River shines clear,
How far the two stars appear!
Full, full, one gulf runs between:
Lorn, lorn, they'd say what they mean.

The above translations reflect the ingenuity of translators at the collocation of reduplicated words which add great force to the message, sound, shape and vividness of the original poems, and then invite the reader's attention. Reduplicated words in Chinese poetry can't be approached mechanically, some of them can be translated in the same way mentioned above, some should be approached flexibly by means of adaptation or adjustment. Consider the following examples:

28. 寻寻觅觅,冷冷清清,凄凄惨惨戚戚。

译文:(1)
  I look for what I miss,
  I know not what it is:
  I feel so sad, so drear,
  So lonely, without cheer.

(2)
  So dim, so dark,
  So dense, so dull,
  So damp, so dank, so dead!

29.
长相思
——白居易
汴水流,
泗水流,
流到瓜洲古渡头。
吴山点点愁。

思悠悠,
恨悠悠,
恨到归时方始休。
月明人倚楼。

Long Longing
Waters of the Bian flow,
Waters of the Si flow,
Flow to the old ferry of Guachow.
The hills in Wu bow in sorrow.

My longings grow and grow,
My grievings grow and grow,
Grow until comes back my yokefellow.
We lean on the rail in moonglow.

  Instead of mechanic collocation of reduplicated words in translation, translators of Example 28 and Example 29 alter the way of expression by means of rhyme and rhythm alliteration (in Example 28) and anadiplosis (in Example 29), but the aesthetic effect of the original poems is reproduced in the translated poems.

The Artistic Mood

The artistic mood is an aesthetic ideal of classical art of Chinese nation, which is frequently mentioned in praise of perfect artistic works like poetry, painting or calligraphy. But what on earth is the artistic mood?

The term "意境" in Chinese was first mentioned by Wang Changling, a famous poet in the middle Tang Dynasty in his "The style of Poetry" (《诗格》):

"诗有三境:一曰物境。欲为山水诗,则张泉石云峰之境极丽艳秀者,神之于心,处身于境,视境于心,莹然掌中,然后用思,了然境象,故得形似。二曰情境。娱乐愁怨皆张于意而处于身,然后驰思,深得其情。三曰意境。亦张之于意而思之于心,则得其真矣。"But before Wang Changling, Liu Xie put forward his point of view:"故思理为妙,神与物游,"which is similar to and based on Zhuang Zi's "游心" which means "thoughts wander with images". Zhuang Zi's doctrine is the essential ground on which the artistic mood is based.

On the basis of what has been mentioned above, the author believes that the artistic mood can be interpreted from the perspective of aesthetics as "the mood formed by various images into which readers can be so naturally ushered and influenced that they will unconsciously feel empathy for the poet (or the artist) and the characters of the poem, and consequently come to realize the true meaning of life, history and the universe".

The literary images are indispensable elements of the artistic mood as they can bring the readers into the atmosphere produced in the poem by the poet, and arouse their sympathetic response to the author. Images can be classified to audio image, visual image, smell image and tactile image according to their attribute and functions. Consider the following examples:

30.　　　　　　　　花谢花飞飞满天,
　　　　　　　　　红消香断有谁怜?
　　　　　　　　　游丝软系飘春榭,
　　　　　　　　　落絮轻沾扑绣帘。

Images in this poem can be classified as follows:
Visual images:花(谢)、花(飞)、(满)天、红、(游)丝、榭、(落)絮、绣帘
Smell image:香
Tactile images:软(系)、轻(沾)、扑(绣帘)

31.　　　　　　　　　绝句
　　　　　　　　　　——杜甫

　　　　　　　　　两个黄鹂鸣翠柳,
　　　　　　　　　一行白鹭上青天。
　　　　　　　　　窗含西岭千秋雪,
　　　　　　　　　门泊东吴万里船。

Images in this poem are as follows:
Audio image:鸣(翠柳)

Visual images: 黄鹂, 翠柳, 白鹭, 青天, 窗, 岭, 雪, 门, 船

A perfect painting with the artistic mood well designed is a good poem depicted with colours. Similarly, a perfect poem with the literary mood well designed is a good painting painted with language, with proper images in particular. Reading the above poems as if readers can see the colourful flowers, smell the fragrance in person, watch the birds flying with their own eyes, hear the orioles sing with their own ears, which is the function of literary images. It is the literary images that cause the readers' imagination to wander into the setting in their mind. When a reader identifies himself mentally with the poem he is reading his imagination which is totally integrated with the feelings and experience for the poet, we may say that he feels real empathy for the poet or he is ushered into the literary mood of the poem. If the literary mood of a poem is reproduced in translation, the functional equivalence can be achieved. Consider the following examples:

32.
江雪

柳宗元

千山鸟飞绝,
万径人踪灭。
孤舟蓑笠翁,
独钓寒江雪。

译文: (1)

River Snowfall

Amidst all mountains, birds no longer fly;
On all roads, no more travelers pass by.
Straw hat and cloak, old man's in boat, head low,
Fishing alone on river cold with snow.

(2)

Angling in Snow

Over mountains no bird in flight,
Along paths no figure in sight.
A fisherman in straw rain coat.
Angling in snow in a lonely boat.

33.
西江月
夜行黄沙道中
——辛弃疾

明月别枝惊鹊,清风半夜鸣蝉。
稻花香里说丰年,听取蛙声一片。
七八个星天外,两三点雨山前。
旧时茅店社林边,路转溪桥忽见。

Tune: "The Moon over the West River"
A Summer Night on My Way Home
from the Yellow Sand Ridge

Startled by magpies leaving the branch in moonlight;
I hear cicadas shrill in the breeze at midnight.
The ricefields' sweet smell promises harvest great,
I listen to the frogs' croak when the night grows late.

Beyond the clouds seven or eight stars twinkle;
Before the hills two or three raindrops sprinkle.
There is an inn beside the Village Temple. Look!
The winding path leads to the hut beside the brook.

34.
天净沙
秋思
——马致远

枯藤老树昏鸦,
小桥流水人家,
古道西风瘦马。
夕阳西下,
断肠人在天涯。

Autumn Thought
To the Tune of Sky-clear Sand

Withered vines, old tree, a raven at dusk crows,
Tiny bridge, thatched cottage, a stream flows,
Ancient road, bleak wind, a bony steed slows.
The setting sun in the west glows,
A heart-broken man at the end of the world sorrows.

35.
Four Ducks
Willam Arningham

Four ducks on a pond,
A grass-bank beyond,
A blue sky of spring,
White clouds on the wing;
What a little thing
To remember for years—
To remember with tears!

四只鸭

塘中鸭戏水，
岸上草如烟，
晴空春日碧，
白云独悠然；
虽然寻常事，
难忘却经年——
思乡泪涟涟！

36. **The Bereaved Swan**
    Stevie Smith

Wan
Swan
On the lake
Like a cake
Of soap
Why is the swan
Wan
On the lake?
He has abandoned hope.

丧偶的天鹅

惨白
无伴
浮在湖面
像块肥皂
影只形单
天鹅缘何
孑然
于湖面？
因为希望已被抛远。

Through a comparative analysis of the above examples and their translations, it can be seen that many elements and factors that add to building up literary mood such as diction, syntactic form, rhyme and rhythm, tropes and so on, have been taken into consideration by translators, hence the literary mood of the original has been reproduced in the translated poems, and then the translations work effectively as the original poems do on readers.

Translation Exercises

Ⅰ. *Translate the following poems into Chinese.*

1.
VAGABONDS
Langston Hughes

We are the desperate
Who do not care,
The hungry
Who have nowhere
To eat,
No place to sleep,
The tearless
Who cannot
Weep.

2.
Fathers that wear rags
Do make their children blind;
But fathers that bear bags
Shall see their children kind.
Fortune, that arrant whore,
Ne'er turns the key to the poor.

Ⅱ. *Translate the following poems into English with enough attention to reproduction of the literary mood in your translation.*

1.
登鹳雀楼
王之涣

白日依山尽，
黄河入海流。
欲穷千里目，
更上一层楼。

2.
敕勒歌
——斛律金

敕勒川，
阴山下。
天似穹庐，
笼盖四野。
天苍苍,野茫茫,
风吹草地见牛羊。

6.6 Translation of Dramatic Texts

Up to the present there is very little material on the special problems of translating dramatic texts, but some translators believe that methodology used in the process of translating dramatic texts is the same as that used to approach prose texts. However, the fact is that drama is different from fiction and most poetry in one essential way: It is meant to be performed. A theatre text is supposed to be read differently. "When you read a play, you miss qualities the playwright intended as a part of the play. For one thing, you miss the audience, whose physical presence and reactions to the performance influence both the performance and your perception of the play. For another, you miss the set designers' vision of the atmosphere and the physical world of the play. You miss the interpretive art of the actors and the illusion they create of real life unfolding before your eyes. You miss the physical and emotional experience of drama that a production gives." (K. Griffith: 77-78) It can thus be seen that a theatre text is read as something incomplete, rather than as a fully rounded unit, since it is only in performance that the full potential of the text is realized. A theatre text is a mere skeleton; performance fleshes out the bones. Hence this presents the translator with a central problem: whether to translate a theatre text as a purely literary text, or try to translate it in its function as one element in another, more complex system. As work in theatre semiotics has shown, the linguistic system is only one optional component in a set of interrelated systems that comprise the spectacle. If it is the former, the translation will not be so complex; if it is the latter, the translation will be more complex than that for other types of translation as the translator is not the only mediator between the source text author and the target reader. A drama translator does not convey a message to the audience. Audiences in theatres receive the message via the actors' performance after the director has carefully planned and monitored the whole process of mise en scene. That is to say, if a theatre text is translated as a purely literary text, the translation will be a reader-oriented translation, otherwise, it will be a performance-oriented one.

6.6.1 A Performance-oriented Translation vs. A Reader-oriented Translation

There is no text in the world that involves more complex linguistic context and paralinguistic context than dramatic text. If we have actors' lines and the words of the dialogue attributed to linguistic context, then paralinguistic context includes: the absent senders (such as the playwright, the director and their intentions), the present senders (the actors and their interpretation of the lines), tone, mimic, gesture, movement, make-up, hairstyle, costume, props, setting, lighting, music, and sound. If a drama translator is faced with a performance-oriented translation, he must be well aware of the distinction between the idea of the text and the performance, between the written and the physical. It would seem more logical, therefore, to proceed on the assumption that a theatre text, written with a view to its performance, contains distinguishable structural features that make it performable, beyond the stage directions themselves. Consequently the task of the translator must be to determine what those structures are and to translate them into the TL, even though this may lead to major shifts on the linguistic and stylistic plans (S. Bassnett:122) Josep Marco, a Spanish scholar summarizes the consequences for the performance-oriented translation in his paper "Teaching Drama Translation" as follows:

1. The text is, above all, spoken and has to be acceptable in the oral conventions of the target culture. This fidelity to conventions is all-important, here as elsewhere, but it should be added that the instantaneous character of dramatic performance lends weight to the claim that conventions exert an even more powerful influence on the stage than on the printed page. The greater the cultural distance between two theatrical environments, the larger the differences in dramatic conventions. Therefore, as Pulvers puts it, "The way is to treat stage language as a problem of theatrical convention, searching for the right new one in which to make the play work" (1984:24);

2. The text has to match the action, and vice versa. On the one hand, this means that players' actions at a given moment will determine what they can say; on the other hand, it implies that their speeches will be reinforced by accompanying gestures. Gestures are often implicit in so-called deictic elements, so that deixis functions as a hybrid signalling device and provides the means for economical expression on stage;

3. Another aspect of the mutual match between text and action is the rhythm of delivery, for variations in the relative speed of delivery depend on such factors as emotional tension, gesture and movement. After all, dramatic dialogue is not measured in space (how many lines a speech takes up) but in time.

It can be seen from the three above points that the close tie between the translator's task and that of the director and the performers is highlighted, and the drama translators will benefit from collaboration with the director and performers of the productions who use their translations. The acceptability, lipsynchronization and the rhythm of delivery must be taken into consideration in a performance-oriented translation. Consider the following example, please.

Waterloo Bridge

电影剧本英语原文:

Screen play by S. N. Behrman, Hans Rameau and George Froeschel

[Candlelight Club. Couples at tables, others dancing, orchestra in background. Myra and Roy seated at table.]

Roy: (looks at Myra, smiles) How nice you look.

Myra: (softly) Thank you.

Roy: (to Myra) What do dancers eat?

Myra: Oh, dull things mostly. Nutritious yet nonfattening.

Roy: Oh, no, not tonight. (to waiter) What could you suggest that would be particularly rich and indigestible?

Waiter: The grouse is very nice, sir.

Myra: Um.

Roy: And wine—it isn't against the rules for a dancer to drink a little light wine, is it?

Myra: Well, tonight.

Roy: Good. Number forty, please.

Waiter: Number forty, sir. (exits)

Roy: The ballet was beautiful.

Myra: Madame didn't think so.

Roy: Well, experts never know. It takes outsiders to know, and I tell you it was beautiful.

Myra: Well, that certainly proves you're an outsider.

Roy: Are you glad to see me again?

Myra: (lower her voice) Yes.

Roy: I sense a reservation.

Myra: Well, I suppose there is one.

Roy: What? Why?

Myra: What's the good of it?

Roy: You're a strange girl, aren't you? What's the good of anything? What's the good of living?

Myra: That's a question, too.

Roy: Oh, now wait a minute—I'm not going to let you get away with that. The wonderful thing about living is that this sort of thing can happen. In the shadow of a deathraid I can meet you and feel more intensely alive than walking around in peacetime taking my life for granted.

Myra: Oh, it's a high price to pay for it.

Roy: I don't think so.

Myra: I do. Do people have to kill each other to give them a heightened sense of life?

Roy: But that's got nothing to do with people killing each other. Either you're excited about life or you're not. You know, I've never been able to wait for the future. When I was very young, a child, in fact, I climbed to the top branch of a high tree, stood like a diver and announced to my horrified Governess: "Now I shall take a leap into the future" and jumped. I was in the hospital for two months.

Myra: You should let the future catch up with you more slowly.

Roy: Oh, no—no—never. Temperament. I can't help it. Look here—if we'd met in ordinary times, in an ordinary way, we'd just about be telling each other what schools we went to. We're much further along, don't you think?

Myra: Are we?

Roy: You know we are.

[Roy looks at waiter as he enters with food. He speaks and he and Myra rise from table. They begin dancing.]

Roy: Oh, I'm too excited to eat. Let's dance.

Myra: All right.

Roy: (proposes a toast) To you.

Myra: Thank you.

Roy: To us. I still don't get it not quite.

Myra: What?

Roy: Your face it's all youth, all beauty.

Myra: What is it you still don't get?

Roy: You know, when I left you this afternoon, I couldn't remember what you looked like, not for the life of me. I thought: "Was she pretty? Was she ugly? What was she like?" I couldn't remember. I simply had to get to that theatre tonight to see what you looked like.

Myra: And do you think you'll remember me now?

Roy: I think so. I think so for the rest of my life?

Myra: But—what is it about me you still don't get?

[Announcer on the band speaks to the patrons, the lights are dimmed and couples begin dancing. Roy and Myra rise and begin dancing.]

Announcer: Ladies and gentlemen, we now come to the last dance of the evening. I hope you'll enjoy the "Farewell Waltz".

Roy: I'll tell you later. Let's dance now.

徐黎鹃、黄群飞的译文《魂断蓝桥》

罗伊:你可真美!

麦拉:谢谢!

罗伊:舞蹈演员都吃些什么?

麦拉:嗯,一般都是些没味的东西。营养丰富、脂肪少的。

罗伊:噢,不,今晚例外。你们这里有什么特别的菜,高脂肪但又特别不好消化的菜?

侍者:松鸡不错,先生。

麦拉:嗯。

罗伊:还有酒。稍喝一点淡酒不算违反舞蹈演员的规矩吧?

麦拉:嗯,今晚不……

罗伊:好,来四十号的!

侍者:知道了,先生。

罗伊:你的舞蹈跳得真美。

麦拉:夫人可不这么看。

罗伊:嗯,内行人不懂,只有外行人才知道。我跟你说,你跳得非常美。

麦拉:这说明你确实是个外行。

罗伊:又见到我高兴吗?

麦拉:是的。

罗伊:我感到你有点保留。

麦拉:嗯,我想是这样吧。

罗伊:是什么?为什么?

麦拉:这又有什么用呢?

罗伊:你是个奇特的姑娘,不是吗?什么事情有什么用?活着又有什么用呢?

麦拉:那也是个问题。

罗伊:嗯,等等,我不想让你转移话题。生活里最美好的就是能发生这样的事情:在空袭

287

的死亡阴影里能遇见你使我感到充满活力,比和平时期悠闲地散步、想当然地生活更有活力。

麦拉:噢,这代价太高了。

罗伊:我不这么认为。

麦拉:我这么认为。难道人们非得互相残杀才能获得生活的活力?

罗伊:可这和人们互相残杀完全是两回事。对生活,不是充满信心就是麻木不仁。要知道,我可从不愿坐等未来。小时候,其实就是个孩子的时候,我爬上一棵大树顶,像一个跳水运动员似的,向着吓呆了的女教师大声宣布:"我要跳向未来。"然后往下一跳。我住了两个月的医院。

麦拉:你应该让未来慢一点儿赶上你。

罗伊:噢,不,不,绝对不行。我天生这样,我也没办法。你看,如果我们在很一般的情况下相遇,我们只怕还在谈我们上的什么学校呢!我们现在可是很进了一步,你说对吗?

麦拉:是吗?

罗伊:你知道是的。

罗伊:噢,我太高兴了,吃不下。我们跳舞去吧。

麦拉:好的。

罗伊:为你。

麦拉:谢谢。

罗伊:为我们。我还是不太明白……不太清楚。

麦拉:什么?

罗伊:你的脸,那么年轻,那么美。

麦拉:还有什么你不明白的?

罗伊:你知道,今天下午我们分手以后,我记不清你长什么样了,怎么也记不起来。我想:"她美吗?她丑吗?她长什么样?"我就是记不起来,我非得赶到剧场去看一看你的模样。

麦拉:现在你不会忘了吧?

罗伊:我想是的。是的,一辈子都不会忘了。

麦拉:那么,对我,你还想知道点儿什么?

罗伊:等一会儿我再告诉你,先跳舞吧。

The above translation generally conforms with the three points mentioned by Josep Marco, but there is still something to be further desired so far as a performance-oriented translation is concerned. Considering the acceptability of the TL readers, lipsynchronization and the rhythm of delivery, the above translation can be polished as follows:

原译	改译
(1)什么事情有什么用?	什么事情有用呢?
(2)我这么认为。	可我是。
(3)对生活,不是充满信心就是麻木不仁。	对生活,不管你是否充满激情。
(4)我住了两个月的医院。	结果,我住了两个月的医院。
(5)我们现在可是很进了一步,你说对吗?	我们现在可前进了一大步,你说呢?

(6) 那么,对我,你还想知道点儿什么? 那么,关于我,你还有什么不清楚的?

6.6.2 Text vs. Subtext

A theatre text is the source of performance which is mainly presented in the form of dialogue. The playwright's most important device for character development is dialogue—what the characters say and what they say about one another. Since performance time is limited, the words of dialogue sometimes cannot describe the character fully. Playwrights, therefore, trust heavily to implication in the dialogue and to "gaps"—information left out—to characterize characters. Critics and scholars mark this distinction with the terms "text" for the written words of the play and "subtext" for the implications and gaps. All literary genres make use of subtext, but it is particularly important to drama as dramatic text involves the most complicated context and paralinguistic context.

Compared with translation of subtext, translation of a theatre text must take cultural specificity of the text into consideration. One reason might be that readers are perfectly able to cope with cultural strangeness in a translated text as they have adequate time for second thought, whereas theatre audiences are not able to make similar adjustments during the ephemeral performance. The reading process allows for reflection on and absorption of strange bodies, whereas performance, on the other hand, has to make the point right away and has no second chances. If the cultural elements are too strange to the audiences, they won't be able to share the information presupposed or implied. Hence culture-loaded words are usually translated by means of domesticating in translation of dramatic text as follows:

1. Fal. Let him be damned like the glutton! Pray God his tongue be hotter! A whoreson <u>Achitophel</u>, rascally yea-for-sooth knave...

<u>福斯塔夫</u>:让他落在饿鬼地狱里!愿他的舌头比饿鬼的舌头还要烫人!一个婊子生的<u>叛徒</u>!一个嘴里喊着是呀是的恶奴!

2. Turn him to any cause of policy.
<u>The Gordian knot</u> of it he will unloose,
Familiar as his garter.

随便什么国家大事到了他手里。
<u>不可解的结</u>也就解开了——
就像随手解他的袜子。

3. Desdemona: To do what?
Iago: To suckle fools and chronicle <u>small beer</u>.

苔丝狄蒙娜:要她干什么呢?
伊阿古:去奶傻孩子,去记<u>油盐账</u>。

The words and phrases like "Achitophel", "the Gordian knot" and "small beer" in the above examples are culture-specific words which are adapted culturally in the TL text for the sake of acceptability of the theatre audiences. Translation is ethnocentric, in drama translation there is always a certain degree of acculturation.

Subtext is closely attached to text. No text, no subtext. A typical example of text and subtext is the scene in Act I of *Hamlet* in which Hamlet, after a long absence, meets his friends Horatio and Marcellus. The night before his meeting, Horatio and Marcellus have seen the ghost of Hamlet's father. But Hamlet doesn't know about the ghost; instead, he complains about his mother's marrying so soon after his father's death:

 Hamlet: Would I had met my dearest foe in heaven.
     Or ever I had seen that day, Horatio—
     My father,—methinks I see my father.
    Horatio: O, where, my lord?
    Hamlet: In my mind's eye, Horatio.
    Horatio: I saw him once; he was a goodly king.
 哈姆雷特:我宁愿在天上遇见顶刻毒的仇人,我也不愿看那天的那种情形,何瑞修! 我的父亲,——我仿佛看见我的父亲。
何瑞修:啊,在哪里,殿下?
哈姆雷特:在我的心眼里,何瑞修。
何瑞修:我见过他一次;他是贤明的君王。

It is clear that there is the "gap" between Hamlet's statement "My father—methinks I see my father" and Horatio's response "O, where, my lord?" If you were the actor playing Horatio, how would you fill the gap. You have to depend on the context, especially the paralinguistic context and to communicate your reaction to the audience by the way you utter the line and by your physical demeanor. "You might" phrase the line as an incredulous question: "What? You see your father? But how could you, he's dead?" Or you might say it as a reflection of what you take to be Hamlet's witty mood: "I know you're joking, Hamlet. But tell me anyway. Where do you see your father?" But another possibility is that you would say it in astonishment, as if you take it literally. After all, you had seen the ghost of Hamlet's father just a few hours before. You probably think Hamlet has now spotted the ghost, and so you say, "Good Lord, do you see it, too? Where?" And you look fearfully around, trying to see the ghost too. When Hamlet indicates that he is only remembering his father, you calm down. At this point you might pause and make appropriate gestures to indicate your shift from fear and astonishment to calmness. The fact that you have made such a shift is indicated by your response to Hamlet: "Yes. Once, when the king was alive, I saw him too. He was an impressive-looking king." This last statement shows that Horatio has moved from thinking about a supernatural phenomenon (the ghost) to thinking about a natural one (Hamlet's father when he was alive). (K Griffith: 87) That is to say, interpretation of subtext is essential for actors, who must figure out how to utter the dialogue and how to perform on stage. But how about the translator? Is it necessary to decode the dramatic text's subtext and to encode it in verbal language? If the translator does, his product must subsequently be decoded by the actors for performance, and then he is actually meddling in director's and actor's affairs. The author of this book believes a drama translator is not supposed to exceed his/her function; enough room should be left for directors and actors to approach the dramatic subtext.

Translation Exercises

Ⅰ. *Translate the following dramatic lines into Chinese with enough attention to rhythm of delivery and lipsynchronization.*

Titanic

ON DECK (Jack and Rose are together.)

Jack: Well, I've been on my own since I was fifteen, since my folks died. And I had no brothers or sisters or close kin in that part of the country, so I lit on out there and I haven't been back since. You can just call me a tumbleweed blown in the wind. Well, Rose. We've walked about a mile around this boat deck and chewed over how great the weather's been and how I grew up, but I reckon that's not why you came to talk to me, is it?

ROSE: Mr. Dawson, I...

JACK: Jack.

ROSE: Jack. I want to thank you for what you did, not just for pulling me back, but for your discretion.

JACK: You're welcome.

ROSE: Look, I know what you must be thinking! "Poor little rich girl. What does she know about misery?"

JACK: No. No, that was not what I was thinking. What I was thinking was, "What could have happened to this girl to make her think that she had no way out?"

ROSE: Well, I... It was everything. It was my whole world, and all the people in it and the inertia of my life, plunging ahead, and me powerless to stop it.

JACK: (looking over the side of the ship) God, look at that thing! You would have gone straight to the bottom!

ROSE: Five hundred invitations have gone out. All of Philadelphia society will be there. And all the while I feel I'm standing in the middle of the crowded room screaming at the top of my lungs and no one even looks up.

JACK: Do you love him?

ROSE: Pardon me?

JACK: Do you love him?

ROSE: You're being very rude. You shouldn't be asking me this!

JACK: Well, it's a simple question. Do you love the guy or not?

ROSE: This is not a suitable conversation.

JACK: Why can't you just answer the question?

ROSE: This is absurd! You don't know me and I don't know you and we are not having this conversation at all! You are rude and uncouth and presumptuous and I'm leaving now, Jack, Mr. Dawson. It's been a pleasure. I sought you out to thank you and now I have thanked you...

JACK: And even insulted me.

ROSE: Well, you deserved it.

JACK: Right.

ROSE: Right.

2. *Translate the following dramatic lines into English with enough attention to the harmonious match between the words of dialogue.*

《雷雨》
曹禺著

周朴园:不许多说话。(回头向大海)鲁大海,你现在没有资格跟我说话——矿上已经把你开除了。

鲁大海:开除了!?

周冲:爸爸,这是不公平的。

周朴园:(向周冲)你少多嘴,出去!
　　　　(周冲愤然由中门下。)

鲁大海:好,好。(切齿)你的手段我早明白,只要你能弄钱,你什么都做得出来。你叫警察杀了矿上许多工人你还——

周朴园:你胡说!

鲁侍萍:(至大海前)走吧,别说了。

鲁大海:哼,你的来历我都知道,你从前在哈尔滨包修江桥,故意叫江堤出险,——

周朴园:(厉声)下去!

仆人们:(拉大海)走!走!

鲁大海:你故意淹死了两千二百个小工,每一个小工的性命你扣三百块钱!姓周的,你发的是绝子绝孙的昧心财!你现在还——

周萍:(冲向大海,打了他两个嘴巴)你这种混账东西!
　　　大海还手,被仆人们拉住。

周萍:打他!

鲁大海:(向周萍)你!
　　　　(仆人们一齐打大海。大海流了血。)

周朴园:(厉声)不要打人!
　　　　(仆人们住手,仍拉住大海。)

鲁大海:(挣扎)放开我,你们这一群强盗!

周萍:(向仆人们)把他拉下去!

鲁侍萍:(大哭)这真是一群强盗!(走至周萍面前)你是萍……凭——凭什么打我的儿子?

周萍:你是谁?

鲁侍萍:我是你……你打的人的母亲。

鲁大海:妈,别理这东西,小心吃了他们的亏。

鲁侍萍:(呆呆地望着周萍的脸,又哭起来)大海,走吧,我们走吧!
　　　　(大海为仆人们拥下,侍萍随下。台上只有周朴园与周萍。)

周萍:(过意不去地)爸爸。

周朴园:你太莽撞了。

周萍:可是这个人不应该乱侮辱父亲的名誉啊。

Appendix

翻译练习参考答案

Chapter Two
2.2.1

II. 1. 一年正逢春,
      一日值清晨,
      清晨正七时;
      山坡露珠新,
      云雀展翅飞,
      蜗牛刚动身;
      上帝居天堂——
      人间万事顺!

2. **Autumn**
   To the Tune of Sky-clear Sand
   Lonely hamlet, setting sun, evening glow,
   Curling smoke, old tree, shivering crow,
   A flying swan casts downwards its shadow.
   Green mountains, limpid water,
   Withered grass, red leaves, daisies are yellow.

2.2.3

III. 1. We would very much appreciate it if you could take our suggestion into consideration.
2. After some hesitation he finally decided to see me himself.
3. I am aware that this is a risky investment.
4. We are all in favour of his suggestion.
5. His excellent performance in the play impressed me deeply.
6. This kind of behavior characterizes the criminal mind.
7. Sooner or later the young will replace the old.
8. His new book is a great success.

9. They gave the famous writer a warm welcome.
10. She has a strong desire to see him.

2.2.4

Ⅱ. 1. He who makes no investigation and (study) has no right to speak.
2. Modesty helps one to go forward, whereas conceit makes one lag behind.
3. The monk may run away, but the temple can't run away with him.
4. Although you may escort a guest a thousand miles, yet must the parting come at last.
5. You can fight a hundred battles without defeat if you know the enemy as well as yourself./You will win one battle and lose one battle if you know yourself but leave yourself in the dark about the enemy./You will lose every battle if you leave both the enemy and yourself in the dark.

2.2.7

Ⅰ. 1. 我向你请教, 你知道信用合作社是怎么回事吗?
2. 他在剑桥大学任植物学教授达30年之久。
3. 我们愿买比这个大一些的房子, 但得量力而行呀。
4. 他很有数学头脑。
5. 一七八三年, 美洲殖民地摆脱了英国统治。
6. A real good friend should be one offering timely help.
7. They maintain the closest relations (ties) with the masses and share their weal and woe.
8. You should take resolute and effective measures to solve these complicated problems.
9. "How stupid of me to forget what I really came for and just to maunder on", exclaimed Granny Lai.
10. If other women are jealous, she's a hundred times so.

Ⅱ. 1. 对我的申请, 我还没有收到回信。
2. 学校里来了一位生力军史密斯先生。
3. 她年轻时是个大美人。
4. 她的财富与美貌成了她进入上流社会的敲门砖。
5. Never wake a sleeping dog.
6. Every life has its roses and thorns.
7. Don't count your chickens before they are hatched, the knotty problem awaits us.
8. He is a man who hoes his own potatoes.
9. We'd better give her rope to hang herself—she's bound to give herself away one of these days.
10. What he said was nothing but a bird in the bush.

Chapter Three

3.2

II. 1. the grand strategy for the development of China's west
2. environment-friendly agriculture
3. environmental protection industry
4. competitive products / knock-out products
5. chain debts
6. three represents
7. bring China's economy more in line with international practice
8. ① to achieve the goal of ensuring our people a relatively comfortable life
   ② to achieve the goal of well-to-do life
9. jerry-built projects
10. all-round responsibility system / lump-sum appropriations operation

3.4.2

II. The moon sheds her liquid light silently over the leaves and flowers, which, in the floating transparency of a bluish haze from the pond, look as if they had just been bathed in milk, or like a dream wrapped in a gauzy hood. Although it is a full moon, shining through a film of clouds, the light is not at its brightest; it is, however, just right for me—a profound sleep is indispensable, yet a snatched doze also has a savour of its own. The moonlight is streaming down through the foliage, casting bushy shadows on the ground from high above, jagged and checkered, as grotesque as a party of spectres; whereas the benign figures of the drooping willows, here and there, look like paintings on the lotus leaves. The moonlight is not spread evenly over the pond, but rather in a harmonious rhythm of light and shade, like a famous melody played on a violin.

Around the pond, far and near, high and low, are trees. Most of them are willows. Only on the path side, can two or three gaps be seen through the heavy fringe, as if specially reserved for the moon. The shadowy shapes of the leafage at first sight seem diffused into a mass of mist, against which, however, the charm of those willow trees is still discernible. Over the trees appear some distant mountains, but merely in sketchy silhouette. Through the branches are also a couple of lamps, as listless as sleepy eyes. The most lively creatures here, for the moment, must be the cicadas in the trees and the frogs in the pond. But the liveliness is theirs, I have nothing.

Suddenly, something like lotus-gathering crosses my mind. It used to be celebrated as a folk festival in the South, probably very far back in history, most popular in the period of Six Dynasties. We can pick up some outlines of this activity in the poetry. It was young girls who went gathering lotuses, in sampans and singing love songs. Needless to say, there were a great number of them doing the gathering, apart from those who were watching. It was a lively season, brimming with vitality, and romance. A brilliant description can be found in Lotus Gathering written by the Yuan Emperor of the Liang Dynasty:

So those charming youngsters row their sampans, heart buoyant with tacit love, pass on to each other cups of wine while their bird-shaped prows drift around. From time to time their oars are caught in dangling algae and duckweed float apart the moment their boats are about to move on. Their slender figures, girdled with plain silk, tread watchfully on board. This is the time when spring is growing into summer, the leaves a tender green and the flowers blooming—among which the girls are giggling when evading an out-reaching stem, their shirts tucked in for fear that the sampan might tilt.

3.5

Ⅱ. I was leaving the old house farther and farther behind, while the hills and rivers of my old home were also receding gradually ever farther in the distance. But I felt no regret. I only felt that all round me was an invisible high wall, cutting me off from my fellows, and this depressed me thoroughly. The vision of that small hero with the silver necklet among the watermelons had formerly been as clear as day, but now it suddenly blurred, adding to my depression.

I lay down, listening to the water rippling beneath the boat, and knew that I was going my way. I thought: although there is such a barrier between Jun-tu and myself, the children still have much in common, for wasn't Hung-erh thinking of Shui-sheng just now? I hope they will not be like us, that they will not allow a barrier to grow up between them. But again I would not like them, because they want to be akin, all to have a treadmill existence like mine, nor to suffer like Jun-tu until they become stupefied, nor yet, like others, to devote all their energies to dissipation. They should have a new life, a life we have never experienced.

As I dozed, a stretch of jade-green seashore spread itself before my eyes, and above a round golden moon hung in a deep blue·shy. I thought: hope cannot be said to exist, nor can it be said not to exist. It is just like roads across the earth. For actually the earth had no roads to begin with, but when many men pass one way, a road is made.

3.6

Ⅲ. 1. ① to drain a pond to catch all the fish
      ② kill the goose that lays the golden eggs
   2. ① to stir up the grass and alert the snake
      ② wake a sleeping dog
   3. ① to be as easy as turning over one's hand
      ② as easy as falling off a log
   4. ① to get burnt by the fire kindled by oneself
      ② fry in one's own grease

5. ① to spend money like dirt
   ② spend money like water
6. ① to play the lute to a cow
   ② cast pearls before swine
7. ① to keep one's mouth closed like a bottle
   ② keep a still tongue in one's head
8. ① to send charcoal in snowy weather
   ② help a lame dog over a stile
9. ① to draw a snake and add feet to it
   ② paint the lily
10. to be like a frog at the bottom of a well
11. take a back seat
12. six of one and half a dozen of the other
13. catch at shadows
14. The leopard can't change its spots.
15. kick down the ladder
16. A friend in need is a friend indeed.
17. Let bygones be bygones.
18. The early bird catches/gets the worm.
19. You cannot eat your cake and have it.
20. fish in the air

3.7

I. 11. There is no smoke without fire.
    12. A quiet conscience sleeps in thunder.
    13. Fine feathers make fine birds.
    14. God never shut one door but He opens another.
    15. All good things must come to an end.
    16. One boy is a boy, two boys half a boy, three boys no boy.
    17. Once bit, twice shy.
    18. An idle youth, a needy age.
    19. A fed-up man do not know how hungry a starved man is.
    20. Even the cleverest housewife cannot cook a meal without rice. / One cannot make bricks without straw.

II. 1. Well, you certainly are a guy! A dog given a bone who doesn't come back for more!
    2. It was as if the sword of Damocles hung over the Japanese sergeant.
    3. He's sure to ask questions but I'll hold my tongue to begin with.

4. When we pass from the old society to the new, each of us shows his true worth.

5. But they were too late for a rescue.

6. No, he's still after my blood. How can you imagine he'd lend me anything?

7. To be quite honest with you, I don't know the first thing about the modern drug business.

8. I'm incapable of running things. I'm too ignorant, blunt and tactless, always getting hold of the wrong end of the stick.

9. Only I feel bad when we lose every fight.

10. Even Chiang Kai-shek can't save himself any more than a clay idol can save itself while swimming across a river.

3.8

II. 1. And these rules, unlike those we have today, do not change all the time.

2. (The Monkey King) woke up with a start. It had all been a dream.

3. Otherwise, standing by with folded arms and waiting for gains without pains will prove to be nothing but long-term nonresistance.

4. He had become so used to setting traps for peasants all these years that it came as rather a shock to him to find he had walked into a snare himself.

5. From time immemorial no one but "the man of Chi Worried lest the sky fall," meaning that only one man from Henan was afraid of it might happen.

6. I failed to recognize your eminence and I hope that you will forgive me for that blunder.

3.9

II. 西 风

西风,和煦的春风,引来百鸟争鸣;
但闻西风起,我便泪水盈盈。
因为它来自西方故土,那褐色的山岗,
吹来人间四月天,还吹开了水仙。

III. 1. It's difficult for us to meet and hard to part.
The east wind is too weak to revive flowers dead.

2. White are the clouds in the azure sky,
Fallen leaves here and there scattering,
Bitter in the west wind wailing,
As swans southward fly.
Frosted trees are dyed red in the morning,
As if their cheeks are flushed with wine,

Or the tears of those who are leaving.

Chapter Four

4.1

Ⅱ. <center>怎样读书?</center>
弗吉尼亚·伍尔夫

　　书既然有小说、传记、诗歌之分,就应区别对待,从各类书中取其应该给予我们的东西。这话说来很简单,然而很少有人向书索取它能给我们的东西,我们拿起书来往往怀着模糊而又杂乱的想法,要求小说是真实的,诗歌是虚假的,传记要吹捧,史书能加强我们自己的偏见。读书时如能抛开这些先人之见,便是极好的开端。不要对作者指手画脚,而要尽力与作者融为一体,共同创作,共同策划。如果你不参与、不投入,而且一开始就百般挑剔,那你就无缘从书中获得最大的益处。你若敞开心扉,虚怀若谷,那么,书中精细入微的寓意和暗示便会把你从有开头就碰上的那些像是山回水转般的句子中带出来,走到一个独特的人物面前。钻进去熟悉它,你很快就会发现,作者展示给你的或想要展示给你的是一些比原先要明确得多的东西。不妨先来谈谈如何读小说吧。一部长篇小说分成32章,是作者的苦心经营,想把它建构得如同一座错落有致、布局合理的大厦。可是词语比砖块更难捉摸,阅读比观看更费时、更复杂。了解作家创作的个中滋味,最有效的途径恐怕不是读而是写;通过写亲自体验一下文字工作的艰难险阻。回想一件你记忆犹新的事吧。比方说,在街道的拐弯处遇到两个人正在谈话。树影婆娑,灯光摇曳,谈话的调子喜中有悲。这一瞬间似乎包含了一种完整的意境、全面的构思。

　　可是当你打算用文字来重现此情此景的时候,它却化作千头万绪互相冲突的印象。有的必须淡化,有的则应该突出。在处理过程中你可能对整个意境根本把握不住了。这时,还是把你那些写得含糊杂乱的一页页书稿搁到一边,翻开某位小说大师,如笛福、简·奥斯丁或哈代的作品来从头读吧。这时候你就能更深刻地领略大师们驾驭文字的技巧了。因为我们不仅面对一个个不同的人物——笛福、简·奥斯丁或托马斯·哈代,而且置身于不同的世界。阅读《鲁滨孙漂流记》时,我们仿佛跋涉在旷野大道上;事件一个接一个;故事再加上故事情节的安排就足够了。如果说旷野和历险对笛福来说就是一切,那么对简·奥斯丁就毫无意义了。她的世界是客厅和客厅中闲聊的人们。这些人的言谈像一面镜子,反映出她们的性格特征。当我们熟悉了奥斯丁的客厅及其反映出来的事物以后再去读哈代的作品,又得转向另一个世界。周围茫茫荒野,头顶一片星空。此时,心灵的另一面,不是聚会结伴时显示出来的轻松愉快的一面,而是孤独时最容易萌生的忧郁阴沉的一面。和我们打交道的不是人,而是自然与命运。虽然这些世界截然不同,它们自身却浑然一体。每一个世界的创造者都小心翼翼地遵循自己观察事物的法则,不管他们的作品读起来如何费力,却不会像蹩脚的作家那样,把格格不入的两种现实塞进一部作品中,使人感到不知所云。因此,读完一位伟大作家的小说再去读另一位的,比如说从简·奥斯丁到哈代,从皮科克到特罗洛普,从司各特到梅瑞狄斯,就好像被猛力扭动,连根拔起,抛来抛去。说实在的,小说是一门困难而又复杂的艺术。要想充分享用小说作者——伟大的艺术家——给予你的一切,你不仅要具备高度的感受能力,还得有大胆的想像力。

III.
A Pickle Pot
—Li Hanrong

Mother came from our home village. She stayed with us for ten days. When she was about to leave, she wanted to buy us something as a present.

"You've got everything," she said, "but you seem to have got nothing. The TV set is yours, but the people who walk back and forth in it are all strangers, even murderers, corrupt officials and thieves come in and out of it from time to time. The radio cassette player is yours, but it's all others who sing in it. The books on the shelf are yours, but they are all written by others. The fridge is yours, but all the year round it's filled with frost that comes from God knows where. Though they make your life easy and comfortable, none of them BELONGS to you in the real sense of the word."

On the day she was to leave for home, she got up early in the morning and brought back a pickle pot from the market.

"Make some pickle in it," she said, "and have something that suits your own palate."

Since then pickles of our own taste had been added to our diet. When we had guests, we often had pickles to go with wine. Slightly intoxicated, everyone would comment, "A country flavor, not bad. Not bad, a country flavor."

So we had something to our own taste. When we looked at the pot, it was standing quietly at the corner. Amid the hustle and bustle of our everyday life and in the apartment of reinforced concrete, the pot stood there by itself, brewing an old and simple flavor.

4.4

I. 6.

维也纳位于维也纳尔瓦德(维也纳森林)树木葱郁的山脚下,蓝色的多瑙河畔,山坡上到处点缀着黄绿色的葡萄园。这是一个富有天然美景的地方。外来的游客固然为之心迷神醉,维也纳本地人也自以为得天独厚。空气中充满了音乐,那是当地的天才弟子,欧洲最伟大的音乐家海顿、莫扎特、贝多芬、舒伯特的高尚优美的音乐,而且在最后那几年回光返照的升平岁月里,还有维也纳自己钟爱的约翰·施特劳斯的欢乐、迷人的华尔兹圆舞曲。对于这样幸运和过惯了巴罗克式生活的人们来说,生活就像一场梦,因此快活的维也纳人都过着纸醉金迷的生活,跳华尔兹舞,喝葡萄酒,在咖啡馆里谈心,在歌场舞榭听曲看戏,打情骂俏寻欢作乐,把一生之中大部分时间消磨在享受和梦想之中。

II. 《第三帝国的灭亡》(节选)
【美】威廉·夏勒

1945年5月8日午夜,欧洲的炮火和轰炸停止了。自从1939年9月1日以来在欧洲整个大陆上第一次出现令人感到有点异样的、但受到欢迎的平静。在这五年八个月零七天中,在上百个战场上,在上千个被轰炸的城镇中,有千百万男女被屠杀;另外又有千百万人在纳粹毒气室里,或在党卫队特别行动队在俄国和波兰挖的死人坑边上被杀害——这一切都是阿道夫·希特勒的征服世界的野心造成的结果。绝大多数的欧洲古城都疮痍满目,一片瓦砾。天气暖和以后,无数没有埋葬的尸体从瓦砾堆中发出了阵阵恶臭。

在德国的大街上,再也听不到冲锋队齐步前进的皮靴声了,再也听不到成群结队的褐衫党徒的喧闹声了,再也听不到元首从扩音器里发出的尖叫声了。

经过十二年四个月零八天以后,"千秋帝国"终于夭折。这十二年四个月零八天对于所有的人来说都是个黑暗时代,只不过对德国人除外,而现在这个黑暗时代结束的时候,对德国人来说也是像一个凄凉的黑夜。我们已经看到,这个"千秋帝国",曾将这个伟大的民族,这个富有才智但又容易被引入歧途的民族,送上他们从来没达到过的权力和征服的高峰,现在它却土崩瓦解了,其突然和彻底,在历史上也是极其罕见的。

人民还在那里,土地也还在那里。但人民却茫茫然,流着血,挨着饿,当冬天到来时,他们在被炸成断垣残壁的窝棚中,穿着破烂衣服不停地打着哆嗦;土地则一片荒芜,瓦砾成堆。曾经企图毁灭其他许多民族的希特勒,在战争最后失败的时候也想要毁灭德国人民,但与他的愿望相反,德国人民并没有被毁灭。

但是第三帝国却成了历史陈迹。

4.5
I.
爱情不是商品
西德尼·J·哈里斯

佛罗里达州的一位读者显然是在个人经历上受过创伤,他写信来抱怨道:"如果我偷走了五分钱的商品我就是个贼,要受到惩罚,但是如果我偷走了他人妻子的爱情,我没事儿。"

这是许多人心目中普遍存在的一种错觉——爱情,像商品一样,可以"偷走"。实际上,许多州都颁布法令,允许索取"情感转让"赔偿金。

但是爱情并不是商品;真情实意不可能买到、卖掉、交换,或者偷走。爱情是志愿的行动,是感情的转向,是个性发挥上的变化。

当丈夫或妻子被另一个人"偷走"时,那个丈夫或妻子就已经具备了偷走的条件,事先已经准备接受新的伴侣了。这位"爱匪"不过是取走等人取走、盼人取走的东西。

我们往往待人如物。我们甚至说孩子"属于"父母。但是谁也不"属于"谁。人都属于自己和上帝。孩子是托付给父母的,如果父母不善待他们,州政府有权取消父母对他们的托管身份。

我们多数人年轻时都有过恋人被某个更有迷惑力、更有吸引力的人夺去的经历。在当时,我们兴许怨恨这位不速之客——但是后来长大了,也就认识到了心上人本来就不属于我们。并不是不速之客"导致了"决裂,而是缺乏真实的关系。

从表面上看,许多婚姻似乎是因为有了"第三者"才破裂的。然而这是一种心理上的幻觉。另外那个女人,或者另外那个男人,无非是作为借口,用来解除早就不是完好无损的婚姻罢了。

因失恋而痛苦,因别人"插足"于自己与心上人之间而图报复,是最没有出息、最自作自受的了。这种事总是歪曲了事实真相,因为谁都不是给别人当俘虏或牺牲品——人都是自由行事的,不论命运是好是坏,都由自己来做主。

但是,遭离弃的情人或配偶无法相信他的心上人是自由地背离他的——因而他归咎于插足者心术不正或迷人有招。他把他叫做催眠师、窃贼或者破坏家庭的人。然而,从大多数事例看,一个家的破裂,是早在什么"第三者"出现之前就开始了的。

（选自乔萍等编著《散文佳作108篇》）

II. Deng on "one country, two systems"

Socialism is to remain dominant in China while capitalism is allowed in certain regions like Hongkong and Taiwan. And the concept of "one country, two systems" which proved successful in solving the Hongkong issue could also be used to settle international problems.

Using a collection of Deng's talks with foreign guests and people from Hongkong and Macao, the article traces the formation of these ideas since they were first discussed after the Third Plenary Session of the 11th Chinese Communist Party Central Committee in 1978.

If the capitalist system is not guaranteed in Hongkong and Taiwan, Deng is quoted as saying, prosperity and stability there cannot be maintained and a peaceful settlement will become impossible...

The idea that the capitalist system in Hongkong should remain unchanged for 50 years after 1997, Deng said, was advanced because China needs 50 to 60 years to realize modernization.

According to Deng, the "one country, two systems" has been adopted to suit China's position and is not an expedient measure. The article quotes Deng saying that the unification of China is a national desire and will be realized even if it takes a thousand years.

"'The one country, two systems' concept is not my personal idea but a principle and law adopted by the National People's Congress and therefore will not change," Deng has said.

The magazine also quoted Deng as saying that it was possible for other countries to use the same concept to settle difficult problems. There are two ways to settle the issues, peacefully or non-peacefully. Since there are many issues that cannot be settled in traditional ways, new methods will have to be found.

Chapter Five
5.1

II. BEIJING ROAST DUCK

Beijing roast duck is a special traditional Chinese recipe which has a history of more than 300 years, originating from the imperial kitchen in Nanjing.

Beijing roast duck is prepared from the Beijing duck. The colour of the Beijing roast duck is purplish red and shiny bright. Its skin is crisp and the meat is tender. Its taste is delicious and has a special aroma which one never tires of. It is also very nutritious.

Beijing Roast Duck No.1 branch

Address: 24 Qian Men Street
Tel: 75.1379

5.4

Ⅰ. 6. Slight modifications of these methods enable the scale of the solar system to be determined.

7. Purpose of the ejector is to increase the pressure of the regenerating air, which, in the circuit, has lower pressure than the dried air, in order to prevent leakage of wet air into the dry air.

8. The early design of lathe had the lead screw fulfilling a dual purpose: as a master screw, and as a feed shaft.

9. Even taking into account possible new discoveries of oil deposits, there may be little or no oil left by the end of this century.

10. The limitations of physical model techniques have, in other branches of engineering, led to the development of mathematical models representing a variety of mechanical structures. The development of the analytical approach has accelerated since the introduction of large digital and analogue computer installations.

5.5

I. JOINT COMMUNIQUE ON THE ESTABLISHMENT OF DIPLIMATIC RELATIONS BETWEEN THE PEOPLE'S REPUBLIC OF CHINA AND THE UNITED STATES OF AMERICA

The People's Republic of China and the United States of America have agreed to recognize each other and to establish diplomatic relations as of January 1, 1979.

The United States of America recognizes the Government of the People's Republic of China as the sole legal Government of China. Within this context, the people of the United States will maintain cultural, commercial, and other unofficial relations with the people of Taiwan.

The People's Republic of China and the United States of America reaffirm the principles agreed on by the two sides in the Shanghai Communique and emphasize once again that:

Both wish to reduce the danger of international military conflict.

Neither should seek hegemony in the Asia-Pacific region or in any other region of the world and each is opposed to efforts by any other country or group of countries to establish such hegemony.

Neither is prepared to negotiate on behalf of any third party or to enter into agreements or understandings with the other directed at other states.

The Government of the United States of America acknowledges the Chinese position that there is but one China and Taiwan is part of China.

Both believe that normalization of Sino-American relations is not only in the interest of the Chinese and American peoples but also contributes to the cause of peace in Asia and the world.

The People's Republic of China and the United States of America will exchange Ambassadors and establish Embassies on March 1.1979.

Chapter Six
6.3

Ⅰ. 1. Pinger decided to invite them in to sit down and accordingly Mrs. Zhou went out to fetch them. As they mounted the steps to the main reception room, a young maid raised a red wool portiere and a waft of perfume greeted them as they entered. Granny Liu did not know what it was but felt she was walking on air. And she was so dazzled by everything in the room that her head began to swim. She could only nod, smack her lips and cry "Gracious Buddha!"

2. The next day he laid his case before Lin Ruhai.

"What a lucky coincidence!" exclaimed Ruhai. "Since my wife's death my mother-in-law in the capital has been worried because my daughter has no one to bring her up. She has sent two boats with male and female attendants to fetch the child but I delayed her departure while she was unwell. I was wondering how to repay you for your goodness in teaching her: now this gives me a chance to show my appreciation. Set your mind at rest. I foresaw this possibility and have written a letter to my brother-in-law urging him to do all he can for you as a small return for what I owe you. You mustn't worry either about any expenses that may be incurred—I've made that point clear to my brother-in-law."

Ⅱ. 毕脱爵士去看弟妇,提到辞退布立葛丝的问题及家里各种难以启齿的事情,着实劝谏了一番。她向他作了解释,说她可怜的丈夫没有斯丹恩勋爵提拔照顾是不行的。至于布立葛丝呢,有了这么好的差使,如果他们不许她去的话,不是太没有心肠了吗？这些话全无效验。她哭也罢,笑也罢,甜言蜜语地讨好也罢,毕脱爵士只是不满意。结果她和他以前最佩服的蓓基很像吵了一次架。他谈到家门和那些年轻的法国男人来往,说他们全是花花公子,行为不检点,他又提到斯丹恩勋爵,说他的马车老停在她门口,他本人每天陪着她好几个钟头,惹出许多闲话来,他以家长的身份恳求蓓基行事小心谨慎,因为外面已经对她说长到短。斯丹恩勋爵纵然地位极高,才识丰富,可是这种人呀,哪个女人接受他的献媚,哪个女人就要遭殃。他要求,他恳求,他命令他的弟妇,要她往后步步留心,少和那位大佬大交道。

6.4

Ⅰ.

春

宋德利　译

春天并非总是一模一样。4月,有时不知怎地一跃,就来到了弗吉尼亚的山坡上—转眼到处生机勃勃。郁金香组成了大合唱,连翘构成了阿拉伯式图案,洋李唱出了婉转的歌声。一夜之间,林木着装,绿叶瑟瑟。

4月也有时又蹑手蹑脚,像我的小孙女一样,羞羞答答地倚在门外,避开视线,偷偷向里窥探,尔后又咯咯地笑着走进门厅。"我知道你在那儿藏着呢,"我喊道。"进来!"于是,春天便溜进了我的怀抱。

山茱萸的蓓蕾,淡绿清雅,表面点缀着褐色斑痕,活像一只完美无缺的小杯,一撮撮种子,半隐半现地藏在里面。我敬畏地观察着这蓓蕾,暗自发问:一个月之前,这些种子在什么地方呢?苹果花开,展示出一片片染了玫瑰红的象牙色薄绸。一切冬眠的东西都在苏醒——美丽的樱草花,纤细的蝴蝶花,还有蓝色的草夹竹桃。大地开始变暖——这,你既可以嗅到,也可以触摸到——抓起一把泥,4月便揉碎在你的手心里了。

黛色的蓝龄山,那是我居住的地方,它像丰乳肥臀的女郎,依然安睡在浩瀚的天幕之下。后来,她终于伸开懒腰,慢慢醒来了。一阵阵和煦的风,像少女的柔发,将帆船似的云朵吹送到温和的天空。下雨了——催人入睡的喜雨——像麦片粥一样微暗的原野,起初淡绿素雅,继而翠绿欲滴。

这使我想到一个话题,它像一首乐曲不断萦绕在我的脑际,平淡无奇,却又奥秘无穷生命绵延不断。一切一切都在于此。任何事物,现在如此,以往如此,将来也必定仍然如此。

我是一个新闻工作者,并不是传道士。我决不会就"上帝的存在"而挥笔撰文,上帝不属于我的工作范围。一天下午,我在院里漫步,无意中停下来,拾起一颗橡子——那是一颗栗色的,光滑的,摸一摸凉凉爽爽的橡子。冠毛茸茸的顶部早已磨平,酷似保险箱的隆起球形旋钮。它没有丝毫出奇之处。成千上万颗这样的种子撒满了草地。

我不知道塔瑟斯的保罗在通向大马士革的大道上突然被圣光包围时看见了什么,但是我知道他的感觉如何。他大吃一惊,情不自禁地颤抖着;而那天下午,我也跟他一样。高耸入云的橡树拔地而起,它不正是从一颗如此这般微不足道的种子迸发出来的吗?而橡树本身蕴藏着的生殖力足以孕育出一片又一片的橡树林。神秘的色彩,雄伟的气魄,壮观的形象,这一切一切,都封锁在这只微小然而奇妙的保险箱内。

这种令人倾倒的时刻,逝去了还会再来。2月里的一天,我下山去拔石楠和忍冬根。我把手伸进腐败的枯叶和碎树皮中去挖。看,在这层毫无生气的枯枝败叶底下,一颗根茎正朝着那看不见的冬日,伸出一个干劲十足的绿芽来。我不想把这说成是神的启示。我发现的大概不过是一颗野生的蝴蝶花罢了。

这株蝴蝶花决不仅仅是为了自己的生存而挣扎,它是在准确无误地按照自然发展进程而生长着,它是在响应那比人类启蒙时期还要古老的节奏与力量。它是在从久久逝去的冬日里那枯叶中奋力挣得生命。于是,我把这只势不可挡的幼芽重新埋好,再用铁锹拍了拍,让它稍安勿躁:春天一定会来的。

这个平凡主题又奏起了一章:春天来了,花园里芸香银莲,花团锦簇,像一列列光彩熠熠的小玩具士兵一样,整齐地排列在石墙头。山茱萸像无拘无束的云朵漂浮在山间。

这是万物复苏的时节。那些已经死去、或貌似死去的东西都复活了——僵硬的枝条柔软起来,暗褐的大地泛起了绿色。这便是奇迹之所在。这里没有死亡,有的只是千真万确的永恒的生命。

春天,我们用铁锹翻开园子里黑油油的沃土,打碎土块,把地面平整好了,再把那些毫无生气的豌豆种子成垅成行地播下去。这都是些平凡至极的劳作,这里有什么激情可言呢?

可是你瞧,雨下起来了。阳光也暖和起来了,接着,奇迹来了。这便是那萌芽的过程。什么样的萌芽?生命的萌芽,神秘的萌芽,奇迹的萌芽。干瘪的种子裂开了,卷曲的绿叶伸展了。这里包含着一种信息,它胜过任何教会的仪式、任何教义、任何有组织的宗教。有谁不信,我的豌豆田可以打消他的疑虑。

春天处处带来赏心悦目的复苏景象,生命在继续,死亡不过是一个早已逝去的季节而已。大自然从不步履蹒跚,从不三心二意。一切都是有条不紊。一切一切,从来都是这么有条不紊。

如果愿意,你就去看一看吧!看一看芸香银莲,看一看萋萋芳草,看一看无边的豌豆田,尤其是那萋萋芳草,早已甩开臂膀,穿过市街。这便是世界何以无止境的原因。过去如此,现在如此,将来也永远如此。春回大地,此时此刻,又有谁还惧怕那遥远的秋天呢?

Ⅱ.
Tea-Drinking
Customs in China
By Wang Congren

China is the home of tea, and drinking tea is a national obsession. The Chinese are the most likely to delight in drinking tea as well as being the most discriminating in the way tea is made and served.

The tea-drinking tradition from the Ming and Qing dynasties, which features infused tea, has been inherited in most of China. But people from different areas favor different teas. Generally, people in northern China, northeastern China and Sichuan Province, love jasmine tea; those living in Jiangsu, Zhejiang and Anhui provinces favor green tea; and along the southeast coast, Oolong tea is preferred. People from Hunan Province have an interesting habit: they chew and swallow the tea leaves after drinking the infusion.

Distinct customs in different areas and minorities compose the variety of China's tea-drinking tradition.

6.5

I. 2.(1) 父亲穿着破衣裳,
　　　　可使儿女瞎了眼;
　　　　父亲佩着大钱囊,
　　　　将见儿女生笑脸。
　　　　命运,那著名的娼妇,
　　　　从不给穷人打开门户。

　　(2) 老父衣百结,
　　　　儿女不相认。
　　　　老父满堂金,
　　　　儿女尽孝心。
　　　　命运如娼妓,
　　　　贫贱遭遗弃。

Ⅱ. 2. **A Shepherd's Song**
　　　　By side of the rill,

At the foot of the hill,

The grassland stretches'neath the firmament tranquil,

The boundless grassland lies,

Beneath the boundless skies.

When the winds blow,

And grass bends low,

My sheep and cattle will emerge before your eyes.

6.6

Ⅰ.   甲板上

（杰克与露丝在一起。）

杰克:我十五岁的时候,父母就去世了,我就自立了。我没有兄弟姐妹,也没有什么亲戚,所以离开家乡以后,我就再也没回去过,人家都说我是无根的小草。噢,露丝。我们绕甲板走了半天了。就谈这些蓝天〈和〉大海,还有我的身世,恐怕你找我还有别的事吧。

露丝:道森先生,〈我〉——

杰克:杰克。

露丝:杰克。我是来向你道谢的。你不仅救了我,还为我掩饰。

杰克:〈欢迎你〉别客气。

露丝:听着,我知道你是怎么想的!〈你〉这个〈可怜的〉阔小姐,身在福中不知福。

杰克:不,不,我没这么想。我只是在想,这〈个〉位姑娘出了什么事？为什么会感到绝望？

露丝:因为——所有的一切。我的环境,还有周围的人使我感到乏味。我想摆脱,可我却无力自拔。

杰克:天哪,〈看看,如果你跳下去,就会一直沉到海底〉这么大,戴着挺沉的吧？

露丝:发出了五百份结婚请柬,〈费城〉所有的名门望族都会来,我觉得自己就像被捆在茫茫的人海里拼命挣扎,大声呼叫却没有人理睬我。

杰克:〈你〉爱他吗？

露丝:你说什么？

杰克:你爱他吗？

露丝:你真无礼,你不应该问我这个。

杰克:这不难回答,你是爱他呢,还是不爱他？

露丝:我们谈论这个问题不太合适。

杰克:〈你为什么不能回答我?〉这不难回答。

露丝:这太荒唐了。我们〈俩互不了解〉两个刚刚认识,你根本就不该问我这个问题。你很无礼,很粗鲁还很放肆。我现在要走了,杰克……道森先生,我不打扰了,我是过来道谢的,我已〈经〉道过谢〈过〉了。

杰克:〈你〉还骂了我。

露丝：啊，那是你自找的。

杰克：是吗？

露丝：是的。

Ⅱ. Zhou: Hold your tongue. (Turning back to Lu Dahai.) You're no longer in a position to speak to me, Lu Dahai—firm's already sacked you.

HAI: Sacked me!

CHONG: That's not playing the game, Father.

ZHOU (turning to Zhou Chong): You shut up and get out! (Zhou Chong departs in high dudgeon through the center door.)

HAI: All right, then, (Grinding his teeth.) Your dirty tricks are nothing new to me. You'd stoop to anything so long as there was money in it. You get the police to mow down your men, and then you—

ZHOU: How dare you!

MA (going to Lu Dahai): Come on, let's go. That's enough.

HAI: Yes, and I know all about your record too! When you contracted to repair that bridge over the river at Harbin, you deliberately breached the dyke—

ZHOU (harshly): Get out of here!

SERVANTS (tugging at Lu Dahai): Come on! Outside! Out!

HAI: You drowned two thousand two hundred coolies in cold blood, and for each life lost you raked in three hundred dollars! I tell you, creature, you've made your money by killing people, and you and your sons stand accursed for ever! And now on top of that you—

PING (hurling himself on Lu Dahai and striking him twice in the face): Take that, you lying swine!

(Lu Dahai returns a blow, but is seized and held by the servants.)

PING: Give him what for!

HAI (to Zhou Ping): You—!

(The servants set upon him. Blood appears on his face.)

ZHOU (harshly): Stop! Leave him alone!

(The servants stop but still keep hold of Lu Dahai.)

HAI (struggling): Let go of me, you hooligans!

PING (to the servants): Hustle him outside!

MA (breaking down): You are hooligans, too! (Going across to Zhou Ping.) You're my— mighty free with your fists! What right have you to hit my son?

PING: Who are you?

MA: I'm your—your victim's mother.

HAI: Take no notice of the rat, Mother. You don't want them setting on to you, as well.

MA (staring dazedly at Zhou Ping's face, then bursting into tears again): Oh, Dahai, let's go! Let's get out of here!

(Lu Dahai is shepherded out by the servants, followed by Lu Ma. Only Zhou Puyuan and

Zhou Ping remain on the stage.)

PING (apologetically): Father.

ZHOU: You might have been less impetuous.

PING: But the fellow had no right to throw mud at you like that.

Bibliography

Bassnett, S. 2004. Translation Studies. Shanghai: Shanghai Foreign language Education Press.

Berman, A. 1984. L'Epreuve de letranger, Paris: Editions Gallimard; trans (1992) by S Heyvaert as The Experience of the Foreign: Culture and Translation in Romantic Germany, Albany: State University of New York.

Catford, J. C. 1965. A Linguistic Theory of Translation. Oxford: Oxford University Press

Chukovsky, K I. 1966. Vysokoe, iskusstvo (A High Art). Collected Works, Vol. 3, 237-627], Moscow: Khudozhestvenaya literature.

Enkvist, N. E. 1978. Constructive Text Linguistics and Translation, in L. Grahs, G. Korlen and [(B. Malmberg (eds) Theory and Practice of Translation, Berne: Peter Lang.)]

Firth, J. R. 1951. Modes of Meaning, Essays and Studies. Oxford: Oxford University Press.

Griffith, K. 2006. Writing Essays about Literature, A Guide and Style Sheet. Beijing: Peking University Press.

Halliday, M. A. K. 1974. The Context of Linguistics, Georgetown University Round Table on Language and Linguistics. Washington, D C: Georgetown University Press.

Holmes, J. 1988. Translated Papers on Literary Translation and Translation Studies. Amsterdam: Rodopi.

Honig, E. (ed) 1985. The Poet's Other Voice: Conversations on Literary Translation. Amherst: The University of Massachusetts Press.

Joos, M. 1962. The Five Clocks. The Hague: Mouton.

Lanham, R. A. 2004. Analyzing Prose. Beijing: Peking University Press.

Lefevere, A. (ed. and trans.) 1992. Translation/History /Culture: A Sourcebook. New York and London: Routledge.

Nabokov, V. 1964/1975. "Foreword", in A S Pushkin Eugene Onegin (ed. and trans by Vladimir Nabokov, 4 Vols.) London: Routledge and Kegan Paul, Vii-Xii.

Newmark, P. 1988. A Text Book of Translation. London: Prentice Hall International (UK) Ltd.

Nida, E. A. and Cherles, R T 1969/1982. The Theory and Practice of Translation. Leiden: E J Brill.

Nida, E. A. 1964. Toward A Science of Translating. Leiden: E J Brill.

Nida, E. A. 2001. Language and Culture: Context in translating. Shanghai: Shanghai

Foreign Language Education Press.

Nord, C. 1991. Text Analysis in Translation. Amsterdam: Rodopi.

Palmer, F. R. 1976. Semantics: A New Outline. Cambridge: Cambridge University Press.

Rumelhart, D. H. 1975. International to Human Information Processing. New York.

Venuti, L. 1995. The Translator's Invisibility. London: Routledge.

Wilss, W. 2001. The Science of Translation: Problems and Method. Shanghai: Shanghai Foreign Language Education Press.

曹雪芹,高鹗. 红楼梦. 北京:人民文学出版社,1975.

冯庆华. 实用翻译教程. 上海:上海外语教育出版社,2002.

郭鸿,彭晓东. 外交英语. 北京:对外经济贸易大学出版社,1999.

顾正阳. 古诗词曲英译美学研究. 上海:上海大学出版社,2006.

郭著章,李庆生. 英汉互译实用教程. 武汉:武汉大学出版社,2002.

黄国文. 翻译研究的语言学探索. 上海:上海外语教育出版社,2006.

黄龙. 翻译学. 南京:江苏教育出版社,1988.

金元浦. 文学解释学. 长春:东北师范大学出版社,1997.

刘宓庆. 文体与翻译. 北京:中国对外翻译出版社公司,1986.

刘宓庆. 翻译美学导论. 北京:中国对外翻译出版公司,2005.

刘勰. 文心雕龙. 北京:长征出版社,1984.

梁实秋译. 莎士比亚全集. 呼和浩特:内蒙古文化出版社,1995.

鲁迅. 鲁迅全集. 乌鲁木齐:新疆人民出版社,1995.

理雅各译. 四书(英文版). 长沙:湖南出版社,1992.

李亚丹. 英汉名篇赏析. 武汉:湖北教育出版社,2000.

乔萍,瞿淑蓉,宋洪玮. 散文佳作108篇. 南京:译林出版社,2002.

谭永祥. 汉语修辞美学. 北京:北京语言学院出版社,1992.

童庆炳等编. 文学理论教程. 北京:高等教育出版社,2000.

涂纪亮. 英美语言哲学. 北京:中国社会科学出版社,1993.

王宝增. 创作空白论. 载:文艺研究,1990(1).

韦勒克,沃伦. 文学原理. 北京:生活、读书、新知三联书店,1984.

文军. 英语修辞格词典. 重庆:重庆大学出版社,1992.

王希杰. 略论语言的词汇和言语的词汇. 载:杭州大学学报,1993(1).

王佐良,丁往道. 英语文体学引论. 北京:外语教学与研究出版社,1987.

徐宏力. 模糊文艺学概要. 沈阳:春风文艺出版社,1994.

徐黎鹃,黄群飞. 经典电影对白欣赏. 武汉:武汉测绘科技大学出版社,1997.

许渊冲. 唐诗三百首(英汉对照). 北京:高等教育出版社,2001.

许渊冲. 最爱唐宋词(英汉对照). 北京:中国对外翻译出版公司,2006.

袁行霈,孟二冬,丁放. 中国诗学通论. 合肥:安徽教育出版社,1994.

杨必译. 名利场. 北京:人民文学出版社,1957.

杨宪益,戴乃迭译. A Dream of Red Mansions. 北京:外文出版社,1978.

张培基. 英译中国现代散文选. 上海:上海外语教育出版社,1999.

张乔. 模糊语义学. 北京：中国社会科学出版社，1999.

张廷琛，魏博思译. 唐诗一百首. 北京：中国对外翻译出版公司，商务印书馆（香港）有限公司，1991.

张振玉. 翻译学概论. 南京：译林出版社，1992.

赵彦春. 翻译学归结论. 上海：上海外语教育出版社，2005.

周邦友. 英语应用文大典. 合肥：中国科学技术大学出版社，2003.

周方珠. 英汉翻译原理. 合肥：安徽大学出版社，2002.

周方珠. 翻译多元论. 北京：中国对外翻译出版公司，2005.

朱生豪译. 莎士比亚全集. 北京：人民文学出版社，1984.